Alabama's Frontiers and the Rise of the Old South

A History of the Trans-Appalachian Frontier

Malcolm Rohrbough and Walter Nugent, editors

Alabama's Frontiers

AND THE RISE OF THE

Old South

Daniel S. Dupre

Indiana University Press

This book is a publication of

Indiana University Press
Office of Scholarly Publishing
Herman B Wells Library 350
1320 East 10th Street
Bloomington, Indiana 47405 USA

iupress.indiana.edu

The paper used in this publication meets the minimum requirements of the
American National Standard for Information Sciences—Permanence of Paper
for Printed Library Materials, ANSI Z39.48–1992.

Manufactured in the United States of America

Library of Congress Cataloging-in-Publication Data

Names: Dupre, Daniel S., 1958- author.
Title: Alabama's frontiers and the rise of the Old South / Daniel S. Dupre.
Description: Bloomington, Indiana : Indiana University Press, [2018] |
Series: History of the trans-Appalachian frontier | Includes
bibliographical references and index.
Identifiers: LCCN 2017033858 (print) | LCCN 2017033313 (ebook) | ISBN
9780253031532 (e-book) | ISBN 9780253031525 (cloth : alk. paper) | ISBN
9780253027276 (pbk. : alk. paper)
Subjects: LCSH: Alabama—History—To 1819. | Whites—Alabama—
Relations with Indians—History. | Southern States—History.
Classification: LCC F326 (print) | LCC F326 .D87 2018 (ebook) | DDC
976.1/01—dc23
LC record available at https://lccn.loc.gov/2017033858

1 2 3 4 5   23 22 21 20 19 18

For
Rachel
and
Joe

Contents

Acknowledgments

I had thought that I'd finished with Alabama's frontier many years ago when I published the book that sprang from my dissertation. I'm grateful that Walter Nugent and Malcolm Rohrbough invited me back into those waters and that they proved to be so patient as they waited for me to make good on that invitation. I have learned so much from many historians, anthropologists, and archaeologists who know far more than I do about their particular areas of expertise. I only hope that I did justice to their work as I sketched out the story of Alabama's frontiers across three centuries.

My academic home, the University of North Carolina at Charlotte, has proved a congenial environment since I arrived back in 1989. The College of Liberal Arts and Sciences gave me a semester off as a reward for a two-year stint as chair of the Department of History. That, in addition to another semester's leave through our department's Cotlow Endowment, gave me valuable time to make progress on this book. Kristopher Steele helped track down sources for my first chapter and the interlibrary loan department at Atkins Library made my research much easier. Many of my colleagues at UNCC, including Lyman Johnson, David Goldfield, Gregory Mixon, Mark Wilson, Janet Levy, and Aaron Shapiro, gave me helpful comments on chapters. Christine Haynes went beyond the call of duty as a French historian by reading and commenting on my early chapters and encouraging me to keep on track. Kathleen DuVal, at the University of North Carolina at Chapel Hill, offered helpful comments on my first couple of chapters. I met Johanna Shields, formerly of the University of Alabama at Huntsville, on my first research trip to Alabama when I was a graduate student in the mid-1980s. She has been a friend and a supporter of my work ever since. Johanna read drafts of most of this book's chapters and offered advice that invariably improved them, along with words that boosted my morale.

My family has also seen me through the process of writing this book. My father, Vladimir Dupre, read portions of it and would always ask about my progress during our phone calls. My brothers and sister—Chris, David, Peter, John, and Susie—have not read the book but they have loved me, which is far more important. Closer to home, my wife, Kathy Consorte, has also offered me her love and encouragement despite having to live with all the preoccupation and mood swings that come with writing a book. She, more than anyone besides me, will be happy that it is done. My two children grew up and left home while I worked on this project. I am proud of this book, but I'm much more proud of Rachel and Joe and the people they have become. So it is to them that I dedicate this book, with much love.

Alabama's Frontiers and the Rise of the Old South

Introduction

In early September of 1540, Hernando de Soto and hundreds of armed and armored Europeans, along with enslaved Africans, captured Indian porters, and a menagerie of horses, dogs, and pigs, marched down from the Appalachian highlands along the Coosa River and passed across an imaginary line that, far in the future, would demark the boundary of the state of Georgia. You could say that Alabama's frontier history began that day, although that geopolitical division of the early nineteenth century would have been meaningless to either de Soto or the Native Americans he encountered. The Indians who witnessed the passage of the horsemen and foot soldiers through the forests and the fields lived, they believed, at the center of the world, on farmsteads and in small hamlets and the occasional larger towns that, together, constituted individual chiefdoms. The chiefdoms of that region were part of the paramount chiefdom of Coosa, which stretched from what would become southeastern Tennessee, through northwestern Georgia, into the northeast corner of Alabama. De Soto himself understood that he was passing through Coosa; he had, after all, fed his army on the maize, fruit, nuts, and meat of the chiefdom for weeks and now was moving southwestward with the chief and his sister in tow as hostages. But to his eyes this was just a small portion of a larger world that the Spanish called *La Florida*, an extensive if indeterminate land stretching north and west from the Gulf and

Atlantic coasts. The king had named de Soto governor of those lands and, in September, he was eager to push on to see if his dreams of wealth might be realized in the next chiefdom.

The Spanish called expeditions like that of Hernando de Soto *entradas*, which literally meant "entrances": part exploratory marches, part treasure hunts, part displays of martial intimidation and conquest. If Howard Lamar and Leonard Thompson are right in their definition of a frontier as "a territory or zone of interpenetration between two previously distinct societies" that opens when "the first representatives of the intrusive society arrive," then de Soto's entrada marked the beginning of Alabama's frontier, not as a straight line between imaginary states but as a contested borderland.[1]

Tracing de Soto's route and pinpointing the various towns and chiefdoms visited by the Spaniards has been an arduous task for historians and anthropologists, one that remains incomplete and debated. They have parsed the written chronicles of the entrada for clues about miles marched and landscape features spied, and have dug through the soil at numerous archaeological sites. Their work, blending European perceptions of an alien landscape with the detritus of everyday life in Indian towns and villages, has brought us closer not just to uncovering de Soto's path but to understanding the character of the southeastern borderlands.

Look at a map of de Soto's route and you are, from one perspective, witnessing an invasion, a penetration; the bold line snaking northward, deep into the interior, before sweeping in an arc through Alabama makes manifest imperial Spain's quest for empire and wealth. It was a mission informed by the earlier conquests of the Aztecs and the Incas but one destined for a different outcome, a failure hinted at in the devolution of the path into a confused meander west of the Mississippi River. The conquistador died on the banks of that river, never having found the gold or the wealthy Indian societies that his previous experiences had led him to believe might lie hidden in the southeastern interior. With that, Spain took one significant step back from its dreams of a northern empire. Look again at that path, however, and this time you discover an Indian world, a tracing of a line from chiefdom to chiefdom as de Soto chased after rumors of gold over the next hill or grimly marched his men on empty stomachs to the next town with stores of maize to be appropriated, all the while being directed by Indian guides. That route was the marriage of the imperial and the indigenous, shaped by the motivations and experiences that propelled the Spaniards into the heart of the interior and by the realities of the land and people that they found there.

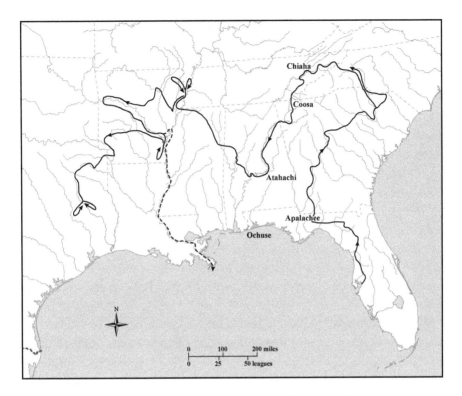

Route of Hernando de Soto's entrada, 1539–1543. Based on a map by
Charles M. Hudson, 1997. Drawn by Patrick Jones.

This history of frontier Alabama begins with Europeans traversing an Indian
world in 1540 and ends in the mid-1830s with the final removal of the Creek Indians from a state that now belonged to American settlers intent on making cotton
king. In between those distant points in time lay a series of "frontiers": the Indians' frontier as they reshaped their world in the wake of de Soto's entrada; the
imperial frontier of the seventeenth and eighteenth centuries as Spain, France,
and Great Britain competed for the trade and allegiance of the Native Americans; and the settlers' frontier as a new nation paved the way for American settlement and the development of a cotton kingdom.

Frontier Alabama, like most frontiers, was at once global and local. Wave
after wave of "outsiders" followed Hernando de Soto to the region, carrying
with them the concerns and motivations of the broader Atlantic world. Like
de Soto, whose path was determined by caches of maize in chiefdom towns, by
rumors of wealth across the next ridge, and by the Indian guides coerced into

service, those later outsiders found their paths shaped by the particularities of the local environment, people, and circumstances. The French trader bartering for deerskins in a Choctaw village in the early eighteenth century was an agent of the European consumer revolution and an informal representative of an empire seeking Indian allies to anchor its position on the continent, but his success largely depended on his ability to navigate the complex web of relations in the village itself. The cotton planter who settled in the Black Belt of Alabama in the 1820s was connected to England's burgeoning industrial revolution and consumers' demands for textiles. His purchase of clear title to acres of surveyed land made him the beneficiary of a federal government determined to develop the Old Southwest. But his success depended on the quality of the soil, on the labor of enslaved men and women, and on the condition of the roads and rivers over which he transported his bales of cotton. The larger forces of economic and political change sweeping through the Atlantic world shaped Alabama's frontier history, but those forces usually played out in largely face-to-face, localized communities.

We are accustomed to thinking of frontiers as beginning with pioneers settling the land. That was my impression many years ago when I wrote my doctoral dissertation on the American settlement of the Tennessee Valley of North Alabama in the early nineteenth century. I was convinced that the roots of the Old South lay in the frontier experience of the Americans, free and enslaved, who migrated west and opened new lands that became the heart of the cotton kingdom. But it turned out that I began my dissertation with the final stages of a complex and old frontier. My notion that "settlers" had "opened" new lands ignored both the generations of Creek, Cherokee, and Chickasaw families and their ancestors who had settled, farmed, and hunted on the land and the wide variety of outsiders who had traversed and often resided in the territory that would become Alabama.

For more than 250 years after de Soto's entrada, the Alabama region remained an interior space on the peripheries of European colonies, dominated by the indigenous peoples. This was the kind of frontier that recent historians have depicted as a "borderland" or "middle ground," a frontier shaped by the cooperation and competition between Indians and Europeans in pursuit of markets and empires. Much of Alabama's first frontier history as a borderland emerged out of the Indians' diplomatic alliances, their wars, their trade, and their migrations. But the Europeans who encircled and probed also defined the region: the Spanish in Florida, the English in Carolina, and, by the late seventeenth century, the French in the lower Mississippi Valley. Emissaries from those worlds,

who Participated

whether missionaries eager to save souls, soldiers claiming territory by building forts, or, especially, traders seeking deerskins or Indian slaves, also created the borderland of Alabama. The indigenous world and the world of markets and empires entwined and, as a growing *métis* or mixed-race population attested, even merged at times, and both sides navigated and negotiated a complex social, political, and economic landscape. Because the precise state boundaries were meaningless through most of this period, this history of frontier Alabama will take an expansive view of the region, following, for example, the Creeks into what is modern-day Georgia and the Choctaws into Mississippi.[2]

Historians have rightly shifted from focusing on Indians as victims acted upon to Indians as historical actors, but the story of America's frontiers was also a story of war and conquest. Some of the largest battles between Indians and people of European descent were fought in Alabama. The long history of a middle ground built on trade and imperial alliances gave way in the nineteenth century to a frontier of land in Alabama, and to starker divisions between American settlers and Indians. While the collapse of the middle ground did not happen abruptly, war narrowed the diplomatic options of Native Americans, beginning with the French defeat in the Seven Years' War. The American Revolution and the creation of a stronger national government in 1789 pushed the process forward in a couple of different ways. First, because the middle ground depended on imperial competition, American consolidation of control over the Old Southwest left Indians less room to maneuver, although Spain's presence in Florida slowed and complicated that process. Second, the new national government's imperial ambitions quickly hinged on westward settlement and not on trade alliances with Native Americans, and ended up facilitating the eager encroachment of pioneers on Indian land by drawing borders, negotiating land cessions, building roads, and surveying and selling the fertile acres. An important component of the government's mission to transform the frontier was the "civilization" policy, designed to transform the Indians' economy and society and encourage the sale of hunting lands, a policy that aggravated tensions within Indian society in the early nineteenth century. The Creek War of 1813–14, which began as a civil war, and the subsequent Treaty of Fort Jackson, which stripped the Creeks of millions of acres of land, marked a turning point in the transition to a federal policy of removal, opening the way for a flood of new settlers.

Andrew Jackson's defeat of the indigenous and imperial enemies of the nation, first at Horseshoe Bend in Alabama and then at the Battle of New Orleans, drove the final coffin nail into the middle ground and helped to create a South that was at once integrated into the nation and deeply conscious of its regional identity. The families who flocked to Alabama and the other Deep South states, and the enslaved people they brought with them, transformed the southeastern borderlands. While African slaves had been present on this frontier since de Soto's entrada, the expansion of cotton cultivation and the Second Middle Passage--the migration of hundreds of thousands of men and women from the Upper South to labor in those cotton fields--turned what had been societies with slaves into a slave society. The development of the cotton kingdom and the expansion and protection of slavery became synonymous with the closing of the frontier. By the 1830s, when Jackson occupied the White House and most of the Creeks and Cherokees were being rounded up and sent west, Alabama stood poised between the president's aggressive nationalism and the defensive sectionalism that ultimately would tear the nation apart. In many ways, then, the story of the end of Alabama's frontier is the story of the beginning of what has come to be called "the Old South."

Notes

1. Howard Lamar and Leonard Thompson, eds., *The Frontier in History: North America and Southern Africa Compared* (New Haven, CT: Yale University Press, 1981), 7.

2. The historiography on the "middle ground" and borderlands is voluminous. Some important works include Richard White, *The Middle Ground: Indians, Empires, and Republics in the Great Lakes Region, 1650–1815* (Cambridge: Cambridge University Press, 1991); Daniel K. Richter, *Facing East from Indian Country: A Native History of Early America* (Cambridge, MA: Harvard University Press, 2001); Jeremy Adelman and Stephen Aron, "From Borderlands to Borders: Empires, Nation-States, and the Peoples in Between in North American History," *American Historical Review* 104 (June 1999): 814–41; and Francois Furstenberg, "The Significance of the Trans-Appalachian Frontier in Atlantic History," *American Historical Review* 113 (June 2008): 647–77.

PART ONE
Beginnings

1

La Florida and the Center of the World

[handwritten: how de Soto interacted w/ Southern NA tribes & the wave of destruction]

[handwritten: Beginnings - de Soto]

By the time he met Chief Tascaluza in the town of Atahachi, somewhere near the confluence of the Coosa and Tallapoosa Rivers, in October 1540, Hernando de Soto knew how to use the rituals of diplomacy and threats of violence to get what he wanted. Since early spring, when his forces left their winter camp in Florida and pushed north, de Soto's entrada had passed through numerous towns, always with the same goals in mind: food, tribute, bodies, and information. He appropriated venison, bear fat, nuts, fruit, and maize to sustain his soldiers on their long march. He accepted gifts of deerskins, pearls, and craft goods. He transformed Indian men into porters, or *tamemes*, shackling and chaining them together to carry the heavy burdens of the expedition, and he impressed Indian women into sexual servitude to satisfy the desires of his men. Information was a more elusive commodity. Did the locals have gold or just the freshwater pearls prized by so many whom de Soto encountered? How fruitful was the land? Could it be settled and could the Indians be subjugated and put to labor? Since it was pearls and not gold to be found and since it was other Spaniards, not these soldiers, who would do the settling, de Soto always came to the final question: where did the next chiefdom lie where he could continue his pursuit of wealth and power as he traversed La Florida, this new land that he now claimed to govern?

The chiefs confronted by these demands often acquiesced. Some understandably were intimidated by horsemen holding lances and armored soldiers wielding crossbows, and might have calculated that the sooner they agreed to provide for the needs of the entrada the sooner those strange men would leave their land. De Soto's ruthlessness reinforced that sentiment. This was a man who, when angered by the misdirection of an Indian guide in Florida, threw him to the greyhounds and wolfhound, war dogs trained to disembowel their victims.[1] But other chiefs might have calculated that they could turn the conquistador's military power to their advantage in their struggles against neighboring chiefdoms. Gifts of food, labor, and women were part of long-standing rituals of diplomacy designed to cement those sorts of alliances. Still others might have viewed de Soto as a visiting paramount chief and pledged fealty through the payment of tribute.[2]

Hernando de Soto's encounters with the Indians of the Southeast reflected an uneasy relationship between the Spaniards' sense of superiority over the local people and their abject dependence on them. He had led his men north and west, deep into the Appalachian highlands in search of gold, which the Spanish associated with mountainous terrain. The way was rugged and food was scarce since there were few towns with stores of maize. As the soldiers trudged over the final range and began moving down the Tennessee River valley, the horsemen on mounts that "were tired and thin" and near starvation, they met a welcoming party that led them to Chiaha, a town situated on an island in the French Broad River. There they stayed for a couple of restorative weeks, filling their bellies with cornmeal porridge, walnut and acorn oil, and bear fat, and living with the residents "in peace," according to one chronicler of the de Soto expedition. He wrote that the Indians "played with them. . . . They swam in the company of the Christians, and in all they served them very well."[3] That idyll ended when de Soto demanded women for his men, prompting the Indians to flee into the surrounding countryside. De Soto responded as he had done at other places in La Florida and earlier in his career as a conquistador in the Incan Empire of Peru: he captured the chief and held him hostage. The townspeople returned and the chief granted de Soto the labor of five hundred tamemes to help carry the supplies to the next chiefdom. The chronicler noted that de Soto softened his demand by agreeing "to leave off collars and chains," but made no mention of whether women were part of the deal.[4]

The Spaniards followed much the same pattern of coercion in the next chiefdom. Coosa was the heart of a paramountcy centered along the Coosawattee River in northwest Georgia that encompassed perhaps as many as ten individual chiefdoms stretching into Tennessee and Alabama. "It was a charming and fertile land," one chronicler wrote, "with good cultivated fields stretching along the rivers. In the open fields were many plums . . . and grapes along the rivers on vines climbing up into the trees."[5] When they reached the principal town of Coosa the chief came out to greet the soldiers, carried on a platform or litter by "sixty or seventy of his principal Indians" who "took turns from time to time, with great ceremony in their manner."[6] A large crowd of Indians accompanied this procession, many playing instruments and singing. The chief, or *cacique*, as the Spanish called Indian leaders, wearing "a robe of marten skins" and "a crown of feathers on his head," welcomed de Soto and ordered that food and lodging be provided to the visitors.[7] Whether he mistrusted the intentions of the people of Coosa or simply followed his usual practice of coercing compliance, de Soto responded to this hospitality by placing a guard over the chief. This effort to ensure the cooperation of the people initially backfired; leaders within the chiefdom, angered by this affront to chiefly authority, "revolted and went away to hide themselves in the woods." De Soto sent his captains off on horseback to round up the deserters and "they seized many Indians, men and women, who were put in chains." The rest returned, "saying that they wished to serve in whatever might be commanded of them." Some of the captured men were released, but the captains kept many in chains as slaves, "without allowing them to go to their lands."[8] After establishing his dominance, de Soto and his men rested and enjoyed the fruits of Coosa for almost a month. When they finally left to continue their southwestward march, they took the cacique and his sister with them.

After traveling for a month, the Spaniards reached Talisi, a border town between the chiefdoms of Coosa and Tascaluza near present-day Childersburg. Here de Soto commandeered food supplies, deerskins, porters, and women and decided to release the Coosa chief, keeping his sister, an important figure in her own right in the matrilineal Mississippian culture. The cacique "was very angry and tearful" over that loss "and because they had brought him so far from his land."[9] It was here, as well, that emissaries from Chief Tascaluza, including his eighteen-year-old son, met de Soto to lead him to the chiefdom's principal town of Atahachi.[10]

When the Spaniards arrived in Atahachi, Tascaluza welcomed them from a position of power, sitting with his retinue on a balcony of his house atop a large ceremonial mound. He wore "a certain headdress," like a turban, "which gave him an appearance of authority, and a *pelote* or blanket of feathers down to his feet."[11] The chief was seated on two cushions surrounded by "his most principal Indians" with "one holding a sort of fan of deerskin which kept the sun from him, round and the size of a shield, quartered with black and white, with a cross made in the middle."[12] The entrada's chroniclers agreed that Tascaluza was a very large man who radiated authority. One claimed that the cacique was "very tall of body, large limbed, lean, and well built" and "was greatly feared by his neighbors and vassals."[13] When de Soto entered the plaza next to the mound, dismounted, and walked toward Tascaluza, the chief "did not rise but rather was quiet and composed, as if he were a king, and with much gravity."[14] Even a display of horsemanship that surely was meant to intimidate the chief and his people failed to disturb his calm. The Spaniards "galloped their horses in front of" Tascaluza, "turning them from one side to the other, and at times toward the cacique. He with great gravity and unconcern from time to time raised his eyes and looked as if in disdain."[15]

Tascaluza might have been more imposing in build and character than other chiefs he had encountered, but de Soto did not hesitate to make his usual demands. After the feasting and dancing had been completed, he got down to the business at hand and called for Indian men to serve as porters and for one hundred Indian women.[16] When Tascaluza replied "that he was not accustomed to serving anyone, rather that all served him before," de Soto ordered him to be confined.[17] Tascaluza acquiesced, rounded up some porters, and offered to lead the entrada to the town of Mabila, where he would hand over more tamemes and the women. De Soto rewarded Tascaluza's cooperation with boots and a red cloak, and found a horse for the chief to ride, a difficult task given the man's height.[18] And so the Spaniards journeyed on to Mabila with the great cacique Tascaluza on horseback, his feet almost scraping the ground, "and always the Indian with the sunshade in front of his lord, and another with a cushion" following behind.[19]

Dressing Tascaluza in European clothes and placing him on horseback might have reinforced de Soto's sense of command over the man and the situation, but a little tickle of doubt could have intruded had he paid attention to that sunshade and cushion. Capture and co-optation did not erase Tascaluza's authority, which was rooted in a complex social structure of clans and a cosmological belief system that linked political leadership to the spiritual world. Tascaluza's people, like those of Chiaha and Coosa, and others along the entrada's route, responded to the Spanish intruders in a variety of ways, including submission, out of necessity, but they did not belong to La Florida. They lived at the center of the world, balanced between the supernatural beings that inhabited the four cardinal directions and the realms above and below, alongside the bones of their ancestors buried in the ceremonial mounds that anchored their towns.[20] De Soto was used to getting what he wanted and he had the military power to enforce compliance, but he would find when he reached Mabila that ultimately he could not govern this land.

prior to break, De Soto's conquest

narrative ↑ analysis ↓

Beginning a history of frontier Alabama with Hernando de Soto's entrada runs the risk of reinforcing false divisions between prehistory and history by suggesting that the appearance of Europeans awakened the indigenous people from a static, timeless past. Certainly the Indians who watched the armored men, horses, and pigs pass by understood that something new had entered their very old world, a world where the everyday routines that sustained life and the spiritual beliefs that gave meaning to those lives evolved slowly over centuries. But archaeologists are increasingly aware of just how fluid the chiefdoms of the fifteenth and sixteenth centuries were before the arrival of Europeans, and just how much the stuff of history—trade, diplomacy, migration, and war—contributed to rapid shifts in the polities of the region. That history shaped the Indians' world long before de Soto's arrival and influenced their reactions to the intrusion of those strangers.[21]

The people whom the Spanish encountered in the Alabama region led very localized lives on scattered farms, or in small hamlets, or perhaps in towns with a few hundred residents, but their chiefdoms were part of a broader culture that stretched through most of the Midwest and the Southeast. The Mississippian culture first emerged in the eleventh century in central Illinois just east of present-day Saint Louis, built on a foundation of intensive maize cultivation that allowed denser settlements. By the thirteenth century at least six thousand and perhaps as many as forty thousand people lived in the city of Cahokia, supported by the surrounding farming villages. Large central plazas and massive ceremonial mounds became symbols of chiefly authority and of hierarchy, both of which were reinforced by prestige goods crafted from nonlocal materials that attested to expanding trade networks. The palisaded walls surrounding the town suggested that diplomacy and war were part of Cahokia's expansion. Central features of the Mississippian culture that began at Cahokia—specific building methods, mounds and plazas, palisades, artistic motifs, and religious iconography—spread throughout the Ohio River valley and the interior of the Southeast, reaching the Alabama region by the thirteenth century.[22]

Alabama, with its relatively mild climate and rich variety of environments, was particularly well suited to sustaining the denser populations of Mississippian chiefdoms. There were five broad physiographic regions in Alabama: the East Gulf Coastal Plain, the Piedmont Upland, the Valley and Ridge, the Cumberland Plateau, and the Highland Rim. The Coastal Plain comprised most of the southern half of modern-day Alabama. Close to the coast the sandy soil supported primarily pine forests, and there were few Indian settlements except for the southwestern corner of the future state. But the interior regions of the Coastal Plain boasted a richer environment, including the Black Belt prairies and oak-hickory-pine forests, especially along the floodplains of the Chattahoochee, Alabama, Black Warrior, and Tombigbee Rivers. The northeastern third of the state had two distinct regions. The Tallapoosa River passed through the rolling hills of the Piedmont Upland in east-central Alabama, cutting narrow valleys through the crystalline bedrock before passing across the fall line hills to the softer sedimentary rock of the Coastal Plain. There the river's flow slowed and broadened in the alluvial floodplain valley before meeting the Coosa River to form the Alabama. To the north of the Piedmont lay a series of south-westward-sweeping ridges that ran along the western edge of the Appalachian Mountains, bisected by broad valleys. The Coosa River was the principal waterway of this region. The Tennessee River in the north flowed through the two remaining physiographic regions, first passing through the more mountainous Cumberland Plateau in the east and then broadening into a valley through the Highland Rim of north-central and northwest Alabama. All of these regions had varieties of oak-hickory forests, interspersed with pines, with the addition of cedars in the Tennessee Valley and a large number of chestnuts in the mountains of the northeastern corner of Alabama.[23]

When Hernando de Soto marched through, there were four major population centers. Stretching along the Tallapoosa, Coosa, and Alabama Rivers were the towns associated or allied with the chiefdoms of Coosa and Tascaluza. Further south, along the Chattahoochee River that later would form a border between Alabama and Georgia, were another group of mound-building chiefdoms. To the west, along the Tombigbee and Black Warrior river system that flowed through the west-central part of Alabama, were a series of towns and farms centered around what has come to be called Moundville, the largest mound site in the Southeast. A fourth cluster of settlements was situated to the south in the Mobile River delta, where the Alabama and Tombigbee Rivers joined. The only major river system without significant Indian populations at the time of the entrada was the Tennessee River valley. Earlier populations of Woodland people had settled along that northern valley, as evidenced by large shell middens, and there had even been Mississippian settlements a century or two before de Soto's visit, but Indians had migrated out of that portion of Alabama by the mid-sixteenth century.[24]

Mississippian Indians built their settlements on bluffs and terraces overlooking creeks, streams, and major rivers.[25] Seasonal freshets deposited along the alluvial floodplains a nutrient-rich, sandy soil that was both fertile and easy to cultivate. They took advantage of canebrakes, the dense thickets of bamboo-like cane that flourished along the riverbanks, to construct their houses, weaving cane matting between posts set in holes or trenches, before daubing the exterior with a plaster of clay and grass. The tough, flexible cane could also be used to make baskets, fishhooks, and knives.[26]

Their towns often straddled ecological zones to maximize resources. For example, archaeologists have discovered town sites clustered in the fall line areas along the Coosa and Tallapoosa Rivers. Those were prized locations, in part because the rocky shoals provided fording places, facilitating travel. More importantly, the Indians could take advantage of two distinct environments. They could plant their maize, squashes, and beans in the alluvial soil deposited just downstream from the fall line, and harvest wild plants and catch fish, turtles, frogs, and small mammals in the ponds and swampy areas where creeks and rivers first flowed out of narrow Piedmont valleys into the Valley or Coastal Plain. The proximity of the Piedmont also had benefits. That was where Indians found minerals such as greenstone, mica, graphite, and quartz that were prized for the crafting of tools and ornaments. Hunters did not have to go far to kill the turkeys, deer, and bear that helped sustain their families. Those animals and others made use of both ecological zones, eating the berries and tender shoots of the Piedmont in the spring and summer before moving into the oak and hickory forests of the river valleys in the fall and winter to eat the mast, the hickory nuts and acorns on the forest floor.[27]

The rich environment and the hard labor, especially in the cultivation of maize, allowed denser settlements, which in turn led to the development of more complex, hierarchical societies organized around the authority of chiefs.[28] In some cases personal attributes, whether prowess on the battlefield, persuasive oratorical skills, or, in the case of Tascaluza, an imposing physical stature, reinforced chiefly power, but for the most part the chiefs' authority sprang from their birth into specific clans.[29] A chief, Marvin Smith notes, was "the highest ranking member of society" who could "prove the closest genealogical link to the founding ancestors."[30] These were matrilineal societies, and while that did not mean that women held political power as leaders, except in rare cases, their bloodlines did determine the social structure of the Mississippian chiefdoms. The fact that the eldest son of the chief's sister would be next in line to lead the chiefdom elevated her, which de Soto undoubtedly recognized when he took both the Coosa chief and his sister hostage. The sons of other women in the ruling clan constituted the elite members of the society. But because clan members could not marry one another, many members of lower-ranking clans married into the ruling clan, broadening the hierarchical structure of the Mississippian chiefdoms. Men far removed from the ruling clan could gain status through wartime exploits, but in most cases one's place within the chiefdom was determined by clan and birth order.[31]

Mississippian Indians lived in a wide variety of settings that, in one way or another, were all related to chiefdoms. Many constructed individual farmsteads strung along creeks and rivers, especially during periods of limited warfare. Others grouped together in small hamlets or larger towns with a few hundred inhabitants, which might or might not have had a ceremonial platform mound and palisade walls for protection. These larger towns served as anchors of simple chiefdoms that bound the neighboring farms and hamlets together into one polity. But in some places, at different times, even bigger towns with over five hundred residents and multiple mounds developed, which seemed to denote the emergence of more complex chiefdoms that dominated the simpler chiefdoms of their region.

The fields of maize along the alluvial floodplains of Alabama's rivers sustained a large and dense population, but it was the platform mounds that made manifest the belief system and economic and political connections that gave life to the Mississippian chiefdoms. The earthen mounds might not have looked very imposing to Spaniards like de Soto who had viewed the stone architecture of the Incan Empire, but they towered over the landscape.[32] The tallest of the twenty platform mounds at Moundville stood at sixty feet, with an estimated volume of over four million cubic feet of earth. A similarly sized mound in Georgia could hold up to three hundred people on top without crowding.[33] Since they were steep, laborers built more gently sloping ramps up one side so that people could reach the tops. De Soto and his soldiers were able to ride their horses up the log steps of one ramp, which they reported was between fifteen and twenty feet wide.[34] The very presence of the mounds augmented the chiefs' authority, since it was they who could mobilize the labor necessary for their construction.[35] But it was the activities associated with the mound centers that reinforced both the communal values and the hierarchical power of chiefdoms.

On the most fundamental level, platform mounds represented the earth and thus anchored towns and chiefdoms to the center of the world. Southeastern Indians of the historic era believed that their natural world, the earth, stood balanced between an Upper World, which represented order and predictability, and an Under World, which represented chaos and change. That balance required rules of behavior and rituals of cleansing and purification. It is likely that Mississippian ancestors of those Indians held similar beliefs. Some archaeologists argue that the stages of construction and layering of soil on platform mounds might have been rituals of renewal and fertility designed to cover surfaces "polluted" by the transgressions of the whole community.[36]

Many southeastern Indian groups told stories about their distant ancestors having emerged from the earth, and mounds played a key role in connecting Mississippian Indians to that distant past. They often built mortuary temples and charnel houses on top of platform mounds, where not only the bones but also carved images of ancestors were laid to rest. The symbolism of the earth, the rituals of purification involved in the mounds' construction, and the link back to the ancestral origins of the people all contributed to the sacredness of platform mounds. That many chiefs built their houses on the highest mound in their town only reinforced the belief that chiefly authority sprang from the chiefs' connections to both supernatural and ancestral forces that were ever present in the world.[37]

The power of chiefs was also associated with one of the primary activities of mound centers: the redistribution of economic goods. Most Indian households were self-sufficient; families fed themselves through farming, hunting, and gathering and made most of the clothing, tools, and vessels, including clay pots, necessary for their day-to-day lives. But both simple and complex mound sites became points of exchange of surplus food and nonutilitarian craft goods. Animal and plant remains, especially of maize and venison, suggest that food supplies accumulated at those towns. Some emphasize the communal purposes of these food stores, suggesting that they were used for periodic ceremonial feasting, for emergencies, or for protection from enemies during times of war. Others speculate that the accumulation of food represented a system of tribute routinely paid by outlying communities to the chief or by vanquished enemies during peace negotiations. Either way, it appears that chiefs controlled access to these foodstuffs and were able to augment their power through communal rituals or by distributing the food to the elites and the craftsmen in the towns.[38]

Those craftsmen made prestige goods, the exotic ornamental pieces, tools, and ceramic vessels found in the burial sites of the Mississippian elite. Copper plates, earspools and pendants, shell and red-slate gorgets, and fancy ceramics became status symbols that differentiated elite from commoner. Since many of these prestige goods were etched with the symbols and animal figures, both real and mythic, that composed the Mississippian cosmological iconography, they also bestowed on their possessors a certain supernatural power. Most of the prestige goods were made out of nonlocal materials that traveled extensive trade routes stretching from the Gulf coast up to the Appalachian Mountains. In some cases it appears that the goods themselves were traded or paid as tribute by a lesser chief to acknowledge allegiance to a paramount chiefdom, while in other cases, craftsmen took the raw materials to create prestige goods for distribution to elites in the neighboring towns of the chiefdom. Scholars believe that it was the chiefs who controlled the distribution of those prestige goods, using them to cement alliances with elites.[39]

The iconography on those prestige goods often depicted clubs and other instruments of war, suggesting the centrality of military conflict in Mississippian culture. The "buffer zones" of empty land between chiefdoms and the palisades surrounding many of the towns confirm that fact. Burial remains with cranial fractures, embedded arrow points, scalping cut marks, mass internments, and severed body parts that appeared to be trophies of war reinforce the notion that late prehistoric Alabama was a violent place.[40]

The introduction of bows and arrows in the late Woodland period brought an increase in mortality rates, and Mississippian Indians responded with defensive measures. In some cases they located their towns on islands in rivers, but more frequently they built palisades. The largest fortified towns, like Moundville, show little evidence of violent deaths, probably because they were too strong to attack. It was another matter in smaller palisaded towns. At Lubbub Creek, about thirty-three miles west of Moundville, there was a town that housed about ninety residents in the fourteenth century, with a larger population of neighbors in small hamlets and farmsteads. This small community had a surprisingly strong defensive structure, with a dry moat or ditch next to a long palisade wall with six bastions for archers. That defense seemed to protect the town's residents and those who fled there during times of war from bows and arrows. But the violent death rate was high, with many killed from blows to the head, perhaps in forays outside the walls to break sieges or during raiding expeditions. The highest mortality from arrow points during the Mississippian period continued to be in the small, undefended hamlets and farmsteads.[41]

Mississippian Indians fought wars not to gain territory but to consolidate or expand the authority of chiefs and chiefdoms. They engaged in small-scale raids and mobilized hundreds of warriors into war parties to attack towns. The goals of this style of hegemonic warfare were to gain captives to enslave or torture, to disrupt or defend the production and exchange of prestige goods, and to bring under vassalage neighboring chiefdoms. Chiefs and elites benefited from successful military engagements because they opened up opportunities for the accumulation of prestige goods. War meant plunder, of course, but the negotiations that followed could also be profitable, with gifts exchanged, restitution for those killed, and ongoing tribute from the conquered chiefdom. Victory also was a sign of favor within the supernatural world, which enhanced the power of the chiefs. Common Indian men could also benefit from war since it gave them opportunities to display the valor and military skill that could improve their status within their communities.[42]

Warfare, of course, brought instability. Massive platform mounds gave the illusion of permanence but in reality chiefdoms were often fragile. Reversals of fortune could signal disruptions or disfavor within the spiritual realm, undermining the authority of chiefs and providing openings for power struggles. Outright conquest was not the only danger. The expansion of a rival chiefdom might cut off the trade route for a particularly important prestige good, or an extended drought might bring about a famine. Both would undermine the redistributive powers of a chief, opening him to challenges. Population growth could also lead to the breaking away of one faction and the migration and founding of a new chiefdom. Finally, the peripheries of larger, complex chiefdoms were often restive. Conquered chiefdoms were rarely tightly controlled but instead were forced into a military alliance that usually required payment of tribute, prompting either passive or active resistance. The rhythm of everyday life and the spiritual beliefs that gave meaning to daily activities created a stable foundation in Mississippian society, but atop that base lay a fluid political landscape of shifting alliances and expanding and contracting polities.[43]

Hernando de Soto was deeply immersed in an indigenous world in the fall of 1540, when he met Chief Tascaluza—a world of ritualized greetings and gift giving, of platform mounds and palisades. But his presence in the chiefdoms of the Southeast and his reactions to people and situations that confronted him cannot be understood without exploring his own background and that of the broader Spanish Empire. As he and his men marched along the Alabama River toward Mabila, they carried with them their Castilian heritage, their Catholicism, and their desires for wealth and power, fueled, in de Soto's case, by decades of experience as an adventurer in the service of Spain's imperial designs in the Western Hemisphere. La Florida was not his first choice for a new land to conquer; rumors of riches deep in the interior persisted but did not erase doubts about the value of this vast territory. Nonetheless, de Soto and his men marched forth, carrying the cross and the sword in the name of Spain, and brought their imaginary vision of La Florida to Tascaluza's world.

The reconquest of Iberia from the Muslim Moors in the second half of the fifteenth century set the stage for Spanish expansion into the Western Hemisphere. The war against the Islamic empire forged a common Christian identity that became the glue that held together a disparate, intensely localistic people and a foundation of what it meant to be Spanish. Christianity itself justified the war and the enslavement of captured Muslims who had explicitly rejected the one "true" faith. Most of the military expeditions against the Moors were privately financed, and officers and common soldiers alike expected compensation through the plundering of booty and land taken from the Muslims. War was the proper path toward wealth and glory in honor-bound Spain. The Crown encouraged and controlled military adventurism through legalistic mechanisms. For example, the government granted the title of *adelantado* to military leaders, which bestowed extensive rights to wealth and land through conquest while ensuring that the Crown received a portion of the booty. The reconquest also militarized the society as a wide swath of the population experienced the hardships of war and learned the tactics of laying siege to towns and responding, both on foot and on horseback, to the surprise attacks of the Moors. When the final group of Moors was pushed out of Granada in 1492, the same year Christopher Columbus set sail across the Atlantic, Spain was ready to harness the military adventurism and aggression and the thirst for personal glory and wealth among its people to further the cause of Christ and Crown in the wider world.[44]

After forays through the Caribbean and encounters with societies deemed disappointingly primitive, Spanish exploration of the Western Hemisphere took a dramatic turn in 1519 with Cortez's conquest of the Aztecs in Mexico. The wealth of that empire sparked new rounds of exploration. Soldiers sought territories that might yield precious metals, or people who could be enslaved, or land that could be transformed into plantations—anything that could bring riches to those bold enough to pursue them. The Church and the Crown oversaw those adventurers, first drawing up contracts spelling out all of the details, especially the division of profits, and then sending priests and government functionaries along on the expeditions.

One of the key points of concern regarded the treatment of the native people. Muslims who refused to convert to Christianity during the reconquest had been enslaved, but could the same action be taken with Indians who had not been exposed to the faith? Certainly, all agreed, they should be made subject to the Spanish Empire. The Crown included a *requerimiento* in the conquistadors' contracts spelling out the duty of the leaders to use force to subject Indians "to the yoke and authority of the Church and their Majesties."[45] There was a fine line between subjugation and enslavement, a line made narrower by the distance from Spain and the perils and exigencies of the entradas. While some lobbied on behalf of the Indians, it was not until 1542 that a royal decree banned their enslavement.[46]

Spain's exploratory efforts in the decade after Cortez defeated the Aztecs took adventurers to the northern reaches of the Gulf and Atlantic coasts, where reports on prospects remained mixed. Ponce de León had skirted the eastern side of Florida back in 1513 and had fought a pitched battle with Indians whom he found very formidable. In 1519, Alonso Álvarez de Pineda sailed along the northern shores of the Gulf, becoming the first European on record to view the land that became Alabama. De Pineda was not impressed and reported back that "all the land is low and sterile."[47] But Spanish slavers on the coast of what would become South Carolina picked up several dozen Indians who spoke of a rich kingdom deep in the interior of the Southeast. Those tales grew into the Chicora legend, which spread throughout the Atlantic littoral and drew sailors and adventurers to the Carolina coast throughout the sixteenth century. The experiences of sailors navigating the Gulf coast during that time gave weight to those rumors of riches; putting onto shore to find provisions or to explore, they sometimes encountered Indians wearing ornamental pieces of gold. Most likely this was part of the flotsam of shipwrecked Spanish treasure ships, refashioned to their own purposes. Many of these coastal Indians were wearing pieces of European clothing that had washed up onshore as well. But the sight of gold reinforced persistent rumors throughout the sailing world that riches lay somewhere deep within the land that had come to be known as La Florida.[48]

After a failed attempt to settle the Atlantic coast, Spain turned to the Gulf. Pánfilo de Narváez, a conquistador experienced in military expeditions in New Spain, received a contract to explore and establish a colony and set out with a force of hundreds from Cuba in 1528 bound for the central Gulf coast. Short on supplies, the expedition landed on Florida's west coast. De Narváez made a fateful decision to march his men overland along the perimeter of the Gulf and sent his ships on ahead to meet them. Unable to find the harbor that was to be the rendezvous point, the ships returned to Cuba, leaving de Narváez's army struggling through marshy land under repeated Indian attacks. Confronted with those difficulties, the men decided to build rafts in order to float across the Gulf to the coast of Mexico, a daunting voyage that proved impossible. The fate of the estimated 250 Spaniards who set off on rafts is largely unknown since they quickly became separated. Most undoubtedly drowned but some washed ashore, including four men who lived among the Indians of Texas for five years before making their way across land to Mexico. One of those survivors, Álvar Núñez Cabeza de Vaca, wrote a celebrated account of the ill-fated de Narváez expedition that proved influential to Hernando de Soto when he undertook his own entrada through La Florida.[49]

One short anecdote in de Vaca's amazing tale of survival involves two men: Teodoro, the Greek, and an African man who may have been a slave. They and others in a small flotilla of rafts, including de Vaca, had made it as far as Mobile Bay in their improbable journey through the Gulf. There a few Indians paddled out in canoes to greet the Spaniards. Teodoro and the African man went ashore, accompanied by the Indians, to search for water and were never seen again. Twelve years later, as he was traveling with Tascaluza along the Alabama River, de Soto came to the small town of Piachi. The residents of the town presented de Soto with a dagger that they claimed had belonged to Teodoro, although it is not clear how it ended up so many miles inland. The fate of the two men is also murky; some say they were killed outright while others suggest that they lived for some time with the Indians of Mobile Bay. In any case, Teodoro the Greek and an anonymous African man became the first recorded nonnative residents of what would become Alabama, even if only for a very short time.[50]

By the time de Narváez set off from Cuba in 1528, Hernando de Soto was already a veteran in the conquests of Central America and would soon become one of the leading conquistadors of the Spanish Empire. He was born around 1497 in the western portion of Estremadura, a poor region of Castile that spawned a large percentage of the military adventurers who ended up overseas. De Soto came from a *hidalgo* family that, despite their upper-class ranking, was relatively poor, and he set his eyes on the New World. In 1514, while still in his teens, de Soto joined the ranks of an army organized by Pedrarias Dávila to oust the famous explorer Balboa from his governorship of Panama and learned firsthand the political intrigue and brutal conditions of New Spain. One-third of the expedition force died within months of their arrival in Panama, felled by disease and malnutrition, but de Soto survived and prospered, largely through his loyalty to Dávila and his military prowess. By 1530 de Soto was the mayor of Leon, owned the best encomiendas in Panama, and was amassing wealth through the sale of Indian slaves. His charismatic leadership and superb horsemanship had gained him a following among the Spanish soldiers in Central America, but he was restless and wanted more.[51]

De Soto's ambitions took him to Peru, where his experiences taught him lessons of conquest and fueled his drive to govern his own colony. Francisco Pizarro recruited de Soto for his invasion of the Incan Empire. Arriving in Peru in 1531 with one hundred horsemen, de Soto found himself in the thick of battle as leader of the mounted vanguard and played an instrumental role in the defeat of the powerful Incas, whose formidable army was undermined by political factionalism and civil war.[52]

Despite being an accomplished and brave officer, de Soto's ambition and personality led to rash decisions that almost resulted in his death. His arrogance was on full display during the march to the Incan capital of Cuzco. Eager to be the first to the city, de Soto broke orders and led his soldiers on a grueling ride, outpacing the rest of the army. The heat and altitude took a toll on his men and horses, and de Soto soon found his forces surrounded by an attacking Incan army. The Spaniards fought fiercely but most likely would have been slaughtered had reinforcements not arrived. Pizarro, perhaps undermining the impact of that lesson on the dangers of overconfidence, rewarded de Soto with the lieutenant governorship of Cuzco. If the message received was that glory and riches came to those who risked all, then that particular Peruvian experience would come to haunt de Soto a decade later in La Florida.[53]

One tactic de Soto did learn in Peru was the efficacy of capturing Indian leaders to control hostile populations. Pizarro took Atahualpa, one of the leaders of an Incan faction, and demanded gold and silver for his ransom. Atahualpa's armies were powerful and far outstripped the Spaniards in numbers, but the imprisonment of Atahualpa paralyzed them and they held back as the treasure poured into the city. Their reticence did not save their leader in the long run; Pizarro later executed Atahualpa. Coming out of Peru, de Soto understood that the authority of Indian leaders could be turned to his advantage if they were under his control.[54]

De Soto gained tremendous wealth in Peru but also was frustrated by limitations on his ambitions. He received 180 pounds of gold and 360 pounds of silver, the third-largest allocation of Incan treasure, and moved into a palace in Cuzco, taking one of Atahualpa's wives as a mistress. But he found himself caught between intriguing factions in Spanish-controlled Peru, his position within the chain of command uncertain. De Soto wanted to be another Cortes and Pizarro, with a governorship of his own, so he left Peru, arriving in Spain in 1536.[55]

Once in Spain, de Soto moved quickly to realize his goal. He solidified his political ties by marrying Isabel de Bobadilla, the daughter of Pedrarias Dávila, his old commander, and then began petitioning the Crown for a position. In 1537 King Charles V finally granted de Soto a contract giving him permission to explore La Florida for four years, with a goal of selecting a site for permanent Spanish settlement. The king even threw in the governorship of Cuba as well. De Soto had to cover the expenses of the entrada himself but he could keep one-seventh of any riches he found, after the Crown took its customary fifth, with the remainder being divided up among his troops. He also had the power to grant encomiendas to any settlers and could set aside twelve square leagues of land for his own estate. La Florida was not his first choice, but with Cabeza de Vaca, the survivor of the de Narváez expedition, back in Spain telling tales about the hints of wealth in the unexplored interior, de Soto had no trouble rounding up soldiers willing to risk their lives for riches and glory.[56]

Six or seven hundred men accompanied de Soto to Cuba in 1538, and the island served as the staging ground for the entrada. They brought armor and weaponry with them from Spain but needed food supplies. De Soto purchased 250 horses and thousands of pounds of bacon, bushels of corn, and baskets of cassava and collected hundreds of pigs to provide a mobile source of food, one that could forage for itself along the trail. Planning ahead, de Soto bought farms in Cuba to grow crops that could later be sent to La Florida to feed his troops. Many of the men who had sailed with him from Spain abandoned the expedition, lured away by opportunities elsewhere, but others in Cuba joined the venture. One was Vasco Porcallo de Figuerora, the wealthiest man on the island. The fifty-year-old seemed an unlikely conquistador but he did have military experience and he agreed to provide many of the pigs, horses, and food supplies for the expedition. Porcallo was more interested in the people of La Florida than in the rumored treasures from the Chicora legend; he was intent on capturing Indian slaves for his plantations and mines on Cuba. But he abandoned the entrada not long after arriving on the mainland, frustrated at the Spaniards' inability to take the fiercely resistant Indians alive.[57]

Only about three hundred of the seven hundred or so members of de Soto's entrada who landed near Tampa Bay in May 1539 survived to make it back to New Spain four years later. Those lucky ones provide a glimpse of the soldiers' backgrounds. As Charles Hudson notes, this "was not an army of strangers."[58] Over 40 percent of the survivors came from Estremadura, de Soto's home region, with most of the rest from other parts of Castile. Nearby Portugal was the birthplace of 5 percent, and there was one Italian and one Frenchman among those who made it out of La Florida. Many officers owned slaves, so an unknown number of Africans came along on the expedition. At least two and probably more women were part of the entrada. The Spanish Crown sent three royal officers—an accountant, a factor, and a treasurer—to make sure that a fifth of the discovered wealth ended up in its coffers. De Soto himself selected priests and scribes, as well as a surgeon and apothecary. The priests might have anticipated measuring success by the number of Indians converted, but the rest of the participants focused on the wealth to be extracted from this largely unknown land. Indian guides captured by scouts in the months leading up to the expedition had been shown gold back in Cuba and they had assured the Spaniards that there was plenty of that precious metal deep in the interior of La Florida.[59]

Those dreams of wealth had largely evaporated by October 1540, when Hernando de Soto and his forces were marching toward Mabila with Chief Tascaluza in tow. No gold or silver had been found, not even in the Appalachian Mountains. The tamemes, or porters, did carry countless bundles of tribute and plunder accumulated along the way: crafted prestige goods of copper and mica, deerskins, and freshwater pearls. But these would not bring riches to de Soto or his men. No great cities to rival Cuzco or empires like the Aztecs or Incas lay hidden in the interior. But the land was fruitful and perhaps could be carved into encomiendas for enterprising Spaniards and farmed by Indians, if they could be subjugated.

The entrada's forces had long since developed a travel routine by the time they reached Alabama. De Soto led a vanguard of horsemen and a few footmen, followed by the main guard of mostly foot soldiers, Indian porters in chains, and a separate group of chained Indian women, all accompanied by dogs and hundreds of pigs trotting alongside. A rearguard of horsemen followed to protect the troops from attack and to round up escaping slaves and deserters. De Soto's foot soldiers wore steel helmets and light armor: either steel plates sewn into their shirts or quilted cloth thickly padded with cotton. They carried a variety of weapons, including swords, matchlock guns, crossbows, and halberds, which were long poles with a spike and axe-like head. The horsemen generally wielded lances and were more heavily armored in chain mail or with steel plates over their torsos and the outsides of their arms and legs. Their horses came from a breed that had been introduced into Spain by the Moors and were small but tough, able to carry heavy loads. They were valuable assets in confrontations with the Indians, who had great difficulty avoiding the deadly lances on open ground. When the Indians fled to swamps or canebrakes to escape the horsemen, the dogs were loosed to flush them out.[60]

De Soto arrived at Mabila on the morning of October 18, 1540, and there were plenty of warning signs that all might not be well. The town was smaller than some they had passed but it was strongly fortified, with thick palisade walls with bastions every fifty feet, each capable of holding seven or eight archers. Some of the Spaniards noted the worrisome fact that the fields around the town seemed to have been recently cleared of all brush and habitations, perhaps in preparation for battle. Even more troubling was the report from scouts that warriors from neighboring settlements had been gathering at Mabila for days and that there were very few women, children, and elderly men in the town. De Soto did not have his full army with him when he arrived. He had moved ahead with his vanguard of forty horsemen and his own personal guard of crossbowmen and halberdiers, along with an assortment of footmen, slaves, and porters. The rest of his forces were strung out along the trail, detained, one chronicler noted, by "pillaging and scattering themselves" across a "populous" land.[61] Despite his limited forces, de Soto decided to accept the invitation of Mabila's leaders to stay in the town and not to camp on the empty plain as some of his officers advised. Perhaps he was reluctant to show fear, or his control of Tascaluza made him overconfident, or he simply operated out of an arrogance bred from a long history of military conquest and a pervasive sense of superiority. Whatever the reason, de Soto left his horses and supplies outside the walls of the town and entered Mabila with perhaps a dozen of his guards and horsemen on foot.[62]

At first, all seemed peaceful. The Spaniards walked "with the Indians" into the town, a chronicler noted, "chatting, as if we had them in peace, because only three hundred or four hundred appeared there." The usual welcoming rituals ensued. "As they made festivity for us, they began to do their dances and songs," the chronicler continued, remembering, especially, that "they had fifteen or twenty women dance in front of us."[63] They had come to Mabila for women, so perhaps this dance distracted them, as they did not at first notice that Tascaluza had slipped into one of the buildings in the town. When de Soto noted his absence, he demanded that Tascaluza leave the building, but the chief refused and de Soto sent Baltasar de Gallegos to bring him out. Glancing through the door, de Gallegos saw a room filled with warriors armed with bows and arrows and called out a warning, before slashing out with his sword and cutting off the arm of a nearby Indian. Immediately, warriors poured out of all the buildings in the town, firing arrows, as others blocked the town's two gates, trapping de Soto and his men inside. The battle of Mabila had begun.[64]

The Spaniards, who were battle-hardened veterans, reacted immediately and began fighting their way to the gates. The chroniclers later claimed that five thousand Indian warriors were in Mabila that day, and while they undoubtedly inflated that number, the dozen Spanish soldiers certainly faced thousands of foes. Despite those unfavorable odds, they had some advantages. They were skilled swordsmen experienced in hand-to-hand combat and they had some armor protecting their bodies. Mabila's buildings and the crowds of people impeded the Indians' ability to get off clean and accurate shots with their bows and arrows. Still they managed to kill five of the Spaniards almost immediately and wounded all of the rest as they retreated back toward the gates. The timely arrival of some of de Soto's horsemen saved the day as they fought off some of the Indians blocking the gates, allowing the surviving soldiers to slip out of Mabila and mount their horses. The Indians brought the baggage and supplies that the Spaniards had left by the palisade wall into the town, along with the porters, closing the gates behind them.[65]

Most of the army still had not reached Mabila and de Soto had only about forty horsemen, but at least he had space to maneuver. The cleared land surrounding the town worked against Tascaluza's people. Hoping to draw them out from behind the palisades, the Spaniards pretended to flee beyond the reach of the arrows, "and the Indians, believing it, ventured from the town . . . in their pursuit," according to one of the chroniclers.[66] The feint worked. When the Indians had advanced far from Mabila's walls, the Spaniards wheeled their horses around and galloped toward them, lancing many before they could run back to the safety of the town. There they stayed, watching de Soto and his horsemen circle Mabila, and only occasionally darting out to fire off an arrow while they waited for the rest of his army to arrive.[67]

When all of de Soto's forces had gathered on the plain outside Mabila, the battle turned in the Spaniards' favor. They first had to breach the strong walls protecting the town. Facing flurries of arrows, the soldiers attacked the clay surface with axes, exposing the horizontal crossbeams that formed the palisade's skeleton and using them as ladders to clamber to the top of the walls. From there they shot flaming crossbow bolts into the town, setting fire to many of the buildings. The Spaniards then were able to break through Mabila's two gates and de Soto led his best-armored horsemen inside, lances lowered and ready. The Indian warriors fought back hard and were able to drive the soldiers out of the town several times. De Soto, while "standing in his stirrups to throw a lance at an Indian," was shot in the buttocks with an arrow and was forced to fight the rest of the battle riding high on his horse. His nephew, Diego de Soto, was not as lucky. He was struck in the eye with an arrow shot so forcefully that it penetrated through the back of his skull. "He fell to the ground at once," one chronicler wrote, "and lay in agony without speaking until the next day, when he died."[68]

Once breached, the sanctuary of Mabila became a trap for Tascaluza's warriors. Ultimately, the flames and smoke and the lances of the well-armored horsemen overwhelmed the Indians. Any who managed to escape the town faced more Spaniards on horseback, lances at the ready. Some of the Indian women picked up the weapons of their men and fought, but to no avail. Nine hours after de Soto entered Mabila, the battle wound down. In the end, a small group of women—survivors of those who had danced for the Spaniards that morning—stood with their hands crossed before them, signaling supplication and surrender. As the soldiers approached, the women stepped aside, revealing three warriors, bows in position. Two were killed instantly and the third climbed a tree and hung himself with his bowstring.[69]

The Spaniards burned Mabila to the ground and, according to the chroniclers, killed three thousand Indians, but that victory left de Soto's entrada close to collapse. Only 22 soldiers died but 143 were wounded, many of them multiple times, and virtually all of their supplies had been destroyed in the fire. The single doctor on the expedition "was stupid and almost useless," and the medicine, olive oil, and bandages that might have been useful had burned up, leaving the soldiers to make do. They tore up the clothing of their fallen comrades to bind their wounds, and one chronicler reported that they resorted to "cutting open the dead Indians and taking the fat to use as ointment and oil in treating wounds."[70] Food supplies were also scarce, so many got busy skinning and butchering the dead horses while others began foraging in nearby towns. It would be almost a month before de Soto and his men left their makeshift camp on the plains outside Mabila.[71]

De Soto had a choice to make after the battle. Before arriving at Mabila he had heard that ships awaited him on the Gulf at Ochuse, a six-day journey away. He originally had planned to lead his men there in order to resupply his entrada and to establish a settlement, but he now had second thoughts. He had not found the riches he had hoped to find and his one treasure, freshwater pearls that he had collected along the way, had burned. If he led his men to Ochuse, some would undoubtedly make their way to Cuba and news of his failure would spread. La Florida "would acquire such a reputation that no man would desire to go thither," one chronicler revealed.[72] De Soto tried to keep the presence of the ships a secret but word leaked out and his officers and soldiers pushed hard to abandon the entrada. The lack of gold and silver had sapped their enthusiasm, but also "the incredible ferocity of the battle" at Mabila "had frightened and disturbed them extraordinarily," according to a chronicler, "making them wish to leave the land and go away from it as soon as they could." Faced with "such bellicose people" who "would allow themselves to be killed first" before being subjugated, some said that it would be better to go to Peru or Mexico, "where they could enrich themselves without so much work."[73]

Determined to salvage his entrada and his reputation, de Soto made his decision. He freed the one Indian guide who knew the way to Ochuse and began to march his forces northwest, away from the ships waiting in the Gulf. What followed was more misery and death in a futile search for some treasure that would make the entrada through La Florida worthwhile. De Soto himself died of fever on the banks of the Mississippi River in the spring of 1542. His soldiers attempted to reach Mexico overland but turned back when they reached arid lands with little food to sustain them. They then built boats and floated down the Mississippi River, finally reaching the Gulf in the summer of 1543. Fewer than half of the Spaniards who embarked on the entrada made it back to New Spain.

Hernando de Soto's vision of La Florida was a fantasy shaped by rumors and by expectations based on past experiences, and, like most fantasies, it collapsed in the face of reality. But even unrealized fantasies have power. De Soto and his men smashed through the South, driven by their pursuit of treasure that did not exist, and quickly departed, leaving behind an Indian world. But while the entrada disappeared from sight like a rock tossed into water, it left ripples in its wake. Thousands had died and thousands had been displaced, chained, raped, and forced to march hundreds of miles from their homes, many never to return. Most were young men and women—hunters and warriors and farmers—and their absence tore holes in the fabric of families, clans, and towns and damaged their communities' ability to feed or defend their people. And could chiefs who had faced the indignity of capture lay claim to the supernatural powers that anchored their authority? If not, then they were vulnerable both to challenges from within their chiefdoms and to attacks from without. Economic, demographic, and political fluctuations had long been part of Mississippian life, but at least along the narrow path of the entrada those disruptions undoubtedly intensified.

Still, ripples subside. De Soto's march did not fundamentally transform the South. Look at those who stayed behind. The pigs that wandered off thrived in the rich environment, evolving into the wild razorbacks that would feed, and sometimes endanger, future pioneers on the southern frontier. Humans wandered off as well, despite de Soto's efforts to round up stragglers. Some of his soldiers fell in love with Indian women during the long encampments in chiefdoms or grew enamored with Indian life and hid when the entrada moved on. A few African slaves also ran away to live among the Indians. Those outsiders were absorbed into families and clans, and in the matrilineal Mississippian culture, their children were not Spanish or African but people of Coosa or Talisi. A "frontier" of sorts began when de Soto and his men tried to make real the imagined La Florida, but when those intruders left the Indians still sat at the center of their world.

Notes

1. Charles Hudson, *Knights of Spain, Warriors of the Sun: Hernando de Soto and the South's Ancient Chiefdoms* (Athens: University of Georgia Press, 1997), 74–76, 85.

2. David H. Dye, "Feasting with the Enemy: Mississippian Warfare and Prestige-Good Circulation," in *Native American Interactions: Multiscalar Analyses and Interpretations in the Eastern Woodlands*, ed. Michael S. Nassaney and Kenneth S. Sassaman (Knoxville: University of Tennessee Press, 1995), 301, 305–6.

3. Rodrigo Rangel, "Account of the Northern Conquest and Discovery of Hernando de Soto," trans. and ed. John E. Worth, in *The De Soto Chronicles: The Expedition of Hernando de Soto to North America in 1539–1543*, ed. Lawrence A. Clayton, Vernon James Knight Jr., and Edward C. Moore (Tuscaloosa: University of Alabama Press, 1993), 1:282.

4. Ibid., 283.

5. *The Account by a Gentleman from Elvas*, trans. and ed. James Alexander Robertson, in Clayton, Knight, and Moore, *De Soto Chronicles*, 1:93.

6. Rangel, "Account of the Northern Conquest," 284.

7. *Account by a Gentleman*, 92–93.

8. Ibid., 93.

9. Rangel, "Account of the Northern Conquest," 288.

10. Hudson, *Knights of Spain*, 228.

11. Rangel, "Account of the Northern Conquest," 290.

12. *Account by a Gentleman*, 96.

13. Ibid.

14. Ibid.

15. Ibid.

16. Rangel, "Account of the Northern Conquest," 291.

17. Luys Hernández de Biedma, "Relation of the Island of Florida," trans. and ed. John E. Worth, in Clayton, Knight, and Moore, *De Soto Chronicles*, 1:232.

18. Hudson, *Knights of Spain*, 232.

19. Ibid.; Rangel, "Account of the Northern Conquest," 291.

20. Hudson, *Knights of Spain*, 2–3, 22–23.

21. James Axtell, *The Indians' New South: Cultural Change in the Colonial Southeast* (Baton Rouge: Louisiana State University Press, 1997), 2.

22. Timothy R. Pauketat, *The Ascent of the Chiefs: Cahokia and Mississippian Politics in Native North America* (Tuscaloosa: University of Alabama Press, 1994), 5, 47, 64.

23. John A. Walthall, *Prehistoric Indians of the Southeast: Archaeology of Alabama and the Middle South* (Tuscaloosa: University of Alabama Press, 1980), 13–19; Donald Edward Davis, *Where There Are Mountains: An Environmental History of the Southern Appalachians* (Athens: University of Georgia Press, 2000), 8, 11.

24. Marvin T. Smith, *Coosa: The Rise and Fall of a Southeastern Mississippian Chiefdom* (Gainesville: University Press of Florida, 2000); John H. Blitz and Karl G. Lorenz, *The Chattahoochee Chiefdoms* (Tuscaloosa: University of Alabama Press, 2006); Ian W. Brown, ed., *Bottle Creek: A Pensacola Culture Site in South Alabama* (Tuscaloosa: University of Alabama Press, 2003); Paul D. Welch, *Moundville's Economy* (Tuscaloosa: University of Alabama Press, 1991); John H. Blitz, *Ancient Chiefdoms of the Tombigbee* (Tuscaloosa: University of Alabama Press, 1993); J. Daniel Rogers and Bruce D. Smith, eds., *Mississippian Communities and Households* (Tuscaloosa: University of Alabama Press, 1995).

25. Charles Hudson, *Conversations with the High Priest of Coosa* (Chapel Hill: University of North Carolina Press, 2003), 7; Tim S. Mistovich, "Toward an Explanation of Variation in Moundville Phase Households in the Black Warrior Valley, Alabama," in Rogers and Smith, *Mississippian Communities and Households*, 161–63; Davis, *Where There Are Mountains*, 21.

26. Bruce D. Smith, "Mississippian Patterns of Subsistence and Settlement," in *Alabama and the Borderlands: From Prehistory to Statehood*, ed. R. Reid Badger and Lawrence A. Clayton (Tuscaloosa: University of Alabama Press, 1985); C. Roger Nance, "A Study of Lamar Ecology on the Western Edge of the Southern Piedmont," in *Lamar Archaeology: Mississippian Chiefdoms in the Deep South*, ed. Mark Williams and Gary Shapiro (Tuscaloosa: University of Alabama Press, 1990); Blitz, *Ancient Chiefdoms*, 33; Hudson, *Knights of Spain*, 154–55; Davis, *Where There Are Mountains*, 15.

27. Blitz, *Ancient Chiefdoms*, 33; Welch, *Moundville's Economy*, 26; Nance, "Study of Lamar Ecology," 142–46; Walthall, *Prehistoric Indians*, 15.

28. John F. Scarry, "The Late Prehistoric Southeast," in *The Forgotten Centuries: Indians and Europeans in the American South, 1521–1704*, ed. Charles Hudson and Carmen Chaves Tesser (Athens: University of Georgia Press, 1994), 21.

29. Blitz, *Ancient Chiefdoms*, 7.

30. Smith, *Coosa*, 14.

31. Ibid., 14–15; Adam King and Jennifer A. Freer, "The Mississippian Southeast: A World-Systems Perspective," in Nassaney and Sassaman, *Native American Interactions*, 275.

32. Patricia Galloway, *Choctaw Genesis, 1500–1700* (Lincoln: University of Nebraska Press, 1995), 14.

33. Walthall, *Prehistoric Indians*, 187; Davis, *Where There Are Mountains*, 21.

34. Charles Hudson, *The Southeastern Indians* (Knoxville: University of Tennesse Press, 1976), 78.

35. David W. Morgan, "A Proposed Construction Sequence of the Mound B Terrace at Bottle Creek," in Brown, *Bottle Creek*, 82; Hudson, *Southeastern Indians*, 78.

36. Blitz, *Ancient Chiefdoms*, 71; Blitz and Lorenz, *Chattahoochee Chiefdoms*, 12–13, 93, 95; Hudson, *Southeastern Indians*, 122–28, 174.

37. Blitz and Lorenz, *Chattahoochee Chiefdoms*, 14.

38. Blitz, *Ancient Chiefdoms*, 14, 100–101; Randolph J. Widmer, "The Structure of the Southeastern Chiefdoms," in Hudson and Tesser, *Forgotten Centuries*, 138–39.

39. Dye, "Feasting with the Enemy," 290–91; Blitz, *Ancient Chiefdoms*, 153, 177–78; Paul D. Welch, "Control over Goods and the Political Stability of the Moundville Chiefdom," in *Political Structure and Change in the Prehistoric Southeastern United States*, ed. John F. Scarry (Gainesville: University Press of Florida, 1996), 81, 86–87, 91; Peter N. Peregrine, "Networks of Power: The Mississippian World-System," in Nassaney and Sassaman, *Native American Interactions*, 252.

40. Patricia S. Bridges, Keith P. Jacobi, and Mary Lucas Powell, "Warfare-Related Trauma in the Late Prehistory of Alabama," in *Bioarchaeological Studies of Life in the Age of Agriculture: A View from the Southeast*, ed. Patricia M. Lambert (Tuscaloosa: University of Alabama Press, 2000), 35; James Taylor Carson, *Making an Atlantic World: Circles, Paths, and Scenes from the Colonial South* (Knoxville: University of Tennessee Press, 2007), 13.

41. Bridges, Jacobi, and Powell, "Warfare-Related Trauma," 39–40; Blitz, *Ancient Chiefdoms*, 29–30, 118–23.

42. David J. Hally, "The Nature of Mississippian Regional Systems," in *Light on the Path: The Anthropology and History of the Southeastern Indians*, ed. Thomas J. Pluckhahn and Robbie Ethridge (Tuscaloosa: University of Alabama Press, 2006), 31–33; King and Freer, "Mississippian Southeast," 272–75; Dye, "Feasting with the Enemy," 302–3, 307.

43. Blitz and Lorenz, *Chattahoochee Chiefdoms*, 18–19, 132–33; Blitz, *Ancient Chiefdoms*, 16–17.

44. Hudson, *Knights of Spain*, 3–9; D. W. Meinig, *The Shaping of America: A Geographical Perspective on 500 Years of History*, vol. 1, *Atlantic America, 1492–1800* (New Haven, CT: Yale University Press, 1986), 4, 11, 45.

45. Luciano Peraña, *La idea de justicia en la conquista de América* (Madrid: Mapfre, 1992), 237–39, quoted in Jerald T. Milanich, "A New World: Indians and Europeans in

Sixteenth-Century La Florida," in *Beyond Books and Borders: Garcilaso de la Vega and* La Florida del Inca, ed. Raquel Chang-Rodriquez (Lewisburg, PA: Bucknell University Press, 2006), 49–50. The translation of the *requerimiento* quoted by Pereña is Milanich's.

46. Hudson, *Knights of Spain*, 8–10; Meinig, *Shaping of America*, 11–12.

47. De Pineda, in the text of Francisco de Garay's contract for the conquest of Amichel, June 4, 1521, in *Colección de los viages y descubrimientos que hicieron por mar los Españoles desde fines del siglo XV*, ed. Martin Fernásdez de Navarrete (Madrid, 1825–1837), 3:160, quoted in Paul E. Hoffman, "Introduction: The De Soto Expedition, a Cultural Crossroads," in Clayton, Knight, and Moore, *De Soto Chronicles*, 1:5.

48. Hoffman, "Introduction," 2–5; Milanich, "New World," 52; Jerald T. Milanich, "The European Entrada into La Florida: An Overview," in *Columbian Consequences*, ed. David Hurst Thomas, vol. 2, *Archaeological and Historical Perspectives on the Spanish Borderlands East* (Washington, DC: Smithsonian Institution Press, 1990), 10–11; Axtell, *Indians' New South*, 12–13.

49. Milanich, "New World," 53.

50. Robert S. Weddle, *The Spanish Sea: The Gulf of Mexico in North American Discovery, 1500–1685* (College Station: Texas A&M University Press, 1985), 193; Hudson, *Knights of Spain*, 38.

51. Curt Lamar, "Hernando de Soto before Florida: A Narrative," in *The Hernando de Soto Expedition: History, Historiography, and "Discovery" in the Southeast*, ed. Patricia Galloway (Lincoln: University of Nebraska Press, 1997), 181–85; Hudson, *Knights of Spain*, 39–41.

52. Lamar, "Hernando de Soto before Florida," 185–88; Hudson, *Knights of Spain*, 41–42.

53. Lamar, "Hernando de Soto before Florida," 191, 196–98.

54. Ibid., 194–95.

55. Ibid., 195, 199–200; Hudson, *Knights of Spain*, 42–44.

56. Ignacio Avellaneda, "Hernando de Soto and His Florida Fantasy," in Galloway, *Hernando de Soto Expedition*, 208; Hudson, *Knights of Spain*, 44–45.

57. Avellaneda, "Hernando de Soto and His Florida Fantasy," 210–12, 215; Hudson, *Knights of Spain*, 55.

58. Hudson, *Knights of Spain*, 48, 87.

59. Avellaneda, "Hernando de Soto and His Florida Fantasy," 213–15; Hudson, *Knights of Spain*, 57, 63–64.

60. Hudson, *Knights of Spain*, 67–69, 76–78, 90; Axtell, *Indians' New South*, 20–21.

61. Rangel, "Account of the Northern Conquest," 292.

62. Hudson, *Knights of Spain*, 235–37; Rangel, "Account of the Northern Conquest," 292; *Account by a Gentleman*, 98.

63. De Biedma, "Relation of the Island of Florida," 233.

64. Hudson, *Knights of Spain*, 237–38.

65. Ibid., 238–39.

66. Rangel, "Account of the Northern Conquest," 293.

67. Ibid.; Hudson, *Knights of Spain*, 240–41.

68. Garcilaso de la Vega, *La Florida, by the Inca*, trans. Charmion Shelby, in Clayton, Knight, and Moore, *De Soto Chronicles*, 2:344; Hudson, *Knights of Spain*, 241–42.

69. Hudson, *Knights of Spain*, 243.

70. *La Florida, by the Inca*, 348–49.

71. Ibid.; Hudson, *Knights of Spain*, 243–44, 246–47, 250.

72. *Account by a Gentleman*, 104.

73. *La Florida, by the Inca*, 356; Hudson, *Knights of Spain*, 248.

2

The Indians' Frontier

[handwritten margin note: differences from de Soto's conquest; possible reasons & explanations]

In the summer of 1560, twenty years after Hernando de Soto and his soldiers marched out of Coosa to rendezvous with Tascaluza, another group of some two hundred Spaniards made their way up the Coosa River toward that celebrated chiefdom. They were a contingent of a much larger force under the command of Tristán de Luna y Arellano, which had left New Spain in 1559 charged with establishing a permanent colony in La Florida. While the main body of that expedition remained encamped and starving far to the southwest in the abandoned Indian town of Nanipacana on the Alabama River, the smaller party scouted ahead, searching for food, for a site suitable for settlement, and for a people willing to accept the authority of a Spanish king and a Christian God. This time there was no talk of gold or silver; de Soto's experiences had taught them the limitations of this land. But the veterans of that earlier entrada who had joined this mission did beguile their foot-weary comrades with stories of the fertile and fruitful chiefdom of Coosa, a "new Andalucia" deep in the interior. Those tales must have provided solace during a difficult journey. The soldiers had passed only a few deserted villages since leaving Nanipacana and had been forced to sustain themselves "on some herbs and blackberries" and "nuts and oak acorns," which they found "too bitter to eat" since they did not know how to prepare them "as the Indians know how to do."[1] That hardship was rewarded when they reached Onachiqui, a border town in the province of Coosa.

There, after fifty-seven days of marching, one chronicler recalled, "the Indians received us with good will, and gave us food without our having to go and forage for it."[2] Another month of travel brought them to the principal town of Coosa, "where the lord of the country resides."[3]

The Spaniards found food in Coosa, which put them in a better position than their comrades back in Nanipacana, but the chiefdom was not the Eden promised by the legends. Each discovery they reported seemed to come with a qualification, a reality that did not quite match expectations. They found "walnuts in great quantity although with very hard shells," and the chestnuts, while "not inferior to those of Spain," were "small and few." The blackberries that had helped sustain them during their long journey were "not so many" as the de Soto veterans "had told us." Coosa had "plums and hazel-nuts, but as they are not yet ripe we do not know how good they are."[4] The towns appeared to be prosperous, with extensive fields of maize along the bottomlands, but the forests pressed in on all sides, leaving little room for Spanish cattle or crops. After three months they rejoined the main force of the de Luna expedition, now back on the coast after having abandoned Nanipacana, and found it even more malnourished than when they left and riven by discord among the officers. Their report on the less-than-promising conditions at Coosa made little difference since the de Luna entrada was desperate and at the point of collapse, unable to take advantage of a new Andalucia even if it had existed. The Spanish soon abandoned their colonization effort and pulled out of the lands that would one day be Alabama.

Over four hundred years later, in 1984, archaeologists working at a site on the Coosawattee River thought to be one of the towns of the Coosa chiefdom made a remarkable discovery. Among the scattering of glass beads, brass bells, and pieces of swords in burial sites—Spanish artifacts dating from the de Luna expedition—they found fragments of a thin copper plate, buried with an Indian child of about ten years of age, and etched with what appeared to be a representation of Catholic/Aztec religious belief. The fragments, when pieced together, depicted three figures, two human and one animal-like. The central figure is of a woman in Aztec dress holding a flowering branch and speaking to a man also dressed in traditional Aztec garb. On the right is an animal that might represent a pig or an ox or perhaps the *axolotl* of Aztec myths, which was usually depicted with a snout and powerful claws. The three figures together represented a syncretic, or blended, religious scene that placed the Catholic imagery within an Aztec cultural context. Some suggest that the plate depicts the Annunciation, when the angel Gabriel visited Mary to announce the coming of Christ, while others argue that the plate is a depiction of a sixteenth-century Mexican legend, the Lady of Guadalupe de Tepeyac, who mysteriously appeared three times before an Aztec convert. Most scholars agree that an Indian in central Mexico created the Coosawattee Plate sometime before 1559, when the de Luna expedition left New Spain.[5]

How did this remarkable artifact find its way into a child's grave in northwest Georgia? No one knows for certain, but most likely one of the two priests who accompanied the scouting party in 1560 carried it to Coosa. One of them, Domingo de la Anunciación, had worked extensively with the Indians of Mexico before coming to La Florida and might have received it as a gift. The plate's size and oval shape was typical of engraved copper plates that adorned both Bible covers and the tops of boxes used to carry Bibles and other religious instruments, boxes that also served as writing desks. Punched holes transformed the plate into a metal gorget hung around a neck.

The Coosawattee Plate is a fascinating curiosity that seems out of place in the soil of northwest Georgia, but in fact it is an apt symbol of the American Southeast in the mid-sixteenth century. It is easy in hindsight to trace the trajectory of that region's development back in time and to discount the presence of Spain, believing that of course the land that became Georgia and Alabama would be "English" before becoming "American." But the origin of the Coosawattee Plate in New Spain reminds us that Spanish ambitions in North America pointed toward an alternate future for the region. If de Luna's colonization efforts had been successful, present-day Alabama would have been part of a northern empire in service to the wealth and power of New Spain as a provider of food supplies, a protector of shipping lanes, and a bulwark against the designs of France and England.

The origins of the Coosawattee Plate as an artifact of an Aztec society transformed by Spanish conquest hint at what might have been, but its burial in an Indian child's grave reminds us of what was. De Luna's expedition failed and the Spanish departed Coosa and Nanipacana and the entire interior of La Florida, leaving behind an Indian world. At some point before then the plate was traded, given as a gift, or stolen. The two priests were not in Coosa long enough to impose their beliefs on the residents but they and their soldier compatriots perhaps embodied an exotic authority as outsiders that might have been transferred to the plate itself. The people of Coosa probably understood the symbolic power of etched figures as representations of supernatural forces that bestowed prestige on the owner. So the Coosawattee Plate became a conveyor of privileged rank, leading to its final resting place in the grave of an elite child. The plate became an Indian artifact, serving the purposes of its new owners.

The mystery surrounding the Coosawattee Plate—how it ended up in Indian hands, who owned it and for how long, and how it was used before being buried—is also an appropriate symbol for the late sixteenth-century Southeast, which in many ways was an unknown world. When the Spanish retreated to the peninsula of Florida and founded Saint Augustine in 1565, the interior of the Southeast reverted back to terra incognita as far as Europeans were concerned. It would be over a hundred years before another European visited the territory that would become Alabama, or at least one who documented that visit. During that period great changes transformed the Indians' world. Spaniards had marched through highly organized hierarchical chiefdoms in the mid-sixteenth century, but by the late seventeenth century Europeans encountered collections of decentralized egalitarian Indian towns that later would form the core of the great Indian confederacies of the eighteenth century, such as the Creeks and the Choctaws. Just what historical forces were in play to bring about those changes is unclear; Charles Hudson calls this period the "black hole" of southern history.[6]

So what kind of frontier existed in Alabama between 1560 and the late seventeenth century? It was not the kind of middle ground or borderland that has been described in other locations, where initial contact was closely followed by European traders, soldiers, and missionaries, all of whom negotiated with Indians of various ethnicities, carving a hybrid society out of their varied agendas. The Spanish left, no other Europeans arrived, and the people of Coosa and Tascaluza and the Chattahoochee chiefdoms remained, farming the bottomlands and hunting up on the ridges as they had done for centuries. This was, emphatically, an Indian world, but it was one in the process of transformation, shaped both by the forces unleashed by Spanish intrusion and by the breathing space granted by Spanish failure and retreat.

In one sense, Alabama in the century after de Luna's entrada was a middle ground created out of what had been and what was to become, a temporal borderland between the old world of the precontact Southeast and the new world that would come with the resurgence of European interest during the late seventeenth century. As they did with the Coosawattee Plate, the Indians took the experience of contact and transformed it within their own framework, precisely because the Spanish left them alone. They had time and space to adjust. This was not a benign process; middle grounds were not harmonious and placid. Contact brought death and wrenching changes to the people of the Southeast, but the passage of time allowed the Indians to create new forms of political organization, to migrate to new regions, and to hold on to old ways of subsisting and of practicing their beliefs. They carved out their own frontier on familiar lands.

The impetus for de Luna's expedition grew out of the wreckage of Hernando de Soto's *entrada*. The conquistador's failure dampened dreams of finding the kind of riches that had been found in Mexico and Peru but did not completely put to rest Spanish desires for a northern empire. If the pearls and furs of the southeastern chiefdoms paled in comparison to the treasures of the Aztecs and Incas, the maize and nuts and bear oil that had sustained starving Spaniards held their own allure. The expedition's survivors told stories of the chiefdoms they had encountered, especially the fertile and powerful Coosa. In doing so they kept alive the idea that deep in the interior of La Florida lay a fruitful land, a new Andalucia, that could provision the wealthier Spanish settlements to the south and even perhaps support profitable commodities like mulberry trees for silk production or grapes for wine.[7]

The stories of dense populations of Indians represented another kind of riches to some Spaniards: that of souls ripe for conversion. Spanish policy toward the native peoples of the Western Hemisphere had undergone a transformation in the years since de Soto embarked on his *entrada* as the court tempered the conquistador impulse to subjugate through terror and enslavement. Around the time that de Soto's men were straggling out of the Mississippi Delta, the Dominican order gained influence in the court and began advocating conversion of the Indians and a voluntary allegiance to Spanish authority. Just as younger conquistadors like de Soto had looked beyond Mexico and Peru for new fields of conquest, priests also looked for new places to establish missions, and La Florida represented the richest field untouched by the word of God.[8]

Spain was also intent on establishing a foothold in the Southeast to counter any colonizing efforts by its rivals. A spate of publications about Spanish exploration of the New World had sparked interest in North America among the French and English, intensifying Spain's determination to solidify its claim over the Gulf and South Atlantic coasts. One major reason for doing so was to protect Spanish shipping lanes from the depredations of pirates and to provide safe havens for ships in distress. La Florida might not contain gold and silver but it could be instrumental in ensuring that those treasures from Mexico and Peru reached Spain.[9]

By the late 1550s an ambitious scheme to colonize La Florida had emerged and was best articulated by Pedro de Santander, an official in New Spain, in a letter sent in 1557 to King Philip II of Spain. He proposed an expedition with 1,500 men from New Spain to pacify the north shore of the Gulf and occupy the Southeast's interior. Memories of de Soto's entrada influenced his proposed route. Beginning at Ochuse, or Pensacola Bay, de Santander would march his forces north to Tascaluza Province, where he would build a town, moving on to do the same at Talisi and Coosa before ending at a proposed colony of Santa Elena on the Atlantic coast of what is today South Carolina. If successful, Spain would control a sweeping arc of land through the heart of La Florida. King Philip II did not agree to de Santander's entire scheme, but it piqued his interest. In December 1557 he called on the viceroy of New Spain, Luis de Velasco, to oversee the colonization of Santa Elena on the south Atlantic coast and of another site yet to be determined on the north Gulf coast, to be financed by the Crown. Here, then, lay the roots of the de Luna expedition, Spain's largest effort to colonize La Florida.[10]

Viceroy de Velasco took great care in planning for a successful expedition. He selected veterans to serve as officers, beginning with Tristán de Luna y Arellano, whom he named governor of La Florida. De Luna came from a prominent family that had long served the Spanish Crown and had been in New Spain for almost thirty years. He had been second in command to Coronado on his march through the Southwest and had later gained some fame for putting down an Indian uprising in Mexico in 1548. De Velasco also sent several ships under the leadership of a de Soto veteran to sail along the Gulf coast in search of a suitable landing site. Bahia Ochuse looked promising, although high winds prevented a thorough exploration, but the sailors also were impressed with Bahia Filipina, or Mobile Bay. The forests of oak, cedar, cypress, and chestnuts were open enough for horses to maneuver and there was plenty of grass and water for livestock. While they did not interact with Indians, they saw them fishing from canoes in the bay and they noted their villages lining the shore, each surrounded by fields tangled with maize, beans, and pumpkins. Since the expedition was focused on settlement, not treasure and conquest, de Velasco made sure that it was well supplied so the settlers could sustain themselves without relying on the Indians for food. One of the soldiers later reported that the viceroy had loaded the expedition's ships with "a great many supplies of corn, biscuit, bacon, dried beef, cheese, oil, vinegar, wine, and some live cattle to multiply in the land" and that he had also included "many tools for building and digging in order to sow." Hedging his bets, de Velasco planned to send regular supply ships from Havana and New Spain to support the new colony.[11]

De Luna recruited four hundred soldiers, half of them mounted, and about one hundred artisans from across the provinces of New Spain to join his expedition, and it was here that planning began to go awry. To begin with, they were a rowdy and undisciplined bunch. The viceroy reported to the king that he would not give the men arms until they had boarded ships "so as to avoid any difficulties which might arise," and confessed that "if I had not made haste to get the men out of Mexico, trouble hard to remedy might have arisen."[12] Then, as de Luna's forces marched from Mexico City to the port of San Juan de Ulúa on the Gulf coast, a ragtag assemblage of almost one thousand family members and servants joined the expedition. Alarmed, de Velasco warned de Luna that the "*canaille* of halfbreeds, mulattoes, and Indians . . . will serve no purpose save to put the camp in confusion and eat up the supplies."[13]

The ships left the port on June 11, 1559, with all of the people, including six Dominican priests, and 240 horses, bound for Ochuse. There they planned to build a town with one hundred house lots, a monastery, a church, and a governor's house that would also be used to store weapons and food supplies, all surrounding a central plaza. Once done, they would march overland through the Southeast to settle Santa Elena on the Atlantic coast. The fact that de Velasco and de Luna considered that inland route to be safer and easier than sending ships around the Keys illustrates the depth of their ignorance about the interior of La Florida.[14]

The first report de Luna sent back to de Velasco was positive. After a brief stop at Bahia Filipina the ships had sailed for Ochuse because they considered it "one of the best ports to be found in the discovered parts of the Indies." Arriving in August, they found "some few Indian huts, which seemed to be for fishermen," and a single cornfield. While that location lacked the dense Indian population surrounding Bahia Filipina, the land appeared fertile, with "many walnuts, grapes, other trees, which bear fruit, and much forest, much game and wild fowl, and many fish of numerous varieties." Best of all, the bay was well protected from storms, and de Luna assured the viceroy that ships anchored there were "so secure that no wind can do them any damage at all."[15]

That confidence was misplaced. In September, soon after their arrival, a hurricane inflicted a devastating blow to the expedition by destroying seven of the ten ships anchored in the bay, drowning a number of colonists who had remained onboard. More importantly, most of the food supplies and tools were lost or ruined in the storm. Suddenly the colonists found themselves in the same situation faced by de Soto's men: an abject dependence on the Indians and on the natural resources of the region.[16]

Unlike his predecessor, de Luna could not command his soldiers to confiscate maize at the point of a lance, since Spanish policy toward the Indians had changed. Viceroy de Velasco in particular was a proponent of a more humane approach to gaining the allegiance of the native peoples, and that stance was reflected in the expedition he organized. He informed the king that he had planned to augment the colony's supplies with relief ships precisely so that the settlers "may not vex the natives, and may be fed until they sow and reap and make a settlement."[17] The oath taken by de Luna when he accepted his position as governor of La Florida specifically charged him with bringing Indians into submission to both Crown and Church "without subjecting them to war, force, or bad treatment."[18]

In any case, indigenous food supplies were scarce. There were few villages in the vicinity of Ochuse so de Luna immediately sent scouting parties deep into the interior to the Alabama River. One group came across the village of Nanipacana, a once-prosperous town near Mabila that, according to one historian, was deserted and ruined. But later testimony by de Luna's soldiers suggests that this was no depopulated ghost town, since the scouts sent word back to de Luna in December that "there was a large quantity of corn" in Nanipacana. They urged him to move the colony inland and join them, but by that time de Luna was suffering from dementia brought on by fevers and he dithered in making a decision. De Velasco had sent a relief ship with food but it was only enough to take the edge off the colonists' hunger. Finally, in February 1560 de Luna brought his people to Nanipacana, only to find that the Indians of the region "had revolted" and "had absented themselves and taken away the supplies," including "a large quantity of maize." Facing a dire situation, de Luna sent scouts up the Alabama River "to discover Indian towns" and, more importantly, bring back food. Once again they passed by many "houses and fields, but no people, it appearing that they had revolted and absented themselves." They returned empty-handed. In desperation, de Luna ordered two hundred of his men to search out the chiefdom of Coosa, for certainly there had to be food there. The rest of the colonists hunkered down at Nanipacana and grew increasingly hungry and mutinous.[19]

Summer brought renewed hopes that the "cornfields and grainfields and certain wild vegetables" along the banks of the Alabama River would help ease their suffering, but that was not the case. Scouting parties once again searched the area around Nanipacana and returned, "not having found one grain of corn;

the cornfields had been pulled up, and all the fields burned and pulled up by the natives, [as had] even the wild herbs, which they had learned that we could make use of and which we eat."[20] Some of de Luna's officers advocated moving the colony down the Alabama River to Bahia Filipina. There "they could sustain themselves on the many shellfish such as oysters, crawfishes, and the many fish which are in the bay," as well as the "great many deer," while "awaiting the succor which the most illustrious viceroy of New Spain might send us." They convinced de Luna and by July 1560 the settlers had returned to the coast.[21]

Why did de Luna's expedition struggle so mightily to find food when de Soto's entrada passed by fields full of maize, squashes, and beans? Some historians suggest that the depredations of de Soto's march had shattered the chiefdoms and emptied the towns. The enslavement of young men and women, the great battle at Mabila, and the epidemics that might have followed in the Spaniards' wake stripped a populous land of its people, they argue. The trauma inflicted by de Soto surely did have an impact, but the Indians had not disappeared. Who, after all, had burned the fields and abandoned the towns? The officers who reported that the Indians had "hidden the food and destroyed the houses" had it right when they told their commander that "the ill will of the natives" had spread across the region. It wasn't that the land that de Luna's men were traversing was depopulated and destroyed by de Soto; rather, its people had been made wary by their violent encounter with Spaniards twenty years earlier.[22]

While de Luna and his officers bickered in Nanipacana, the scouting party made their way toward the chiefdom of Coosa through the spring and summer months of 1560. Their reports drew a decidedly mixed portrait of the people and land that they encountered. They faced no real opposition, although many of the villages they passed early in their journey had been recently deserted. When they did finally reach inhabited towns along the Coosa River, the Indians willingly provided food and porters but seemed eager to be rid of the intruders. The leader of the party, Mateo del Sauz, wrote to de Luna in July from Apica, a town near the border with Coosa, to report that the Indians "give us burden-bearers and all we ask for in order to get us out of the country." He feared that "the people here may rise against us when they harvest their crops." One of the friars in the party acknowledged that "the people of this land are very peaceable" but then wondered if the fact that "they do not keep their women and clothing in their houses" meant "that when they have gathered their corn they will also themselves go into hiding."[23] The prospect of starvation left the Spaniards uneasy.

As they got closer to the core of the chiefdom the towns were more frequent and the people more friendly. When they finally arrived in the chief's town they were welcomed and given dried maize and roasting ears and pumpkins. They were pleased that the Indians were "at ease with all the Spaniards" and that the chief "made no move to take away their food or women." The scouting party ended up staying three months.[24]

It soon became clear why the people of Coosa welcomed the Spanish soldiers: they were seeking allies. "It seems that certain Indians have entered their lands," Father de la Anunciación wrote, and "have caused them injuries and vexations." The troubling interlopers were actually the Napochies, a former tributary chiefdom in the eastern Tennessee Valley that had broken away and now were controlling important trade paths. The armed Spaniards were a godsend and the Coosa chief was quick to take advantage. He asked the soldiers to fight for him, reminding them, as de la Anunciación wrote to de Luna, that "they were our friends" and that they "had given us of whatever they had, and had placed themselves under the protection of the king."[25] Del Sauz agreed to send a small detachment of fifty soldiers and cavalrymen with three hundred of Coosa's warriors to launch an attack against the Napochies, which proved successful.[26]

The people of Coosa might have been welcoming, but the land itself seemed less than desirable and certainly did not match the glowing reports of the de Soto veterans. The heart of the province of Coosa was a collection of eight small towns, none with more than fifty houses. They were strung along rivers and streams to take advantage of the bottomlands for cultivation, but, as de la Anunciación observed, "all the rest is so densely wooded that it can by no means be inhabited."[27] When reports from the scouting party began filtering back to the Spaniards' main encampment at Ochuse, officers who wanted to abort the mission used the discouraging news to plead their case, arguing against de Luna's rather weak-willed desire to move the colony to Coosa. "The country is not fit to settle in," one group of officers complained, "for, aside from there being no lands on which to plant crops save those the Indians occupy, these are so scant that as soon as an ear of corn is gathered they immediately plant again at the foot of the selfsame stalk." The Indians even had difficulty cultivating the land, the officers said, and they "sustain their lives" on "bitter acorns, shoots of canes, and roots."[28] Two others argued that "there is no place to settle nor plant a town of Spaniards" throughout the land, "not even in Coosa itself; for that country is shut in by forests full of marshes and swamps."[29]

Those observations cannot be taken at face value as accurate depictions of Coosa. The junior officers faced insubordination charges after the failed expedition and used exaggerated descriptions of unsuitable land in legal depositions to justify their reluctance to obey de Luna's commands. Still, it is clear that the reality of Coosa brought crushing disillusionment to the Spaniards who had been primed by the legends of the de Soto veterans. Davila Padilla recounted that Coosa "looked so much the worse to the Spaniards for having been depicted so grandly," and added that the veterans guiding the scouting party "declared that they must have been bewitched when this country seemed to them so rich and populated as they had stated."[30]

The colony continued to collapse through the fall of 1560, brought low by malarial fevers, starvation, and mutinous discord among the officers. Relief ships arrived at Ochuse, but never with enough supplies to sustain the Spaniards. De Luna abandoned plans to move the colonists to Coosa and recalled the scouting party in November. Word of de Luna's indecision and periodic dementia filtered back to New Spain and in March 1561, de Velasco relieved him of command and appointed in his place Ángel de Villafañe, a veteran of Mexican conquests. When de Villafañe arrived in Ochuse he found the colonists in dire straits, living on grass and shellfish after having eaten up all their leather products. By that time rumors of French designs on the South Atlantic coast had renewed the viceroy's interest in establishing a colony in present-day South Carolina. Accordingly, de Villafañe gathered up the settlers at Ochuse and, leaving behind a small garrison, sailed in April 1561 for Havana to prepare for the settlement of Santa Elena. Many of his forces, fed up with the hardships of colonization, deserted de Villafañe in Cuba. He finally set sail, but while searching for a good port around Cape Hatteras, the expedition was beset by a hurricane that sank two of his ships and drove the rest back to Hispaniola. Conceding defeat, he sent ships to pick up those left behind at Ochuse, marking the end of Spain's largest and best-organized attempt to settle La Florida.[31]

After de Luna's failures in the Gulf and de Villafañe's aborted attempt to settle Santa Elena, Spain abandoned its larger vision of a northern empire and concentrated on gaining a foothold on the peninsula. They succeeded in doing so when they founded Saint Augustine in 1565 and then focused on converting Indians by establishing mission towns stretching west to the Apalachicola River. The collapse of Spain's dreams of La Florida would have important repercussions many decades down the road as the Atlantic and Gulf coasts remained open to English and French exploration and settlement. But the more immediate effect was that the Indians of the southeastern interior were left alone to absorb the impact of the Spanish entradas that had transformed their world into a frontier.

The chroniclers of Hernando de Soto's march through the Southeast described towns anchored by massive earthen mounds and surrounded by palisades, and recounted rituals of greeting with chiefs carried on platforms, resplendent in robes of fur and feathers. But in the last decades of the seventeenth century, when English traders began probing the western interior from their bases in Virginia and Carolina and Spanish soldiers marched north from Florida, they encountered a very different Indian world. A wide variety of ethnic groups clustered in towns, or *talwas,* along Alabama's waterways, most, but not all, Muskogee speaking. Cowetas, Cussitas, and Hitchitis lived on the Chattahoochee River, while Abihkas, Tuckabatchees, and Alabamas built their homes near the confluence of the Tallapoosa, Coosa, and Alabama Rivers. Instead of mounds, each talwa centered on the square ground, a clearing surrounded on all four sides by the houses of leaders and their advisors. Vestiges of the great plazas of the Mississippian towns, the square grounds nonetheless exemplified a more egalitarian political system that placed a premium on debate and discussion. They, along with the absence of mounds and of elite burial sites in the newer towns along the Coosa, suggest a shift away from hierarchical social organization and chiefly claims to divine authority.[32]

Historians sum up those complex changes as the "collapse" of the Mississippian chiefdoms, but just how and why that happened is still a mystery. Some emphasize the impact of the Spanish entradas, conjuring images of powerful yet brittle societies shattered by European intrusion. Others suggest that shifts in population and in political authority were part of the ebb and flow of Indian societies, both before and after the Spaniards came and went.

In the eyes of some historians, diseases were the engines of change, spreading out, in both time and space, far beyond the Spaniards who introduced them to the Southeast. Some suggest that epidemics led to massive depopulation, which in turn contributed to the rapid crumbling of the social and political foundations of the chiefdoms, the migrations of survivors, and the coalescence of more decentralized Indian confederacies. One of the strongest proponents of this view, Henry Dobyns, argues that Old World diseases brought about the "wholesale depopulation of the Southeast" and the "collapse of the aboriginal way of life" soon after European contact.[33] Smallpox, influenza, measles, bubonic plague, and other diseases "biologically invaded the peoples of the Americas"; those viruses and germs were "the true shock troops with which the Old World battered the New."[34] Even before de Soto passed through the Southeast, Indians of the interior were dying off, Dobyns claims, the victims of various diseases that had moved inland from coastal contact points with the Spanish. The conquistador's entrada left its own destructive wake of violence and disease. So rapid was the collapse of the chiefdoms, Dobyns argues, that when de Luna arrived twenty years later towns were empty of people and the fields devoid of crops.[35]

Dobyns's depiction of the decimation of Indian society is the most exaggerated version of a common perception of the "virgin soil" of America defiled by Old World diseases. Before that cataclysm, the eighteen million Indians that he estimates resided north of Mesoamerica had lived "in almost a paradise of well-being" because of the "near-absence of lethal pathogens in the aboriginal New World."[36] That "virgin soil" provided a fertile field for the virulent spread of new diseases to which native people lacked immunity. Dobyns and others assume that the smallpox carried by a Spanish sailor on the coast of Florida in the 1530s, or even the influenza of a resident of Mexico, swept north along trade paths, passing from one Indian to another, deep into the interior of the Southeast.

Not all accept Dobyns's argument. Some challenge his precontact population figures and the numbers killed by disease. Others accuse him of exaggerating the spread of illnesses. As one critic, David Henige, notes, in Dobyns's view "there was scarcely a disease incident that was not also an epidemic, and very few epidemics that did not evolve into pandemics."[37] Dobyns's model hinges on vague reports of sickness in the documentary record and on long-distance trade routes that have been misrepresented. Mississippian elites did trade prestige goods made from exotic materials from distant sources, but most of the food, clothing, and tools of the interior Indians were local in origin, and contact with coastal regions was very limited.[38] But could the Spaniards have carried disease into the heart of the Coosa and Tascaluza chiefdoms, as Dobyns assumes? The documentary evidence suggests not. Both de Soto's and de Luna's expeditions camped for weeks and months in some locations, yet the chroniclers never reported outbreaks of illness among the Indians in the vicinity. If the men had been carrying smallpox, measles, whooping cough, or other major diseases then illness would have struck their own ranks early in their marches. The chroniclers did mention that some soldiers got sick, but not until many months into their expeditions, and it is likely that they were laid low by bacterial infections or malaria, not more deadly diseases like smallpox or influenza. Old World diseases certainly killed large numbers of indigenous people and played a major role in the conquest of some empires, like the Aztecs and Incas. But current research suggests that, at least until the late seventeenth century, the more isolated interior of the Southeast escaped epidemics associated with European contact.[39]

The image of epidemics sweeping through virgin soil creates too stark a division between the "paradise" of precontact America and the fallen world of collapsed chiefdoms, one that obscures more than it reveals. Alabama, and the rest of the Southeast, was not a pristine land that was timeless and somehow removed from history, just waiting for the disasters triggered by the invasion of disease. De Luna's men did not travel through a land emptied of people, cut off from its precontact past, as Dobyns suggests. They marched through a changing land, where some had died, some had migrated, and the many who remained chose to desert their towns and hide their corn because of past experiences. The dislocations of the late sixteenth and seventeenth centuries that have come to be called "the collapse of the chiefdoms" were not sharp transitions but a more muddled middle ground of decline and adaptation, of change and continuity built on the Indians' own cycles of history and on the intrusions of outsiders.

A closer look at Alabama's frontier in the late sixteenth and seventeenth centuries complicates our picture of the "devolution" of chiefdoms. Some historians argue that there was a wider range of Indian polities in the Mississippian Southeast than de Soto's chroniclers have led us to believe. The Spaniards viewed La Florida through the prism of their own feudal society and their experiences with the great empires of Aztecs and Incas. They brought their own cultural preconceptions about the organization of provinces and subject towns to their descriptions of chiefdoms like Coosa and might very well have overemphasized the extent of control exercised by the paramount chief over tributary towns like Chiaha and Talisi. For example, what the Spaniards saw as tribute flowing from peripheral chiefs to the paramount chief within a centralized political unit might just have been ritualized gifts to seal a military alliance between largely independent chiefdoms. Patricia Galloway, for one, suggests that "a patchwork of variation in social organization" existed in the Southeast and that simple chiefdoms and even tribal confederations were more common at the time of European contact than previously thought.[40]

Paying attention to the longer cycles of history before European contact is also helpful in putting the collapse of the Mississippian chiefdoms in context. The kind of migrations and depopulation of specific regions that historians point to when discussing the devastating impact of epidemics were constantly occurring in the centuries before the Spanish arrived in the Southeast. Neal Salisbury points out that, throughout North America, "the continent's demographic and political map was in a state of profound flux" when Europeans arrived.[41] Chiefdoms were inherently unstable political organizations, and migration, according to Ned Jenkins, served as a "safety valve for social tensions among competing elites." In matrilineal societies, power flowed through the lineages of the chief's sisters. Their sons, the nephews of the chief, had legitimate claims to the position and sometimes wrangled over ascension to power. One solution was for one challenger to break away and take a portion of the chiefdom's population to a new site to establish an independent, but ethnically related, chiefdom. Anthropologists call this "budding," and it probably was a major factor in the spread of Mississippian culture across the Southeast. But chiefdoms also collapsed periodically, in a process archaeologists call "fissioning." Environmental crises such as drought, which could deplete agricultural surpluses, or disruptions in the trade of prestige goods could undermine the authority of chiefs and contribute to the breaking apart of established chiefdoms and the out-migration to new territories.[42]

The shifts in residential patterns in the Black Warrior Valley associated with the chiefdom of Moundville illustrate that process of consolidation and dispersal. By the eleventh century, the valley's population was spread out among a series of fairly large villages interspersed with farmsteads. Intensive cultivation of maize led to surpluses that allowed for denser populations organized around simple chiefdoms. During the twelfth century a platform mound was built at the town of Moundville but most of the people lived along the river and its tributaries. It was during the next century that Moundville sprang to life, as the approximately one thousand residents built twenty major platform mounds topped with public buildings, mortuary temples, and elite homes, all surrounding a central plaza and encircled by a large palisade. Perhaps as many as two thousand others continued to live along a fifty-kilometer stretch of the river on farmsteads and in towns, many of which had their own platform mounds and palisades. Archaeologists disagree about the exact nature of the relationship between those varied communities, but it appears that the outlying simple mound centers and farmsteads fell within the economic and political gravitational pull of Moundville. Yet that dominance did not last. By the end of the fourteenth century, while the population within the broader valley continued to grow and smaller mound centers proliferated, Moundville itself declined. Only about three hundred people lived in Moundville itself by the early fifteenth century, and the site was now devoted to the production of craft goods and the burial of Indians from the entire valley. By the end of that century, the burials had ended and Moundville was largely abandoned.[43]

Climate changes might account for the decline of Moundville. After more than a century of warm, rainy weather that was favorable to maize cultivation, the Southeast experienced a series of droughts in the late fourteenth century and the first half of the fifteenth century. That environmental stress might have contributed to the collapse of the Moundville chiefdom. Some of the chiefdom's people stayed in autonomous towns along the Black Warrior Valley, while many of those in the Tombigbee River area moved into what would become Mississippi and helped to form the Chickasaws. Many, though, moved into small stream valleys along the upper Alabama River, areas that had limited arable land and thus could not support denser chiefdoms. They organized themselves in simpler, more egalitarian tribal polities, decades before de Soto's men marched through the area.[44]

Recognizing the internal and environmental factors that might have led to dislocations does not mean denying the impact of the entradas, especially de Soto's violent intrusion into the Mississippian Southeast. Those incursions might not have triggered major epidemics but they did create stresses among Indian societies along their paths. As Patricia Galloway notes, both "the natural cycle of chiefdom development and devolution" and "the unnatural chaos" introduced by the Spanish shaped the long transition from more centrally organized chiefdoms to decentralized confederacies.[45] The horrors of de Soto's expedition contributed to higher rates of mortality in a variety of ways. Even if the Spaniards were not carrying smallpox or influenza, their presence had health consequences, especially in places like Coosa where they camped for several weeks. They ate up stores of food all along the route of their entrada, and left copious quantities of human and animal waste in their encampments, generating a deadly combination of bacterial infections and malnutrition from famine. De Soto's army also disrupted populations in town after town by impressing men and women into service as porters and sexual slaves. Although some were released to return home, many died along the way. Finally, there were those killed at the great battle of Mabila. One does not have to accept the Spanish estimates of Indian deaths, which no doubt were inflated, to realize that the towns and villages along the Alabama River lost a great many warriors and some women on that October day in 1540.[46]

Death and the depletion of resources destabilized chiefdoms, like Coosa, that lay along de Soto's path. Chiefs gained authority as embodiments of the supernatural world. To illustrate their power they relied on their ability to gather and distribute surplus food, to control the trade of prestige goods among elites, to mobilize labor for mound construction, and to wage war. Setbacks like those depredations associated with the Spaniards would have signaled a falling out of divine favor and would have encouraged the kind of elite competition that led to fissioning. Tributary towns on the borders of a paramount chiefdom might also have been emboldened to break away when the chief was weakened. De Luna's men perhaps found themselves in the middle of just such a conflict when the Coosa chief asked for their assistance in regaining military control over Napochies. Mississippian chiefdoms had long dealt with the ebb and flow of border town loyalties, but the challenges must have intensified in the wake of de Soto's entrada. Threats at its borders might have contributed to the southwestward migration of Coosa's principal towns over the course of the next century. But towns along the Tallapoosa River appeared very stable through the sixteenth and seventeenth centuries. Like large swaths of Alabama and the Southeast in general, they avoided the Spanish expeditions and seemed to have remained largely untouched by the organizational disruptions of the postcontact period.[47]

While the "collapse" of the chiefdoms suggests a dramatic break, the actual rhythm of day-to-day life for Alabama's Indians in the seventeenth century reflected a deeper continuity. People generally lived in familiar environments, immersed in a flow of time structured around the seasons as they followed many of the same practices of farming, hunting, and gathering as their Mississippian ancestors. Men went out in the fall and winter to hunt the white-tailed deer using bows and arrows and trapped raccoons, opossums, squirrels, and rabbits throughout the year with snares that had changed little over the century. They also did the heavy labor of burning brush and clearing canebrakes to prepare the large communal fields along the floodplains. The women planted the maize in spring, along with the squashes and beans that entwined the stalks, and tended to the "kitchen" gardens next to their houses on the bluffs overlooking the rivers and streams, much as their grandmothers had done. They were the ones who processed the environment's bounty for their families' use. Women scraped the fur off the deerskins, soaked them in water treated with pulverized deer brains, pounded them until soft, and stretched them on a frame to dry over a smoldering fire before stitching the leather into clothing. They made hominy by soaking dried maize kernels in water and lye made from hardwood ashes and then used a mortar and pestle to grind the hominy into a fine meal that could be used to make fried cakes or, more commonly, a porridge they called *sofkee*. They gathered the hickory nuts, walnuts, acorns, and pecans and extended their usefulness into the winter and spring months by parching them and grinding them into a meal or by boiling them in water and skimming the oil off the top with a feather to collect in a pot. None of that work was different from the labors that had filled the days of their ancestors.[48]

The beliefs that undergirded those daily activities were also much the same, although some of the forms of expression had changed. At the center lay the concept of balance through rules of behavior and rituals. Both the Upper World and the Under World, between which the material world lay suspended, had a place within the world of humans, but the trick was maintaining a harmonious balance. The division of labor, with women in charge of planting and men of hunting, was one such rule, as was the rigid gender segregation of many of the Indians' ceremonies. Another way to create balance was to respect the animals that shared the material world as representatives of the spiritual realms. Mississippians etched serpents and falcons onto the surfaces of their pottery to capture some of the supernatural energy of those creatures. Their descendants a century later no longer did that, but they still venerated, through stories, songs, and dance, the snake as a denizen of the Under World and birds as messengers from the Upper World.

Purification rites also played a role in restoring balance. The mounds were the focal point of those rituals for Mississippians as symbols of the earth. Some scholars suspect that, along with serving as burial grounds, mounds were places for communal ceremonies of renewal. Indians would add a new layer of dirt each year to cover the "polluted" surface to represent the fertility of the earth, probably followed by a harvest feast. Echoes of that ritual resonated in the busk ceremony that marked the beginning of communal access to the corn and produce grown on town land. In the early summer months, families relied on corn from their individual kitchen gardens, but by late July or so the "green" corn in the bottomland fields would be ready for harvest. The ceremony began with a cleaning of houses and the square ground and the burning of all the old grain and other foodstuffs, including any remaining kitchen garden crops, to reinforce the spiritual importance of the communal crops. Families also extinguished their hearth fires before gathering in the square ground to renew the talwa's fire, a symbol of the sun, and then carried that fire back to their individual homes. As with the mound ceremonies, the busk coupled purification with renewal of both the fertility of the earth and the community itself.[49]

Still, continuity of beliefs cannot erase the fact that chiefly authority eroded in the seventeenth century, although echoes of the past persisted. Tascaluza, resplendent in his feathered robes, lived high above his chiefdom on a platform mound, built by the people he commanded. One hundred years later, the headmen, or *micos*, in the towns along the Chattahoochee, Tallapoosa, Coosa, and Alabama Rivers lived on the same level as their people and conferred with councilors on the square grounds. They still augmented their power among their own people by distributing food from communal stores during hard times and decorative items crafted by artisans, much as their Mississippian ancestors had done. Although towns in the late seventeenth century were largely autonomous, headmen also negotiated alliances with other chiefs, cementing new relationships with rituals of gift giving that resembled earlier tribute ceremonies. Their authority increasingly sprang from their talents as speakers and negotiators, although some familial lineages still carried vestiges of supernatural power through tales of distant origins among the gods of the Upper World. Those spiritual beliefs also reinforced a red-white dichotomy that contributed to divided power within towns. Red came to symbolize the chaos and violence of the Under World, while white represented the order and peace of the Upper World. Red chiefs who had authority over war and external relations shared power with white chiefs who governed internal civil affairs, and some talwas became known as red or white towns.

Multiple identities complicated the political landscape. Sometimes townspeople who migrated to a new location created satellite, or "daughter," villages and retained a link to the original town even if they were a hundred miles away. They shared one fire, both symbolically and literally, since burning embers were carried from town to village during the annual busk. Clan networks also transcended towns and even geographic regions as well. In addition to being born into a matrilineal lineage, Indians belonged to clans that societies throughout the Southeast recognized, all with roots in the distant past. Some, like the Wind Clan, had higher standing and spawned a greater share of headmen, serving as faint reminders of the more hierarchical chiefdoms.

❧ ————————————————————————

When Europeans reentered the Indian world of the Gulf lands around the turn of the eighteenth century they encountered vestiges of the Mississippian past. In 1702, while scouting out a site for the new French settlement along the Mobile River, Jean-Baptiste LeMoyne de Bienville, brother of Louisiana's leader Pierre LeMoyne d'Iberville, came to a cluster of low islands in the swampy delta land north of Mobile Bay. This was the territory of the *petit* nations of Mobilians and Tohomes, but this particular group of islands was uninhabited. According to d'Iberville, his brother's Indian guide told de Bienville that they were "the place where their gods are . . . and to which the Mobilians used to come and offer sacrifices," and he had to be bribed with a gun to show the Frenchman where the spot was. Even then the man refused to come close. There, "on a little hill among the canes, near an old village," stood the gods, "five images—a man, a woman, a child, a bear, and an owl—made of plaster in the likeness of the Indians of this country." The guide had said that "a person cannot touch them without dying on the spot," but de Bienville took them back to the expedition's encampment and noted that the Indians who saw them "are amazed at our boldness and amazed that we do not die as a result."[50]

Archaeologists call the site where de Bienville found the statues Bottle Creek, a large island in the middle of swampy land that once boasted at least eighteen mounds, some dating back to 1250. Bottle Creek was home to the elite of a chiefdom, a place where they could monitor trade along east-west paths and, most especially, along the rivers that flowed into the Gulf. Remains suggest that neighboring Indians brought large quantities of corn to the island as tribute, but as time wore on fewer people lived on the island, and by the early sixteenth century the mounds there were being used as burial sites. Some argue that the island must have been sacred to the chiefdom's people since other, more suitable locations along the river's bluffs could have been selected. By 1702, echoes in the shape of sculptures and the guide's reverence and fear were all that remained of the once-powerful mound site.

De Bienville's encounter with the sacred world of Alabama's Indians was a pivot point between worlds lost and worlds yet to come. It is easy to focus on the loss that accompanied the "collapse" of the chiefdoms, to suggest that, because there were no more Tascaluzas striding across mound tops in feathered robes, Alabama's Indians had devolved. Certainly the Frenchman's theft of the statues and his casual dismissal of their significance hint at future depredations. But the towering mounds of the past masked a brittle vulnerability; shifts in trade patterns, or environmental changes, or challenges by outsiders could undermine the chief's claim to supernatural authority, causing the chiefdom to collapse. The Indians who would have to deal with the English, Spanish, and French imperial powers lived in dispersed and largely autonomous towns with headmen more accustomed to negotiation and persuasion than command. That gave them some flexibility and resilience to cope with the massive changes to come when Europeans once again entered their world deep in the heart of Alabama.

Notes

1. "Fray Domingo de la Anunciación and Others to Velasco, Coosa, August 1, 1560," in *The Luna Papers: Documents Relating to the Expedition of Don Tristán de Luna y Arellano for the Conquest of La Florida in 1559–1561*, ed. Herbert Ingram Priestley (DeLand, FL: Florida State Historical Society, 1928), 1:235, http://palmm.digital.flvc.org

/islandora/object/uwf%3A46938#page/spine/mode/2up. Also see Robert S. Weddle, *The Spanish Sea: The Gulf of Mexico in North American Discovery, 1500–1685* (College Station: Texas A&M University Press, 1985), 261–72.

2. "Fray Domingo de la Anunciación and Others to Velasco, Coosa," 237.

3. Ibid.

4. Ibid., 239.

5. James B. Langford Jr., "The Coosawattee Plate: A Sixteenth-Century Catholic/ Aztec Artifact from Northwest Georgia," Proyecto Guadalupe, accessed March 12, 2017, http://www.proyectoguadalupe.com/PDF/cosawatee_plate.pdf.

6. Charles Hudson, "An Unknown South: Spanish Explorers and Southeastern Chiefdoms," in *Visions and Revisions: Ethnohistoric Perspectives on Southern Cultures*, ed. George Sabo and William Schneider (Athens: University of Georgia Press, 1987), 6–24, quoted in John E. Worth, "Bridging Prehistory and History in the Southeast: Evaluating the Utility of the Acculturation Concept," in *Light on the Path: The Anthropology and History of the Southeastern Indians*, ed. Thomas J. Pluckhahn and Robbie Ethridge (Tuscaloosa: University of Alabama Press, 2006), 197.

7. Paul E. Hoffman, *A New Andalucia and a Way to the Orient: The American Southeast during the Sixteenth Century* (Baton Rouge: Louisiana State University Press, 1990), 84, 95–97.

8. Ibid., 99.

9. Ibid., 102, 105–6, 125–26, 136–37, 148–51.

10. Weddle, *Spanish Sea*, 256–57; Hoffman, *New Andalucia*, 149–52.

11. "Testimony and Report Given by Certain Soldiers concerning What Happened on the Journey to La Florida. . . .," in Priestley, *Luna Papers*, 2:285, https://palmm .digital.flvc.org/islandora/object/uwf%3A8101#page/spine/mode/2up; Weddle, *Spanish Sea*, 258–59, 265–66.

12. De Velasco to King Philip II, May 25, 1559, in *New American World: A Documentary History of North America to 1612*, ed. David B. Quinn (New York: Arno, 1979), 2:213.

13. De Velasco to de Luna, May 12, 1559, in Quinn, *New American World*, 2:212.

14. Weddle, *Spanish Sea*, 260–62; de Velasco to King Phillip II, May 25, 1559, in Quinn, *New American World*, 2:214.

15. "Narrative of Don Luis de Velasco, Viceroy of New Spain, to His Majesty. . . .," in Priestley, *Luna Papers*, 2:275; Weddle, *Spanish Sea*, 267.

16. Weddle, *Spanish Sea*, 268; "Testimony and Report," 285.

17. "Narrative of Don Luis de Velasco," 271.

18. "Oath and Covenant of Luna," November 1, 1558, in Quinn, *New American World*, 2:208.

19. "Testimony and Report," 287–91; Weddle, *Spanish Sea*, 268–71.

20. "The Reply of the Maestre de Campo to the Decision of the Governor," in Priestley, *Luna Papers*, 1:155; Weddle, *Spanish Sea*, 271.

21. "Reply of the Maestre de Campo," 157; "The Captains Represent the Many Obstacles to Prevent Going Inland," in Priestley, *Luna Papers*, 1:161, 163, 165; Weddle, *Spanish Sea*, 273–74.

22. Weddle, *Spanish Sea*, 268–71; "Testimony and Report," 287–91.

23. "Mateo del Sauz to Luna, Apica, July 6, 1560," in Priestley, *Luna Papers*, 1:221; "Fray Domingo de la Anunciación and Others to Luna, Coosa, August 1, 1560," in Priestley, *Luna Papers*, 1:227, 229.

24. "Fray Domingo de la Anunciación and Others to Luna, Coosa," 229, 231.

25. "Fray Domingo de la Anunciación and Others to Luna, Coosa," 231; "Mateo del Sauz to Luna," 221.

26. Matthew H. Jennings, "Violence in a Shattered World," in *Mapping the Mississippian Shatter Zone: The Colonial Indian Slave Trade and Regional Instability in the American South*, ed. Robbie Ethridge and Sheri M. Shuck-Hall (Lincoln: University of Nebraska Press, 2009), 274–75; Ian K. Steele, *Warpaths: Invasions of North America* (New York: Oxford University Press, 1994), 18.

27. "Fray Domingo de la Anunciación and Others to Velasco, Coosa," 241.

28. "Opinion of the Captains," in Priestley, *Luna Papers*, 1:215.

29. "Opinion of the Officials," in Priestley, *Luna Papers*, 1:207.

30. John R. Swanton, *Early History of the Creek Indians and Their Neighbors* (Washington, DC: Smithsonian Institution, Bureau of American Ethnology, 1922), quoted in Marvin T. Smith, *Coosa: The Rise and Fall of a Southeastern Mississippian Chiefdom* (Gainesville: University Press of Florida, 2000), 42–43.

31. Weddle, *Spanish Sea*, 273–78; Hoffman, *New Andalucia*, 172–74.

32. Marvin T. Smith, *Archaeology of Aboriginal Culture Change in the Interior Southeast: Depopulation during the Early Historic Period* (Gainesville: University Press of Florida, 1987); Smith, *Coosa*.

33. Henry F. Dobyns, *Their Number Become Thinned: Native American Population Dynamics in Eastern North America* (Knoxville: University of Tennessee Press, 1983), 267.

34. Ibid., 24.

35. Ibid., 267–68.

36. Ibid., 35, 42.

37. David Henige, *Numbers from Nowhere: The American Indian Contact Population Debate* (Norman: University of Oklahoma Press, 1998), 79.

38. Paul Kelton, *Epidemics and Enslavement: Biological Catastrophe in the Native Southeast, 1492–1715* (Lincoln: University of Nebraska Press, 2007), 38–39.

39. Ibid., 60–69; Henige, *Numbers from Nowhere*, 177.

40. Patricia Galloway, *Choctaw Genesis, 1500–1700* (Lincoln: University of Nebraska Press, 1995), 106–7, 110–15; John H. Blitz, *Ancient Chiefdoms of the Tombigbee* (Tuscaloosa: University of Alabama Press, 1993), 15.

41. Neal Salisbury, "The Indians' Old World: Native Americans and the Coming of Europeans," *William and Mary Quarterly* 53 (July 1996): 449.

42. Ned J. Jenkins, "Tracing the Origins of the Early Creeks, 1050–1700 CE," in Ethridge and Shuck-Hall, *Mapping the Mississippian Shatter Zone*, 191–95.

43. Margaret J. Schoeninger, Lisa Sattenspiel, and Mark R. Schurr, "Transitions at Moundville: A Question of Collapse," in *Bioarchaeological Studies of Life in the Age of Agriculture: A View from the Southeast*, ed. Patricia M. Lambert (Tuscaloosa: University of Alabama Press, 2000), 63–77; Blitz, *Ancient Chiefdoms*, 118; John F. Scarry, "The Nature of Mississippian Societies," in *Political Structure and Change in the Prehistoric Southeastern United States*, ed. John F. Scarry (Gainesville: University Press of Florida, 1996), 20.

44. Jenkins, "Tracing the Origins," 191–95; Galloway, *Choctaw Genesis*, 64–72.

45. Patricia Galloway, "Confederacy as a Solution to Chiefdom Dissolution: Historical Evidence in the Choctaw Case," in *The Forgotten Centuries: Indians and Europeans in the American South, 1521–1704*, ed. Charles Hudson and Carmen Chaves Tesser (Athens: University of Georgia Press, 1994), 393.

46. Galloway, *Choctaw Genesis*, 128–32; Kelton, *Epidemics and Enslavement*, 65–66; Jenkins, "Tracing the Origins," 223–24; Cameron B. Wesson, *Households and Hegemony: Early Creek Prestige Goods, Symbolic Capital, and Social Power* (Lincoln: University of Nebraska Press, 2008), 69–70.

47. Marvin T. Smith, "Aboriginal Population Movements in the Postcontact Southeast," in *The Transformation of the Southeastern Indians, 1540–1760*, ed. Robbie Ethridge and Charles Hudson (Jackson: University Press of Mississippi, 2002), 4; Wesson, *Households and Hegemony*, 71–73.

48. Charles Hudson, *The Southeastern Indians* (Knoxville: University of Tennessee Press, 1976), 80–82; Blitz, *Ancient Chiefdoms*, 124; Donald Edward Davis, *Where There Are Mountains: An Environmental History of the Southern Appalachians* (Athens: University of Georgia Press, 2000), 25.

49. Blitz, *Ancient Chiefdoms*, 70–71; Joshua Piker, *Okfuskee: A Creek Indian Town in Colonial America* (Cambridge, MA: Harvard University Press, 2004), 117–18.

50. Richebourg Gaillard McWilliams, ed., *Iberville's Gulf Journals* (Tuscaloosa: University of Alabama Press, 1981), 168–69.

PART TWO

The Imperial Frontier

3

The Birth of the Creeks

[handwritten margin notes: Creek formation. English, Spanish, French influences & interaction 17 – 18th C (mainly events)]

Two groups fleeing past lives came to Mobile in the summer of 1704, one crossing the Atlantic to bolster that fledgling outpost on the margins of the French Empire and the other traveling overland to seek refuge from the ravages of imperial warfare. The women arrived first, in July, disembarking from the *Pelicán* at Massacre Island, later called Dauphin Island, in the bay before being ferried twenty-five miles up the Mobile River to the settlement that had been founded just two and a half years earlier. Pierre LeMoyne d'Iberville, the governor of the new colony of Louisiana, had recruited young women from Parisian convent schools and orphanages who were willing to trade limited prospects at home for an uncertain future on the Gulf coast frontier. He hoped that they would settle the restless Frenchmen and Canadians of Mobile and encourage them to raise both crops and families. One wonders if those women might not have regretted their decision when they caught sight of Fort Louis situated on a bluff on the western shore of the river, its bastions already rotting in the humidity, and spied the small town stretched behind on lower, swampy ground. But the sixty or so bachelors crowding the shore in welcome might also have been disappointed when they counted only twenty-seven women in the small boats, not the one hundred that d'Iberville had hoped to recruit. The competition of courtship promised to be fierce.[1]

The following month, hundreds of Talimali and Chacato Indians from towns east of Pensacola set up camp on the shore of Mobile Bay while their leaders came to Fort Louis to confer with the French officers. The Talimalis were Apalachees, a chiefdom once famed for its spirited resistance to Spanish incursions in the sixteenth century. One of Hernando de Soto's chroniclers wrote of their "great courage and boldness," and noted that "although the Spaniards pursued them and burned them" in response to their ambushes, the Apalachees "were never willing to make peace."[2] That recalcitrance softened over the next century as trade goods facilitated the spread of the mission system. By the end of the seventeenth century most of North Florida's Indians, including the Apalachees, had converted to Catholicism, and many, especially the elites, had taken on the names, titles, and language of the Spanish. The Chacatos had originally been enemies of the mission Indians and had raided Apalachee towns from their homeland west of the Apalachicola River. But in the late seventeenth century, faced by attacks from the Chiscas, they moved east to live among the Apalachees and many converted to Catholicism.[3]

The French had tried to recruit the Chacatos and the Talimalis, so their appearance in the area that August was not a complete surprise. After establishing Mobile in early 1702, Jean-Baptiste LeMoyne de Bienville, the commander of the outpost and younger brother of d'Iberville, worked quickly to develop good relations with the two large Indian confederacies in the region, the Choctaws and Chickasaws, and with the petit nations, the small towns of Mobilians and Tohomes in the Mobile River delta. He knew that France's success in the region depended on close alliances with as many Indian nations as possible. With that in mind, in 1703 de Bienville sent an emissary east to invite the Apalachee to migrate to the Mobile area, emphasizing that the French, too, were Catholic, but that they also had more guns than the Spaniards and could provide better protection from enemies.[4]

De Bienville's intent was not to undermine Spain. The ragtag garrison at Pensacola posed no real threat and in fact suffered chronic food shortages that forced its commander to turn repeatedly to Mobile for aid. He instead cast his worried eye toward the English in Carolina, who had been busy for over twenty years establishing an extensive trade empire throughout the Southeast. Slaves, not just deerskins, had become the commodity of choice in Charles Town at the turn of the century as Carolinians and their Indian allies staged a series of attacks on mission towns across Spanish Florida. The English had to be checked if Louisiana was to succeed.[5]

The Chacatos and Talimalis had no interest in moving west to Mobile until the slaving raids finally reached their towns in 1704. That August around two hundred of the Chacato refugees built a village called Oignonets on the west bank of the Mobile River where it flowed into the bay, near where Mobile is situated today. The four hundred or so Talimalis split into two towns, with about half settling on the east side of the bay and the other half up north, closer to where the Tombigbee and Alabama Rivers formed the Mobile River.[6]

The Talimalis and Chacatos arrived in the Mobile area at a strange time when death and courtship played against one another, each hinting at alternate futures for the new settlement. The *Pelicán* had stopped in Havana en route to Louisiana and had picked up yellow fever. By the time the ship arrived in Mobile Bay many of the sailors and young women had taken ill. Most of the prospective brides recovered in short order, but not before the virus had spread. By the middle of August half of the townspeople were sick and over forty would die as summer slipped into autumn. The success of the new colony seemed precarious in the wake of the epidemic. Still, in the midst of all that illness the women and the eligible men began pairing up. The officers and the more prosperous men arranged engagements within weeks, leaving the women who remained to make the best possible deals with the less reputable settlers rather than face a single life in this remote outpost. Feasting, fiddling, and dancing accompanied the marriages that began taking place almost every day by the middle of the month, offering comforting reminders of home and a celebratory counterpoint to the grim business of burials. The marriages and the prospects of children pointed toward the possibility of stability and growth for this French colony on the Gulf coast.[7]

Many of the Apalachee refugees escaped the horrors of the slave raids only to succumb to yellow fever. The Talimalis in particular, along with members of the petit nation of Tohome, took sick and died in large numbers that August. As devout Catholics, the refugees flocked to the priests stationed in Mobile to be ministered to and to have their children baptized before illness led to death. The lead priest, Henri Roulleaux de La Vente, who was ill himself, felt overwhelmed by the influx of Indians and complained of the "Apalache savages . . . who have all been Christians for a long time and who give us proof every day of this by coming here when they are ill and bringing their children for baptism." Indeed, the first recorded baptism performed in the new parish of Mobile was of an Apalachee child, long before the coupling of August bore the fruit of French children to sustain the colony.[8]

That the first child baptized in Mobile was a refugee Apalachee is more than just an interesting fact; it speaks volumes about the forces that were reshaping lives on Alabama's frontier at the turn of the eighteenth century. Decades of close contact with the Spanish had brought the most dramatic transformation to the mission Indians of Florida. The mother and father who sought the baptism probably spoke Spanish along with their Muskogean language, might very well have given their child a Spanish name, and probably wore a European-style dress and coat. But Spain's missionary efforts had bypassed the Indians of the interior in towns strung out along the Savannah, Ocmulgee, Chattahoochee, Coosa, Tallapoosa, Alabama, Black Warrior, and Tombigbee Rivers. In the last decades of the seventeenth century traders from the new colony of Carolina entered those interior towns as far west as the Mississippi River, offering guns, cloth, and other goods in exchange for deerskins and slaves. Some of those same traders accompanied the Yamasee, Apalachicola, and Alabama warriors who swept south into Florida, killing and capturing thousands and sending the rest fleeing into exile. Disease traveled the paths of trade and war, contributing its own destruction, as the Talimalis and Chacatos discovered when they sought refuge near Mobile.[9]

The forces of trade, violence, enslavement, and sickness that swept up the Talimalis and Chacatos and altered the political landscape of the entire Southeast unfolded within an imperial context. Their journey from the Spanish mission towns of Florida to the sanctuary of French Mobile to escape Carolina's fearsome slave raiders encapsulates the roles played by the Europeans at the turn of the eighteenth century. From their precarious footholds on the Atlantic and Gulf coasts, all three empires looked inward to the interior for resources and alliances that would solidify their nations' claims to the Southeast. The Spanish hoped to revitalize their weakening empire and foster trade by extending their missionary efforts up the towns along the Chattahoochee River. The English traders in Carolina reached across to those same towns and beyond to the Chickasaws, in part to form political alliances but mostly to reap profits generated by their hunters and warriors. That the pursuit of those gains resulted in the destruction of Spanish towns and the enslavement of Spain's Indian allies was simply a bonus. France also pursued trade relations with Alabama's Indians but always with an eye toward forging bonds that might help them push back English penetration of the interior South. Their control of the Mississippi River depended on that.

We often think of the frontier as a peripheral region on the edge of Atlantic empires that was defined by the motives of the colonizers. Indian reactions played a role, of course, but the energy, it seemed, lay on the "civilized" side of the dividing line; it was their missionaries, their traders, and their militias who entered into and thus created the frontier. Imperial policies and decisions about war and peace made in Britain, France, and Spain spilled over into towns deep in the heart of Alabama. Deerskins made their way to Europe and captives found themselves in the sugar fields of the Caribbean as cloth and guns from Britain and the Continent flowed into the southern interior. The actual settlements in Charles Town, Pensacola, and Mobile might not have been imposing but they carried the political, military, and economic weight of the European empires, encircling and thus helping to define the frontier interior.

Of course, that interior was not simply an empty space, a terra incognita defined by its colonial periphery and the inward gaze of the Europeans. The Indians of the Southeast inhabited that center and looked outward toward the English, French, and Spanish, weighing the opportunities and perils those outsiders presented with their own interests in mind. The Indians controlled the resources and alliances coveted by the Europeans. It was the Apalachicolas and Alabamas, after all, who ransacked Florida's mission towns and took Apalachee captives to sell in Charles Town. They and other Indians responded to the guns and trade, disease and war that swept through the southeastern interior at the turn of the century in ways that reshaped their world.

The tensions generated by the interplay of the Indian center and the European periphery shaped the emergence of the Creeks, a seminal development in the story of Alabama's frontier. In the 1670s there were no Creek Indians. Instead there were a wide variety of talwas clustered in certain ethnic groups along Alabama's waterways, most, but not all, speaking Muskogee. By 1715 the Cowetas, Cussitas, and Hitchitis who had lived along the Chattahoochee River were now known to the English as the Lower Creeks, while the Abihkas, Tallapoosas, and others to the west had claimed the title of Upper Creeks. That identity was in some ways a fiction; Cowetas and Abihkas still saw themselves as Cowetas and Abihkas, and talwa autonomy was sacrosanct. But it was a fiction shaped by the Indians themselves as they navigated the crosscurrents of the new imperial frontier.

When Marcos Delgado marched northwest from Florida with twelve Spanish soldiers and forty Apalachee warriors in 1686, he became the first recorded European to enter the interior of today's Alabama since de Luna's men passed through the region over one hundred years earlier. Delgado was on a fact-finding mission for officials anxious about Spain's increasingly shaky hold on the Southeast. Already contending with the repercussions of English settlement on the Atlantic coast, officials in Mexico had heard worrisome rumors that the

French were intent on planting a foothold in the Gulf to anchor an extension of their northern colony of New France through the Mississippi Valley. Having forgotten what little they had learned a century earlier about the land and people that lay northwest of their missions in Apalachee, they sent Delgado toward the Mississippi River to find out what he could about French intentions. The expedition made it as far as the Indian towns clustered where the Tallapoosa and Coosa Rivers formed the Alabama, a region the Spanish called Tawasa. There, Delgado found that the English posed the real threat, not the French, who ended up waiting another fifteen years to settle the region. What Delgado discovered deep in the heart of Alabama was a ripple effect of violence unleashed by the English colonies of Virginia and Carolina.[10]

Tawasa had become a refuge for migratory groups in the 1680s, signaling some upheaval in the southeastern interior. Delgado visited two large towns of the "Qusate" nation that had recently settled on the Alabama River, after traveling "a great distance from the north." These were Koasatis, a people who, centuries earlier, had shared a linguistic connection and ancestral past with the Alabamas before moving to the Little Tennessee River valley in the Appalachian highlands, where they became the chiefdom of Coste. What uprooted them from their mountain homes, according to Delgado, was "persecution from the English and Chichumecos and another nation called chalaque."[11] Chichumeco was the name the Spanish gave to the Westos, the most feared Indian raiders in the Southeast in the 1670s. The Westos were refugees themselves, Eries who had fled Iroquois slave raids in the north, moving to Virginia in the early 1650s and eventually to the Savannah River in the 1670s. They first established relationships with Virginia traders but were quickly wooed away by the Carolinians in the 1670s. Amply supplied with guns, they ranged throughout the interior, killing warriors and capturing women and children to sell into slavery, first to Virginia planters and then to merchants in Charles Town. But their favored status among the English deteriorated, and in the early 1680s the Carolina traders turned against the Westos and ended up killing or enslaving many of their former allies. Once the Westo monopoly on the slave trade ended, other groups like the Yamasees and Cherokees, or Chalaques, stepped in, eager to gain access to the guns and trade goods offered by the English. The Cherokees raided to the south and west, pushing the Koasatis and the remnants of the Coosa chiefdom out of Appalachian river valleys, deeper into what would become Alabama.[12]

The potent mixture of trade, guns, and slaves fractured Indian communities throughout the Southeast, forcing survivors to seek refuge in safer regions. Two such places were the Chattahoochee River and the area around the confluence of the Tallapoosa and Coosa Rivers. It was there that the coalescence of long-standing residents, recent migrants, and refugees gave birth to the Creek confederacy.[13]

Delgado hoped that the violent displacement of the Koasatis and others at the hands of English allies would brighten Spanish prospects in Tawasa. The people there were long familiar with various Spanish trade goods, including decorative brass bells and glass beads and more utilitarian iron hoes and axes. The Indians along the Chattahoochee River, known to the Spanish collectively as the Apalachicolas, had traded with the Apalachees in the mission towns to the south for years, and they, in turn, had passed those goods along to the people in the Coosa and Tallapoosa towns. Eager to reinforce those connections Delgado gathered together an assembly of Indians in Tawasa and told them that the Crown would treat them with "affection, love and benevolence" and that "the friendship of the Christians was not like that of the English" but "would be quiet and peaceful." They thanked Delgado "for having opened the road to their lands and provinces, that now they have a way to come to the province of Apalache to receive their presents and enjoy friendship with the Spaniards and Christians."[14]

The Koasatis soon dashed Delgado's hopes of monopolizing Indian trade in Tawasa. Putting aside diplomatic niceties, they told him "the presents of the English were better" than those of the Spaniards, since "they gave more powder, balls and muskets." He was incredulous and asked them "how could such be, if they actually had fled their former lands because of the English and Chichumecas"? This would not be the last time an imperial agent would be confounded by Indians' pursuit of their own interests. Delgado recorded no response to his query, but the Koasatis' blunt assessment of the superiority of English trade goods provided a valuable lesson in the flexibility and survival instincts of the southeastern Indians. Persecutors could become allies if they offered something more tangible than "affection, love and benevolence": access to the power of guns.[15]

The roots of the slave raiding and the trading that upended southeastern Indian communities lay in the founding of the English colony of Carolina in 1670, granted by Charles II to a group of proprietors in thanks for their loyalty to the Crown during the English Civil War. The proprietors and settlers expected that one or more profitable commodities would thrive in the environment, whether sugarcane, or olives, or silkworms and the mulberry leaves they ate, but none panned out. Eventually rice, indigo, and cotton became the cash crops that brought wealth to Carolina, but for several decades the colony made do with lesser commodities like cattle, timber, and naval stores. In that context of diminished expectations both the proprietors and the planters turned to the Indian trade in deerskins and captives to reap profits, and in the process helped shape the history of frontier Alabama.

Carolina relied on the diplomatic skills of Dr. Henry Woodward to extend its trade network west of the Savannah River in the 1670s and 1680s. Trained as a surgeon in London, Woodward had come to the coast of Carolina in 1666 on a ship that was reconnoitering settlement sites for the future colony. He stayed with Indians in the Port Royal area for several months and learned a variety of languages. Captured by the Spanish, he escaped prison in Saint Augustine in 1668 when English pirates attacked the city, and returned to Carolina when Charles Town was founded in 1670. His knowledge of Indian languages and customs made Woodward a valuable asset to the proprietors, who had begun hearing of a powerful nation to the west named "Cussitaws" that possessed an abundance of freshwater pearls and silver. In 1674 they sent Woodward up the Savannah River to the Westo towns to investigate. There, the Westos told him that they had been fighting against the Cussitas and the Cowetas on the Chattahoochee River and that, despite their advantage in weaponry, they had been unable to best them. Woodward negotiated a truce between the combatants in 1677 but it was not until 1685 that he brought a trade caravan to those Chattahoochee towns.[16]

Woodward's journey to Coweta and Cussita in 1685 was a pivotal moment in the history of Alabama and the entire southeastern frontier. He introduced English trade to the Indians along the Chattahoochee and drew one step closer to those living to the west along the Coosa, Tallapoosa, and Alabama Rivers, the Tawasa region that Marcos Delgado would visit the following year. That trade would be transformative over time but the immediate impact was the opening of a new arena of competition between the Spanish and British Empires in North America and new opportunities for alliances with the native people. Woodward's push deep into the interior reflected Carolina's expansionist energies and the continual search for new resources to be sold to the consumers in the broader Atlantic world.

Looking at that momentous encounter from the perspective of the Indian center rather than the colonial periphery complicates our picture of just who initiated contact. Woodward undoubtedly was pursuing profits for himself and for merchants back in Charles Town but he traveled along paths carved out of

Indian relationships. The micos of Coweta and Cussita took advantage of far-flung connections and invited the Englishman into their communities. They re-shaped their frontier, Alabama's frontier, by looking eastward toward Carolina in order to strengthen their power among the Apalachicola towns and counterbalance the growing influence of the Spanish. That decision had far-reaching consequences for the Indians of the Southeast.[17]

The Cussitas and Cowetas were recent arrivals on the Chattahoochee, having settled there in the 1660s and 1670s, but their influence quickly grew. From their location on the river's fall line they extended their power southward down the Chattahoochee and toward the west and east along trading paths. Cussitas had once lived on the Coosa and Tallapoosa Rivers and retained close kinship, clan, and trade ties with their former neighbors to the west. Coweta and Cussita also forged connections eastward, largely through refugees who temporarily sought safety in their towns. Westos, Yamasees, and Shawnees from the eastern edges of the frontier all spent time in the northern Chattahoochee towns, and residents of Coweta and Cussita often visited their towns in return. By the mid-1680s, leaders from the two Muskogean talwas had created an extensive network built on trade, kinship, and political influence that stretched down the Chatta-hoochee toward Apalachee, west to the Tallapoosa and Coosa confluence, and east to the very borders of settled Carolina.[18]

Those leaders were troubled by Spain's efforts to extend its sphere of influence beyond the Apalachees and up the Chattahoochee among the people the Spaniards called Apalachicolas. By 1675 the Spanish had established two mission towns, Sabacola and Sabacola el Grande, on the border north of the Apalachees and had sent Franciscan friars to live in some of the Hitchiti towns on the lower Chattahoochee. Because of their long history of trade and kinship relations with the Apalachees, the Apalachicolas were familiar with the Spanish, coveted their trade goods, and even recognized the protective benefits of living in the mission towns. Less appealing, however, were the burdens associated with Spanish oversight. Apalachee micos had to send groups of men to carry goods to Saint Augustine and to work twice a year under the *repartimiento*, Florida's contract labor system. Catholic missionaries even restricted cultural traditions like ball games and dances, further evidence that Spanish influence threatened Indian independence along the Chattahoochee.

While they were worrying about Spanish incursions from the south, the Apalachicolas were hearing mixed reports about the English from Indians to the east. On the positive side, Carolina's traders reputedly had access to better goods, especially guns, and seemed disinclined to interfere in Indian ways of

life or to require special labor. However, they did have a troubling habit of sending slave raiders to the region and of turning against their former allies. Refugees from the Yamasees and Yuchis flocked to the Chattahoochee towns with
tales of Westo raids, only to be followed several years later by Westo refugees be-
wailing the Carolinians' betrayal. Their stories convinced many of the Chattahoochee Indians to keep their options open. The Cowetas pressed the Hitchitis
to throw out the Catholic missionaries, even as their mico joined other Apalachicola leaders in Saint Augustine in the early 1680s to pledge their friendship
with the Spanish. At the same time, they explored the possibility of English
trade.[19]

The Coweta and Cussita headmen reached out to Woodward through their
Indian contacts to the east. They asked a Yamasee named Niquisaya to be a go-
between and to invite Woodward to visit their towns. Niquisaya made the connection and agreed to provide fifty porters to accompany Woodward's caravan,
which included several other traders. They arrived in Coweta first, in June 1685,
and there Woodward and the mico, an influential leader named Brims, exchanged gifts and negotiated trade arrangements. In order to bind Woodward
within a web of both rights and responsibilities, Brims arranged a marriage between his niece and the Englishman, effectively making Woodward a member
of the ruling clan. The English traders left their mark in the form of a blockhouse
outside Coweta and a defensive palisade at Tasquique, the northernmost town
on the Chattahoochee River.[20]

Alarmed by Woodward's venture, the Spanish immediately responded with
a show of force, ushering in a brief tug-of-war over Apalachicola. To prevent
the English from establishing a foothold to the north, Antonio Matheos, an officer stationed in Apalachee, led soldiers up the Chattahoochee River twice in
the fall and winter of 1685–86 to capture the traders and restore the allegiance
of the Indians. Focusing on the towns on the upper Chattahoochee, Matheos
confiscated supplies of maize and interrogated captured Indians to force them
to reveal the whereabouts of the English traders, who had gone into hiding.
Frustrated by the lack of cooperation, he burned Coweta, Cussita, Colone, and
Tasquique, the four northernmost towns on the Chattahoochee, and then retreated.

Far from being cowed, Coweta's leaders responded by encouraging the
southern Hitchiti towns that were closest to Apalachee to welcome the English traders. One Englishman, accompanied by forty-five Yamasees, came to
the principal Hitchiti town of Apalachicola and presented the mico, Pentecolo,
with twenty-six guns, machetes, hatchets, and other goods as gifts from the gov-

ernor of Carolina. Henry Woodward followed later that summer of 1686 and gave Pentecolo and other gathered chiefs gifts of cloth and beads, and returned to Charles Town with a delegation of headmen and 150 warriors. Woodward took ill during his journey and died sometime soon after returning to Carolina, but Spanish officials continued to receive reports of English traders throughout the province of Apalachicola. To reassert control, Florida's governor ordered a fort constructed near Coweta in 1690 and manned the garrison with Spanish and Apalachee warriors. That drove the Chattahoochee Indians into the arms of the English and ultimately planted the seeds of the destruction of the Apalachee missions over the next two decades.[21]

The struggle over the Chattahoochee region in the late 1680s led to the out-migration of the Apalachicolas and proved to be a significant step in the creation of Creek identity. The Cowetas and Cussitas led the way by packing up their belongings and transporting their sacred fires to new homes along the rivers and creeks that flowed into the Ocmulgee, Oconee, and Savannah Rivers in what is today north-central Georgia, a region depopulated over the years by Westo and Yamasee raiders. Soon others from the Chattahoochee followed, including the Hitchitis, driven east by Spanish harassment and the lure of English trade. Even the talwas of Tuckabatchee and Tallassee on the Tallapoosa River created "daughter" towns in the Ocmulgee region. By the mid-1690s the Chattahoochee River was almost completely depopulated. Twenty years later, when the Cowetas, Cussitas, Hitchitis, and others returned to their old homeland, they would be known as the Lower Creeks.[22]

The naming of the Creeks was in part an English construct that obscured the diversity of groups that composed that nation, but it was a construct built on connections rooted in the Indian world. Carolina traders and the Apalachicolas had easy access to one another after the migration of the early 1690s, and that bred familiarity. The English began to call the Cowetas, Cussitas, and other Indians who lived on the creeks and rivers that flowed into the Ocmulgee River "Ochese Creeks." Before the migration, Woodward and other traders had quickly used their connections with the Apalachicolas to reach out to the Indians on the Tallapoosa and Coosa Rivers, many of whom shared clan and kinship ties and a common Muskgogean language with the Indians to the east. In the 1690s the Carolinians established a trade path that swept first past the various Ochese Creek towns on the Ocmulgee River and then across the Chattahoochee to the confluence of the Coosa and Tallapoosa Rivers before turning northwest to the Chickasaw lands of today's northern Mississippi. Over time the traders began to call the Abihkas and Tallapoosas and eventually even the

Alabamas the Upper Creeks. The Creeks themselves never lost their local identities based on kin lineages, clans, talwas, and ethnic groups, but the connection between the various components of the Creeks was not purely imaginary, especially in their dealings with the outside world. A basic level of trust and acceptance of local autonomy cemented relations between the groups and helped them navigate the treacherous landscape of the imperial frontier.[23]

After 1690 the various Indian groups that would make up the Creeks found themselves increasingly enmeshed in a world of trade that was principally built on two commodities: deerskins and captives. Hunting deer and taking captives in war were traditional practices, and participation in English trade did not completely transform Indian life, nor lead immediately to dependency. Deep into the eighteenth century, women continued to tend the fields of maize, squashes, and beans and gather wild plants, and men still continued to hunt and trap to provide meat. But trade did alter many aspects of their society and economy and entangle the Indians in the imperial competition of the Europeans.

The Indians of the Southeast, including the Creeks, desired English goods because they conferred power on their owners and made life easier and more comfortable. Decorative items that denoted status, such as beads, bells, and brass armbands, remained popular, but Indians increasingly wanted guns, cloth, iron tools such as hatchets, and smaller implements such as scissors. Many of these goods were utilitarian, as the worn blades of axes attest, but they might also have conveyed a supernatural quality that would enhance the status of their owners. Burial remains suggest that in the earliest years of the trade around the turn of the century, many goods were hoarded by elites in ways that resembled the accumulation of prestige goods by their Mississippian ancestors. Traders probably dealt most frequently with micos and other officials within talwas, who then would distribute goods in ways that augmented their influence.

As the eighteenth century wore on, trade goods began appearing in virtually all graves, suggesting a pattern of economic democratization as traders began dealing with Indians on an individual basis as consumers. These goods made life easier. An iron hatchet saved hours of labor crafting a stone blade. Woolen cloth was easier to stitch together to make clothing, remained warm when wet without shrinking the way deerskin did, and came in decorative colors of bright red and blue. Leggings for men and skirts for women were popular but Indians also bought a wide array of clothing and accessories, from shirts, belts, and hats to ostrich feathers and ribbons. Guns, of course, enhanced power by facilitating both the hunting of deer and the capture of slaves. One English official estimated that by 1710 a third of Abihka's warriors, almost two-thirds of Tallapoosa's warriors, and virtually all the warriors among the Alabamas owned muskets.[24]

The deerskin trade grew increasingly important to the Indians after 1715, but in the decades before that it was the exchange of slaves that brought them the consumer goods they desired. In 1700, Charles Levasseur surveyed the Mobile Delta region in preparation for French occupation and discovered the extent to which the English traders had penetrated the towns along the Alabama, Coosa, and Tallapoosa Rivers. The English "were in those nations every day" with "pack horses burdened with clothing, guns, gunpowder, shot, and a quantity of other goods" to be "traded to the savages for cured deer hides, for fresh deer hides with hair, and for the buffalo" hides. But this trade paled in comparison to "the trade of slaves" from "their neighbors whom they war with continuously," he was told. "The men take the women and children away and sell them to the English, each person being traded for a gun."[25] Eight years later, the value of slaves seemed to have increased, at least according to Thomas Nairne, one of Carolina's leading traders. While they lived in excellent hunting territory, "no imployment pleases the Chicasaws so well as slave Catching," Nairne wrote in his journal. "A lucky hitt at that besides the Honor procures them a whole Estate at once, one slave brings a Gun, ammunition, horse, hatchet, and a suit of Cloathes, which would not be procured without much tedious toil a hunting."[26]

Nairne's brief mention of "honor" in the capture of slaves reminds us that war captives were very much part of the traditional culture of the southeastern Indians, stretching far back into the Mississippian era. Various fates awaited those brought back from raids on enemies. Male captives were frequently tortured and killed to satisfy the blood vengeance of those who wanted to settle the spirits of slain kinsmen. Women and children who were captured might be adopted into a clan in order to augment the population of the town and would then obtain the full rights and responsibilities of any other clan member. Between torture and death and adoption into the clan lay an intermediate role as a kind of "nonperson" who lacked a clearly defined status. Male captives who dishonored themselves by pleading for their lives sometimes were spared but then became workers who lived among but were not part of the clans and townspeople. Choctaws often made these men dress and work in the fields like women. While all of the major southeastern Indian groups had a place for these subjugated laborers within their traditional societies, none perceived of these "slaves" as commodities to be bought and sold before contact with the Europeans.[27]

English demand for slaves and Indian desire for consumer goods drove the raiding by Ochese Creeks, Tallapoosas, Alabamas, and Chickasaws in the 1690s and the early eighteenth century, just as they had decades earlier with the Westos. Tobacco planters in Virginia, farmers and merchants in New York and New England, sugar planters in the West Indies, and Carolinians carving out plantations around Charles Town all wanted labor. African slaves were costly at this time, in part because the North American colonies remained backwaters on the Atlantic slave trade. But Indian captives were close at hand and had been enslaved from the very beginning of the colonies. In general, owners preferred women and children because they could be controlled more easily and because they were more accustomed to farming than were Indian men. And from the owners' perspective, and that of the colonial leaders, it made sense to purchase captives from distant lands. Enslaved Indians from Carolina knew the terrain and could run away or, worse, provoke retaliatory raids from kinsmen. Far better to enlist Indian allies in their quest for captives from faraway regions to labor in the fields.[28]

Besides providing labor and profits, the raids were also tools of imperial warfare. Trade begat political and military alliances, and slave raids against the mission Indians undermined Spanish authority in Florida even as they lined the pockets of traders. The political benefits of slave raids became more evident after 1702 when the War of Spanish Succession broke out in Europe, pitting England, Holland, and Austria against Spain and France. Attacks against Saint Augustine and Florida's mission Indians, and later against France's Indian allies in the Gulf, intensified during this conflict, which in America was called Queen Anne's War, and which lasted until 1713. The flow of slaves out of the Southeast was especially strong in the early stages of the war.[29]

The Yamasees, Ochese Creeks, Tallapoosas, Alabamas, and Chickasaws who participated in those slave raids were not puppets doing the bidding of the Carolinians. English traders encouraged rivalries and warfare but found it impossible to control Indian allies, who often had their own motives for fighting. For example, the Ochese Creeks joined with the Yamasees in a series of attacks on Timucuan mission towns in north-central Florida from 1691 to 1694, much to the displeasure of Carolina officials since England and Spain were not yet formal enemies. The raiders were intent on capturing slaves who could be sold in Charles Town for guns, cloth, and other goods, but the vehemence with which the raiders destroyed churches, crosses, and convents suggests that hos-

which not enslaved

tility toward Catholicism was another motivation. The destruction of Catholic buildings and symbols echoed Mississippian traditions of warfare, when raiding parties destroyed platform mounds and looted sacred objects as a way of undermining the spiritual power of their rivals. But more recent events also played a role; the Ochese Creeks remembered Matheos's burning of their towns along the Chattahoochee and had no love for the Spanish.[30]

When Queen Anne's War broke out in 1702 Indian allies drew closer to Carolina. Governor James Moore's attack on the Spanish fortress at Saint Augustine late that year ended in a failed, drawn-out siege that contributed to his ouster from office, but many of the interior Indians were impressed with the effort. The English had succeeded in torching the surrounding countryside and town and had retreated with many captives, both standards of success in Indian warfare. In 1703 the Alabamas and some of the other neighboring Indians asked Carolina officials for drums and flags to carry into battle so that they could be identified as English allies. The following year, Moore, who was one of the largest slave traders in Carolina, led fifty of his fellow colonists and over a thousand Ochese Creeks, Alabamas, and Yamasees against the Apalachees. An even larger force of Indian warriors returned later that year without English guidance to destroy the remaining towns in Apalachee province, capturing thousands more slaves and sending the Talimalis and Chacatos fleeing to Mobile for refuge. By participating in the wars against the mission Indians, the Creeks curried favor with Carolina and accumulated valuable commodities, both of which could be converted into the coveted goods that made them the wealthiest of the southeastern Indians.[31]

The trade relationship that began with Henry Woodward's visit to Coweta in 1685 and was cemented by the migration of the Apalachicolas eastward became a military alliance formalized in the first Anglo-Creek treaty in 1705. The treaty was negotiated and signed in Coweta, and the word "Creek" was not to be found in it. Instead, twelve representatives from constituent talwas were labeled "kings," or "captains," or "head warriors." The English had not yet blurred together all of the varieties of people into one nation but they did treat the occasion as a kind of royal court. Brims, as "king" of the Cowetas, was first to sign, followed by representatives from the other Apalachicola towns, including Cussitas, Hitchitis, and Chiahas, and then, finally, by leaders of the western towns of the Tallapoosas, Abihkas, and Alabamas. These micos and war chiefs saw themselves as representatives of distinct communities; they were not Creeks. But, as Steven Hahn argues, "the treaty signing forced the Native leaders to imagine themselves, even if only briefly, as one people and to invent a suitable hierarchy for the whole." The English encouraged that unanimity since it eased their diplomatic tasks. At the bottom of the treaty an Englishman wrote that the leaders at the meeting had signed "In the Name of the rest," banding an even larger coalition of Indian peoples together in an imaginary confederacy.[32]

As the English worked to secure their alliance with the powerful groups that would form the Creek confederacy, they faced a potentially more formidable foe, one skilled in forming close relations with Indians. Spanish power might have crumbled in the face of attacks but France was busy establishing a presence in the Gulf and was determined to make inroads among the very Indians being wooed by Carolina traders. The French established Mobile in 1702 in part to protect the new colony of Louisiana from the aggressive expansion of the English, in order to maintain control over the Mississippi River. But from the beginning of the settlement, French officials looked up the Alabama River toward the heart of what would become Upper Creek country, determined to forge friendships with the Indians who would help them press back against Carolina.

The settlement of Mobile marked a shift in French policy toward the fledgling colony of Louisiana. Since Cavelier de La Salle had voyaged down the Mississippi River to its mouth in 1682, France had only tentatively accepted responsibility for holding on to what he had claimed for the nation. The strategic importance of the Mississippi to the burgeoning fur trade in the Great Lakes and upper Midwest was obvious, but officials were focused more intently on New France and did not have the resources to commit to this new colony of Louisiana. Canadian *voyageurs* traded with the Indians, and Jesuit missionaries sought their conversion, but no settlement was planned and not much happened for a number of years. Spain established a garrison at Pensacola by the late 1790s in reaction to French exploration of the Gulf, which in turn prodded France to lay claim to a foothold on the Gulf coast. The Crown commissioned Pierre LeMoyne d'Iberville, the Canadian hero of naval battles against England in Hudson Bay who had grown rich off the fur trade, to search for an outpost that would secure the Mississippi's mouth for the French. After an initial settlement at Biloxi Bay in 1698, d'Iberville shifted his focus east to Mobile Bay, which was larger and deeper and, most importantly, drained an extensive river system that was home to a large number of Indian communities that could prove useful in checking the expansion of their imperial rivals in the Southeast.[33]

Early in 1702, d'Iberville and his brother, Jean-Baptiste LeMoyne de Bienville, chose a settlement site on a bluff about twenty-five miles up the Mobile River from the bay. The proximity to the towns of the Mobilians and the Tohomes, who welcomed the French, played a role in the selection, but the location was problematic. While the fort they built on the bluff overlooking the river remained dry, the lower land that lay behind where the houses were built routinely flooded. Finally, a particularly high spring flood in 1711 convinced de Bienville that they must abandon the site and they relocated to Mobile's current location on the east side of the bay, where a larger plateau provided plenty of room for houses as well as a fort.[34]

As construction on the fort and houses for the 179 settlers began, d'Iberville and de Bienville turned their attention to the Indians of the region. Everywhere they looked revealed alarming evidence of the far reach of English trade. Reports filtered in that Carolina traders were regular visitors to Chickasaw towns and to those along the Coosa, Tallapoosa, and Alabama Rivers, and that they were inciting extensive slave raiding. Evidence of those attacks lay close to home, in the abandoned villages of the Tohomes and Mobilians on some of the delta islands. All along the Gulf coast, slaving raids forced smaller communities to cluster together in compact settlements and in some cases to forgo hunting and planting for fear of capture. That was one reason why those petit nations welcomed the French in their midst. Even more galling was the fact that a number of French trappers in the Illinois country were trading with the English. One group of five journeyed along the Tennessee River east to Charles Town in 1701 to exchange pelts for English goods. They claimed no allegiance to France, raising fears that they might guide the Carolinians in attacks on Louisiana settlements. If the French were going to challenge the English, d'Iberville would have to move quickly to win over the Indians, and the place to start was with the two large confederacies of Choctaws and Chickasaws.[35]

While the French were unfamiliar with the southern Indians, they were experienced in the art of negotiation with Native Americans. D'Iberville was sensitive to the nuances of Indian rituals and understood the importance of exchanging gifts to cement alliances. His brother, de Bienville, shared that ability and was adept at picking up Indian languages. They also had with them at Mobile veterans of trade and military campaigns in New France and explorations down the Mississippi. One of those old hands was Enrico di Tonti, an Italian raised in France who became a fur trader in the Great Lakes. He became a legend among the Indians of that region in part because he had an iron hook replacing a hand lost to a grenade while fighting the Spanish in Sicily. In February 1702, d'Iberville sent the fifty-two-year-old soldier and trader on a crucial mission to the villages of the Choctaws and the Chickasaws north and west of Mobile. His task was to convince the leaders of those perennially warring confederacies to make peace and to ally themselves with the French against the English.[36]

Di Tonti got off to a good start with the Choctaws. The meager supply of trade goods he carried—nine cooking pots, eight axes, six compasses, several pairs of red stockings, and a few guns—did not much impress the Indians but it did whet their appetite for more guns to stave off the slaving raids of the Chickasaws and Creeks. As he journeyed north, di Tonti almost stumbled into the path of one of those raiding parties, a group of four hundred Chickasaws led by an Englishman, but managed to skirt around the warriors and made it to one of the Chickasaw towns, where he encountered another trader. "He was seated," di Tonti later reported, "holding a gun in his hands and a sword beside him," and was dressed in "a very dirty blue shirt, no pants or stockings or shoes, a red blanket and necklaces around his throat like a savage." Di Tonti scolded the man, whom he called Ajean, for trading in slaves and "causing the destruction of these nations." Perhaps that bold confrontation impressed his hosts, since di Tonti managed to convince the assembled Chickasaw leaders to send a small delegation of influential men to join the Choctaws in Mobile.[37]

When di Tonti's party of four Choctaw and seven Chickasaw leaders arrived back in Mobile in March 1702, d'Iberville prepared to make his case for peace and an alliance with the French, a first step in pushing back against Carolina. The Choctaws, as victims of English-sponsored raids, were amenable, but the Chickasaws would take more persuading. He first handed out to each nation large quantities of gunpowder and shot, a good number of guns, axes, and knives, and "some kettles, glass beads, gun flints, awls, and other hardware." The presents distributed, d'Iberville then cajoled the assembled headmen with a skillful blend of threats and promises, focusing on the dangers of the Chickasaw alliance with the English. While they had captured and sold many Choctaws over the years, d'Iberville reminded the Chickasaws that many of their warriors had been killed during those slaving raids. "The ultimate plan of the Englishman, after weakening you by means of war," he warned, "is to come and seize you in your villages and then send you to be sold somewhere else, in faraway countries from which you can never return." If they refused to shun the English, d'Iberville promised to arm the Choctaws, Mobilians, Tohomes, and the Illinois to the northwest and set them upon the Chickasaws. But if they did "drive the Englishman . . . who likes nothing except blood and slaves," from their towns, they could sell the "skins of buffalo, deer, and bear"—the only "slaves I want," he added—to the French for "all kinds of goods." The Chickasaw delegation agreed to d'Iberville's proposal and also promised to pressure the Alabamas to suspend their slave raids against the Choctaws and the petit nations as well.[38]

Negotiations with the Alabamas in the coming months revealed the difficult path that lay ahead for the French. One party of Alabama micos came in the summer of 1702 and left bearing gifts in exchange for a promise of peace. The following spring a second group, led by a principal headman named Deerfoot, arrived in Mobile during hard times. D'Iberville had left for France to drum up recruits, leaving de Bienville in charge during a severe food shortage and unable to provide his visitors with trade goods. Deerfoot offered to send maize to Mobile in exchange for future goods. When his party traveled back upriver, five Canadian residents of the settlement went along to continue negotiations. One evening, men from the nearby town of Koasati visited Deerfoot's camp on a bluff overlooking the Alabama River, smoked the pipe of friendship, and then left. Later that night they returned and attacked the Canadians, killing four. The fifth man was wounded but managed to roll down the bluff into the water, climbed into a pirogue, and drifted downstream to Mobile to raise the alarm.[39]

De Bienville did not retaliate immediately but waited until November, after harvest time, when Alabama men would begin leaving their towns to hunt. Then he gathered a force of 280 French and Indian warriors, including Mobilians, Tohomes, and Choctaws, not at Mobile's fort but in the principal Mobilian town. There, de Bienville and the French and Canadian soldiers witnessed and participated in the ritual preparations for war, including purification, dancing, and oratory around the fire. De Bienville, who was only in his early twenties, got so caught up in the excitement that he agreed to have his chest tattooed in the manner of Mobilian warriors. After that he spoke to the assembled warriors and then distributed guns and swords. But this impassioned buildup to war and display of French and Indian solidarity broke down in the field. The plan was to paddle up the Alabama River part of the way and then to travel overland to Koasati and the other offending towns. As the forces marched through the woods de Bienville became suspicious that his guides were leading them in circles and were apparently reluctant to take on the Alabama warriors. The Mobilians seemed to share that fear since they continually lagged behind. Then illness struck, whittling down his army. The mico of the Tohomes got sick and returned with his men to their village. Some of the French soldiers also took ill and retreated. With almost one hundred miles to go and his forces reduced to 120, de Bienville abandoned his retaliatory mission and returned to Mobile.[40]

Why did the Alabamas ambush the Canadians and why were the Mobilians reluctant to join forces with the French in war? The simple answer to the first question is that the English most likely swayed the Alabamas. Thomas Nairne, Carolina's leading Indian agent and trader, was in the Alabama towns in 1703 just before Deerfoot went to Mobile. The Apalachicolas and Tallapoosas were firmly in England's camp and he was eager to ensure that the Alabamas remained allied. He warned Deerfoot and his advisors that the French had united the Choctaws and Chickasaws and were arming them to make war on their enemies to the east, including the Alabamas. And he reminded them of the superiority and abundance of English trade goods. But the fact that English traders like Nairne had influence over the Alabamas does not mean that the Alabamas went to Mobile as spies with treachery on their minds. It is just as likely that their numbers were divided as to which side to support and that some perhaps simply wanted to benefit from both the French and the English. The Mobilians and Choctaws were traditional enemies of the Alabamas, and that, more than the imperial competition between England and France, might have driven their betrayal of the Canadians. In any case, there was no unified policy between the talwas and it is possible that the Koasati warriors who ambushed the Canadians acted on their own without Deerfoot's knowledge or approval. As for the Mobilians, they too were navigating tricky terrain. They needed French support but they also recognized Mobile's weakness compared to the English. Their towns, which lay between the French settlement and the Alabamas, were vulnerable. Better perhaps to offer noisy encouragement for de Bienville's quest for vengeance while quietly lagging behind to preserve the men needed to protect their homes.[41]

D'Iberville and his brother de Bienville were adept at Indian diplomacy but they could not counter the influence of the English or maintain the consistent allegiance of Indians who had their own agendas. They were unable to woo the Alabamas and Apalachicolas away from the Carolina traders in that first decade and were frustrated to discover that the Chickasaws fell back into trade with the English and resumed raids against the Choctaws. The real weakness of the French was their inability to match England's supply of trade goods. For all their skill at understanding Indian rituals of gift exchange, they simply had fewer guns, blankets, cloth, axes, and other goods to give or sell than the Carolina traders did.

Mobile itself suffered periodic shortages of supplies and grew very slowly. In 1704, after the *Pelicán* brought the French women to the town, Mobile's population stood at 231. By 1711, when they relocated to the bay, it had only grown to 348. Residents lived in houses that were quickly constructed but also quick to rot, with vertical posts and plastered mud forming the walls and roofs made from palmetto leaves. Small gardens grew around the houses but few settlers took to farming. Many of the Canadians who came south with d'Iberville preferred trading and drifted off to local Indian villages. Others left for France when their terms of service were completed. The people who stayed were dependent on the Indians for maize and regular shipments of supplies from France. The women of the *Pelicán*, who had been promised fresh starts, quickly tired of the cornmeal mush that composed the bulk of their diet, and of the primitive conditions that were a far cry from the picture d'Iberville had painted when he recruited them.[42]

Still, Mobile struggled on as the first sustained European settlement in what would one day be Alabama, and that persistence was important. For all its weaknesses, Mobile did provide a counterweight to English power in the southeastern interior. Certainly the Chacato and Talimali Indians who were driven out of their Spanish mission towns appreciated the refuge that French Mobile provided. Even after France began investing more energy and funds in the development of their Mississippi settlements to the west in the coming decades, Mobile remained Louisiana's center of Indian diplomacy. While the Chickasaws, the Alabamas, and the various groups that would become the Upper Creeks remained in the English camp in the early eighteenth century, they all began to build connections with Mobile. In time, the French presence on their frontier would allow them to pursue the shifting alliances and neutrality that became a hallmark of Indian diplomacy through most of the century.

The superiority of English trade networks throughout the Southeast did not mean that Carolina got all that it wanted from the Indians either. That became evident when colonial leaders turned their attention to the French. After the successful raids on the Apalachee province and the damaging attacks on the Spanish fort at Pensacola in 1704, the English began to plan an attack on Mobile and sent Thomas Nairne to recruit Indian warriors from the Savannah River to the Mississippi in the winter of 1707–8. Nairne's journal offers a window onto English perceptions of Indian society. His failure to generate much enthusiasm among the warriors illustrates the limitations of English power.[43]

The egalitarian and decentralized character of Indian society immediately stood out to Nairne. "Plato . . . could never contrive a Government where the equallity of mankind is more Justly observed than here among the savages," he wrote. A visitor "would have seen a prince, nobility, and the Mobb all at work or play together," and it was impossible to tell "whose Cloths was of the most value, and the same in their diet[,] house and furniture." But the negative side to that equality, according to Nairne, was their political divisions. They could have lived happily "if they had not been infatuated to divide and rent themselves into so many petty Tribes and by that means have endless feuds and warres one with another." Perhaps projecting his own vision of English expansion, he argued that it would have "been infinitely better for these infedils, if some powerful tribe had subdued the rest, and brought them under government and to a peaceable life, rather then they should thus have consumed themselves, by their savage quarrels."[44]

Nairne did not hesitate to intrude in Indian rituals to impose his English vision of good order and, in so doing, reshape Alabama's political map. While in Okfuskee, a town on the Tallapoosa River, Nairne presented the mico Cossittee with a war commission from Carolina's governor "to be head of all the Tallapoosies settlement." Any Tallapoosas present at what Nairne called a "coronation" must have been surprised, since the people of Okfuskee were Abihkas. Cossittee insisted "that he might be installed in his dignity," and what followed was a hybridized ritual that reveals the emergence of a middle ground on this frontier. The leading warriors of Okfuskee picked up Cossittee and his chosen deputy and carried them around the fire four times, accompanied by singing and drumming. Nairne "saluted the Chief and wished him Joy" as he presented him with the commission from the governor. Cossittee and his deputy then washed themselves with cold water, fasted for a day and a night to ward off "all manner of spells, and enchantments that may be formed against them," and then washed again to purify themselves. It is hard to know what Cossittee and the Okfuskees thought of this ceremony. Nairne claimed that it was the usual way of "investing their Chiefs with Authority," but it took place in winter and not during the summer busk when such elevations usually occurred. In any case, it is unlikely that Cossittee believed he was now "head" of all the Tallapoosas. They would have quickly dispelled him of that notion if he did. But the English were powerful and their commissions carried weight. So instead of rejecting Nairne's offer, the Okfuskees accepted the fiction and patched together an appropriate ceremony that included the words of the visiting dignitary.[45]

Cossittee might have accepted the commission but that did not mean the Abihkas or Tallapoosas or Alabamas were eager to serve as England's foot soldiers in an imperial war against the French. Mobile's Fort Louis, despite its damp rot, was formidable, and an assault there would probably require an extended siege, not a tactic favored by the Indians. It took the English a year to organize enough warriors for an attack, and then they quickly retreated before reaching Mobile when they were attacked by French, Mobilian, and Tohome soldiers. Nairne's efforts to recruit warriors for an imperial war were a failure and, in the case of the Alabamas, might have backfired. Soon after the failed campaign against Mobile, the Alabamas began making peace overtures to the French. De Bienville carefully tended the tentative rapprochement and by 1712 had negotiated a truce not just with the Alabamas but also with the Abihkas and others in the region.[46]

The English had better luck among the Lower Creeks in 1711 when Thomas Welch and Theophilus Hastings, two well-known traders and militia captains, recruited war parties. The men brought gifts of musket balls, shot, gunpowder, and red war paint to the Creeks and chose seven chiefs to reward with coats and hats. They singled out Brims, the mico of Coweta, offering him a war commission from the governor that named him "emperor." Brims and Hastings then led 1,300 warriors against the Choctaws, burning their towns, killing 80, and capturing 130 to be sold into slavery. The Creeks could see the point of slave raids against the Choctaws, which fit their style of warfare and, more importantly, brought them profits. They followed their own terms. As Nairne noted in his journal, "The savages . . . have not a right notion of Alegiance. . . . They're apt to believe themselves at Liberty, when they please to turn to those who sell them the best pennyworths."[47]

Some of the Indians' reluctance to do Carolina's bidding during Queen Anne's War might have stemmed from their growing disillusionment with English trade. The Creeks and Chickasaws had sought out and welcomed traders like Henry Woodward in part because they were far removed from Carolina and could profit from the sale of skins and slaves alike without facing the negative consequences, but they found it impossible to avoid the pitfalls of engagement in the Atlantic economy.

One such danger was disease. Despite the Spanish entradas of the sixteenth century and sporadic trade with Florida mission towns in the seventeenth century, much of the southeastern interior had remained isolated from the Old World pathogens that decimated coastal populations. But as traders led their pack horses along the paths to towns on the Ocmulgee, Tallapoosa, Coosa, and Tombigbee Rivers and as Indian warriors led their captives east to Charles Town, that isolation was shattered. Between 1698 and 1700, smallpox swept through the Southeast along the trading paths from Carolina, fracturing some communities and leading to new migrations and coalescence. The hardest hit were the smaller Indian societies in the Florida mission towns and the petit nations near Mobile. They were vulnerable to slave raids, which not only disrupted their normal subsistence practices but also forced them to cluster in tightly packed towns, intensifying the impact of illnesses. The mortality rates in the large Creek, Cherokee, Chickasaw, and Choctaw confederacies were not as high; they were powerful enough to retain their decentralized settlement patterns and continued hunting and farming, minimizing the spread of disease.[48]

Carolina traders could be disruptive despite their efforts to fit into Indian society. Di Tonti's encounter in 1702 with the trader in the Chickasaw town whom he "had trouble recognizing" as English reminds us that many traders adopted the clothing and lifestyles of the people with whom they lived.[49] Quite a few found marriage the easiest way to establish close connections with towns, with the added benefit of forging kinship ties to clans that extended far beyond the town's boundaries. "It is the easiest thing in the world, for an English Traveller to procure kindred among the Indians," according to Nairne. Once married, "he has at once relations in each Village, from Charles Town to the Missisipi."[50] But the traders were a rowdy bunch and they often caused trouble in towns. They killed horses and burned down houses, they stole goods and got their customers drunk to confuse them, and they sometimes beat their Indian wives. Even reputable traders cheated. John Musgrove, one of the two translators employed by Carolina during treaty meetings with the Creeks, was brought before the assembly and charged with imposing a "tax" of four deerskins on each Creek he traded with, ostensibly to be paid to the governor as a form of tribute. What particularly troubled Carolina's leaders was that the scheme had discouraged the Creeks from warring against the colony's enemies once they found out they had been fooled. Traders were the forward agents of the British Empire but their avid pursuit of profits, often in unscrupulous ways, tended to undermine the broader imperial interests.[51]

Carolina's officials tried using regulations to tackle the problem of traders who "lead loose, vicious lives" and who "oppress the people among whom they live, by their unjust and illegal actions." The Indian trade act of 1707 required traders to purchase an annual license and give a bond promising good behavior upon penalty of one hundred pounds. The bill banned liquor sales to all Indians, prohibited the sale of ammunition to enemy tribes, and restricted enslavement to war captives, not free Indians. It also established a commission to meet twice a year to hear Indian complaints against traders, giving aggrieved Indians, at least those who could travel to Charles Town, a place to be heard. But the litany of complaints recorded by the commission over the next several years, ranging from rape and assault to theft, cheating, and unlawful enslavement, illustrates the impotency of the new regulations.[52]

The precarious position of Indian traders within a commercial system based on credit actually encouraged those abuses. Indian traders usually purchased a year's worth of trade goods on credit from Charles Town merchants and then loaded up their packhorses for the long trek to the Indian towns. Once they had collected all the deerskins and slaves they could transport, they returned to Charles Town to pay what they owed and to gather up a new load of merchandise. Debt along the entire chain generated pressures. The large Charles Town merchants were in debt to British merchants, and their success depended on the steady arrival of shiploads of supplies from Britain and pack trains of deerskins and slaves from the interior. Delays could mean ruin for them so they imposed high interest on loans and stiff penalties if payments were not made on time. The traders had to navigate the transatlantic financial world represented by the Charles Town merchants, but their success in satisfying their debts depended on their negotiation skills with Indians deep in the interior. Forging those connections required a certain commitment to adopting Indian ways, but their immersion in that world sometimes undermined their reputations among the coastal merchants. Failure to collect enough deerskins or slaves, sudden declines in their prices, robberies, or wars could prevent traders from paying off debts and spell ruin. Unscrupulous and even brutal practices proliferated in that atmosphere of intense pressure.[53]

Debt was increasingly a problem for the Indians as well after the turn of the century. Gun ownership had become commonplace but it generated a constant demand for gunpowder and shot, along with the other consumer goods that Indians so avidly craved. Like others along the trade chain, Indians usually purchased those goods on credit and paid off the traders later with either deerskins or slaves. That debt ballooned. By 1711, the Ochese Creeks owed traders about 100,000 deerskins, or 250 per adult man, a quantity that would take several years of hunting to supply. Slaves were becoming a problematic alternative. The destruction of the Apalachees meant that raiders had to go farther down the Florida peninsula or far to the west to find captives. The demand for Indian slaves was also declining in large part because the British mainland colonies were becoming more deeply integrated into the African slave trade, and Carolina planters had a cheaper, less troublesome source of labor.[54]

Those planters were pushing the boundaries of settlement deeper into the interior beyond Charles Town, exacerbating tensions with Indians already angry about trade abuses. The Yamasees, who lived closer to the Carolina coast, grew particularly alarmed by the erosion of their independence. Early in 1715 rumors that they were forming alliances with the Cherokees and Creeks in preparation for war reached officials' ears, as did stories of Spanish and French provocations. Hoping to head off violence on the frontier, Carolina's governor sent a delegation of high-ranking negotiators to the Yamasees, including Thomas Nairne. Their reassurances seemed to placate the Yamasee hosts, but that apparently was a subterfuge. On the night of April 15, the Yamasees attacked their sleeping guests, killing most outright and capturing a few, including Nairne. The Yamasees tortured him for several days by piercing his skin with pieces of burning wood before he finally succumbed. Within days of the assault, Creek, Chickasaw, and Cherokee warriors slew about ninety Carolina traders in towns across the Southeast. Meanwhile, raiding parties of Yamasees and various Indians from the Piedmont to the north pushed toward Charles Town, burning plantations and killing hundreds of Carolinians. The Cherokees and Creeks hung back from those offensive raids, and eventually Carolina defeated the Yamasees with assistance from Virginia, armed African slaves, and allied Indians.[55]

The Creeks remained on the periphery of the Yamasee War as half-hearted participants in large part because of their place within the southeastern system of trade and empire. They were enmeshed in the Atlantic economy, suffering some of the same abuses and struggling under similar debt as the Yamasees, but their geographic distance from the Carolina settlements permitted a certain detachment. Feeling little threat from the plantations that were beginning to push inland from the coast and fearing entanglement in a larger war, they refused to send warriors east. But they did take advantage of the Yamasees' plunge into warfare to kill the traders in their towns. They did so because they were angry about abuses but also because the Spanish and especially the French were on their southern and western borders. The Creeks were eager to make British Carolina aware that they had alternative sources of trade. France's decision in 1717 to build Fort Toulouse, a small, fortified garrison near the junction of the Coosa and Tallapoosa, reinforced that message in the decades after the war. Still, English goods were superior; the Creeks had no interest in a permanent rupture and neither did Charles Town's merchants and officials. Peace delegations on both sides quickly settled their differences and trade resumed. But the allure of English trade that had drawn the Apalachicola towns east to the rivers of Georgia had palled. In the years following the Yamasee War the Ochese Creeks moved back to the Chattahoochee River. They and their kindred towns on the Coosa and Tallapoosa Rivers would become adept in the coming decades at playing the imperial powers off one another.

Notes

1. Jay Higginbotham, *Old Mobile: Fort Louis de la Louisiane, 1702–1711* (Tuscaloosa: University of Alabama Press, 1977), 132–35, 175–86.

2. Rodrigo Ranjel, "Narratives of the Career of Hernando de Soto," in *Voices of the Old South: Eyewitness Accounts, 1528–1861*, ed. Alan Gallay (Athens: University of Georgia Press, 1994), 11.

3. John F. Scarry, "Resistance and Accommodation in Apalachee Province," in *The Archaeology of Traditions: Agency and History before and after Columbus*, ed. Timothy R. Pauketat (Gainesville: University Press of Florida, 2001), 39–41, 52–53; John H. Hann, *The Native American World beyond Apalachee: West Florida and the Chattahoochee Valley* (Gainesville: University Press of Florida, 2006), 28–51; Higginbotham, *Old Mobile*, 189–90.

4. Higginbotham, *Old Mobile*, 192.

5. Ibid.

6. Higginbotham, *Old Mobile*, 190–93; Hann, *Native American World*, 50–51; John E. Worth, "Razing Florida: The Indian Slave Trade and the Devastation of Spanish Florida, 1659–1715," in *Mapping the Mississippian Shatter Zone: The Colonial Indian Slave Trade and Regional Instability in the American South*, ed. Robbie Ethridge and Sheri M. Shuck-Hall (Lincoln: University of Nebraska Press, 2009), 300–302.

7. Higginbotham, *Old Mobile*, 183–87, 196–202.

8. La Vente to Séminaire de Québec directors, September 20, 1704, Archives du Séminaire de Québec, quoted in Higginbotham, *Old Mobile*, 193–94; Scarry, "Resistance and Accommodation," 53.

9. Scarry, "Resistance and Accommodation," 53–55.

10. Mark F. Boyd, introduction to "The Expedition of Marcos Delgado from Apalache to the Upper Creek Country in 1686," *Florida Historical Quarterly* 16 (July 1937): 3–6.

11. Marcos Delgado, "Delgado's Report, January 5, 1687," in "Expedition of Marcos Delgado," 26; Sheri M. Shuck-Hall, "Alabama and Coushatta Diaspora and Coalescence in the Mississippian Shatter Zone," in Ethridge and Shuck-Hall, *Mapping the Mississippian Shatter Zone*, 254–59.

12. Robbie Ethridge, "Creating the Shatter Zone: Indian Slave Traders and the Collapse of the Southeastern Chiefdoms," in Ethridge and Shuck-Hall, *Mapping the Mississippian Shatter Zone*, 211–12; Eric E. Bowne, "'Carying Away Their Corne and

Children': The Effects of Westo Slave Raids on the Indians of the Lower South," in Ethridge and Shuck-Hall, *Mapping the Mississippian Shatter Zone*, 105–6.

13. Vernon James Knight Jr., "The Formation of the Creeks," in *The Forgotten Centuries: Indians and Europeans in the American South, 1521–1704*, ed. Charles Hudson and Carmen Chaves Tesser (Athens: University of Georgia Press, 1994), 385.

14. Delgado, "Delgado's Report," 26–27.

15. Ibid.

16. Paul Kelton, *Epidemics and Enslavement: Biological Catastrophe in the Native Southeast, 1492–1715* (Lincoln: University of Nebraska Press, 2007), 129–32; Steven C. Hahn, *The Invention of the Creek Nation, 1670–1763* (Lincoln: University of Nebraska Press, 2004), 32–33; Alan Gallay, *The Indian Slave Trade: The Rise of the English Empire in the American South, 1670–1717* (New Haven, CT: Yale University Press, 2002), 54–55; Steven C. Hahn, "The Mother of Necessity: Carolina, the Creek Indians, and the Making of a New Order in the American Southeast, 1670–1763," in *The Transformation of the Southeastern Indians, 1540–1760*, ed. Robbie Ethridge and Charles Hudson (Jackson: University Press of Mississippi, 2002), 86–87.

17. Hahn, *Invention of the Creek Nation*, 40–41.

18. Joshua Piker, *Okfuskee: A Creek Indian Town in Colonial America* (Cambridge, MA: Harvard University Press, 2004), 9; John E. Worth, "The Lower Creeks: Origins and Early History," in *Indians of the Greater Southeast: Historical Archaeology and Ethnohistory*, ed. Bonnie G. McEwan (Gainesville: University Press of Florida, 2000), 272; Hahn, *Invention of the Creek Nation*, 41; Kelton, *Epidemics and Enslavement*, 133.

19. Hahn, *Invention of the Creek Nation*, 30–31, 34–39; Kelton, *Epidemics and Enslavement*, 133–34; Joel W. Martin, "Southeastern Indians and the English Trade in Skins and Slaves," in Hudson and Tesser, *Forgotten Centuries*, 311.

20. Hahn, *Invention of the Creek Nation*, 41–44; Kelton, *Epidemics and Enslavement*, 134; Martin, "Southeastern Indians," 311; Worth, "Razing Florida," 300.

21. Hahn, *Invention of the Creek Nation*, 44–46; Hahn, "Mother of Necessity," 92–95; Kelton, *Epidemics and Enslavement*, 134; Hann, *Native American World*, 106, 115, 121; Eric E. Bowne, "Dr. Henry Woodward's Role in Early Carolina Indian Relations," in *Creating and Contesting Carolina: Proprietary Era Histories*, ed. Michelle LeMaster and Bradford J. Wood (Columbia: University of South Carolina Press, 2013), 89; Marvin T. Smith, "Aboriginal Population Movements in the Postcontact Southeast," in Ethridge and Hudson, *Transformation of the Southeastern Indians*, 5.

22. Worth, "Lower Creeks," 278–82; Hahn, *Invention of the Creek Nation*, 48–52; Hahn, "The Cussita Migration Legend: History, Ideology, and the Politics of Mythmaking," in *Light on the Path: The Anthropology and History of the Southeastern Indians*, ed. Thomas J. Pluckhahn and Robbie Ethridge (Tuscaloosa: University of Alabama Press, 2006), 77; Joseph M. Hall Jr., *Zamumo's Gifts: Indian-European Exchange in the Colonial Southeast* (Philadelphia: University of Pennsylvania Press, 2009), 77.

23. Cameron B. Wesson, *Households and Hegemony: Early Creek Prestige Goods, Symbolic Capital, and Social Power* (Lincoln: University of Nebraska Press, 2008), xxii–xxiii; Hahn, *Invention of the Creek Nation*, 91; Hall, *Zamumo's Gifts*, 118.

24. Gallay, *Indian Slave Trade*, 124–25; Martin, "Southeastern Indians," 311–12; Hall, *Zamumo's Gifts*, 105; Wesson, *Households and Hegemony*, 33–35, 39–40, 92–93, 125–26; Gregory A. Waselkov and Marvin T. Smith, "Upper Creek Archaeology," in McEwan, *Indians of the Greater Southeast*, 246–48, 250–51.

25. Vernon J. Knight Jr. and Sherée L. Adams, "A Voyage to the Mobile and Tomeh in 1700, with Notes on the Interior of Alabama," *Ethnohistory* 28 (Spring 1981): 182.

26. Alexander Moore, ed., *Nairne's Muskhogean Journals: The 1708 Expedition to the Mississippi River* (Jackson: University Press of Mississippi, 1988), 47–48.

27. Kelton, *Epidemics and Enslavement*, 103–4; Hahn, *Invention of the Creek Nation*, 52–53; Hall, *Zamumo's Gifts*, 80.

28. Kelton, *Epidemics and Enslavement*, 104.

29. Hahn, *Invention of the Creek Nation*, 58–59.

30. Hahn, *Invention of the Creek Nation*, 53–56.

31. Gallay, *Indian Slave Trade*, 137, 144–49.

32. Hahn, *Invention of the Creek Nation*, 66–67; Gallay, *Indian Slave Trade*, 138–40.

33. Jay Higginbotham, "Discovery, Exploration, and Colonization of Mobile Bay to 1711," in *Mobile: The New History of Alabama's First City*, ed. Michael V. R. Thomason (Tuscaloosa: University of Alabama Press, 2001), 14–17; Higginbotham, *Old Mobile*, 22–25.

34. Higginbotham, *Old Mobile*, 33–34, 43–48, 453–55.

35. Richebourg Gaillard McWilliams, ed., *Iberville's Gulf Journals* (Tuscaloosa: University of Alabama Press, 1981), 166, 168; Higginbotham, *Old Mobile*, 541; Kelton, *Epidemics and Enslavement*, 139, 141; Knight and Adams, "Voyage to the Mobile," 182; Galloway, "Confederacy as a Solution to Chiefdom Dissolution: Historical Evidence in the Choctaw Case," in Hudson and Tesser, *Forgotten Centuries*, 406; Marcel Giraud, *A History of French Louisiana*, vol. 1, *The Reign of Louis XIV, 1698–1715*, trans. Joseph C. Lambert (Baton Rouge: Louisiana State University Press, 1974), 81.

36. Gallay, *Indian Slave Trade*, 128; Higginbotham, *Old Mobile*, 53–56.

37. Di Tonti to d'Iberville, March 14, 1702, Archives de la Marine, Paris, quoted in Higginbotham, *Old Mobile*, 64; Higginbotham, *Old Mobile*, 57–64

38. McWilliams, *Iberville's Gulf Journals*, 171–73; Higginbotham, *Old Mobile*, 78.

39. Higginbotham, *Old Mobile*, 117–23; Gallay, *Indian Slave Trade*, 140.

40. Higginbotham, *Old Mobile*, 125–28.

41. Ibid., 124.

42. Ibid., 541; Giraud, *History of French Louisiana*, 146–49, 155.

43. Hahn, *Invention of the Creek Nation*, 68–69.

44. Moore, *Nairne's Muskhogean Journals*, 58, 64.

45. Ibid., 35–36; Hahn, *Invention of the Creek Nation*, 69–70.

46. Hahn, *Invention of the Creek Nation*, 71; Hahn, "Mother of Necessity," 102.

47. Hahn, *Invention of the Creek Nation*, 71; Moore, *Nairne's Muskhogean Journals*, 56.

48. Kelton, *Epidemics and Enslavement*, 143–58.

49. Di Tonti to d'Iberville, quoted in Higginbotham, *Old Mobile*, 64.

50. Moore, *Nairne's Muskhogean Journals*, 60–61.

51. Hall, *Zamumo's Gifts*, 119; Hahn, "Mother of Necessity," 100; Gallay, *Indian Slave Trade*, 213–14.

52. Gallay, *Indian Slave Trade*, 216–17, 243–45.

53. Ibid., 246; Hall, *Zamumo's Gifts*, 119–20.

54. Hahn, *Invention of the Creek Nation*, 76–77.

55. Gallay, *Indian Slave Trade*, 328–29.

4

Trade and the Search for Order

[handwritten note: sim to last ch - Spa, Fra, Eng, NA interactions, but w/ a focus on trade & dipl incl a few major events]

When violence once again descended on the traders in the Upper Creek towns forty-five years after the Yamasee War, life and death depended on luck and on the power of personal relationships. John Ross had neither that day in May of 1760 as he loaded his packhorses with deerskins at his storehouse in Sugatspo-ges, a village offshoot of the larger town of Okfuskee. He had just collected the skins from the local Abihkas' winter hunt as payment for the guns, cloth, and other merchandise he had advanced them the previous fall and was now pre-paring to leave for Augusta, where he would purchase new goods to bring back to Indian country. Traders had been making that trek for decades since the reso-lution of the Yamasee War, usually without incident. But tensions were high in 1759 and 1760, enough so that Ross, "considering the dangers I am daily exposed to," had recently written his will, leaving his entire estate to "the only friend I have got in this part of the world."[1] His foreboding proved prescient. Ross was killed before he could leave the village, "chopped to pieces, in a most horrid manner," according to fellow trader James Adair. A small group of warriors led by Handsome Fellow, the son of an Okfuskee headman, also killed the two men working alongside Ross, one of whom was described as "a negroe" and was prob-ably a slave, but they did so quickly, without "any kind of barbarity." Perhaps be-cause Ross had a reputation for being "surly and ill-natured," he was singled out for a particularly gruesome death. One of his trade partners had the good for-tune of being out in the woods when the warriors struck and, hearing the attack,

[handwritten note in right margin: more violence/power?]

hid under a fallen tree, avoiding detection by two scouting parties. That night his Creek wife brought supplies to his hiding place and he fled to Augusta on foot, arriving "exceedingly torn with the brambles, as his safety required him to travel though unfrequented tracts."[2]

Another trader in a nearby town benefited from the quick thinking of his Creek wife. Two unarmed warriors "anointed with bear's oil, and quite naked, except a narrow slip of cloth for breeches, and a light blanket," visited them at their storehouse on the day of the attacks. The trader, who "was nearly in the same light dress" and also unarmed, prepared "to give them some tobacco" as hospitality demanded, even while growing suspicious of their "gloomy and fierce" expressions. His wife was also watchful. When one of the warriors grabbed her husband and the other lunged for an axe lying on the floor, "she seized it at the same instant, and cried, 'husband fight strong, and run off, as becomes a good warrior.'" He broke free, dashed out of the house down to a river, and swam across to the far shore while his wife fought off the two men. She knew that because "her family was her protection," they would not harm her. Eventually the trader made it to the Spanish settlement of Pensacola, 150 miles away.[3]

Not all were so lucky. Creek warriors in Okfuskee shot William Rae, the son of John Rae, a leading partner in one of Augusta's largest trading firms. Three other traders in the Upper Creek towns of Calilgies and Fushatchie were also killed, along with four employees. In all, eleven men involved in the Creek trade died that day in May.[4]

Echoes of the Yamasee War, which began with the wholesale slaughter of English traders throughout the southeastern frontier, reverberated in this event, raising the specter of a general Creek uprising at the worst possible time. Britain and France, after periodic conflicts throughout the eighteenth century, were once again embroiled in a war that spanned Europe and both nations' far-flung colonies. Most of the fighting between the imperial powers and their Indian allies during the Seven Years' War in North America occurred in the Great Lakes and Ohio Valley regions, but the potential for violence in the Southeast was certainly on the minds of colonial and native residents of the frontier. The French in Louisiana had extended their reach as far east as Fort Toulouse, and officials in Savannah and Charlestown (whose name generally evolved from Charles Town around 1719) feared that they might unite the Creeks and the Cherokees in a war against the settlers of the Carolina and Georgia backcountry. If the British could cement the allegiance of the Creeks, on the other hand, they could forestall French expansion and perhaps destroy Fort Toulouse and push on to Mobile. Creek country was a pivot point in the imperial contest: tilt it in one direction or the other and the whole of the Southeast could swing to either the English or the French.

Even before the attacks of 1760, the British feared that they were losing influence among the Creeks and that the French were making inroads on the frontier. Rumors spread in the late 1750s that a French spy, posing as a trader licensed by South Carolina, was distributing gifts from Louisiana's governor among Cherokee headmen, and that the Creeks were acting as go-betweens. Reports in the summer of 1759 of a wampum belt that was circulating through both Cherokee and Creek towns and was sent by the Nottawagas, members of the Canadian Iroquois allied with the French, heightened fears of a widening theater of war, particularly because it reputedly depicted "three headless Englishmen garnished with red paint." When the Cherokees began attacking backcountry settlers in South Carolina and Georgia in early 1760, the British blamed French influence and worries about Creek entanglement intensified.[5]

One Creek headman in particular troubled colonial officials. Yahatustunagee, the Okchai headman whom the Anglo-Americans called the Mortar, had close connections in Cherokee towns and was known to be friendly with the French. He and his followers had built a camp in 1759 far up the Coosa River from which Cherokee and Creek warriors and French soldiers could stage attacks against English backcountry forts. Yahatustunagee's sympathies probably lay more with the Cherokees than with the French. He was a traditionalist—"the compleatest Red man in principle," according to Edmond Atkin, the British superintendent of Indian affairs—who rejected both European trade and European trappings of political power. When the Creek warriors murdered the traders in May, officials were quick to blame the Mortar and his followers.[6]

The Creeks might have seemed primed to join the Cherokees in a backcountry war, but the fact that the violence of May 16 sputtered to a quick halt paints a more complex picture of Creek allegiance. The assaulting warriors themselves probably intended the attack to be a limited statement and not a prelude to war, but divisions among the Creeks also prevented the intensification of hostilities. Robert French, a packhorseman who worked for a trader in Okfuskee, later reported that he was grabbed by Creeks who said "they were sent to take his Goods away and to kill him but that they would not do the latter." Instead they "hurried him forceably away to a Place of Safety."[7] As word of the bloodshed filtered from town to town, a small group of panicked traders fled to Mucculassee, a town near Fort Toulouse governed by the mico known as the Wolf or Wolf-King. He armed the traders and led them into a nearby swamp to hide, before sending "them safe at length to a friendly town," as James Adair reported, and then on to Savannah.[8] Other headmen in Upper Creek towns, including the Mortar's brother-in-law (the Gun Merchant at Okchai), Devall's Landord at Pucantallahassee, and the Okfuskee Captain, offered refuge to the vulnerable traders.[9]

Within days of the uprising, Creek headmen were making peace overtures by sending messages, or "talks," to officials in Georgia and South Carolina. The Okfuskee Captain insisted that his "'People were always reckoned one People and one Fire with the English'; the 'mad Affair' threatened to 'put the Fire out,' but he hoped it would burn 'as long as the Sun shines and the Rivers empty themselves into the Sea.'"[10] Devall's Landlord and the Wolf both laid blame for the violence on disorderly young warriors and reasserted their commitment to the English. Despite some panic among backcountry settlers, Governor Henry Ellis reacted calmly and sent a talk to Okfuskee signaling acceptance of their peace efforts. To seal the rupture in their relations, the Creeks gave the dead traders a proper burial. They scraped away the men's flesh and wrapped the bones in deerskins that had been bleached white to signify peace and unity before burying them in the ground. Later that summer, Handsome Fellow, one of the leaders of the violent uprising, brought the scalp of a Cherokee warrior to Augusta. He hoped that the trophy would help "restore peace and good understanding with the English" and "wipe away a few of the tears for the murder of the traders in their nation."[11]

What are we to make of this brief flurry of violence followed by such elaborate exertions to put things right? In many ways it illustrates the workings of a middle ground on Alabama's frontier, a world shaped by Indians and "outsiders," by the everyday reality of personal relationships in Creek towns, and by the rumors, fears, and hopes that fueled the imperial contest between Britain, France, and Spain. The middle ground was, in Richard White's words, a place where "diverse peoples adjust[ed] their differences through what amount[ed] to a process of creative, and often expedient, misunderstandings." Indians seeking advantage responded to what they perceived as European interests, and Europeans did the same, with both groups often fumbling in the dark.[12]

The details that emerge in this drama of life and death on the Alabama frontier speak to the blended cultures and personal relationships that created the middle ground. A trader, dressed much like the Creek warriors who came to kill him, followed the native protocol of offering tobacco even while suspicious of his guests. Creek wives challenged their people in order to save their husbands, and solicitous headmen protected favored traders. Talks traveled from Okfus-

[handwritten margin note: A middle ground]

kee and Savannah along well-trodden paths, carried by emissaries, Indian and Anglo-American "beloved men," long accustomed to the journey between two worlds. Bones scraped and buried with honor amended the violence of murder, while a Georgia governor declined to take retaliatory action against the murderers. This was a frontier where neither Europeans nor Indians fully dominated, because both depended on the other. The Creeks needed European trade goods, especially guns, powder, and shot, far more than the French and English needed their deerskins, as lucrative as they were. Alliances with the Indians were the coin of the realm for the Europeans, crucial to the protection and expansion of the colonies and the realization of their imperial dreams. "The prosperity of our Colonies on the [American] Continent, will stand or fall with our Interest and favour among" the Indians, Edmond Atkin informed the king in 1755. "While they are our Friends, they are the Cheapest and strongest Barrier for the Protection of our Settlements; when Enemies, they are capable by ravaging in their methods of War, in spite of all we can do, to render those Possessions almost useless."[13]

The murders, along with the acts of protection and contrition, were components of a middle ground that had developed in Alabama in the decades after the Yamasee War. The calculations of individual towns and headmen within the decentralized Creek political system might have triggered the attacks, but the British, viewing the volatile situation through an imperial filter, elevated the French to a featured role in the killings. It was as if all the vexing power of French Louisiana had found its way through Mobile to the ramshackle stockade on the Coosa River called Fort Toulouse. The British exaggerated the extent of French power in the region but the Creeks could benefit from that misperception. Governor Ellis, fearing that too aggressive a response to the uprising would push the Creeks deeper into the French embrace, accepted the necessary fiction uttered by conciliatory headmen that rash young warriors had been to blame. Meanwhile, the murders provided a useful reminder to the British that their hold on the Creeks' loyalty was precarious.

Traders helped to shape the middle ground, not simply because they took Indian wives and adopted Indian clothing but because they occupied the place in between the day-to-day realities of Creek towns and the often imaginary world of imperial dreams. While primarily focused on making profits, they became forward agents of the British Empire. But colonial officials intent on imposing some order over an often unruly frontier and countering the maneuverings of their European rivals also influenced the political landscape of Indian country. They hosted delegations of headmen in Charleston and Mobile and sometimes traveled to the Indian towns to distribute gifts and medals and to deliver talks. But those diplomatic rituals generally ratified relationships that had formed over the exchange of deerskins for merchandise.

By 1760 the system of trade and empire in Creek country that had developed through the eighteenth century was on the cusp of major changes. The proliferation of unlicensed traders, many of whom bypassed the town headmen, and the increasing use of alcohol signaled growing pressures in the everyday transactions that underpinned the deerskin trade. At the same time, French defeat in the Seven Years' War left Britain in control of the Gulf, undermining the tradition of Indian diplomacy that depended on imperial competition. But British domination of Alabama's frontier borders proved short-lived as the American Revolution once again reshuffled the political landscape.

————————————————

The slaughter of perhaps as many as ninety traders during the onset of the Yamasee War forty-five years earlier shattered the trade networks that had developed around the turn of the eighteenth century, but only temporarily. By 1720 packhorse caravans were once again plodding along the paths through Indian country. By that time, slaves were no longer the commodities of choice. The Apalachees and other mission Indians in Florida had been killed, captured, or scattered in the great raids earlier in the century. Other potential victims, such as the Choctaws, were being armed by the French and were no longer easy to capture and sell. The markets for Indian slaves were also disappearing by the time of the Yamasee War. The northern colonies, alarmed by the disorderly nature of southeastern captives, prohibited or taxed their importation. Carolina planters, meanwhile, were increasingly relying on African slaves to labor on the newly emerging indigo and rice plantations along the coast. So as traders once again ventured into the Indian towns along the Chattahoochee, Tallapoosa, Coosa, and Alabama Rivers and beyond, they sought not slaves but deerskins.[14]

Avid consumers on both sides of the Atlantic fueled the expansion of the Indian trade through the eighteenth century. Europeans demanded large quantities of deerskins because leather products were ubiquitous, far beyond the gloves, belts, and shoes that we might imagine today. Of course, the largely rural society needed leather bridles and saddles, but there was an array of utilitarian products that required a supple yet tough and water-resistant material, including buckets and covers for trunks and coach seats. The dictates of fashion also popularized leather trousers and coats and broad-brimmed "South Carolina" hats, as they were known at the time. Cowhides could provide that leather, but a cattle plague in the early eighteenth century had reduced their availability in Europe. Britain, and to a lesser extent France, turned instead to deerskins, or what came to be known as buckskin.[15]

The indigenous people of Alabama were equally interested in trade, and long before settlers "opened" the frontier they had become suppliers and consumers within a global market economy. Guns, powder, and shot were some of the most desirable commodities, necessary for both hunting and warfare. The most common guns were smooth-bore muskets made in Birmingham, often adorned with decorative plates depicting fanciful creatures like dragons. Guns were expensive, however, and thus cloth in a wide variety of forms was the most common trade good. Indians made blankets and coats out of duffel, a coarse, heavy woolen cloth woven in Belgium, and sewed leggings, skirts, and breechcloths out of stroud, a cheaper English woolen cloth designed specifically for the Indian trade. They coveted decorative items like ribbons and utilitarian commodities made of iron, including axes, knives, kettles, scissors, and needles. When they painted their faces in preparation for war they used vermilion, a pigment made in China and shipped through England.

The process of transforming the skins of deer into buckskin trousers, gloves, or countless other goods sold to Europeans began in the woods of the Southeast. From October to March Indian men left their towns and roamed the hunting grounds, but they did not travel alone. Women and children accompanied men to the winter hunting camps, leaving the towns sparsely populated with the elderly, the sick, and unmarried or widowed women. Men hunted with guns and were often disguised in the heads and skins of deer, combining modern technology with traditional stalking techniques, but their labor ended after killing and skinning the animals. Their wives butchered the deer and smoked the meat and then processed the skins, much as they would have before the commercial trade developed. After scraping the fat and tissue from the undersides, they stretched the skins across wooden frames to dry. Sometimes Indians sold skins in this "raw" state to traders, but throughout most of the eighteenth century "half-dressed" deerskins more commonly made their way to the Atlantic market. Those skins had their hair scraped off after soaking and were then lightly smoked to help preserve them during shipping. Deerskins that were "fully dressed" were the most valuable but least common in the Indian trade. Indian women, just as they had in the seventeenth century, soaked the dried deerskins in water, rubbed them with deer brains, and then pounded them until soft and supple before stretching them out on a frame to dry.[16]

Indian families killed and processed deer one by one in the wooded ridges and valleys of the lands that would become Alabama and its neighboring states, adding their take to the flood of skins that flowed out to the wider world every year. Over 53,000 skins were being shipped out of Charlestown annually in the 1720s, and that figure doubled by the mid-1730s. By the late 1750s over 355,000 pounds of deerskins passed through the South Carolina port each year, and a decade later Savannah was closing in on Charlestown with just over 300,000 pounds of skins exported annually, all traded for guns, powder, shot, cloth, tools, kettles, ribbons, and vermilion.[17]

The conduits for that exchange were the Carolinians, and later Georgians, who set up stores in towns throughout Indian country and guided packhorses laden with merchandise or deerskins along the trade paths. The traders relied on the small, hardy horses common on the frontier, each able to carry two sixty-pound bundles slung over the sides of their saddles, with a third on top. The journey was long and difficult, taking about eight days from Augusta, the center of the Indian trade, to the Lower Creek towns along the Chattahoochee River, and as many as twenty days to reach many of the Upper Creek towns.[18]

Colonial officials watched those traders pushing west with some trepidation, mindful that abuses and conflict could trigger warfare. The Yamasees, who had retreated to Florida, and their Spanish allies still posed a threat to the colony's backcountry, and the allegiance of the Creeks and Cherokees was uncertain. In order to discourage disreputable men from flooding Indian country, South Carolina's assembly raised the fees required for trade licenses and imposed heavy fines for unlicensed traders. But as always, enforcement out on the frontier proved difficult.[19]

The founding of the Georgia colony in 1733 by James Oglethorpe brought renewed efforts to regulate the Indian trade. South Carolina's leaders at first welcomed Oglethorpe's enterprise since it promised to provide a buffer against Spanish and Indian threats, but his determination to assert authority over Indian trade between the Savannah and Mississippi Rivers generated some intercolonial conflict. Oglethorpe established a fort and settlement at Augusta and sent agents into Cherokee and Creek country to confiscate the goods of traders not licensed by Georgia. Oglethorpe's philanthropic nature predisposed him against the rapacious actions of the Carolina traders, especially when it came to the sale of alcohol, but his geopolitical concerns also reinforced his desire to regulate trade. Georgia occupied a vulnerable position, with Spanish Florida to the south and French Louisiana to the west, and preserving the allegiance or

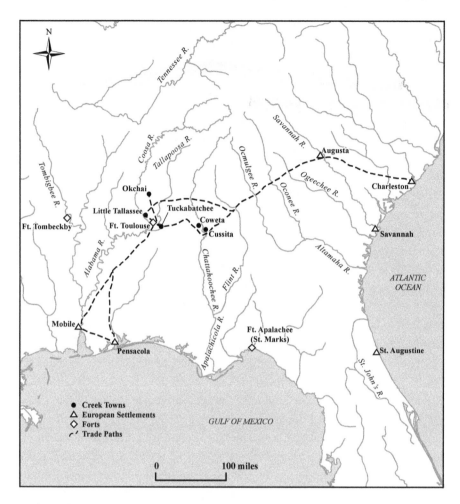

Eighteenth-century trade routes to Upper and Lower Creek towns.
Drawn by Patrick Jones.

neutrality of the Indians, especially the Creeks, was crucial to its survival. In 1739 war broke out between Spain and Britain, heightening tension along the border with Florida. At the same time, France, which did not formally enter the war until 1744, was engaged in a full-scale assault against the Chickasaws, who were allied with the British. In that precarious atmosphere, Oglethorpe traveled to the towns of Coweta and Cussita on the Chattahoochee River to solidify his relations with the Lower Creeks. He promised to regulate traders to prevent abuses and told the Creeks that the backcountry settlement of Augusta would be "the Key of the Indian Countrey." From the garrison at that town colonial officials could monitor the Creek and Cherokee traders.[20]

Augusta did turn out to be the key to the British colonial frontier by mid-century, but that had less to do with official regulations and oversight than with the economics of the Indian trade. Charlestown's merchants had access to the credit necessary to purchase merchandise, but their unsuccessful attempts very early in the century at establishing stores in Indian towns had convinced them that wholesaling was the more prudent path to follow. They turned instead to the Indian traders who clustered in Augusta to serve as middlemen, collecting the deerskins of the Indian hunters and sending them along to Charlestown, and later Savannah, in pirogues in exchange for the merchandise they transported to Indian towns as far west as the Mississippi River. Those master traders formed shifting partnerships, utilizing their personal relationships with wholesale merchants in the colonies and with merchants and leather brokers in Britain to increase their access to credit in order to expand their operations. By the 1740s those partnerships had solidified. One of the biggest trading firms was Brown, Rae and Company, also known as the Augusta Company. Patrick Brown and John Rae, two of the biggest master traders, joined forces and ended up controlling about 75 percent of the Creek and Chickasaw trade by the mid-1750s. Independent traders complained about the power of firms like Brown, Rae and Company, but their influence brought some order to the Indian trade and helped keep abuses in check.[21]

The deerskin trade might have depended on transatlantic credit networks but it also hinged on the personal relationships between traders and Indian headmen and townspeople. In the mid-eighteenth century, firms like Brown, Rae and Company sent individual traders to specific towns and kept out competition. Some were simply employees of the companies, but others were master traders themselves who were partners in the firms and often hired their own employees, including packhorsemen, servants, and slaves. Augusta merchants like Patrick Brown and John Rae benefited from having trusted men anchored in the important Creek towns, men who could navigate the rituals of smoking the calumet, or pipe, and tolerate the vomiting induced by the "black drink," a tea made from the yaupon holly customarily drunk before important talks.

Two members of Brown, Rae and Company were especially important to the Creek trade. George Galphin came from Ireland in 1737 and established himself as the leading trader among the Lower Creeks, with a home and storehouse in Coweta. Lachlan McGillivray, who had come to Georgia the year before with a contingent of Highland Scots, had kinsmen who had been involved in the trade.

He accompanied a trade caravan to the Creeks and quickly learned their language. By the 1740s, McGillivray was one of the principal traders with the Upper Creeks and had established his storehouse in Little Tallassee.[22]

The trading firms wanted to restrict competition on the frontier but the Indians had their own reasons for limiting the number of traders in their towns. A Creek trade delegation to England in 1734 informed their hosts that they wanted "but one English dealer to every town, and he to be licensed, that they might know who to complain of, and be Sure of redress if ill used, for multitude of Traders only bred confusion and misunderstanding."[23] The traders and their merchandise represented an outside world that was both spiritually powerful and potentially chaotic. If the talwa represented order, the woods beyond represented disorder. Hunters returning from the forests underwent rituals of purification to restore their spiritual order. In much the same way, traders from beyond the town borders had to be integrated into talwas, and it was the micos, the protectors of and providers for their people, who played that role. They had to develop a close relationship with traders in order to control the disorderly forces of the outsiders and to utilize their power. Access to trade goods was widening among Creek townspeople by the mid-eighteenth century but headmen still played a role in the distribution of merchandise, so a close association with traders bolstered their authority. Thomas Devall, a South Carolina trader who worked on the frontier from the 1720s until his death in 1761, must have had a particularly close relationship, for example, with the Upper Creek headman known as Devall's Landlord.[24]

The most direct way to contain the disorderly force of outside trade was through marriage. Most traders established in towns married Creek women, often the politically powerful nieces of headmen. In the matrilineal societies of the southeastern Indians, marriage integrated outsiders into the clan system, the foundation of community order. Traders who married Indian women became "countrymen," not full-fledged adoptees into the towns but no longer outsiders. Both partners benefited greatly from those marriages. The wives provided food for traders, performing the traditional labor of processing both meat and agricultural products to help their husbands survive. They also served as linguistic and cultural translators. There were a myriad of customs and traditions to master that were crucial to facilitating the goodwill necessary for successful trade relations. As Theda Perdue notes, "Learning to extinguish fire, the earthly representative of the sun and the upper world, with soil, the mediating substance of this world, and not water, which led to the under world, reassured a trader's customers and neighbors that he was not violating the carefully ordered harmony of the cosmos." The wives gained access to a wider range of goods that they could use in their day-to-day chores or as ornamentation, as well as goods that they could distribute as gifts, enhancing their power. They also had access to information from the outside world through their husbands and thus could serve as informal counselors in debates over foreign policy with their kinsmen. This enhanced power linked them closely to their husbands' trading enterprises and made them watchful and shrewd business partners.[25]

The Indians of the South had become avid consumers of European goods, but they had not abandoned their traditional ways. Traders did carry with them the energies of an Atlantic economy of consumption, manufacturing, and credit but their success depended on the relationships, rituals, customs, and structures of life in the Creek towns of Alabama. In the first half of the century there is little evidence that trade generated a capitalistic spirit of accumulation among the Indians, despite their eagerness to get their hands on guns, cloth, tools, and decorative trinkets. The Creeks still celebrated the riches of nature with the midsummer ritual of the busk and, as they had for generations, burned most of their possessions to begin the new year afresh. They also continued to be buried with both Indian and European goods instead of passing them down to their children. Still, while those practices signaled that consumption did not equal dependence, they did generate increased trade. More deer needed to be hunted and new goods purchased with each passing year, and over time that would erode the economic base of traditional Creek life.[26]

During the first half of the eighteenth century the deerskin trade created a web of connections that helped give shape to the frontier that would become Alabama, but from the perspective of Charlestown and Savannah it was far from being an orderly or predictable frontier. The Creeks and the Cherokees were forever at war with one another, as were the Creeks and the Choctaws, and the Choctaws and the Chickasaws, and while none of those conflicts directly threatened the security of the Carolinas or Georgia they were troubling reminders that the people inhabiting the vast frontier had their own political agendas. The traders themselves created disorder. As much as they forged bonds between the British Empire and the Indians, they also created animosity through trade abuses, or found themselves victimized by war parties, necessitating some response by the colonial officials. The fact that the Spanish in Florida continued to woo the Lower Creeks along the Chattahoochee River and that the French based in Mobile maintained their frontier outpost at Fort Toulouse heightened the tension, adding an imperial veneer to every meeting, war party, or trade transaction conducted by the Indians. Both South Carolina and Georgia periodically sent agents into Indian country, primarily to the Cherokees and the Creeks, to try to impose their vision of an orderly frontier, one that would generate trade, provide protection to the plantations that were quickly becoming the foundation of the southern colonial economy, and further Britain's imperial goals.

The colonial agents, or beloved men, who carried talks into Indian country had some weapons in their diplomatic arsenals. First and foremost was the power of trade. Charlesworth Glover understood that power when he traveled to Okfuskee in 1728 to challenge Creek flirtations with the Spanish and the Yamasee refugees in Florida. There, before delegations from the Upper and Lower Creek towns, he boasted of the superiority of British trade. "Show me one of your Women or Children cloathed by the French or Spaniards," he told his audience, "and I'll show you 500 cloathed by the English."[27] These were not empty words. Glover backed up his boast with a trade embargo, calling on all the traders in the Lower Creek towns to leave until further notification. Traders did not always cooperate with such pronouncements but this time they did, and the Creeks in Coweta and the other towns along the Chattahoochee began to feel the pinch, especially as their gunpowder and shot began to run out. In the end, Carolina lifted the embargo when some of the Lower Creek headmen reaffirmed their loyalty to the English.[28]

Colonial agents also used gifts and commissions to create connections to Creek headmen, hoping to impose some semblance of order on the frontier. Parleys with colonial agents or journeys to Charlestown or Savannah connected Indian leaders to both the spiritual forces and the material goods of the outside world. The British officials who negotiated with Indians were careful to follow indigenous rituals of deliberation and hospitality even as they emphasized the power of their king across the water and of their trade goods. That meant that headmen selected to participate in those negotiations, whether in Okfuskee, Coweta, or Charlestown, could claim they had carried their talk to the beloved men of the king and that some of his power had become a piece of them. More tangibly, they could return to their towns bearing gifts from the king to distribute among their advisors and people as they saw fit. Medals with the imprint of the royal arms and brightly colored and decorated uniform coats, the personal gifts of the colonial agents, became visible symbols of an authority that extended beyond the confines of the talwa or the Creek nation as a whole. The mico of Okfuskee and his "head warrior," for example, each returned from a diplomatic mission to the colonies with "a red coat with silver buttons, a ruffled shirt, a hat with lace trim, a pair of shoes, and red stockings."[29]

The diplomatic mission of Tobias Fitch, the first Carolina agent to visit the Creeks since Thomas Nairne, illustrates Britain's efforts to assert control over the Indians and the myriad difficulties posed by the frontier. It is worth examining in some detail. Fitch, a young but well-respected planter and veteran of the Yamasee War, set out in 1725 with several goals in mind. The most immediate was to get redress for an attack on an English trader that had occurred in November 1724 at the Cherokee town of Tugaloo. A large group of Upper Creek warriors led by Steyamasiechie, better known by the English as Goggle Eyes, had descended on John Sharp's storehouse and had shot the trader in the leg before dragging him out of the building, stripping him, and then beating him. They then had looted the store, taking an enslaved woman and her two children. Beyond gaining restitution for the assault and theft, Fitch hoped to broker a peace in the long-standing war between the Creeks and the Cherokees, and to steer the Lower Town Creeks away from the Spanish and the Yamasees.[30]

Fitch arrived in Okfuskee after a seventeen-day journey from Charlestown and met with quick success in the Sharp affair. Steyamasiechie admitted his guilt, apologized, and promised to return the enslaved woman and her children to Sharp along with his "Best Case of Pistoolls." The rest of the stolen goods had been distributed and could not be restored but could be replaced. Okchai Captain, another of the Upper Creek headmen, stepped forward and told Fitch that while Goggle Eyes had been "at the head of that Mischieff that Happen'd at the Cherokeys," all of the headmen would be responsible for paying off the goods with deerskins after the next hunting season. That was the kind of unified response that the Carolinians sought, one that seemed to reflect a kind of national identity that the British could work with and understand.[31]

The headmen's willingness to pay for Sharp's plundered goods, however, did not signal an interest in pursuing peace. The Cherokees had "Latly Killed Several of the Leading Men of Our Nation," they informed Fitch, "and till we have had Satisfaction We will heare of No peace."[32] Fitch tried to browbeat the headmen with a history lesson, reminding the micos that before English trade their people "had nothing But Boes and Arrow's To kill Dear. . . . But now you have Learn'd the use of Firearm's As well to Kill Dear and . . . To War agst Your Enemies." The Abihka and Tallapoosa headmen would not budge. Perhaps someday they would consider peace, they told Fitch, but not before they had had a chance to send their war parties out to wreak revenge on the Cherokees for the blood they had spilled. Fitch later tried to salvage the situation with deception when he traveled down to Coweta to meet with the Lower Creek headmen. When he lied and told Brims that the Upper Creeks had agreed to negotiate peace with the Cherokees, the aging but still powerful mico replied, "The Tallapoop's and Abecas may do As they please But we have Nothing of Makeing a peace with The Cherokeys." As much as Carolinians might have wanted a "nation" and a "king" with whom to negotiate, agents like Fitch were stuck with a wide variety of micos with often competing agendas.[33]

Fitch also confronted the continued lure of the Spaniards when he visited the Lower Town Creeks. Brims was eager to extend his power to his son, Sempeyoffee, in the form of a British commission allowing him to carry the mico's talk to various negotiations with Carolinians. Fitch, aware of Sempeyoffee's active support of the Yamasees and the Spanish during the recent war, refused. Brims attested to his son's loyalty to the British and angrily reminded the young agent that the king had customarily granted headmen the right to choose their representatives. Fitch reluctantly assented and, swallowing his mistrust, granted Sempeyoffee the commission in the form of a metal plate inscribed with the royal arms. Soon after, Fitch encountered two Spaniards in Coweta's square ground and demanded to know their business. One replied that Brims had sent for them, "That he wanted to here a Talk, and Likewise to Send a Talk to [Saint] Augustin[e]." Brims denied that claim but the presence of the Spanish unsettled Fitch.[34]

Even more troubling was the Spaniards' companion, a "Negro" who "Sat in the Square in a Bould Maner." Fitch recognized him as an enslaved Carolinian who had been taken by the Yamasees some years earlier. At some point that man had learned both Spanish and Muskogee, since the Spaniards said that he was "the Mouth" that they had "Brought to Talk with them" and that he was "a Good Christian." They must have valued his work as a translator, because when Fitch demanded his return they offered either two Indian slaves in his stead or payment so that they could "Redeem him." Fitch refused. Unable to trust Brims and the other leaders of Coweta, Fitch went to the neighboring town of Cussita to recruit men to help him capture the former slave. They returned to Coweta and met with no resistance when they seized the man, although Brims was angry and insulted that his honor and loyalty had been questioned. The captive escaped as he was being led back to Carolina and, with the assistance of food and a canoe supplied by some Creeks, made his way back to Florida. Later in his mission, Fitch pursued a runaway slave who had found refuge with the French near Fort Toulouse.[35]

Fitch's determination to capture former slaves in the midst of diplomatic negotiations reflected the Carolinians' growing preoccupation with protecting the Low Country's emerging plantation economy and their fears of Indian and African alliances. Indian war parties striking eastward posed a threat, but so did fugitive slaves escaping to the frontier, especially if France and Spain were offering enticements to those doing the running. Colonial officials encouraged Creek and Cherokee leaders to return runaway slaves in exchange for goods like blankets and guns. Driving a wedge between Africans and Indians would not only help secure valuable property and an increasingly essential labor force, but also ensure the safety of the colonies by preventing dangerous alliances from forming on the frontier. For the same reason, Carolina and Georgia prohibited deerskin traders from employing Africans, free or enslaved, in their caravans or in Indian towns. Men engaged in the trade often learned at least a smattering of Muskogee or other Indian languages, and officials did not want news about colonial affairs passed to the Creeks or friendships to develop.[36]

Despite those concerns and restrictions, Africans had a presence on Alabama's frontier in the decades following the Yamasee War. As Fitch discovered, runaways from the British colonies sometimes found refuge with the Spanish or the French, or with allied Indians. Others made their way west, only to replace one form of captivity with another. David George, an enslaved man living in Virginia, ran away from a brutal master and headed toward Georgia's backcountry in 1770. He was caught at the Ocmulgee River by a party of Creeks led by a headman named Blue Salt and was taken to their camp, where they fed him "bear meat, turkeys and wild potatoes." George became Blue Salt's "prize" and "made fences, dug the ground, planted corn, and worked hard" for about four months, although he later reported that he was treated kindly. His master's son tracked him down and "paid King Blue Salt for me in rum, linen, and a gun," but George managed to escape again and this time he made it further west to a Natchez town. There he went to work in the deerskin trade, traveling once a year in packhorse caravans some four hundred miles to George Galphin's trading post on the Savannah River near Augusta. Galphin, one of the most prominent merchants in the Indian trade, had no problem with George's involvement with the Indians. Deerskin traders had long ignored the laws against hiring free blacks or using slaves in their business and were willing to pay the fines if caught. Even colonial officials violated their own regulations, sometimes employing as interpreters Africans who had picked up Indian languages.[37]

Fitch left Creek country early in 1726, frustrated by his inability to knit together the disparate factions and towns to nudge them toward peace with the

Cherokees and away from the influence of the Spanish and French. The depth of his failure became clear that spring when a war party comprising Cherokee and Chickasaw warriors staged a devastating attack on Cussita. The attack itself was not surprising since the Creek and Cherokee war continued apace. What was a shock to the Cussitas, however, was that the attacking warriors were waving a British flag as they slaughtered the people who, among all the Creeks along the Chattahoochee River, were most loyal to Carolina. Meanwhile, a Cherokee war party intercepted Miles MacIntosh, a Carolina trader, and several of his companions on the path between Charlestown and the Upper Creek towns and "stripped [them] naked as ever they was born and beat them and told them they did that in revenge of Sharp."[38] John Sharp, the trader who had been attacked and robbed in Tugaloo, was frustrated by Fitch's disinclination to punish Goggle Eyes. When he learned that his Cherokee customers were preparing to raid the Creek towns, Sharp asked them to avenge his humiliation. Better to rely on the personal relations he had built through trade than on the imperial agents who seemed impotent before the complexities of the frontier.[39]

In the decades following Fitch's mission, colonial agents continued to be frustrated by the Indians' dealings with their imperial rivals, despite the superiority of British trade. Spanish influence among the Creeks declined in the 1730s with the defeat of the Yamasees in Florida, but the French threat persisted. Patrick MacKay, Oglethorpe's Indian agent, was particularly offended by Fort Toulouse and pressed the neighboring Creeks and Alabamas to attack the French outpost in 1734. He was incredulous when they refused to do his bidding. A Creek trade delegation had recently returned from London, and while they were impressed with the city, MacKay noted with disgust that they remained "overawed by the silly place in possession of the French called fort Thoulouse."[40] MacKay might have scoffed at the "silly" fort, but in the midst of the war that broke out between England and France in the late 1740s, the danger seemed real. Worried that the French might rally Creek and Alabama warriors to attack the colonial backcountry, Governor James Glen called the fort "an Eyesore" to South Carolina.[41]

That the French could ever pose a threat to the English colonies might have come as a surprise to Antoine de la Mothe Cadillac when he first saw the residents of Mobile in 1713. "Here there is nothing more than the piled up dregs of Canada," he observed, "jailbirds who escaped the rope, without any subordination to Religion or to Government, steeped in vice, principally in their concubinage with savage women, whom they prefer to French girls."[42] Cadillac, who had just assumed the governorship of Louisiana, was confronting the implications of France's neglect of its new Gulf colony. Founded largely for strategic purposes, Louisiana was intended to anchor French control over the North American interior by protecting the Mississippi artery from English and Spanish expansion. The more lucrative colonies in the Caribbean and Canada had diverted resources and attention from Louisiana, and France had been unable to do much more than secure a foothold on the Gulf by 1713.

In the early decades of the eighteenth century, France turned Louisiana over to various financiers with ambitious plans to profit from the colony, all of which failed. For a time in the 1720s, though, it looked as if Louisiana might succeed. The Company of the Indies, which then controlled the colony, sponsored the immigration of thousands of settlers, many of them indentured servants and exiled debtors and criminals, and shipped in thousands of enslaved Africans to labor on the growing number of tobacco plantations along the Mississippi River north of the new town of New Orleans. But the colony suffered a serious blow in 1729 when the Natchez Indians, alarmed at the influx of settlers, struck back in a series of attacks, killing over 230 men, women, and children. They were joined by a large number of newly arrived African slaves, the kind of alliance that imperial officials throughout the Southeast feared most. The Natchez revolt struck at the heart of the company's efforts to develop a plantation economy, and in 1731 its directors relinquished control of the colony back to the royal government.[43]

Mobile became something of a backwater to a backwater colony once New Orleans became the focal point of Louisiana. At its heart stood Fort Conde, the brick-walled replacement for the old Fort Louis. There were just under 550 people living in Mobile in 1726, including about 200 slaves, 50 of whom were Indians. By 1746 the population of both groups, free and enslaved, had changed very little. Settlers had established farms in the Mobile River delta region just north of the town and along the bay, but plantation agriculture had not taken hold. Instead the residents of Mobile and the vicinity raised livestock and fowl, and grew corn, rice, and other food crops, which they consumed themselves and traded to soldiers at the fort and in Pensacola. Settlers also took advantage of the pine forests in the region and began making tar and other naval stores. They also participated in the deerskin trade with the Indians of the petit nations, along with the Choctaws to the northwest as well as the Alabamas and, to a lesser extent, the Creeks to the northeast. Despite its small population and straggling economy, Mobile remained important as a center of Indian trade and diplomacy throughout the period of French rule.[44]

The paradox of the imperial competition over the lands that would become Alabama is that the very fragility of Louisiana, especially of Mobile, strengthened France's relationship with the indigenous people of the Gulf South. The Natchez revolt, the difficulty enticing settlers and importing slaves and keeping both alive, the limited resources and attention of the Company of the Indies and the Crown, and the competition from France's West Indies colonies all conspired to long delay the development of plantation agriculture. One wonders what would have happened if settlers and slaves had poured into Mobile in the 1720s and 1730s and pushed up the Mobile, Alabama, and Tombigbee Rivers, carving the fertile land into tobacco or cotton plantations. Certainly the delicate diplomatic dance that governed France's relationship with the Creeks, Alabamas, and Choctaws would have been upended and probably would have turned increasingly violent. But plantation agriculture did not develop in Alabama, and French settlement of any kind did not spread much beyond Mobile and the outposts at Fort Toulouse on the Coosa River and, in the 1730s, Fort Tombeckbe on the Tombigbee River. The significance of Mobile and Louisiana to France's imperial enterprise was not economic but strategic, and that, coupled with the weakness of their colony, heightened Louisiana officials' awareness of their dependence on the Indians. That dependence, in turn, helped create the middle ground of frontier Alabama in the eighteenth century.

French and Indian trade differed dramatically from that fostered by the English, who were more aggressively capitalistic in their pursuit of economic opportunities. Trade, while entwined with diplomacy, took precedence. Merchants in Charlestown and, later, in Savannah and Augusta sent traders into the towns of Indian country and funneled the profits into land and slaves, building their own plantation enterprises. The French, on the other hand, were conscious of their vulnerability. For example, the Choctaws, the largest of the southern tribes, were right next door, and large delegations of as many as a thousand journeyed to Mobile every year, making their presence felt. Military and diplomatic alliances held priority, especially since an elite class of military officers and administrators, not merchants, dominated the Indian trade. Of course, they profited from that trade, but they also kept their eyes on the larger imperial goals of securing French control of the Gulf. Gifts and services were the keys to alliances with the Indians.[45]

Indians saw advantages and disadvantages to trade relations with the British and the French. Traditional animosities shaped some of those relations. The Chickasaws and the Choctaws, for example, were longtime enemies and each gravitated toward a primary trade partnership: the Chickasaws with

Carolina traders and the Choctaws with the French in Mobile. Others, like the Creeks and Alabamas, kept their options open. The advantage of dealing with the Anglo-American traders was the robustness of the British commercial economy. Those traders had a wide variety of good merchandise in large quantities and they usually offered a good exchange rate for the Indians' deerskins. But the growing number of private traders also unsettled the good order of Indian towns and led to the proliferation of trade abuses. Conscious of the developing plantations of South Carolina and Georgia and of the press of settlement into the backcountry, Creeks feared that eventually the pursuit of trade could shift to a pursuit of Creek land.

France's deerskin trade with the large Indian nations was less extensive than that of the English. Their traders had trouble matching the quantity and variety of goods of their English competitors. The commander of Fort Toulouse, Commandant Hazeur, confronted those limitations when he encouraged the nearby Abihkas and Tallapoosas to join the Alabamas within the French sphere of influence. The English traders among the Upper Town Creeks "set the Indians against us," he reported in 1743, "by supplying them with all the things they need, even with several trifles that appeal to their tastes such as ribbons, braid, earrings, mirrors, buckles, belts, shoes, and stockings for men and women, coats of fine materials, fine hats, fine and often decorated shirts, in a word with everything that can flatter their imagination."[46] He even went so far as to arrange to have a sample of ribbon sold by the English sent to French manufacturers to duplicate in order to cater to the discriminating consumers in Indian country. Still, Choctaws, Alabamas, and Creeks enjoyed the diplomatic gifts and services offered by French emissaries, who represented a colony that was far less threatening than Carolina and Georgia, one that could be used as a countervailing force to keep the English in check.[47]

The French at Mobile developed their closest relationship with the petit nations, the cluster of small tribes like the Tohomes and Mobilians who had long been in the region and the newer refugee groups like the Apalachees. Small to begin with, these groups had suffered population declines because of disease and increasingly came to rely on their economic connections to the Europeans. Men sold venison and corn to neighboring settlers, and women marketed various foodstuffs and craft items like baskets on the town's streets. Many of the men found work transporting goods and people up the rivers in their traditional pirogues and in the large boats built to supply the French forts in the interior. The Mobilians in particular became important go-betweens in French trade and diplomacy with the Choctaws, Alabamas, and Creeks. Not only did they man the oars of the boats and lead parties on foot to Indian towns, but their own village became a stopping point for both Indian and French delegations. There, Mobilian headmen counseled and, at times, argued with Indian and French diplomats and traders, carving out a semi-independent niche in this borderland world.[48]

French diplomatic efforts in the mid-eighteenth century focused on wooing the large Indian nations. The Choctaws were solidly in France's camp and the Alabamas leaned in that direction, although both groups made sure that colonial officials did not take their allegiance for granted. The Abihkas and Tallapoosas who stood between Mobile and South Carolina and Georgia were up for grabs and often played the British and French off one another. Hundreds of Choctaw headmen and warriors traveled to Mobile every year for a series of celebrations and meetings with colonial officials that often lasted weeks, while the French hosted frequent Indian councils at Fort Toulouse. At the center of those occasions was the distribution of gifts, ranging from practical goods like tools, gunpowder, shot, and cloth that could be shared with townspeople back home to ornamental goods like uniforms and medals that headmen could keep as symbols of their authority. Indians periodically visited Charlestown and Savannah and demanded gifts during negotiations, but those encounters rarely came close to matching those grand councils with the French in frequency or scale. When the British took control of Mobile in the fall of 1763 after the Seven Years' War, they were astounded to discover, as Lieutenant Colonel James Robertson noted, "about five thousand Choctaw Indians encamped around the Town," who had come at the invitation of the French for the annual distribution of gifts.[49]

Providing services to the Indians also fostered good relations for the French. A blacksmith stationed at Fort Toulouse repaired muskets for the Creeks and Alabamas free of charge, while Choctaws and members of the petit nations regularly visited Mobile for the same services. As many as nine hundred Indians came to Mobile in the winter of 1731–32 in order to have their muskets repaired. That kind of service, made possible by the proximity of the French and by their culture of diplomacy, generated a tremendous amount of goodwill among the Indians, a fact not lost on the English. Edmond Atkin, the British agent for the southern Indians, noted that while his nation's traders sold guns "at an extravagant price," the French, when the gun was "spoiled," repaired the weapon "for nothing. This endears the Frenchman to him. He is glad to have such a Friend near him. Their mutual Convenience unites them."[50] Alabama's Indians also turned to the French for gunpowder and shot, as well as liquor; those bulky items were easier and cheaper to paddle up the rivers from Mobile than to transport on packhorses from Augusta.[51]

Diplomatic talks and the exchange of goods took place within a ritualized context that often blended European and Indian cultures. French traders and officials, like their English counterparts, quickly understood that smoking the calumet or patiently listening to long speeches were necessary adaptations to the process of negotiation. They often were in the Indians' world and they had to follow the rules of the square ground. But Indians also came to the French world and at times adopted European customs. Colonel James Robertson noted that "French manners are in vogue" among the Choctaws who came to Mobile in 1763. "Every Indian affects them, and is esteem'd in some measure as he succeeds," he observed. "A Chief bows like a dancing Master, kisses both your cheeks and makes you a French compliment."[52]

Clothing and personal possessions served as visual reminders of cultural blending and competition on the imperial frontier. A young "prince" who traveled with his entourage of advisors and warriors from Coweta to Fort Toulouse in 1759 was riding "a Spanish mount with an English saddle" and wore "a scarlet coat with gold braid and English cuffs" along with deerskin boots, white shirt, loincloth, and feathers in his hair, according to a French soldier named Jean-Bernard Bossu. After a salute from the fort's cannons and the smoking of the calumet, the commander invited the visitors to rest since "it is customary among the Indians to wait until the next day before discussing political matters so that they may have time to think." The following morning the young Creek was no longer wearing his red coat. Perhaps he did not want to offend his hosts, although Bossu suspected that he "thought it politic to take it off, hoping that the French would give him another one." If that was his ploy, it worked. "Since the Prince was my size," Bossu reported, "the Commander asked me to give him a blue coat, a waistcoat with gold braid, a plumed hat, and a white shirt with embroidered cuffs." Headmen in Creek and Alabama towns hoarded gifts like medals and military uniforms and took them to their graves. Indeed, the competition between English and French trade goods followed Indians into the afterlife. Archaeological research conducted by Gregory Waselkov in the towns near Fort Toulouse shows that after 1720, "an increasing number of Creeks were buried with either French *or* English goods, suggesting symbolic representation of factional affiliation."[53]

French, African, and Indian people participated in more informal exchanges of goods and services in addition to the diplomatic gift giving. The focal points of those encounters were the French settlements around Fort Toulouse and Mobile. There, a different sort of middle ground emerged, one that was more localized and less connected to the imperial construct of the frontier.

Fort Toulouse, located about ten miles from present-day Montgomery, had little military significance but was vital to France's imperial goals. Several Alabama towns were close by, and it was their residents who first invited the French to build the fort in 1717. The towns of the Tallapoosas and Abihkas were not far beyond and they were of special concern since their people had stronger connections to the English traders. Toulouse projected a French presence deep into the frontier at a time when the English colony of Carolina was still reeling from the Yamasee War, but the stockade itself was flimsy and housed only a small garrison in the early years. A British spy reported in 1720 that the fort had three or four small swivel guns, and by 1732 there were a couple of cannons as well. The wooden palisades and buildings were always rotting and the earthworks eroding, both needing constant repair. Warfare between Britain and France in the 1740s convinced Louisiana's governor to build a new fort with stronger walls in the 1750s, and by 1763, at the end of the Seven Years' War, Fort Toulouse housed fifty soldiers and officers. But one English officer who toured the fort after its surrender had it right when he noted that the French "depended more on the Indian friendship than on the strength of the places for the safety of their garrisons."[54]

French officials encouraged soldiers at Fort Toulouse to interact with the local Alabamas and Creeks in order to build goodwill. One way to do that was to limit the supply of provisions. The large boats manned by up to twenty-eight oarsmen carried a lot of goods up the Alabama River from Mobile but they did not bring much in the way of food. The Marquis de Vaudreuil-Cavagnal, who served as governor of Louisiana from 1743 to 1753, explained the policy in 1745, stating that "this garrison must necessarily trade in order to get a living," which would allow the local Indians to "find a market for their products."[55] Using the gunpowder, shot, cloth, and other merchandise that filled the supply boats, the soldiers bartered with the Indians in the surrounding towns for venison, corn, beans, and other food products. They also turned to the local women to provide the labor necessary to survive, trading goods, for example, in exchange for their work grinding corn into meal or making clay storage jars. Some of those soldiers stayed after their term of service ended and married Indian women and raised métis children, while others brought French wives. By 1758 a small community of about two dozen families numbering about 160 people, including one African slave, clustered around the fort. Mixed-race families and day-to-day encounters with people in neighboring villages reinforced the integration of Indians and French on Alabama's frontier.[56]

Blurred racial boundaries were even more common in and around Mobile. In the early years enslaved Indians and Africans often lived in the same French households. Just over 200 of the 241 Africans listed in Mobile's 1721 census lived with at least one Indian slave, while 92 of the 110 Indians belonged to masters who owned at least one African slave. The character of slavery shifted some over the next decade as several hundred more men, women, and children from the West African regions of Senegambia and the Bight of Benin were transported to Mobile as part of Louisiana's unsuccessful efforts to develop plantation agriculture. But the flow of African slaves slowed to a trickle after the Natchez revolt in 1729 and failed to replace Indian slaves completely, which meant that cross-cultural encounters persisted deep into the eighteenth century. The newly arrived Africans most likely learned the local trade language, Mobilian Jargon, from both their French masters and their Indian comrades. Some French settlers lived in Indian villages with their slaves. One carpenter named La Carie Drapeau, for example, lived in a Tohomes village with his wife and children, and two African and five Indian slaves. Frontier work also brought people together and promoted informal connections. Members of the petit nations developed close ties to the French by rowing their boats, serving as guides, and selling goods to settlers. Africans who herded livestock and tapped pine sap to make tar moved freely through the delta land and piney woods beyond the bluffs, encountering both French and Indian people. Many enslaved Africans participated in trade, selling chickens and eggs, crops grown on their own small patches known as provision grounds, or crafts such as baskets that they made in their off hours to the people who lived in the area.[57]

The middle ground that emerged out of the deerskin trade and diplomacy after the Yamasee War began to crumble in the 1760s and 1770s. Britain's victory in the Seven Years' War in 1763 altered the imperial landscape of the Gulf South by expelling France from North America and Spain from Florida, leaving the British in control of East and West Florida. The Creeks and other southeastern Indians could no longer play one empire off another. At the same time, pressures within the system of trade intensified, challenging the economic and social traditions of Alabama's Indians. Britain found it hard to control Alabama's traders and Indians even in the absence of their European rivals, and ultimately discovered just how difficult it was to maintain the loyalty of their North American colonists. Their command over the Gulf region proved short-lived.

British officials knew that a well-ordered frontier depended on the goodwill of the Indians and they adopted policies with that reality in mind. Their Proclamation of 1763, for example, prohibited colonial settlements beyond the Appalachians. They also were determined to regulate contacts between traders and Indians and appointed officials to monitor trade, including John Stuart, the Indian agent for the South. But effective imperial control and oversight proved elusive across the vast trans-Appalachian West. Settlers began to push into the backcountry and traders ignored the regulations imposed from on high, generating stresses on Alabama's frontier.

One source of conflict was the proliferation of unregulated traders in Indian country. Long-established traders from South Carolina and Georgia found themselves competing with new men from Pensacola and Mobile now that West Florida was in British hands. More troubling was the fact that those upstarts took to trading in the woods when they were unable to get a foothold in the Creek towns. Southern Indians had long believed that the woods were realms of disorder and chaos, even as they provided sustenance. Hunters and their families and warriors on the warpath passed through them, of course, but always with the protection of purification rituals. But increasingly in the 1760s, new traders were conducting business in the woods outside the towns. One of the driving forces behind that shift was the growing demand for raw skins that had been only minimally processed. Young hunters without wives could kill and skin deer and trade directly from their hunting camps. The fact that alcohol was increasingly the "currency" of exchange for the skins only compounded the sense of disorder. Drunkenness was a cause for worry in and of itself, but also because it invited trade abuses and cheating. Both the regular traders connected to towns who had advanced supplies to those hunters and expected payment of skins and the Indian leaders cut off from sources of authority complained to John Stuart about the proliferation of trading in the woods.[58]

More established traders also brought changes to Indian towns that hinted at transformations to come in the next decades. Traders who married Indian women, developed friendships with headmen, and became "countrymen" sunk roots into Indian towns and began to supplement their trading activities with farming and herding. Complaints about their livestock trampling the corn in the communal bottomland fields increased in the 1760s, and many of the traders moved their homes and storehouses beyond the town borders in order to claim land to till and to forage their livestock. Some used slave labor, despite colonial prohibitions against bringing blacks to the frontier. Trade still forged connections but alternate enterprises like livestock herding diminished traders' reliance on their Creek neighbors.[59]

One of those traders was Lachlan McGillivray, whose son, Alexander, would come to embody the transition from trade to farming. The Scottish trader was well established in the Upper Creek town of Little Tallassee by the 1740s, in part because of his marriage to Sehoy, a Creek woman whose father was a French officer stationed at Fort Toulouse. Sehoy had political clout as the sister of a Koasati headman and as a member of the prestigious Wind Clan. McGillivray maintained plantations in Georgia but spent a good part of the year at his trading post and farm on the Coosa River. Unlike many traders, Lachlan did not divide his affections between an Anglo-American wife in the East and an Indian wife on the frontier. His only wife was Sehoy and his only family was the four children they had together. Indian custom demanded that Sehoy's brothers teach Alexander the hunting and warring skills required of Creek men, but Lachlan also wanted him to learn how to navigate the Anglo-American world. He sent him to live for a time with his brother in Charleston where he received schooling, and then in 1765, when Alexander was about fifteen, Lachlan apprenticed him out to a Savannah mercantile firm so that he could learn more about the fur trade business.[60]

Alexander McGillivray might have become a trader like his father had the revolution not intervened to draw him back more deeply into Creek society. As protests over parliamentary acts evolved into outright political rebellion in 1775, colonists, including the traders of South Carolina and Georgia, began to choose sides. George Galphin chose the cause of independence while Lachlan McGillivray remained loyal to King George. When Patriot leaders in Georgia confiscated his plantations, McGillivray returned to Scotland, leaving his son behind. Alexander and his sister, Sophia, had been living at their father's plantation outside Savannah for a decade or so, but now they returned to their homeland. There Alexander reestablished connections, first renewing his relationship with the Upper Creek mico Emistisiguo, an old friend of his father's, and then taking time to tour the numerous towns along the Coosa, Tallapoosa, and Alabama Rivers. As a Loyalist with important kinship and clan connections in Creek country, Alexander proved valuable to the British. He accepted a position

Facing page: Bernard Romans's map illustrates the central position of Creek country in the South in 1776. Courtesy of the Library of Congress, Geography and Map Division.

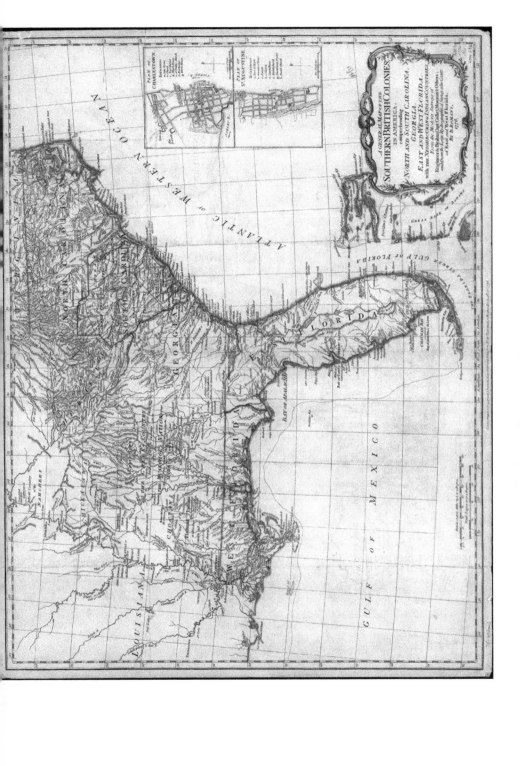

as a commissary to the Upper Creek towns and began funneling royal gifts to headmen to promote loyalty to the Crown.[61]

The British needed all the help they could get as the Revolutionary War ground on. Their army and navy established control over the South Atlantic seaboard by taking Savannah and Charleston, but pacifying the southern interior proved more difficult. Loyalist and Patriot militias staged vicious guerrilla raids that left the Carolina backcountry in a state of virtual civil war. The British had recruited Cherokee warriors to make common cause in driving frontiersmen from their settlements, but that too had not gone as planned. Georgians and Carolinians had struck back with a vengeance, wreaking havoc in Cherokee towns. Now, with British attention, guns, and manpower focused on the rebellious eastern colonies, West Florida was vulnerable. The problem was not outright political rebellion; the polyglot residents of Baton Rouge, Mobile, and Pensacola, while not fervently loyal, were not inclined to throw in with the Patriot movement. But the old imperial rivals, France and Spain, might take the opportunity to pluck West Florida from Britain's grasp.

To shore up their defenses of their Gulf outposts, the British turned to the Creeks, Choctaws, and Chickasaws, but their efforts to rally support yielded limited results. Alexander McGillivray worked hard to bring Creek towns into the Loyalist fold, reminding headmen that Britain's Proclamation Line of 1763, however imperfect, impeded American settlers eager to claim Indian hunting territory. But many Creek leaders opted to remain neutral. The assault on Cherokee towns was enough to convince them of the perils of British allegiance.

In the end, Britain's fears came true at the hands of an ambitious Spanish governor. British officials had worried that France, which had allied with the Americans, would try to reclaim their former Gulf possessions. Instead, Bernardo de Gálvez, the governor of Louisiana, took advantage of the distractions of war to move against West Florida. After capturing Baton Rouge, de Gálvez set his sights on Mobile, which he took after a brief siege in March 1780. Few allied Indians made it to Mobile in time to aid in its defense, but Choctaws, some Chickasaws, and a small contingent of Creeks led by McGillivray did come to the aid of the British in Pensacola. The governor's fleet arrived in March 1781, and his forces began the arduous process of digging trenches and inching closer and closer to Fort George on the bluff overlooking Pensacola. The Indian warriors harassed the Spanish soldiers but could not stop their slow advance. In April, the British surrendered the fort and abandoned the town, leaving their Indian allies to make their way back to their towns in the interior. Later that year Britain's efforts to hold on to its rebellious colonies collapsed when the

Continental Army and its French allies defeated General Cornwallis at York-town.[62]

The events in Pensacola and Yorktown in 1781 pushed Britain to the negoti-ating table and ended up altering the geopolitical landscape surrounding fron-tier Alabama. Thanks to Gálvez's bold maneuvers Spain gained control over East and West Florida when the treaty was signed in 1783, while the fledgling American nation secured the independence it had claimed in 1776. The Creeks and other southern Indians who occupied the territory in between would have to find ways to protect their own autonomy in this postrevolutionary world. Perhaps a resurgent Spanish Empire would help them counterbalance the pressures of a new country whose people hungered for western land across the mountains.

Notes

not move table of Any rev?

1. *Abstracts of Colonial Wills of the State of Georgia, 1733–1777* (Spartanburg, SC: Reprint Company, 1981), 120, quoted in Joshua Piker, *Okfuskee: A Creek Indian Town in Colonial America* (Cambridge, MA: Harvard University Press, 2004), 58.

2. James Adair, *The History of the American Indians*, ed. Kathryn E. Holland Braund (Tuscaloosa: University of Alabama Press, 2005), 276–77.

3. Adair, *History of the American Indians*, 279.

4. Ibid., 277, 521n285; Piker, *Okfuskee*, 52, 222n19; Steven C. Hahn, *The Invention of the Creek Nation, 1670–1763* (Lincoln: University of Nebraska Press, 2004), 254; David H. Corkran, *The Creek Frontier, 1540–1783* (Norman: University of Oklahoma Press, 1967), 216.

5. Hahn, *Invention of the Creek Nation*, 250–52.

6. Hahn, *Invention of the Creek Nation*, 251–53.

7. "The Narration of Robert French Pack-Horse-man. . . ." in *The Colonial Records of the State of Georgia*, vol. 8, *Journal of the Proceedings of the Governor and Council, March 8, 1759, to December 31, 1762, Inclusive*, ed. Allen D. Candler, Kenneth Cole-man, and Milton Ready (Atlanta: Franklin-Turner, 1907), 314, quoted in Piker, *Ok-fuskee*, 60.

8. Adair, *History of the American Indians*, 278; Hahn, *Invention of the Creek Nation*, 254–55.

9. Hahn, *Invention of the Creek Nation*, 255; Corkran, *Creek Frontier*, 217.

10. "The Headmen's Answer of the Upper Creeks. . . ." in Candler, Coleman, and Ready, *Colonial Records*, vol. 8, 420–21, quoted in Piker, *Okfuskee*, 55.

11. *South Carolina Gazette*, September 27, 1760, quoted in Piker, *Okfuskee*, 62; Piker, *Okfuskee*, 61–62; Hahn, *Invention of the Creek Nation*, 255; Corkran, *Creek Fron-tier*, 218.

12. Richard White, *The Middle Ground: Indians, Empires, and Republics in the Great Lakes Region, 1650–1815* (Cambridge: Cambridge University Press, 1991), x.

13. Wilbur R. Jacobs, ed., *The Appalachian Indian Frontier: The Edmond Atkin Report and Plan of 1755* (Lincoln: University of Nebraska Press, 1967), 3–4, quoted in James Axtell, *The Indians' New South: Cultural Change in the Colonial Southeast* (Baton Rouge: Louisiana State University Press, 1997), 45.

14. William L. Ramsey, "'All & Singular the Slaves': A Demographic Profile of Indian Slavery in Colonial South Carolina," in *Money, Trade, and Power: The Evolution of Colonial South Carolina's Plantation Society*, ed. Jack P. Greene, Rosemary Brana-Shute, and Randy J. Sparks (Columbia: University of South Carolina Press, 2000), 177–79.

15. Axtell, *Indians' New South*, 48–49; Kathryn E. Holland Braund, *Deerskins and Duffels: The Creek Indian Trade with Anglo-America, 1685–1815* (Lincoln: University of Nebraska Press, 1993), 42, 49, 88, 121–23.

16. Axtell, *Indians' New South*, 48–49; Braund, *Deerskins and Duffels*, 64–69; Seymour Feiler, ed., *Jean-Bernard Bossu's Travels in the Interior of North America, 1751–1762* (Norman: University of Oklahoma Press, 1962), 46.

17. Braund, *Deerskins and Duffels*, 98; Robert M. Weir, *Colonial South Carolina: A History* (Millwood, NY: KTO, 1983), 143; Joseph M. Hall Jr., *Zamumo's Gifts: Indian-European Exchange in the Colonial Southeast* (Philadelphia: University of Pennsylvania Press, 2009), 134.

18. Braund, *Deerskins and Duffels*, 92.

19. Hall, *Zamumo's Gifts*, 126–27; Steven J. Oatis, *A Colonial Complex: South Carolina's Frontiers in the Era of the Yamasee War, 1680–1730* (Lincoln: University of Nebraska Press, 2004), 228–31; Braund, *Deerskins and Duffels*, 108–9.

20. Oglethorpe to Trustees, March 8, 1739, Georgia Historical Society Collections, Savannah, quoted in Edward J. Cashin, *Lachlan McGillivray, Indian Trader: The Shaping of the Southern Colonial Frontier* (Athens: University of Georgia Press, 1992), 28; Cashin, *Lachlan McGillivray*, 18–20, 27–34; Braund, *Deerskins and Duffels*, 81; Oatis, *Colonial Complex*, 292–93, 296.

21. Eirlys M. Barker, "Indian Traders, Charles Town and London's Vital Link to the Interior of North America, 1717–1755," in Greene, Brana-Shute, and Sparks, *Money, Trade, and Power*, 144–45; Braund, *Deerskins and Duffels*, 44–45, 48, 81–83.

22. Braund, *Deerskins and Duffels*, 45–46.

23. "Talks with the Trustees on Trade Regulation," in *Early American Indian Documents: Treaties and Laws, 1607–1789*, ed. Alden T. Vaughan, vol. 2, *Georgia Treaties, 1733–1763*, ed. John T. Juricek (Frederick, MD: University Publications of America, 1989), 25, quoted in Braund, *Deerskins and Duffels*, 49.

24. Braund, *Deerskins and Duffels*, 84, 87; Hahn, *Invention of the Creek Nation*, 166–67; Theda Perdue, "'A Sprightly Lover Is the Most Prevailing Missionary': Intermarriage between Europeans and Indians in the Eighteenth-Century South," in *Light*

on the Path: The Anthropology and History of the Southeastern Indians, ed. Thomas J. Pluckhahn and Robbie Ethridge (Tuscaloosa: University of Alabama Press, 2006), 174; Piker, *Okfuskee*, 34, 138; Barker, "Indian Traders," 150.

25. Perdue, "'A Sprightly Lover,'" 168–74; Piker, *Okfuskee*, 168–69; Braund, *Deerskins and Duffels*, 83–85.

26. Claudio Saunt, *A New Order of Things: Property, Power, and the Transformation of the Creek Indians, 1733–1816* (Cambridge: Cambridge University Press, 1999), 43–44.

27. Glover to the Governor's Council for South Carolina, March 14, 1727/1728, Records in the British Public Record Office Relating to South Carolina, South Carolina Department of Archives and History, Columbia, 13:130–31, quoted in Oatis, *Colonial Complex*, 281.

28. Oatis, *Colonial Complex*, 279–86; Hall, *Zamumo's Gifts*, 156–57.

29. Piker, *Okfuskee*, 140.

30. Hall, *Zamumo's Gifts*, 142, 145–46; Oatis, *Colonial Complex*, 144–45.

31. "Tobias Fitch's Journal to the Creeks," in *Travels in the American Colonies*, ed. Newton D. Mereness (New York: Antiquarian, 1961), 176, 178–79, 180.

32. Ibid., 180–81.

33. Ibid., 181, 183.

34. Ibid., 184.

35. Ibid., 184–87, 200, 210.

36. Sylviane A. Diouf, *Slavery's Exiles: The Story of the American Maroons* (New York: New York University Press, 2014), 30.

37. "An Account of Life of Mr. David George from S. L. A. Given by Himself," Black Loyalists: Our History, Our People, Canada's Digital Collections, accessed July 30, 2015, http://blackloyalist.com/cdc/documents/diaries/george_a_life.htm.

38. *Transcripts of the Journal of the Commons House of Assembly*, ed. John S. Green, 3:279, South Carolina Department of Archives and History, Columbia, quoted in Hall, *Zamumo's Gifts*, 152.

39. Oatis, *Colonial Complex*, 147–48.

40. MacKay to the Trustees, Coweta, March 29, 1735, in *General Oglethorpe's Georgia: Colonial Letters, 1733–1743*, ed. Mills Lane (Savannah, GA: Beehive, 1990), 1:148, quoted in Hall, *Zamumo's Gifts*, 162.

41. Glen to Duke of Bedford, February 3, 1747/1748, quoted in Daniel H. Thomas, *Fort Toulouse: The French Outpost at the Alabamas on the Coosa* (Tuscaloosa: University of Alabama Press, 1989), 24.

42. Charles Edward O'Neill, *Church and State in French Colonial Louisiana: Policy and Politics to 1732* (New Haven, CT: Yale University Press, 1966), 91, quoted in Richmond F. Brown, "Colonial Mobile, 1712–1813," in *Mobile: The New History of Alabama's First City*, ed. Michael V. R. Thomason (Tuscaloosa: University of Alabama Press, 2001), 30–31.

43. Brown, "Colonial Mobile," 30–33, 37–38; Ira Berlin, *Many Thousands Gone: The First Two Centuries of Slavery in North America* (Cambridge, MA: Harvard University Press, 1998), 79–82, 88.

44. Brown, "Colonial Mobile," 38–39, 41; Feiler, *Jean-Bernard Bossu's Travels,* 126–27.

45. Axtell, *Indians' New South*, 47; Brown, "Colonial Mobile," 34.

46. Dunbar Rowland, Albert G. Sanders, and Patricia K. Galloway, eds., *Mississippie Provincial Archives, French Dominion* (Baton Rouge: Louisiana State University Press, 1984), 4:208–9, quoted in Gregory A. Waselkov, "French Colonial Trade in the Upper Creek Country," in *Calumet and Fleur-de-Lys: Archaeology of Indian and French Contact in the Midcontinent*, ed. John A. Walthall and Thomas E. Emerson (Washington, DC: Smithsonian Institution Press, 1992), 42.

47. Brown, "Colonial Mobile," 36, 39; Waselkov, "French Colonial Trade," 36.

48. Brown, "Colonial Mobile," 35; Feiler, *Jean-Bernard Bossu's Travels*, 128; "Journal of De Beauchamps' Journey to the Choctaws, 1746," in Mereness, *Travels in the American Colonies*, 262–64.

49. Hahn, *Invention of the Creek Nation*, 177; Feiler, *Jean-Bernard Bossu's Travels*, 135–36; Brown, "Colonial Mobile," 37; Robertson to Sir Jeffrey Amherst, November 15, 1763, Sir Jeffrey Amherst Papers, William L. Clements Library, University of Michigan, Ann Arbor, quoted in Robert R. Rea, "Lieutenant Colonel James Robertson's Mission to the Floridas, 1763," *Florida Historical Quarterly* 53 (July 1974): 43.

50. Jacobs, *Appalachian Indian Frontier*, 10, quoted in Gregory A. Waselkov, introduction to Thomas, *Fort Toulouse*, xxvii; Brown, "Colonial Mobile," 36.

51. Waselkov, "French Colonial Trade," 36, 41–42.

52. Robertson, "Report of Florida," Great Britain, Public Record Office, Colonial Office, US Library of Congress transcripts, quoted in Rea, "Lieutenant Colonel James Robertson's Mission," 44.

53. Feiler, *Bossu's Travels*, 151–54; Waselkov, "French Colonial Trade," 45; Cameron B. Wesson, *Households and Hegemony: Early Creek Prestige Goods, Symbolic Capital, and Social Power* (Lincoln: University of Nebraska Press, 2008), 129–31.

54. Robertson, "Report of Florida," quoted in Rea, "Lieutenant Colonel James Robertson's Mission," 45; Thomas, *Fort Toulouse*, xiii, xix, 6–12, 52.

55. Rowland, Sanders, and Galloway, *Mississippie Provincial Archives*, 4:250, quoted in Waselkov, introduction to Thomas, *Fort Toulouse*, xxv.

56. Waselkov, introduction to Thomas, *Fort Toulouse*, xxiii; Thomas, *Fort Toulouse*, 26–31; Waselkov, "French Colonial Trade," 36, 44.

57. David Wheat, "My Friend Nicolas Mongoula: Africans, Indians, and Cultural Exchange in Eighteenth-Century Mobile," in *Coastal Encounters: The Transformation of the Gulf South in the Eighteenth Century*, ed. Richmond F. Brown (Lincoln: University of Nebraska Press, 2007), 120–23. See also Berlin, *Many Thousands Gone*, 77–92, 195–215.

58. Braund, *Deerskins and Duffels*, 144–46.

59. Ibid., 181.

60. Michael D. Green, "Alexander McGillivray," in *American Indian Leaders: Studies in Diversity*, ed. R. David Edmunds (Lincoln: University of Nebraska Press, 1980), 42; Cashin, *Lachlan McGillivray*, 73–75; Saunt, *New Order of Things*, 67; Kathleen Du-Val, *Independence Lost: Living on the Edge of the American Revolution* (New York: Random House, 2015), 28–29.

61. Green, "Alexander McGillivray," 42; DuVal, *Independence Lost*, 76–77.

62. DuVal, *Independence Lost*, 166–71, 190–216.

PART THREE

The Settlers' Frontier

5

Ordering Alabama's Frontier

The delegation of almost thirty Creeks led by Alexander McGillivray caused quite a stir when they journeyed from their towns along the Tallapoosa, Coosa, and Chattahoochee Rivers to meet with George Washington in New York City in the summer of 1790. Colonel Marinus Willett, the president's personal envoy, accompanied the traveling party, and local and state leaders feted the Indian dignitaries every step of the way. In Richmond they dined "with the governor, council, judges, a number of the gentlemen of the bar, and other persons of distinction." A visit with George Washington's sister awaited them in Fredericksburg, along with a viewing of the president's birthplace and "the cottage in which his mother died." Pennsylvania's governor and members of the council greeted the delegation on the outskirts of Philadelphia before escorting them into the city. There the Creeks enjoyed a visit by a committee of Quakers and attended both a public dinner and the theater.[1] The president, who was eager to shower "attention" on McGillivray and the headmen and warriors, had provided funds to encourage the governors of Virginia, Maryland, and Pennsylvania to treat the Creeks lavishly so that they "might be kept in good humour."[2]

One impromptu celebration on the journey drove home the necessity of peace negotiations. At Guilford Courthouse, the site of a fierce and bloody Revolutionary War battle in North Carolina, Jane Brown renewed her friendly acquaintance with Alexander McGillivray in a reunion that Marinus Willett thought "was truly affecting." Like thousands of other Virginians and Carolinians after the war, Brown had set out from Guilford County in early 1788 with her husband, James, and their children, with the aim of settling beyond the Appalachian Mountains in the Cumberland region of present-day Tennessee, then the westernmost district of North Carolina. Rather than tackling the physically arduous overland path through the Cumberland Gap, the Brown family had instead boated down the Tennessee River, only to be ambushed by a party of Cherokee and Creek warriors. The raiders struck James Brown a mortal blow, nearly decapitating him, and took Jane and her children captive. After dividing up the children, one warrior claimed Jane and took her to a Creek town on the Tallapoosa, where she was put to work doing typical women's labor, hoeing fields and grinding maize. A chance encounter with Sophia Durant, Alexander McGillivray's sister, brought her plight to the leader's attention. McGillivray interceded and bought off her captor, and then tracked down those in nearby Creek towns who held two of her children and persuaded them to release their captives to his custody. Jane and her two children lived as guests on McGillivray's plantation for over a year before he took them with him to treaty negotiations at Rock Landing, Georgia, in November 1789. There, Jane Brown was reunited with all but one of her other children who had escaped their Cherokee captors, and the family returned to North Carolina.[3]

The reunion between captive and redeemer might have augured goodwill in the impending negotiations but it was also a reminder of the bloody border war being fought on the southwestern frontier in the years after the revolution. McGillivray had taken Jane Brown into his home, but he also most likely had ordered the raid that killed her husband and led to her captivity in the first place. He and most of the other Creek headmen and their Cherokee allies were determined to staunch the flood of settlers and drive out those intruding on their hunting grounds to the north and east of their homelands.

Why, then, were McGillivray and the other Creek leaders traveling to New York to negotiate peace? Because the conflict with the settlers had taken its toll. "A number of our frontier towns are getting weary of a Contest & war that diverts their attention . . . from their Indespensible occupations," he informed Esteban Miró, Louisiana's Spanish governor, just before leaving Little Tallassee that summer. McGillivray had no illusions about the motivations of the Americans. Washington's offer to talk stemmed not from "principles of Justice & humanity," he believed, but from the new nation's "poverty & Inability to Support & maintain a Vigorous Contest to reduce us by force." Far better "to treat with an enemy under Such circumstances," he informed Miró, "than a more powerful one."[4] Even an enemy could be useful in relieving the relentless pressure of settlers on the borders of Creek country.

None of the festivities along the road prepared the Creeks for what awaited them when the sloop carrying them across the Hudson docked in Manhattan as nearby ships fired their cannons in salute. There stood members of New York's Tammany Society lining the piers, bedecked in "Indian" headdresses. The Tammanies led the delegation in parade through the streets of the nation's capital, first past the Federal Hall where members of Congress had gathered to cheer the visitors and then to the house of General Henry Knox, the secretary of war, before finally being presented to Washington at his presidential mansion. Those headdresses were not meant to mock the visiting dignitaries; rather, they were an integral part of the patriotic organization's culture. Founded by artisans in Philadelphia in the 1770s, the society took its name from Tamanend, the chief of the Lenni-Lenape people who reportedly had pledged peace with William Penn and the original settlers of Pennsylvania almost a century earlier. Chapters spread throughout the eastern cities, each with a different "clan" name, and members wearing fanciful Indian garb gathered together in "wigwams" and elected "sachems" as their leaders. By playing Indian, the Tammanies appropriated an indigenous past to celebrate a new American identity, one differentiated from European origins and rooted in republicanism.[5]

It was fitting, then, that the Tammanies, symbols of peaceful cooperation between settlers and indigenous people on a long-ago, almost mythic frontier, escorted the Indian leaders to the president. The Creeks had traveled from the violent Alabama frontier, one distant in miles from New York but very present in the minds of Washington and Knox. Faced with the seemingly intractable problems of a Southwest that threatened to fracture the new nation itself, they could only hope that the Creek leaders were ready to embrace Tamanend's legendary spirit of cooperation.

Violence plagued the Southwest in the late 1780s in large part because of the blurring both of boundaries and of lines of authority. Spain had expanded beyond Louisiana to regain control of East and West Florida during the war and now claimed territory stretching far to the north, all the way to the Tennessee River and even the junction of the Ohio and Mississippi Rivers, land the United States called its own. Complicating that international boundary dispute was Georgia's contention that it owned most of the land west to the Mississippi and was eager to sell that vast territory to speculators. Of course neither Spain nor the United States nor Georgia actually controlled the interior lands; the Indians did. But they too faced challenges as settlers pressed against the eastern and northern margins of Indian country. Border conflicts threatened to pull the nation into a large-scale Indian war for which it was not at all prepared and which it could not afford.

A successful treaty with the Creeks could go a long way toward solving some of the problems associated with the postrevolutionary frontier. Direct diplomacy with the Creek delegation would undercut Georgia and assert federal authority over the southwestern territory. Clear boundaries would give Knox the power to police the frontier, removing the squatters who were infiltrating hunting grounds and inciting border raids. At the same time, trade concessions would woo the Creeks away from the influence of the Spanish in Florida and help tilt the balance of power in the Southwest toward the new American nation.

For several weeks in July and August 1790, the Creeks and Henry Knox, with assistance from Secretary of State Thomas Jefferson, hammered out a treaty that met both sides' goals, at least on paper. Establishing boundaries was the first priority since, as the preamble noted, removing "the causes of war" between the United States and the Creek nation required "ascertaining their limits." The treaty fixed the Creek-Georgia boundary at the Oconee River, and guaranteed "all their lands within the limit of the United States to the westward and southward" of that line. The Creeks gave up a small portion of land between the Ogeechee and Oconee Rivers already settled by squatters in exchange for a $1,500 annuity to the nation. Americans were prohibited from attempting "to hunt or destroy game on the Creek lands," and anyone settling across the boundary would "forfeit the protection of the United States," leaving the Creeks to "punish him or not, as they please."[6] Two secret articles were designed to augment McGillivray's power and cement Creek loyalty: a commission for McGillivray as a brigadier general with an annual salary of $1,200, and a trade deal, to be implemented two years later, which would allow the Creeks to import, through an American port, sixty thousand dollars' worth of duty-free goods, much of which would be controlled by McGillivray.[7]

The Treaty of New York passed the Senate, the first treaty to be ratified by that body under the new Constitution, and the formal signing ceremony before the members of Congress at Federal Hall the following week was a festive occasion. Washington and Knox followed the rituals of Indian treaty ceremonies, with gifts of tobacco and wampum beads and a reading of the treaty, with a translation by Joseph Cornell, McGillivray's brother-in-law, who had served as an interpreter during the negotiations. After Washington spoke, McGillivray, dressed in a red-and-blue military jacket, addressed the crowd. The ceremony

Hopoithle Mico, of Tallassee, traveled with the Creek delegation to New York City in 1790. There the artist John Trumbull sketched this portrait.
Courtesy of the New York Public Library.

closed with shakings of hands and a Creek song of peace. When the delegation departed New York to return to their towns in Creek country, McGillivray left his young nephew behind, to live with and be educated by Henry Knox, who had hosted the leader during his stay in the city.[8]

Despite being a constitutional milestone, the Treaty of New York failed to solve the problems of the southwestern frontier. Georgians who saw "their" western lands blithely guaranteed to the Creeks were outraged, but so too were many of the Lower Towns' micos, who believed that McGillivray had betrayed them by giving away some of their hunting grounds beyond the Oconee. The surveyor commissioned to draw the boundary line between Georgia and the Creek nation waited for the Creek witnesses required by the treaty to appear so that he could get to work, but they never arrived and he eventually gave up. McGillivray continued to receive his salary from the United States government, but ever the adroit politician, he turned against the treaty provisions in the face of his compatriots' hostility. He rebuilt his alliances with the Spanish and by 1792 was once again sending Creek warriors on border raids. By that time, Jane Brown, the redeemed captive he had reunited with at Guilford Courthouse in 1790, had returned with her children to the Cumberland region, one of thousands who continued to press into the frontiers of the Creek nation.[9]

Echoes of the old imperial frontier reverberated through the meeting of Creeks and the Washington administration in 1790. The president's fears of full-scale Indian war and the pernicious influence of European rivals would have been familiar to South Carolina's leaders in the early eighteenth century. McGillivray and the other headmen's deft manipulation of those fears and their ability to play one power off another—Spanish, American, and Georgian—had been a hallmark of Creek diplomacy throughout the entire century. Journeys from the heart of Creek country to colonial centers of power had been occurring for almost a hundred years. New York, it is true, was further away than Augusta or Mobile, signaling a shift in the locus of authority after the revolution. But even that distance was not so new; after all, in the past, Creek delegations had traveled to Havana, Mexico City, and London. They were accustomed to dealing with distant imperial powers. The rituals of negotiation—the gift of tobacco, the use of wampum to communicate, the depositing of a beloved nephew in Knox's household—all carried vestiges of ancient rites of peaceful alliances.

Despite those reminders of the past, the treaty proved a turning point in two ways. First, it marked a shift in perceptions of what was of value in the Southwest. For almost a hundred years, Carolinians, the French, and the Spanish had focused on trade and alliances in their negotiations with the Indians, each at-

tempting to harness the economic and military might of the native peoples for
the glory of empire. The Treaty of New York touched on trade as a tool to secure Creek loyalty, but land was the central concern of all the parties. Competition over land generated the bloody conflict that necessitated the treaty in the
first place, and establishing peace and order began with boundaries, by marking
what was American and what was Indian. Second, the treaty extended federal
authority over Indian diplomacy. By undermining the claims of both the Spanish and the Georgians, Knox and Washington circumscribed the Creeks' ability
to maneuver between competing powers. That authority was not complete and
would take some time to consolidate. The Spanish presence on the Gulf delayed
the collapse of imperial gamesmanship, new rounds of speculation called into
question just who owned Georgia's western lands, and schemers tempted by
Spanish alliances and tantalizing dreams of land profits continued to flirt with
separatist plots, complicating the imposition of governmental authority over
the borderlands. But by the turn of the nineteenth century the federal government had assured American dominance over the southwestern frontier, opening the door to the expansion of settlement.[10]

The story of Jane Brown and her family captures popular conceptions of
the initial encounter between settlers and Indians, of Americans brought
face-to-face with the tomahawk on a bloody ground. That Brown was willing to
cross the mountains again in 1792 after the killing of her husband and her own
captivity attests to the land hunger and the individual fortitude of pioneering
settlers. That she and her neighbors continued to fear raids attests to the determination of the Indians to defend their homelands. What gets lost in that
story of bloody beginnings are the ways in which the political powers—Indian, Spanish, and American—sought to mediate and shape those encounters
to their respective advantages. A new frontier in Alabama began to emerge out
of those struggles over the boundaries of land and authority in the decades after
the revolution. The fate of the southern Indian nations, Spain's northern empire,
and the new United States hung in the balance.

Years before he met with Alexander McGillivray, George Washington worried
about the dangers that westward expansion posed to American security. Back
in 1784, as he traveled to the Ohio River revisiting the region he had fought in
during the French and Indian War over twenty years earlier, Washington reflected on the flow of settlers across the Appalachians. Their distance from the

Eastern Seaboard and their isolation from governmental authority were troubling, but more disturbing was the fact that "other powers, and formidable ones too" controlled "the flanks and rear" of the nation. If the government did not "apply the cement of interest to bind all parts of [the union] together, by one indissolvable band . . . what ties[,] let me ask, should we have upon those people . . . if the Spaniards on their right, or Great Britain on their left, . . . should envite their trade and seek alliance with them?" The settlers of the West, Washington believed, "stand as it were on a pivet [pivot]—the touch of a feather would almost incline them any way."[11] Washington echoed the concerns of the Carolinians who had turned a wary eye toward the French in Mobile and Fort Toulouse in the 1750s. Then the future of the British Empire in North America seemed up for grabs; in 1784, the security of the West seemed to control the fate of the new American nation.

Alexander McGillivray had worked hard, with limited success, to rally Creeks to the British cause during the revolution, but he took some solace in the seeming fragility of the fledgling nation. The war had set people in motion: first the southern Loyalists who retreated with their families and their slaves to the western interior, and then the Americans who pushed deeper into the Carolina and Georgia backcountry and crossed the mountains into the lands that would become Kentucky and Tennessee.[12] As alarmed as he was about those new settlers, McGillivray delighted in the problems they posed for the Americans. Calling the pioneers a restless and rowdy bunch that resisted taxation and governmental authority, he noted in a letter to Arturo O'Neill, governor of West Florida, in 1784 that "the whole Continent is in Confusion." McGillivray predicted that America's victory in the revolution and its independence would be short-lived. "Before long," he said, "I expect to hear that the three kings must Settle the matter by dividing America between them."[13] While skeptical of America's republican experiment, McGillivray did share General Washington's clear-eyed assessment of the perils that lay ahead. An expanding frontier peopled by settlers with tenuous attachments to the East, and the presence of Spain and Britain in the Gulf and the Great Lakes, threatened the territorial integrity of the new nation. Looking ahead from the perspective of 1784, McGillivray predicted collapse and dismemberment, and he relished that prospect; Creek power could flourish in terrain contested by the Europeans.

Spanish forces had moved aggressively during the revolution to take control of Gulf lands, and the treaties of 1783 granted them East and West Florida, but the exact boundaries of their possessions remained ambiguous. The United States, taking its cue from the original line drawn in 1763 between British West

Florida and the Indian nations, argued that Spanish territory lay south of the 31st parallel. That line ran just below the confluence of the Alabama and Tombigbee Rivers and excluded the Natchez settlements on the Mississippi River. The Spanish contended that the official border stretched from the Chattahoochee to the Mississippi River along the 32° 28′ north latitude, a line that had marked the border of British West Florida from 1764 until the end of the revolution, which left Natchez and significant portions of the Tombigbee and Alabama Rivers under their control. Beyond that, the Spanish at times asserted their rights to all the territory between Georgia and the Mississippi River that lay south of the Tennessee River, based on their victories over the British during the revolution. Under that expansive claim, all of what would soon become Alabama, except for the narrow strip north of the Tennessee River, was Spanish in the 1780s and early 1790s.[14]

Spain's empire, a new La Florida, might have been vast on paper, but it was also largely hollow. Florida as well as Texas and the other northern frontier outposts were, in the words of historian J. H. Elliott, "the orphans of Spain's empire in America." While the Anglo-American backcountry was drawing a steady stream of migrants "hungry for land," New Spain's borderlands remained depopulated and economically stagnant, "envisaged primarily as buffer zones" to protect the more valuable Mexican colony to the south.[15] Few Spanish settlers flocked to Mobile and Pensacola, which remained primarily military garrisons and trading posts. In 1800, Louisiana's non-Indian population stood at about 50,000, a polyglot mixture of Americans, Germans, Britons, and Frenchmen, along with Spaniards. Compare that to the rapidly rising populations of America's western territories, like Kentucky, where the 12,000 non-Indian settlers at the end of the revolution grew to 73,000 by 1790 before reaching 221,000 ten years later.[16] That growth alarmed Spain. East Florida's governor, Vicente Manuel de Zéspedes, portrayed those American settlers pushing against the margins of the Spanish Empire as "nomadic like Arabs and . . . distinguished from savages only in their color, language, and the superiority of their depraved cunning and untrustworthiness."[17]

Spanish officials responded to this imbalance of power by trying both to harness and to repel the energies of American expansion. Building off the migrations of Loyalists during the war, Spain moved toward a policy of attracting American settlers to the Floridas and Louisiana. McGillivray lobbied on behalf of one group of Georgia Loyalists, assuring Governor O'Neill that they would be "contented & happy under the king of Spains Government," but only if they were granted "Liberty of Conscience" and not required to convert to

Catholicism.[18] By the mid-1780s local officials in the Floridas and Louisiana had begun giving land grants to American settlers, and that practice became official policy in 1788. Migrants could forgo religious conversion but had to swear an oath of allegiance to the Crown. Most of the Americans willing to become Spanish subjects moved to the Mississippi Valley, especially around the growing Natchez district. The rich soil and easy access to shipping on the river made Natchez an early outpost of the cotton kingdom. But some, like McGillivray's Loyalist friends, were drawn to Pensacola, Mobile, and the Tensaw region in the delta lands to the north.[19]

While trying to attract settlers willing to become subjects, Spain also tried to inhibit American expansion in the West. One way to do that was to block access to the Gulf, hindering commercial development in the trans-Appalachian interior. In 1784 the Spanish closed the lower Mississippi River to American shipping. They eased that policy in 1788 and opened the Mississippi and Mobile Rivers to American boats but imposed a 15 percent duty on the goods being transported.[20] Spanish control over the western river system frustrated settlers in Kentucky and Tennessee, and the national government's seeming impotency in the face of those restrictions contributed to their sense of isolation and alienation.[21]

McGillivray leveraged Spain's concern regarding American expansion to gain trade concessions for the Creeks. In a letter to West Florida's Governor O'Neill, he explained why a Spanish-Creek alliance was so important. Georgia and Carolina were doing all they could to seduce the Indians with trade in order to "make use of them in all the designs they may form against Pensacola & Mobile or elsewhere." McGillivray argued that the best way "to frustrate the americans Schemes" was for the Spanish to provide "a plentifull Supply of Goods" to the Creeks "on the footing that the English used to do." After all, he reminded O'Neill, "Indians will attach themselves to & Serve them best who Supply their Necessities." That being done, "the Crown of Spain will Gain & Secure a powerfull barrier in these parts against the ambitious and encroaching Americans."[22] This was not idle boasting, since officials estimated that the Creeks could muster between 3,500 and 6,000 warriors at that time, far more than either the Spanish or the Americans could gather.[23]

Spanish authorities took McGillivray up on his offer of an alliance in 1784, meeting first with Creek leaders and later with the Alabamas, Chickasaws, and Choctaws in Pensacola to negotiate treaties. The Indians agreed to maintain order in the borderlands by returning runaway slaves and military deserters and by refraining from robberies and horse and cattle thefts in Spanish settlements.

The Spaniards promised to help protect Creek land from Georgian settlers and provide consumer goods such as cloth and tools and, more importantly, guns, powder, and ammunition in exchange for deerskins.[24]

The problem was that Spain was in no position to provide the goods required and desired by the Indians. The Spanish had struggled to compete with Britain's economic might for a century, but this time they found a solution through McGillivray's connections. He knew the Scottish trader William Panton, whose mercantile firm had been pushed out of Georgia to East Florida during the war, and he had already told Governor Miró that Panton's company was "the only Means to Keep the Americans from teaking [taking] all the trade" of the Creek nation.[25] So at McGillivray's urging, the Spanish turned to Panton, Leslie and Company to supply the trade goods necessary to maintain peace with the Indians and check the expansion of American settlers on the frontier. Over time, Panton pressed the Spanish for trade concessions and steadily moved their outposts westward, first to Pensacola and then to Mobile.[26]

Alexander McGillivray's métis heritage and upbringing, and his familiarity with the wider Atlantic world, helped him navigate the shifting political landscape of the postrevolutionary southwestern frontier and bolstered his authority in the eyes of many Creeks, as well as Americans and Spaniards. Some historians admire his diplomatic flexibility but others suggest that his ability to maneuver smacked of self-interest rather than leadership. This was a man, after all, who accepted a commission from the United States as brigadier general with an annual salary of $1,200 while being paid $600 a year as Spain's trade commissioner to the Upper Creeks and maintaining his partnership with William Panton's firm. Historian Claudio Saunt, for one, questions McGillivray's commitment to the Creeks. Saunt argues that the leader, who was only one-quarter Creek by blood, was more his father's son than his mother's, and that he stood apart from Creek society. Unlike more traditional Creeks, McGillivray did not hunt and instead invested in livestock and slaves, pursuing the kind of agricultural activities that over time would transform Creek country. He also challenged the decentralized nature of Creek government by seeking to cement his authority by augmenting the power of the National Council. McGillivray even used members of the Wind Clan as bodyguards or "constables" to enforce his policies with threats of violence and to punish those he deemed disorderly. While he might have presented himself to outsiders as the most important Creek leader, McGillivray was, according to Saunt, an outsider himself, one who represented alien political, social, and economic ideas encroaching on traditional ways of life.[27]

McGillivray emerged out of the changes wrought by trade and imperial competition, but traditional patterns still shaped his behaviors. His multiple dealings with the Spanish and Americans and Georgians were reminiscent of the Creek policy of neutrality practiced almost a century earlier by Brims, who, like McGillivray, exaggerated his clout within the decentralized political system of his people when negotiating with outsiders. While McGillivray's literacy and immersion in the trade and political discourse of the Atlantic world distanced him from most other Creeks, they also connected him to powerful allies. As far back as the Mississippian chiefdoms, leaders had gained authority by forging commercial and political links with external polities. Like earlier micos who distributed prestige goods, McGillivray sought to control the flow of both information and goods, especially of weaponry, in order to cement the allegiance of other chiefs and warriors. While he challenged Creek traditionalism in his economic pursuits and in some of his attempts to consolidate power, McGillivray's diplomacy echoed older practices.

McGillivray began mobilizing support among the Creek headmen for armed resistance to check American expansion in the Georgia backcountry and the Cumberland. Not all were willing to go along. Hopoithle Mico of Tallassee and Eneah Mico of Cusseta had supported the Americans during the revolution. Honoring the long tradition of trade with Georgia they promised to "always look to the sun rising for any sup[p]ly," and were ready to negotiate with American commissioners in the mid-1780s.[28] But in the spring of 1786 the majority of Creek leaders agreed "to take arms in our defence & repel those Invaders of our Lands, to drive them from their encroachments & fix them within their own proper limits." McGillivray assured Spanish officials that they were not seeking to "engage in general Hostilities with the whole American States."[29] Instead he had instructed warriors "to conduct themselves with moderation" in driving settlers off their land, making sure "to shed no blood on no pretence but where Self defence made it absolutely necessary." A war party cleared out Georgian settlers on the Oconee lands without inflicting casualties, and a second one forced the Cumberland settlers to retreat to their fortified stations while "they ravaged & destroyed the plantations." Warriors also investigated rumors that "Americans were forming a New Settlement" at Muscle Shoals on the Tennessee River, but they found "only a few working utensils & some preparations for buildings . . . which they destroyed."[30] Faced with those attacks, the settlers on Georgia's frontier warned the governor that "their Plantations will be broke up, their Crops left to parish and the largest part of this fertile County Abandoned."[31]

This was the opening salvo in a border war that, despite McGillivray's assurances of restraint, intermittently brought terror and bloodshed to the southwestern frontier over the next ten years. The whole point of the raids was to intimidate encroaching settlers, to scare them so much that they would abandon their farms. That meant that Creek and Cherokee raiders went beyond burning houses and stealing livestock and killed, scalped, and dismembered men and sometimes women. Two of McGillivray's nephews joined a raiding party that attacked a surveying party in the Cumberland region. Surveyors were particularly vulnerable as symbols of the appropriation and sale of hunting lands, and this group of six fared poorly. The raiders killed and scalped all six, singling out the chief surveyor for torture before finally putting him out of his misery when "he cried and beged so much for his life."[32] Enslaved men and women, forced by their owners to clear the frontier land for settlement, were also vulnerable to Indian attack. One young girl hid and watched as Creeks attacked the farm where she and her family worked as slaves. She survived and "later reported that 'her Father & Mother & Sister were all Killed by the Indians & the houses all burning—that She Seen the Indians plain by the light of the Burning Houses—that they shot her Father & Tomahaweked her Mother.'"[33]

Indian raids scared the settlers. Georgia's governor described the bloodshed in the autumn of 1787: "Our frontiers have been the scene of blood and ravages; they have killed thirty-one of our citizens, wounded twenty, and taken four prisoners; they have burnt the court house and town of Greensburgh, in the county of Greene, and a number of other houses in different parts of the country."[34] Residents of Cumberland informed North Carolina governor Samuel Johnston in January 1788 that "forty-one of our Inhabitants have been massacred within twelve Months" and blamed the deaths on "those Barbarians," the Creeks.[35] Between 1787 and 1789, the Creeks burned eighty-nine houses and killed seventy-two white settlers in the frontier counties of Georgia.[36] Roger Parker Saunders wrote Georgia governor George Walton in 1789 that while he was "much Attached to Georgia" and was "loth to brake up My Plantation in Liberty County," he felt "compeld by Necessity" to move to Charleston. Another planter worried that if "Liberty County break Chatham & Effingham will soon follow."[37]

Others were more defiant. One settler in Georgia assured the governor that "the Upper part of this state is thick settled and strong and will kill Indians every chance and are not afraid."[38] Benjamin Harrison, a settler accustomed to the rough-and-tumble violence of frontier life—and who, to prove it, was missing an eye that had been gouged out in a brawl—led an attack on a Creek town, killing and dismembering sixteen men. Trumpeting his own martial spirit, he bragged "that there Sould Nevr be a peace with the Indians whilst his Nam was Ben Harrison for he was abel to raise men enough to kill half the Indians that might cum to aney Treaty."[39] After detailing the ways in which Creek raiders had run settlers off their farms, one report to Georgia governor Edward Telfair noted that "it is now time you take your Gun up. [T]he field is now open for execution."[40]

The men who headed frontier households and faced the very real possibility of their family members being scalped, mutilated, and killed or captured did not hesitate to pursue raiders and initiate retaliatory strikes into Indian country. Men like Andrew Jackson, who left North Carolina for the Cumberland settlements in 1788 and quickly became a leader in the border wars, developed a localist mentality and were ready to take the defense of their lives and their livelihoods in their own hands since no governmental forces were at their disposal. The harshness of frontier life, their hatred and fear of the Cherokees and Creeks, and their determination to wrest lands from the Indians all encouraged a violent response. Settlers often did not discriminate between different Creek towns when striking back. When Upper Creek warriors killed two Georgians in the summer of 1787, backcountry raiders attacked a hunting party from Cusseta, the Lower Creek town most closely allied with the Americans. McGillivray reported that the settlers had killed thirteen and had "shockingly mangled the dead Carcasses by Scalping & cutting to pieces."[41] Cusseta's headman, Eneah Mico, had pursued close relations with Georgia since the revolution, but the slaughter of his people convinced him to join McGillivray's border war.

The violence of the border wars was intended to drive settlers away from hunting lands, but it was also part of a broader culture of warfare that stretched back hundreds of years. Young men gained status within their clans and their talwas through martial exploits, but the traditional military rivalries between the Creeks and the Choctaws and Cherokees had quieted by the 1780s. The raids against frontier settlements offered another avenue for displays of bravery, symbolized by the trophies of scalps and body parts carried back home. Scalps could also serve the spiritual motivations of wars fought for blood vengeance, historian Christina Snyder notes: "Placed atop blood poles or the houses of slain relatives, those emblematic trophies of war allowed for the release of dead kinspeople's souls into the afterlife."[42]

Raiders killed and scalped when they had to move quickly, but they also captured settlers to bring back to their towns in Creek country. White male captives fared the worst. Difficult to control and potentially disruptive or violent, they were rarely absorbed into Creek society. Instead, those who were brought to the towns were often tortured and killed to avenge the deaths of kinfolk, a practice that stretched back generations. Captured children faced a different fate. Hannah Hale, a young girl taken by Creek raiders during the border wars, was adopted into a clan and ended up marrying a Creek man and raising a family.[43] Children were more adaptable, better able to learn the language and customs and to become part of a Creek society that had long used young captives to replenish populations. Adult women like Jane Brown, however, often found themselves bound to labor in positions that lay somewhere between adoption and chattel slavery. Christina Snyder recounts the story of Lillian Williams, who was taken in a raid on the Cumberland settlements in 1788. Pregnant at the time of her capture, she gave birth to a daughter named Molly and was then put to work in the cornfields. Williams did the work of Creek women but she was not adopted into a clan, nor did she marry. Instead she had a master who "treated her 'with much severity, having been often beat until she was black and blue.'" But her daughter had a different life in Creek country. Molly was adopted into a clan, renamed Esnahatchee, and raised as a Creek. When Lillian Williams was finally released, most likely after receiving a ransom paid by her relatives, "the Creeks informed her that Esnahatchee would remain with them 'because [she] was born in their Nation.'" Captives like Lillian Williams were *este-vpuekv*, or "owned people." Snyder writes that "Creeks treated these captives as vessels for exploitation—flesh and bone for work or sale—rather than as mediums for vengeance or social reproduction."[44]

Ransoming captives like Williams could be a lucrative sideline to the border raids. John Franklin paid $150 to the Creek captors of his wife, and an Indian trader paid eight hundred pounds of dressed deerskin worth over $250 to redeem a Miss Thompson, who had been taken near Nashville in 1792. Other Indians refused to accept ransom offers, preferring instead to keep captives for their labor. Snyder writes of one Creek master who turned down a trader's offer to exchange an African American slave for his two female captives by noting that "they did not bring the prisoners there to let them go back to the Virginia people [Americans], but had brought them to punish and make victuals and work for them, the Indians."[45] The women's labor might have been important, but one suspects that the Creek man also used the humiliation of captivity as a weapon against encroaching settlers.

All settlers on the borders of Creek country were vulnerable to attack, but enslaved pioneers ran the greatest risk of capture. Georgia officials compiled a list of those killed in raids during a two-year period in the late 1780s and found that while 72 whites were killed, only 10 Africans died at the hands of the raiders.

However, 110 blacks were taken captive while only 30 whites met the same fate.[46] The Creeks had long been exposed to chattel slavery, primarily through the European traders and soldiers who passed through and resided in their country. Despite laws prohibiting slaves from joining traders, enslaved African Americans had accompanied packhorse trains for decades and could often be found working the fields around trading stores in Creek towns. Slaves who ran away to the frontier during the Revolutionary War sometimes found refuge among the Creeks but also were taken up to be sold. So the raiders who struck the farms and plantations of Georgia and the Cumberland knew that captured slaves could be treated as commodities in ways that white captives could not. They often passed through several hands, sold and resold, as Christina Snyder writes, "in order to pay debts or obtain cash for goods." White and métis traders were the usual customers, but Creek headmen also purchased captive slaves to be retained as laborers or distributed as gifts to augment their political power. Often Creek raiders or subsequent owners of captured slaves took them to Pensacola where merchants were eager to buy them to resell in the Havana slave market.[47] That enslaved men and women—some African, some born in Virginia, the Carolinas, and Georgia—found themselves on the sugar plantations of the Caribbean after being taken by their masters to the borderlands between America and Creek country is a reminder of just how connected Alabama's frontier was to a wider Atlantic world.

Raiders also plundered livestock, stripping settlers of valuable property for their own use or to sell for profit. Creeks stole almost 650 horses from Georgia between 1787 and 1789, and took just under a thousand head of cattle.[48] As with slaves, cattle and especially horses could be sold for cash or trade goods in the Creek nation or in Pensacola or even back east. William Blount, the governor of the Southwest Territory organized in 1790, argued that white bandits and Indians worked together, "and as soon as a Horse is Stolen he is conveyed through the Indian nation to north or South Carolina or Georgia and in a Short time to the principal towns on the Sea board for sale so as to effectually prevent a recovery."[49]

The border raids, then, offered opportunities to Creek men to retaliate against American encroachment, assert their traditional status as warriors, and profit from a shifting frontier economy all in one blow. The deerskin trade was already on the decline because of decades of overhunting driven by the desire for consumer goods and especially for alcohol. After the revolution, American settlement in the Lower Town hunting territories of Georgia and the Upper Town territories between the Tennessee and Cumberland Rivers only exacer-

bated that problem as pioneers and their slaves cleared forests to plant and let
free-ranging livestock compete with deer for forage. Ransoming captives and
selling the war booty of slaves and livestock offered an easy and lucrative source
of income. The infusion of cattle and of enslaved men and women quickened the
pace of acculturation among some Creek and métis men who turned away from
hunting altogether to pursue ranching and agriculture. So the raids to protect
the borders of the Creek nation and their traditional ways of life ended up contributing to the economic and social changes that ultimately would fracture the
Creeks and lead to civil war a couple of decades later.

As bloody as the border raids of the 1780s and early 1790s were, various factors limited the spread of violence. The decentralized nature of Creek society
inhibited coordinated efforts; warriors from individual towns might strike
out against settlers while other headmen held back. The isolation of American
settlements encouraged a violent "do-it-yourself" mentality but also prevented
large-scale military responses to Indian threats. The larger imperial interests
of both Spain and the United States also tamped down frontier violence. The
Spanish wanted to check American expansion and knew that well-armed Indian warriors served as a buffer against American incursions into Pensacola,
Mobile, and New Orleans. At the same time they did not want the Creeks entangled in a damaging full-scale war with the new nation. After one season of
border raids, Louisiana's governor Miró wrote Arturo O'Neill in Pensacola to
discuss McGillivray's request for more guns to prepare for further attacks in
the spring of 1787. Miró urged O'Neill to encourage McGillivray to hold off
making another attack. "If they exasperate the Georgians with new hostilities,"
he wrote, "all the states will make common cause."[50] The Spaniards grudgingly
acquiesced to a new round of raids but by 1789 they had dramatically slowed
the flow of guns, powder, and ammunition to the Creeks. They might have
pressed their advantages more aggressively if they had understood America's
reluctance to prosecute a war on the southwestern frontier. A report commissioned by Secretary of War Henry Knox in 1789 suggested that, while a string
of frontier forts might shelter settlers from attack, the only way to eradicate
the threat was to carry "the arms of the Union into the very heart of the Creek
country." But that would require "five regiments of infantry . . . one regiment
of cavalry . . . and a corps of artillery" totaling over four thousand soldiers.[51]
President Washington had invested what limited funds and manpower the federal government had to conduct war in the Ohio Valley, where Indians allied
with the British were attacking settlers. Finally, Knox was aware of the culpa-
bility of white settlers in provoking Indians. Border wars, he understood, were

complicated and ambiguous affairs. Both groups of people held "deep rooted prejudices, and malignity of heart, and conduct," Knox argued, which ignited "the flames of a merciless war" that swept up "the innocent and helpless with the guilty." Better to find diplomatic solutions that would clarify boundaries and keep settlers and Indians separate even as the government worked to purchase land.[52]

Complicating matters on a frontier already rife with violence were a series of speculative ventures that both took advantage of and intensified the crisis of authority in the Southwest. The revolution unleashed a flood of American settlers across the mountains, opening opportunities for men with financial and political clout to buy and sell vast quantities of land. William Blount, for example, had an avid interest in the Cumberland region that comprised the western lands of his home state of North Carolina, and as a state legislator, member of the Continental Congress, and later a delegate at the Constitutional Convention, he had the connections to profit. Veterans of the war had been issued military scrip that could be used to purchase land in payment for their services, but the depression of the mid-1780s depreciated the value of the scrip and heightened the desperation of many. Blount, like other powerful men who commanded capital and credit, was able to buy up scrip at a great discount from impoverished veterans to use in buying western land. He relied on his agent James Robertson, one of the first settlers in the Cumberland region, to scout out and survey the best acreage, making sure to establish a clear title to facilitate resale to settlers. Numerous partnerships like this transformed paper money into landed reality and converted the energies of westward settlement into profits for eastern and western speculators alike.[53]

As settlers moved into the Cumberland region, speculators began to turn their attention to grander schemes involving lands further south along the Tennessee River. The Tennessee had long been a central artery for Virginia and Carolina traders traveling to Chickasaw towns and to the various Indian nations along the Mississippi River. The Great Bend of the river that swept across what would become North Alabama bisected the hunting territory of Chickasaws, Creeks, and Cherokees. To American eyes, however, the Great Bend appeared to be a natural site for settlement. Centered between Nashville, Kentucky, and the Ohio River valley to the north and the headwaters of the Black Warrior and Tombigbee Rivers, which joined together to flow into the Gulf of

WILLIAM BLOUNT
Nat 1744 – Ob 1800

From Photograph of the Original Painting furnished by Dr Thomas Addis Emmett

William Blount of North Carolina was the first governor of the "Territory South of the River Ohio," which encompassed lands that became Tennessee, Mississippi, and Alabama. Creeks called Blount "the Dirt King" because of his extensive land speculation. Courtesy of the New York Public Library.

Mexico at Mobile, to the south, the Great Bend seemed poised to command much of the trade of the trans-Appalachian West.[54]

William Blount, in partnership with John Sevier and other speculators, tried to gain control over the Great Bend almost immediately after the revolution by negotiating with those who had authority over the region. Blount petitioned the state of Georgia for a land grant while some of his partners approached the Cherokees to negotiate a cession of their hunting territory. No one bothered to consult the Chickasaws or the Creeks. The Cherokees sold some of their land and Georgia's legislators agreed in 1784 to create Houston County, leaving the Blount group in control of all the public offices and land sales. Commissioners picked by Blount and by Georgia leaders met at Muscle Shoals that summer to select militia officers and to plan their land surveys, but at that point the project stalled because of Sevier's political adventures. An early pioneer in the Watauga region of today's northeastern Tennessee, Sevier gained prominence as a Revolutionary War officer and Cherokee fighter. In 1784 he and some of the other partners in the Houston County venture from Watauga created the state of Franklin and declared independence from North Carolina. Their attempt to break away ultimately failed but it did prove distracting, and Houston County remained a paper project that never resulted in actual settlement.[55]

Four years later, Sevier set his eyes further west to Muscle Shoals and the upper reaches of the Tombigbee River. He apparently turned to Alexander McGillivray for help since the Creek leader reported in 1788 that Sevier, as governor of the rapidly collapsing state of Franklin, was "in rebellion to Congress" and had "Sent me word that he wants much to come to me with his desperados." McGillivray rejected the request, writing that he gave Sevier "no encouragement, tho he might do me Service against his Country."[56] The following January, Bennett Ballew, Sevier's representative, wrote to McGillivray on behalf of a "Company of Gentlemen" interested in the "Business of Speculation in the Western Country, that is opening a trade with the Spaniards in Tombigbee & opening large Stores of Goods imported from Europe."[57] William Panton, alarmed perhaps at the possibility of new competitors in the Indian trade, was relieved to report that McGillivray ignored the "wild schemes of Trade & of settling stores on Tombigby."[58]

McGillivray's brief communications with Sevier and Ballew hint at one of the most troubling problems associated with speculative ventures in the Southwest: a willingness on the part of speculators to deal with and perhaps join the Spanish. Ironically, Spanish policies designed to slow American expansion sometimes encouraged separatist impulses among settlers and speculators alike. Settlements in Kentucky, Cumberland, and the Holston region confronted Spanish obstacles to shipping on the Mississippi as well as Indian warriors armed with Spanish-procured guns, powder, and shot, and ended up railing against the impotency of the federal government to protect their interests. Speculators with large landholdings were particularly angry as they watched their investments depreciate in value under the threat of restricted trade and violence. That sense of isolation and alienation fueled a willingness on the part of some westerners to consider joining the Spanish Empire, a willingness encouraged to varying degrees by Spaniards in the 1780s and 1790s. Don Diego de Gardoqui, Spain's representative to America, actively recruited both Sevier and Robertson in the Cumberland settlement in 1788, promising a stop to Indian raids and large grants of land along the southern banks of the Tennessee River and the headwaters of the Tombigbee if they pledged loyalty to Spain.[59]

Georgia was the instigator of a more alarming speculative venture late in 1789 when the legislature, eager to cash in on western lands they claimed but did not really possess, sold over twenty-five million acres of land in today's Mississippi and the northwestern corner of Alabama to three speculative companies: the South Carolina Yazoo Company, the Virginia Yazoo Company, and the Tennessee Yazoo Company. The Yazoo speculators, who included John Sevier, Patrick Henry of Virginia, and Alexander Moultrie, the brother of South Carolina's governor, got a good deal, paying only an average of one cent per acre. They could reasonably expect to make a solid profit selling the land to the settlers pushing across the Appalachians and flocking to the Mississippi Valley. Of course, to realize that dream they would need to contend with a federal government that claimed authority over the territory and with the people who actually lived, farmed, and hunted on that land. They never got that chance. When the Georgia legislature decided to require payment in specie, or hard cash, the deal fell apart.[60]

The Yazoo sale of 1789 got the attention of both Alexander McGillivray and George Washington. In February 1790, McGillivray received a letter from Alexander Moultrie on behalf of the South Carolina Yazoo Company, enlisting his support in the enterprise. Moultrie boasted that "a very large Migration is now about to move on from the Waters above us," which, along with a "Large Emigration from Europe" and "an African Trade on a very extensive Basis," would help establish a prosperous settlement and, ultimately, a state on the southwestern frontier. But his company still faced the challenge of Indian occupancy. He hoped that McGillivray could promote "Amity & mutual interest" between the Creeks and Choctaws, on the one hand, and the company and Georgia on the other, by helping to develop "a plan . . . to engage them on the Terms of Commerce and Civilization." Moultrie informed McGillivray that "a person of Your Character Should take the lead in so brilliant a Scene, which I think would . . . raise your already respected Character to everlasting fame." In case that flattery was not sufficient, he also told McGillivray that his assistance would gain him "four hundred thousand Acres which we have no doubt will soon bring a Guinea an Acre."[61] Other representatives also tried to enlist his aid; McGillivray reported to Panton that during a tour of the Upper Creek towns he was pestered "by the Rambling Agents of the Yassou Companys."[62]

The scale of the Yazoo sales alarmed McGillivray. The Tennessee Company grant, the smallest of the three, encompassed much of the Tennessee River valley and "includes every foot of our, the Cherokees & Chickasaw Hunting Grounds," he informed Panton. McGillivray was incredulous at the brazen attempt of the speculators to entangle him in their schemes. "These fellows must think me as mercenary, base & unprincipled as themselves by presuming to address me on such a Subject," he wrote, warning that "it is the avowed intention & view of the Georgians in this business to effect a Strong Settlement at our Backs." To avoid being "hemmed in among them," he vowed "to guard our Common Interest against these Vagrant Emigrants" and "to resist them (even if our allys & friends give their Sanction to them) at every risk." Apparently the Creeks, along with their Cherokee allies, had already put those words into action by attacking three large boats armed with swivel guns and small cannons, which were carrying settlers to a proposed Tennessee Company settlement at Bear Creek south of the Great Bend of the Tennessee River. The warriors killed twenty-seven men and wounded five others.[63]

A pitched battle on the banks of the Tennessee River did not bode well for the peaceful expansion of federal authority in the Southwest. The president feared that Georgia's Yazoo sale might drag the nation into disputes with the Indians, a fear later confirmed when he dined with Patrick Henry, one of the Yazoo speculators. When Washington asked the Virginian "if the Company did not expect the Settlement of the lands would be disagreeable to the Indians," Henry replied "that the Co. intended to apply to Congress for protection—which, if not granted they would have recourse to their own means to protect the settlement."[64] The president also believed the land sale violated the Constitution and undermined the authority of his new government. Still, Washington thought it more politic to allow anti-Yazoo factions to emerge in Georgia instead of alienating the people through a proclamation opposing the sale. A heavy federal hand on the frontier might arouse localist resentments.[65]

Even as the Yazoo sale was collapsing, Washington's administration took several steps in 1790 to establish authority over the Southwest. One was to negotiate the Treaty of New York with McGillivray and the Creeks in an attempt to define boundaries, quiet the border war, and take treaty making out of the hands of states like Georgia. The Indian Intercourse Act codified the precedent established by that treaty; Indian land could be purchased only through public treaties under the auspices of the federal government, not by private individuals or states. Finally, Congress gave some semblance of political order to the Southwest by creating the "Territory South of the River Ohio." By creating this territory, which included much of present-day Alabama and Mississippi but centered on the settlements that soon would become Tennessee, Congress co-opted troublesome local leaders into a political structure under the authority of the federal government. Washington appointed William Blount territorial governor and Blount promptly named both Sevier and Robertson commanders of regional militias in the new territory. In one stroke, three men who had been deeply involved in speculation and who had flirted with separatist schemes now owed some allegiance to the new federal government. That shift was not complete. Blount, who was known as "the Dirt King" by the Creeks because of his extensive landholdings, continued to speculate, and all three men gained more power by representing local interests than through their federal connections. But the territorial government changed the context in which they operated. "The Treaties with the Indians must be observed inviolate and it is the duty of every officer so to speak and act for they have sworn to support the Constitution," Blount informed General Robertson in 1791. "Let the officers support the Government and the Government will support them."[66]

But the federal efforts to order the frontier in 1790 did not bring peace or stability to the Southwest in the first half of the decade. Rumors of an American settlement at Muscle Shoals sponsored by Zachariah Cox, one of the members of the Tennessee Yazoo Company, angered both Upper Town Creeks and Cherokees known as Chickamaugas, who lived along the Tennessee River in the north Georgia highlands. McGillivray received reports in April 1791 that 150 armed men were intending to build a fort at Muscle Shoals and he "Immediately Sent out a Considerable party of my Warriors to attack & destroy such settlement" but found no one there. Cox continued to promote his venture and recruited members in the Holston region by arguing the legality of such a settlement, much to the displeasure of Blount and other government officials. Cox might "triumph in the Eyes of ignorant People," Blount told Robertson, "but be assured the United States have other means in store to prevent them from form-ing a settlement at the Muscle Shoals or on any Indian Lands." Still, he worried that although Cox and his followers "cannot succeed I forsee they will yet give more trouble."[67] Blount and McGillivray might have agreed that Cox's settle-ment plan should be stopped, but that accord did not create harmony. Settlers continued to pour into the territory between the Cumberland and Tennessee Rivers, land used by the Indians for hunting. By the summer of 1792, Creeks and Chickamaugas were launching new raids against the Americans, and the am-ity of New York seemed a distant memory. "It is really painful to reflect, after all our efforts for peace with the southern Indians, that affairs in that quarter are so critical," Knox wrote Blount in August 1792. "It would seem from representa-tions, that a few more sparks would light up a pretty general flame."[68]

Knox had good reason to worry about a frontier conflagration in 1792. The previous year the government's efforts to pacify the Ohio country had gone di-sastrously wrong. Major General Arthur St. Clair, the governor of the North-west Territory, led a force of some 1,400 men, both regular army and militia, from Fort Washington near present-day Cincinnati northwest toward the Wa-bash River in November 1791. He was intent on defeating the Shawnees and other Indians who were routinely killing settlers in Kentucky. Instead, the In-dians staged a surprise attack and succeeded in killing over six hundred of his troops and wounding three hundred more, one of the worst defeats the United States ever suffered at the hands of Native American opponents. Unable to bring order to the Ohio Valley, the federal government could ill afford to confront a large-scale Indian war to the south as well. But worrying rumors of pan-Indian alliances between northern and southern nations filtered back to Knox. Back in 1787, Shawnee, Mohawk, and Iroquois headmen journeyed to Little Tallas-see, McGillivray's town, and in 1792 Creek emissaries headed north to the Ohio country of the Shawnees to attend a general meeting of Indians. Those early ef-forts to form military alliances came to naught, but they did intensify govern-ment efforts to maintain the peace on the southwestern frontier.[69]

The resumption of the border raids also coincided with a shift toward a more aggressive anti-American policy on the part of Spanish Louisiana. Governor Miró had fostered commercial alliances with the southern Indians in order to check American expansion, but he also feared entanglement in a full-scale war and periodically counseled peace. Late in 1791, Miró was replaced as governor by Francisco Luis Héctor de Carondelet, who was much more intent on forg-ing military alliances with the Indians to protect Louisiana. In 1793 Carondelet met with headmen of the Creeks, Cherokees, Chickasaws, and Choctaws at Fort Nogales on the Yazoo River and signed a treaty forming a confederation of all the southern tribes, united in defense of the Spanish Empire. This compact carried little weight in reality but it signaled the Spaniard's willingness to, in Carondelet's words, "'make the most destructive war' on the Americans."[70] That sentiment was troubling, especially when the governor backed it up by patrolling the Mississippi with a newly constructed fleet and by building forts along the river's banks as far north as present-day Memphis. He also extended Spain's reach into the interior north of Mobile by constructing Fort Confederación about two hundred miles up the Tombigbee River in 1794. It appeared to Washington's administration that Spain was poised to contest American control over much of the disputed territory of the Southwest.[71] Washington informed his secretary of war that he could not decide which was more to blame for the violent discord: the "lawless settlers and greedy (land) Speculators on one side, and the jealousies of the Indian Nations and their banditti on the other." But he did know that "the interference of the Spaniards . . . add not a little to our embarrassment."[72]

Washington's frustrations with the southwestern frontier were matched, if not exceeded, by the settlers. Residents of Tennessee County petitioned James Robertson to express their concerns in February 1792. They voiced their "Dread from the Indians as the Spring Season Approaches" in the wake of "The Recent Murders & ravages," and complained, "We already feel the Effects of the Navigation of the river being Shut up." The settlers warned "that the Frontiers will brake unless some speedy method is Taken to secure them from the Inroads of the Savages."[73] Spanish control over the Mississippi and the Gulf ports of Mobile and Pensacola inhibited the agricultural and commercial development of the Southwestern Territory, and the resumption of the border raids discouraged settlement. Political leaders like Blount, who pinned their political authority on their connections to local settlers rather than on federal patronage, continually pressed Washington's administration to deal with both problems. That those solutions would also encourage stability and enhance the value of their massive landholdings throughout the Southwest was no small inducement to their efforts.

Some eastern politicians sympathized with the frontiersmen. Andrew Pickens of South Carolina toured the West in 1792 and "found that Country particularly Cumberland, in a most pitiable and distressed situation almost continually harassed by the Creeks and the four lower Towns of the Cherokees on the Tennessee." Like his predecessors earlier in the century he worried about the possibility of Indian raids against his own state's western frontier. He warned South Carolina governor Charles Pinckney "that the Spaniards are using all their influence with the Southern Indians to engage them against the United States, and I am clearly of Opinion that the Creeks are on the eve of going to War with us." Pickens suggested that troops "carry a vigorous campaign into the Creek Country" in order to "convince the Southern Indians in general that we are able and determined to protect ourselves and . . . chastise their insolence."[74]

Petitions and politicians' letters calling for a military response to the Creek and Chickamauga attacks in the early 1790s largely fell on deaf ears. The Washington administration had committed the nation's limited military resources to the Indian war in the Ohio Valley. The Northwest was the nation's first federal territory, the Ohio River was a crucial east-west artery for future development, and many of the Federalists who held the reins of government had speculative interests in the region. For all of those reasons, the northern frontier took precedence over the Southwest. Settlers there were largely left to fend for themselves.[75]

Federalist perceptions about southern Indians and settlers also shaped the administration's muted response to the renewed border wars in the region. They differentiated between northern Indians like the Shawnees and the large southern nations. Creeks, Cherokees, Chickasaws, and Choctaws had been trading with Europeans and Americans for almost a century and many of their leaders were mixed-race men perceived by federal leaders as amenable to diplomatic persuasion. "The great object in managing Indians . . . is to obtain their confidence," Henry Knox wrote in 1792, but that was hard to do when "the Indians have constantly had their jealousies and hatred excited by the attempts to obtain their land." Knox later warned Blount that the United States "never will enter into a War to justify any sort of encroachment of the Whites."[76]

Administration figures were skeptical of Blount's claims that Indian raids were unprovoked and routinely blamed both speculators and squatters for challenging Indian rights to land and triggering conflict. Thomas Jefferson, Washington's first secretary of state, hoped in 1792 that "encroachments on the Indian lands" would end since "an Indian war [was] too serious a thing, to risk incurring . . . merely to gratify a few intruders." He thought the idea of making "war against the intruders as being more just & less expensive."[77] Washington himself despaired that "scarcely any thing short of a Chinese Wall, or a line of Troops will restrain land Jobbers, and the Incroachment of Settlers, upon the Indian Territory."[78] Timothy Pickering, Knox's successor in the War Department, believed that Indians played a vital role in shaping an orderly western frontier. If they were conquered, he wrote, "lawless emigrants [would] spread over the whole of it."[79]

Mistrust characterized the relationship between territorial leaders like William Blount and federal officials like Knox. The problem was not just that the southwestern leaders were speculators with a vested interest in taking Indian land. Most of the territorial officials and military officers appointed in the Northwest were deeply involved in speculation—Knox himself had invested in land companies with ventures stretching from the Ohio Valley through New York to his home region of Maine. But those officials owed their positions of power to the patronage of the federal government, and most were rooted in institutions close to the heart of the Federalist administration. Many had been officers in the Continental Army during the revolution, for example. In other words, they could be trusted to enact and enforce Federalist policy in the West, which envisioned a slow, orderly expansion under elite leadership. The leaders of the Southwestern Territory, men like Blount, Sevier, and Robertson, had forged connections to the settlers west of the mountains long before Washington elevated them to official positions. Their authority grew out of those associations, many of which involved land transactions. They too had fought in the revolution but invariably in the state militias, not the Continental Army, and had acquired reputations as Indian fighters. None were opposed to a strong federal presence in the Southwest if it solved the problems of Indian attacks, uncertain boundaries, and blocked navigation that depressed the value of their holdings. But their allegiance was to their own private interests and to the settlers who bought their land and who respected their power. Like the old colonial Indian traders, local officials sometimes furthered and sometimes complicated the agendas of the federal government. In general, both they and their constituents wanted to unleash the energies of westward expansion in order to foster a rapid development of the frontier. Their alienation deepened when the government failed to heed their cries for military support in the face of Indian attacks.[80]

🔊————————————————————————

Fortunes began to shift in the middle of the decade in ways that both strengthened and challenged federal control over the Southwest. First came Anthony Wayne's defeat of the northern Indian alliance at the battle of Fallen Timbers in 1794. Wayne was a Georgian interested in western land speculation who had long advocated an offensive approach against the Indians. Back in 1789 he had written James Madison asking for permission to "organize & discipline a *Legionary Corps*" to attack the "insolent" Creeks and transform the Southwest into "a field for *National speculation* vastly superior to all the Country between the Ohio & Mississipi [*sic*]."[81] Washington must have appreciated that bellicose sentiment even if he did not agree with Wayne's estimation of the Southwest's importance, and after St. Clair's humiliating defeat in 1791, he appointed the Georgian to command the nation's forces in the Ohio Country. Fallen Timbers and the Treaty of Greenville that followed in 1795 did not have a direct impact on the Southwest but they did end American fears of a pan-Indian alliance and of a general frontier war stretching from the Gulf to the Great Lakes. From that point forward, Creek and Cherokee raids on American settlers quieted.[82]

The position of Spain in the Southwest also shifted in 1795. Governor Carondelet had been pursuing an aggressive strategy of encouraging separatist schemes among westerners and forging military alliances with the various Indian nations. Both were probably pipe dreams since they depended on a unanimity of sentiment among groups of settlers and Indians that really did not exist, but Carondelet remained optimistic. Still, the international situation concerned the Spanish government far more than what was happening in the interior regions east of the Mississippi. Spain feared the possibility of war with Britain and could no longer afford to alienate the United States by wrangling over boundaries, navigation on the Mississippi, and Indian raids. Negotiations with the American diplomat Thomas Pinckney in Madrid resulted in the Treaty of San Lorenzo in 1795.

The Treaty of San Lorenzo was significant for the future development of the American Southwest for two reasons. First, it opened up trade along the Mississippi River to the Gulf of Mexico, breaking the trans-Appalachian interior free of its commercial isolation. Second, it dramatically scaled back Spanish claims on territory by drawing the new international boundary at the 31st parallel, just north of Mobile. Growing settlements in the Tensaw and Tombigbee region that had been under Spanish authority now were incorporated into the new American nation. Those residents still faced navigational restrictions since the treaty did not address shipping through Mobile, but the clarity of a boundary line encouraged more settlers to take a chance on that corner of the Southwest in the coming years.

Just as the United States was quieting Indian hostilities and establishing firmer control over the Southwestern borderlands, a new challenge to its authority emerged. In January 1795, the Georgia legislature sold thirty-five million acres of western land to four speculation companies in what was known as the second Yazoo sale. The scope of the transaction was astounding. Two of the companies received land limited to what would become the state of Mississippi, but two others bought vast tracts of land in Alabama. The Tennessee Company gained control over the entire Tennessee Valley and the Georgia Company was granted a wide swath of land from the Mississippi to the Coosa and Alabama Rivers. Some familiar characters, including John Sevier, William Blount, and Zachariah Cox, were involved, but most of the speculators were northern or European financiers. What had changed since the 1789 speculation was popular perceptions of the southern frontier's economic prospects. Thomas Pinckney was negotiating with Spain and many expected navigation to open on the Mississippi, a key factor in the future of the Yazoo lands. More importantly, Eli Whitney's gin had helped to launch a cotton boom in the upcountry of South Carolina, and the land to the west gave every indication of equaling or surpassing that region in cotton production. Although the Creeks, Chickasaws, and Cherokees occupied most of the Yazoo lands, the conditions were right for families to migrate into the Gulf lands, if the speculative energies could be channeled into organized settlement ventures.[83]

But the Yazoo speculation of 1795 was short-lived, in one respect at least. Popular anger boiled over in Georgia because the state's western domain had been sold so cheaply—for less than two cents an acre—and because revelations of bribery exposed the venality of the state's legislators. An anti-Yazoo political movement emerged in the state that elected large numbers of new members to the legislature, and they swiftly passed a Rescinding Act in February 1796 that nullified the Yazoo sale. No settlements, then, emerged out of the speculation. However, many company members had sold their shares to various capitalists in the year before the Rescinding Act was passed, and many of those new owners of Yazoo land sold their interests to others, and on down the line. What that meant was that the Yazoo speculation created a tangle of claims that persisted long after the original sale was declared fraudulent and voided. Eventually the Supreme Court would have to sort out the mess.

The federal government, alarmed by this assertion of state power, moved quickly to establish its authority over the western lands. In 1798 it created the Mississippi Territory and formed a commission to negotiate the state's relinquishment of Georgia's western lands. It was not until 1802 that it succeeded. Despite these efforts, the legacy of the Yazoo sale endured and would end up having an impact on the settlement of Alabama down the road.

One wonders what Alexander McGillivray would have made of the events of 1795. He had died two years earlier while spending the winter in Pensacola.

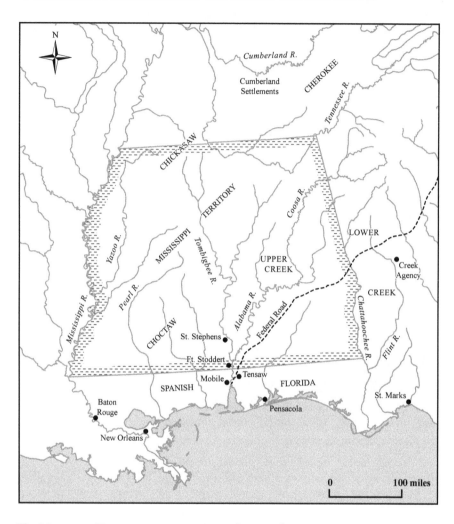

The Mississippi Territory, circa 1805. Drawn by Patrick Jones.

In the years following the revolution he confidently predicted the breakup of the new nation, which he believed would fracture either from dissension from within or from dismemberment by European powers. But that did not happen. Instead, by 1795 the Spanish had pulled back from their most aggressive claims to the Southwest, the Indians of the north had been defeated, and the United States had gained more authority over the borderlands. Washington had gone a long way toward realizing his goal of consolidating the trans-Appalachian West through the authority of the federal government. But McGillivray and other headmen, by waging war, negotiating treaties, and playing the Spanish and Americans off one another, had also managed to maintain the integrity of their nation despite the pressures on their frontiers. Still, new speculative energies had been unleashed in 1795 with the Yazoo sale, and American settlers continued to move across the mountains, threatening the Creek nation, the heart of Alabama's frontier, in the coming decades.

Notes

1. William M. Willett, *A Narrative of the Military Actions of Colonel Marinus Willett, Taken Chiefly from His Own Manuscript* (New York: G. & C. & H. Carville, 1831), 111–12.

2. Donald Jackson and Dorothy Twohig, eds., *The Diaries of George Washington*, vol. 6, *January 1790–December 1799* (Charlottesville: University Press of Virginia, 1979), 85.

3. Willett, *Narrative of the Military Actions of Colonel Marinus Willett*, 111; John Frost, "The Captivity of Jane Brown and Her Family," in *Heroic Women of the West: Comprising Thrilling Examples of Courage, Fortitude, Devotedness, and Self-Sacrifice, among the Pioneer Mothers of the Western Country* (Philadelphia: A. Hart, 1854), 122–63.

4. McGillivray to Miró, Little Tallassee, June 2, 1790, in *McGillivray of the Creeks*, by John Walton Caughey (Norman: University of Oklahoma Press, 1938), 265–67.

5. Joseph J. Ellis, *American Creation: Triumphs and Tragedies at the Founding of the Republic* (New York: Alfred A. Knopf, 2007), 152.

6. "Treaty with the Creeks, 1790," August 7, 1790, in *Indian Affairs: Laws and Treaties*, ed. Charles J. Kappler, vol. 2, *Treaties* (Washington, DC: US Government Printing Office, 1904), 25–27, http://digital.library.okstate.edu/kappler/Vol2/treaties/creo025.htm.

7. Michael D. Green, "Alexander McGillivray," in *American Indian Leaders: Studies in Diversity*, ed. R. David Edmunds (Lincoln: University of Nebraska Press, 1980), 56–57; Ellis, *American Creation*, 157–58.

8. Ellis, *American Creation*, 158; "Treaty with the Creeks, 1790," 29.

9. Angela Pulley Hudson, *Creek Paths and Federal Roads: Indians, Settlers, and Slaves and the Making of the American South* (Chapel Hill: University of North Carolina Press, 2010), 32–33.

10. Ibid., 32.

11. Memorandum following diary entry of October 4, 1784, in *George Washington's Diaries: An Abridgement*, ed. Dorothy Twohig (Charlottesville: University Press of Virginia, 1999), 265–66, quoted in Fred Anderson and Andrew Cayton, *The Dominion of War: Empire and Liberty in North America, 1500–2000* (New York: Viking, 2005), 183.

12. Kathryn E. Holland Braund, *Deerskins and Duffels: The Creek Indian Trade with Anglo-America, 1685–1815* (Lincoln: University of Nebraska Press, 1993), 180.

13. McGillivray to O'Neill, Little Tallassee, February 5, 1784, in Caughey, *McGillivray of the Creeks*, 70.

14. David J. Weber, *The Spanish Frontier in North America* (New Haven, CT: Yale University Press, 1992), 277–78.

15. J. H. Elliott, *Empires of the Atlantic World: Britain and Spain in America, 1492–1830* (New Haven, CT: Yale University Press, 2006), 272–73.

16. Weber, *Spanish Frontier*, 274.

17. Zéspedes to Capt. Gen. Luis de las Casas, St. Augustine, June 20, 1790, in "Cracker—Spanish Florida Style," ed. and trans. James A. Lewis, *Florida Historical Quarterly* 63 (October 1984): 191, quoted in Weber, *Spanish Frontier*, 272.

18. McGillivray to O'Neill, Little Tallassee, February 5, 1784, in Caughey, *McGillivray of the Creeks*, 69.

19. Weber, *Spanish Frontier*, 281.

20. Ibid., 277–79.

21. Andrew R. L. Cayton, "'Separate Interests' and the Nation-State: The Washington Administration and the Origins of Regionalism in the Trans-Appalachian West," *Journal of American History* 79 (June 1992): 39–67.

22. McGillivray to O'Neill, Little Tallassee, January 1, 1784, in Caughey, *McGillivray of the Creeks*, 65–66.

23. Green, "Alexander McGillivray," 47.

24. Jack D. L. Holmes, "Spanish Treaties with West Florida Indians, 1784–1802," *Florida Historical Quarterly* 48 (October 1969): 140–43.

25. McGillivray to Miró, Little Tallassee, March 24, 1784, in "Papers Relating to the Georgia-Florida Frontier, 1784–1800," by D. C. Corbitt, *Georgia Historical Quarterly* 20 (December 1936): 360.

26. Holmes, "Spanish Treaties," 140–43.

27. Claudio Saunt, *A New Order of Things: Property, Power, and the Transformation of the Creek Indians, 1733–1816* (Cambridge: Cambridge University Press, 1999), 67–89. More admiring scholars include J. Leitch Wright Jr., "Creek-American Treaty of 1790: Alexander McGillivray and the Diplomacy of the Old Southwest," *Georgia Historical Quarterly* 51 (December 1967): 379–400; Gregory Evans Dowd, *A Spirited Resistance: The North American Indian Struggle for Unity, 1745–1815* (Baltimore: Johns Hopkins University Press, 1992), 90–99; Eliga H. Gould, "Entangled Histories, Entangled Worlds: The English-Speaking Atlantic as a Spanish Periphery," *American Historical Review* 112 (June 2007): 779; Green, "Alexander McGillivray."

28. "A Talk from the Young Tallassee King from the Up[p]er and Lower Towns," December 15, 1778, Edward E. Ayer Collection, Newberry Library, Chicago, quoted in Hudson, *Creek Paths*, 28; Dowd, *Spirited Resistance*, 96–98; Green, "Alexander McGillivray," 49–52.

29. McGillivray to O'Neill, Little Tallassee, March 28, 1786, in Caughey, *McGillivray of the Creeks*, 104–5.

30. McGillivray to Miró, Little Tallassee, May 1, 1786, in Caughey, *McGillivray of the Creeks*, 109.

31. Principal planters and other inhabitants of Liberty County to Governor George Handley, undated, in *Georgia Indian Depredation Claims*, ed. Donna B. Thaxton (Americus, GA, 1988), 487, quoted in Christina Snyder, "Conquered Enemies, Adopted Kin, and Owned People: The Creek Indians and Their Captives," *Journal of Southern History* 73 (May 2007): 269.

32. Affidavit of John Fitzpatrick, October 7, 1791, in "Indian Letters, 1782–1839," typescript, ed. Louise F. Hays, Georgia Archives, Morrow, GA, 14–16, quoted in Snyder, "Conquered Enemies, 264–65.

33. Snyder, "Conquered Enemies," 269.

34. George Mathews to "Sir," Augusta, November 15, 1787, in *American State Papers, Indian Affairs*, vol. 1, ed. Walter Lowrie and Matthew St. Clair Clarke (Washington, DC: Gales and Seaton, 1832), 23, https://memory.loc.gov/cgi-bin/ampage?collId=llsp &fileName=007/llsp007.db&recNum=4.

35. Anthony Bledsoe and James Robertson to Samuel Johnston, January 4, 1788, Colonial and State Records of North Carolina, 21:437–38, Documenting the American South,. accessed March 20, 2017, http://docsouth.unc.edu/csr/index.php/document /csr21-0003.

36. Table appended to Governor George Walton to Indian commissioners, Augusta, October 4, 1789, in Lowrie and Clarke, *American State Papers*, 77.

37. Saunders to Walton, March 29, 1789, in "Creek Indian Letters, Talks, and Treaties, 1705–1839: In Four Parts," typescript, ed. Louise F. Hays, Georgia Archives, Morrow, GA, part 1, 194, quoted in Snyder, "Conquered Enemies," 269; James Maxell to Walton, May 24, 1789, in Hays, "Creek Indian Letters," part 1, 204, quoted in Snyder, "Conquered Enemies," 269.

38. Lemuel Lanier to Walton, April 21, 1789, in Hays, "Creek Indian Letters," part 1, 200, quoted in Snyder, "Conquered Enemies," 270.

39. Affidavit of William Scarborough, January 9, 1796, in Hays, "Creek Indian Letters," part 2, 462, quoted in Snyder, "Conquered Enemies," 271.

40. Captain Joshua Inman to Telfair, Augusta, May 23, 1786, C. Mildred Thompson Collection, Southeastern Native American Documents Database, 1730–1840, Digital Library of Georgia, http://dlg.galileo.usg.edu, quoted in Hudson, *Creek Paths*, 30.

41. McGillivray to O'Neill, Little Tallassee, June 20, 1787, in Caughey, *McGillivray of the Creeks*, 154.

42. Snyder, "Conquered Enemies," 267.

43. Kathryn E. Holland Braund, "The Creek Indians, Blacks, and Slavery," *Journal of Southern History* 57 (November 1991): 621.

44. Snyder, "Conquered Enemies," 272, 274–75.

45. "Deposition of James Ore," June 16, 1792, in Lowrie and Clarke, *American State Papers*, 274; Braund, "Creek Indians," 622.

46. "Report of the Commissioners," 77.

47. Snyder, "Conquered Enemies," 280–81.

48. "Report of the Commissioners," 77.

49. Blount to Secretary of War Henry Knox, Knoxville, May 5, 1792, in *The Territorial Papers of the United States*, ed. Clarence Edwin Carter, vol. 4, *The Territory South of the River Ohio, 1790–1796* (Washington, DC: US Government Printing Office, 1936), 148–49.

50. Miró to O'Neill, New Orleans, March 24, 1787, in Caughey, *McGillivray of the Creeks*, 145–46.

51. "The Commissioners to the Secretary of War," November 20, 1789, in Lowrie and Clarke, *American State Papers*, 78.

52. Report of the secretary of war to Congress, July 10, 1787, quoted in Anderson and Cayton, *Dominion of War*, 193; Stuart Banner, *How the Indians Lost Their Land: Law and Power on the Frontier* (Cambridge, MA: Harvard University Press, 2005), 130–34; Ellis, *American Creation*, 138, 141, 148.

53. Daniel M. Friedenberg, *Life, Liberty, and the Pursuit of Land: The Plunder of Early America* (Buffalo: Prometheus Books, 1992), 249; Buckner F. Melton Jr., *The First Impeachment: The Constitution's Framers and the Case of Senator William Blount* (Macon, GA: Mercer University Press, 1998), 64–65.

54. Friedenberg, *Life, Liberty*, 252.

55. Friedenberg, *Life, Liberty*, 252–55; Thomas D. Clark and John D. W. Guice, *Frontiers in Conflict: The Old Southwest, 1795–1830* (Albuquerque: University of New Mexico Press, 1989), 72.

56. McGillivray to O'Neill, Little Tallassee, August 12, 1788, in Caughey, *McGillivray of the Creeks*, 192.

57. Ballew to McGillivray, Cherokee Nation, Coosawatee, January 17, 1789, in "Papers Relating to the Georgia-Florida Frontier, 1784–1800," *Georgia Historical Quarterly* 21 (September 1937): 289.

58. Panton to unknown recipient, September 14, 1792, in "Papers Relating to the Georgia-Florida Frontier, 1784–1800," *Georgia Historical Quarterly* 21 (December 1937): 373. This letter references a letter sent to Miró in June 1789.

59. Thomas P. Abernethy, *A History of the South*, vol. 4, *The South in the New Nation, 1789–1819* (Baton Rouge: Louisiana State University Press, 1961), 45–50.

60. Clark and Guice, *Frontiers in Conflict*, 69; Banner, *How the Indians Lost Their Land*, 124; Shaw Livermore, *Early American Land Companies: Their Influence on Corporate Development* (New York: Octagon Books, 1968), 147–50; George R. Lamplugh, *Politics on the Periphery: Factions and Parties in Georgia, 1783–1806* (Newark: University of Delaware Press, 1986), 66–71.

61. Moultrie to McGillivray, Charleston, February 19, 1790, in Arthur P. Whitaker, "The South Carolina Yazoo Company," *Mississippi Valley Historical Review* 16 (December 1929): 393.

62. McGillivray to Panton, Little Tallassee, May 8, 1790, in Caughey, *McGillivray of the Creeks*, 259.

63. Ibid., 259–60, 262.

64. Donald Jackson and Dorothy Twohig, eds., *The Diaries of George Washington*, vol. 5, *July 1786–December 1789* (Charlottesville: University Press of Virginia, 1979), 108; also see ibid., 69.

65. Ibid., 73.

66. Blount to Robertson, September 3, 1791, in Carter, *Territorial Papers*, vol. 4, 79; Banner, *How the Indians Lost Their Land*, 135–36; Abernethy, *History of the South*, vol. 4, 60.

67. McGillivray to Miró, Little Tallassee, June 8, 1791, in Caughey, *McGillivray of the Creeks*, 291–92; Blount to Robertson, September 3, 1791, in Carter, *Territorial Papers*, vol. 4, 79; Acting Governor Daniel Smith to Secretary of State Thomas Jefferson, October 4, 1791, in ibid., 83.

68. Knox to Blount, August 15, 1792, in Carter, *Territorial Papers*, vol. 4, 163.

69. Eric Hinderaker, *Elusive Empires: Constructing Colonialism in the Ohio Valley, 1673–1800* (Cambridge: Cambridge University Press, 1997), 243; Richard White, *The Middle Ground: Indians, Empires, and Republics in the Great Lakes Region, 1650–1815* (Cambridge: Cambridge University Press, 1991), 454; Dowd, *Spirited Resistance*, 103–5.

70. Carondelet, "Military Report," New Orleans, November 24, 1794, quoted in Weber, *Spanish Frontier*, 285.

71. Weber, *Spanish Frontier*, 284–85.

72. John C. Fitzpatrick, *George Washington's Writings* (Washington, DC: Government Printing Office, 1938), 32:108, quoted in David W. Miller, *The Taking of American Indian Lands in the Southeast: A History of Territorial Cessions and Forced Relocations, 1620–1854* (Jefferson, NC: McFarland, 2011), 61.

73. "Petition of Tennessee County to James Robertson," February 1, 1792, in Carter, *Territorial Papers*, vol. 4, 117.

74. Pickens to Pinckney, September 13, 1792, in Carter, *Territorial Papers*, vol. 4, 169–70.

75. Cayton, "'Separate Interests,'" 47–48.

76. Knox to Blount, April 22, 1792, in Carter, *Territorial Papers*, vol. 4, 141; Knox to Blount, November 26, 1792, in ibid., 221; Cayton, "'Separate Interests,'" 48–49.

77. Jefferson to David Campbell, March 27, 1792, quoted in Miller, *Taking of American Indian Lands*, 83.

78. Washington to Timothy Pickering, quoted in Miller, *Taking of American Indian Lands*, 63.

79. Pickering to Rufus King, May 30, 1785, in *The Life and Correspondence of Rufus King: Comprising His Letters, Private and Official, His Public Documents and His Speeches,* ed. Charles R. King, vol. 1, *1755–1794* (New York: G. P. Putnam's Sons, 1894), 120, quoted in James E. Lewis Jr., *The American Union and the Problem of Neighborhood: The United States and the Collapse of the Spanish Empire, 1783–1829* (Chapel Hill: University of North Carolina Press, 1998), 21.

80. Cayton, "'Separate Interests,'" 56–59.

81. Wayne to Madison, Richmond, GA, June 15, 1789, in *The Papers of James Madison,* vol. 12, *2 March 1789–20 January 1790 and supplement 24 October 1775–24 January 1789,* ed. Charles F. Hobson and Robert A. Rutland (Charlottesville: University Press of Virginia, 1979), 221, quoted in Cayton, "'Separate Interests,'" 46.

82. Cayton, "'Separate Interests,'" 45–46, 53.

83. Clark and Guice, *Frontiers in Conflict,* 73–74.

6

Settlements and Transformations

When Alexander McGillivray and the other Creek headmen traveled back to their homeland in 1790, Major Caleb Swan accompanied them, sent by Secretary of War Knox to report on the character and mood of the Creek nation. This time the delegation sailed from New York City, arriving at the mouth of the Saint Mary's River in Georgia in mid-August and then journeying overland, reaching the Chattahoochee in early October. After visiting some of the Lower Creek towns, Swan continued on with McGillivray to the communities along the Tallapoosa, Coosa, and upper Alabama Rivers, spending some time with him at his plantation at Little Tallassee. His sojourn in Creek country was short; by Christmas, Swan had crossed the Flint River and was heading back to the coast to catch a ship up to New York. Perhaps anticipating some displeasure with his abbreviated visit, Swan explained in a letter to Knox that McGillivray had left for Pensacola, as he did every winter, and that "without an associate or companion" he faced the prospect of "suffering the inconveniences of cold, and probably of *hunger*" if he remained "through the winter season."[1]

Swan himself took on the role of goodwill ambassador during his visits to the Creek towns, countering "the jealous minds of the Indians" with promises "that the white people of the United States were sincere and candid in all their overtures of peace and friendship."[2] His assurances met with some skepticism and even his host seemed to have been wary of Swan's intentions. The major informed Knox that he feared "General M'Gillivray viewed me for some time rather in the light of a spy" and that while taking notes "I found myself watched with an eye of jealousy." He "thought it prudent to keep them out of sight . . . even from my only friend, Mr. M'Gillivray himself."[3]

The Creeks had reason to be wary. While much of Swan's report offered a cursory account of their customs, language, and social structure, he also described the physical features of the country with an enthusiasm based more on fantasy than on actual experience. How else to explain his confident assertion, after spending a couple of autumn months there, that "the climate of this inland country is remarkably healthy," with "constant breezes" that "render the heat of summer very temperate," and his declaration that "the summers [are] sweet and wholesome"? Or his observation that the winters were "soft and mild," an assessment that flew in the face of his fearful admission to Knox that staying past December would mean "suffering the inconveniences of cold, and probably of *hunger*"? The rivers had "no stagnant waters or infectious fogs," according to Swan, which meant "neither alligator, mosquitoes, or sand-flies, have ever been known to infest this pleasant country."[4] Mild summers and no mosquitoes? Here was frontier boosterism, not a hard-nosed geographical report.

Swan described the landscape with an eye toward the future, casting every natural feature in a context of what could be—indeed, what inevitably would be. "Having no shoals, or sand spits," he wrote, the Alabama River "might be navigated with large boats up to M'Gillivray's, at Little Tallassie, through the centre of an inviting, fertile and extensive country, capable of producing every thing necessary to the comfort and convenience of mankind." The "medicinal plants and herbs" he knew existed would "without doubt . . . be found as valuable and important as any hitherto discovered." The "abundance of small waterfalls" would provide "mill-seats of constant water," while the "minerals" he had collected promised "useful mines." Central Alabama's "soil and climate seem well suited to the culture of corn, wine, oil, silk, hemp, rice, wheat, tobacco, indigo, every species of fruit trees, and English grass," and "with a free navigation through the bay of Mobile, may probably, one day or other, be the seat of manufacture and commerce."[5]

Swan was not the first outsider to get carried away with dreams of frontier possibilities, but his report, with its emphasis on the transformation of the land itself, reflected a dramatic shift. Hernando de Soto, colonial officials, and traders alike had pegged their visions of wealth or empire, whether grandiose or more prosaic, on the Indians themselves. But to Swan the Creeks, far from being necessary partners in the extraction of a resource or in an alliance, had become impediments to progress. The hunting territory east of the Chattahoochee was "a forlorn rude desert," he claimed, one that, with a little labor, might be made to 'blossom like the rose.'" And if the soil along the Alabama was of such a quality that "with the slovenly management even of the savages, it produces most abundantly," think what could be done if it were properly farmed. While Swan did not foresee cotton fields on the banks of the Alabama River—he wrote his report just a year before Eli Whitney invented his cotton gin—his litany of potential cash crops to be marketed down the river and out to the world anticipated the rapid expansion of the cotton kingdom. The whole of Creek Country was "but a rude wilderness, exhibiting many natural beauties, which are only rendered unpleasant by being in the possession of the jealous natives."[6] Swan in effect stripped the "savages" from his vision of Alabama's future. Untapped potential was waiting to be released from the dead weight of Indian occupation, a process that could only begin with American possession of the land. No wonder he felt compelled to hide his notes from his Creek hosts.

Swan's brief portrait of Creek country, present and future, captures a common perception of America's frontiers as dividing lines between the "wilderness" that belonged to the Indians and settled land "civilized" through cultivation. Settlement, he believed, would make the Indians' "desert" "blossom" into the white man's paradise, and that idea has stuck in the popular imagination. But that depiction conflicted with what he witnessed on his sojourn: fields cultivated by Creek women and herds of livestock tended by Creek men in town after town, and the sixty or so slaves toiling on McGillivray's plantation, Little Tallassee. It also contradicted the vision of his employer, Henry Knox, who believed that, with help, the Indians themselves could transform the land. One provision in the Treaty of New York promised "useful domestic animals and implements of husbandry" in order to lead the Creek nation "to a great degree of civilization."[7]

Swan's preoccupation with imagining what could be instead of reporting what actually was, and his rendering the native inhabitants invisible, reveals some of the energies that drove settlement. In the eyes of many, the frontier was wilderness until occupied by Americans. In the twenty years after Swan's visit, settlers did press deeper into two regions on the margins of Creek territory: the Tensaw-Tombigbee delta north of Mobile, and the Tennessee Valley. They began to transform Alabama's frontier even as some of their Indian neighbors changed their ways of life. The process of American settlement was often far messier and more complex than Swan's binary progression from wilderness to civilization would suggest.

The Tensaw-Tombigbee and Tennessee Valley settlements differed dramatically from one another. By the time Swan dipped into Creek country in 1790, settlers were already flocking to the pine-forested bluffs and rich bottomlands, swamps, and canebrakes north of Mobile, and many more would come after the Treaty of San Lorenzo settled the international boundary at the 31st parallel and the federal government established Washington County as part of the Mississippi Territory. They brought slaves with them, but plantation agriculture failed to take hold. Instead, families grew food crops and raised cattle and hogs for barter and sale, living lives not much different from those of their Creek and Choctaw neighbors, with whom they exchanged goods and services. Tensaw-Tombigbee's diverse population lived in a frontier world that was more blurred borderland than stark divide between Indian "wilderness" and settler "civilization."

The Tennessee Valley settlements grew out of the expansive energies of the new cotton kingdom. Squatters filtered down from the Cumberland settlements just after the turn of the nineteenth century, but it was not until 1806, when a group of Cherokee leaders ceded the hunting land that would become Madison County, that settlers came in great numbers. Many were small farmers with few or no slaves, but the first federal land sale in 1809 also drew wealthy settlers from Nashville and Georgia who brought large numbers of enslaved laborers to carve out cotton plantations in the Great Bend of the Tennessee. That "log cabin aristocracy" laid the foundations for Alabama's first cotton frontier just a few years after the land passed from Indian hands. The rapid transplantation of an elite planter class whose wealth depended on the transformation of land came closer to Swan's vision than did the frontier economy of the Tensaw and Tombigbee settlements.

In 1799, Andrew Ellicott, who was charged with surveying the line along the 31st parallel dividing the United States from Spanish West Florida, described the Mobile as "a fine large river, and navigable some distance above the boundary for any vessel that can cross the bar into the bay." Together with the Tensaw River, which entered the eastern head of the bay, it provided "the easiest way from the Gulf of Mexico by water into the United States," as well as access to the Alabama and Tombigbee River systems that were home to the Creek, Choctaw, and Chickasaw nations. Flowing south from deep in the interior, those two rivers merged about six miles north of the Spanish border and then split again after a few miles, into the eastern and western channels of the Tensaw and Mobile and out to the bay. Navigation might have been easy but the land along the rivers posed some problems. The soil of the upland bluffs that ranged along the western banks of the Mobile and Tombigbee was "of an inferior quality" and produced "little beside pitch-pine and wiregrass," according to Ellicott. The eastern bank was more fertile but that was due largely to frequent flooding, which replenished the nutrients in the soil but understandably proved "a great inconvenience" to those farming the land. Ellicott claimed that farmers often had to wait until well into the spring season to plant their crops to avoid the flooding, but they sometimes were surprised by later "inundations." That happened in May 1799 "after the corn was two feet high." Cypress forests and pastures became swamps when the Tensaw and Mobile, and the myriad of lesser streams bisecting the delta, overflowed their banks.[8]

Ellicott's task was to make real the line laid out on paper in the Treaty of San Lorenzo, to turn a borderland claimed by both Spaniards and Americans into a bordered land. That proved difficult in a very literal sense. Flooding along the Mobile and Tensaw Rivers left a swamp ten miles wide, forcing the surveyors "to pass our Horses over in Boats by a rout(e) of at least sixteen Miles by Water" and "to make large openings on both sides of this Swamp on the High Lands, build large fires, hoist up flags, as signals in order to ascertain the true course of the line."[9] Surveying frontier land was often arduous, but establishing the 31st parallel north of Mobile was particularly so.

Ellicott's efforts to draw a line through a swamp are an apt symbol of the character of the Tensaw-Tombigbee region at the turn of the century; attempts to impose geometric and legal order could not completely erase the tangled and blurred borderland nature of those settlements. In the twenty-five years after the revolution, waves of diverse migrants—white, African, and Indian—came to the river lands north of Mobile, set in motion by the forces of war and social change. Some in the early years were drawn to the region as a place of refuge from a newly independent America, while others came to pursue economic opportunities, enticed by the liberal policies of the Spanish. What had been contested land became American in the late 1790s, and fresh streams of settlers pushed into Tensaw and especially the Tombigbee, now joined together as Washington County and part of the Mississippi Territory. By 1804 about two hundred families lived along the Mobile and Tombigbee Rivers from the Spanish border sixty miles north to Choctaw country. Of those, fifty or sixty families, "the most opulent and respectable" in the area, lived in Tensaw, the wedge of land between the confluence of the Alabama and Tombigbee Rivers and the waterway known as the "cutoff," eight miles to the north. The rest of the households were scattered along the west side of the Tombigbee.[10]

Like the floods that routinely replenished the soil and delayed cultivation, and sometimes washed away homes, Tensaw-Tombigbee was a place of promise and of frustrations. Despite a steady flow of migrants, the region seemed unable to fulfill its potential. Isolation from American settlements in Georgia, the Cumberland, and Natchez, and Spanish control of Mobile and the outlet to the Gulf, blunted the full development of a plantation economy. Instead a more diversified frontier economy persisted through the first decade of the nineteenth century, one that bound many of the diverse inhabitants together in networks of exchange.

Much like Swan, visitors to the region expressed a kind of bipolar vision, one that acknowledged a ragtag present while lauding future prospects. Lorenzo Dow, the great eccentric itinerant minister who ranged through much of the Old Southwest, "found a thick settlement" near the Tensaw in 1803, "and then a scattered one seventy miles long" up the west bank of the Tombigbee River. The settlers "are like sheep without a shepherd," he noted in his journal. "Whilst under the Spanish government," the settlements were "a place of refuge for bad men; but of late, since it fell to us, seems to be in a hopeful way, and there is still room for great amendment." If the future held promise for the character and morals of the settlers, it also seemed bright in more worldly ways. "The river Tombigbee . . . will one day become the glory of the southern part of the United States," Dow wrote, "as the trade of Tennessee, &c., will pass through it."[11]

Ephraim Kirby, the newly appointed territorial land commissioner, painted a more jaundiced portrait of the residents of Tensaw-Tombigbee in an 1804 report to Thomas Jefferson, even as he lauded the region's prospects. Most of the settlers were "illiterate, wild and savage, of depraved morals, unworthy of public confidence or private esteem; litigious, disunited, and knowing each other, universally distrustful of each other." The officers and institutions of governmental authority did not inspire much confidence either. "The magistrates [were] without dignity, respect, probity, influence or authority.—The administration of justice, imbecile and corrupt. The militia, without discipline or competent officers."[12] Nature promised a brighter future even if the residents were a sorry lot. Mobile, then "a depressed colonial establishment," was "at the mouth of one of the finest navigable waters in the United States." Once Mobile became American, "the produce of an extensive and fertile interior country" would flow down the Alabama and Tombigbee and out to the world.[13] Like Dow's, Kirby's optimism sprang not from any confidence in the virtues of the settlers but instead from a sense of geographic destiny.

Before gazing forward, Kirby looked back to explain to the president how the motley collection of frontiersmen came to inhabit Tensaw and Tombigbee. "The most antient [ancient] inhabitants of the country" were the French, who, though "few in number," were "generally peaceable honest, well disposed citizens." Next came the Loyalists, mostly "emigrants from the Carolina's and Georgia," who "not only hate the american government, but . . . are now hostile to all law and to every government." But once the United States established the Mississippi Territory, the "most meretorious" group of emigrants arrived, consisting primarily of "poor people who have come hither to avoid the demands of creditors, or to gain a precarious subsistence in a wilderness."[14]

There was some truth and a lot of exaggeration to Kirby's tossed-off history of settlement. The French were the most "antient inhabitants" among the Europeans but they arrived in a region that had long been an Indian borderland with very ambiguous boundaries. Mobilians had built several towns on the western bluffs of the Mobile River, and the Tohomes did the same further north along the Tombigbee before the French arrived, but the Taensas, who lent their name to the river, were more recent arrivals. De Bienville had encouraged them to leave their homelands near New Orleans sometime between 1711 and 1715 to join the other petit nations as a buffer to protect Mobile from Creek attack. All three Indian nations abandoned the region and moved to Louisiana after the French defeat in the Seven Years' War, when Britain took control.[15] The Creeks, who had fought against the petit nations, claimed the Tensaw-Tombigbee region as their own by right of conquest but ended up compromising with the British. They drew a line across the Alabama River just a bit above the split into the Mobile and Tensaw Rivers. British settlers could carve out their farms south of that line, leaving the rest of the Alabama River to the Creeks. Still, Creek and Choctaw hunters ranged widely through the delta land north of Mobile.[16]

Before the British drove them from Mobile, some French families ventured north of the bay, often building their homes on the same bluffs vacated by the Mobilians and farming the rich soil on the eastern banks. While most abandoned their plantations when the British took control in 1763, some, like the Chastang family, remained. Joseph Chastang had immigrated to New Orleans and in 1760 ended up in Mobile when he married a local woman. His younger brother, John, followed and became a prominent doctor in Mobile and at Fort Saint Stephens. They established plantations along the bluffs of the Mobile River, one of which came to be known as Chastang Landing, and remained there through the shifts in imperial control of the region. British settlers joined the French who had remained behind, both along the Mobile and further north up the Tombigbee River. Many were absentee owners who hired overseers to manage the slaves on their plantations, but one British settler actually resided on his plantation and became a nucleus of the early Tensaw settlement. Major Robert Farmar, the British commander of Mobile, lived at Farm Hall, the main house of his plantation on the east side of the Tensaw River. William Bartram, the botanist, visited Farmar in 1778 and noted that other houses "inhabited by French families; who are chiefly his tenants," surrounded Farm Hall, which offered "a spacious prospect up and down the river, and the low lands of his extensive plantations on the opposite shore."[17] Other landowners, both British and French, joined Farmar on the Tensaw, but none matched the commander's wealth, marked by the fifty-five slaves laboring in his fields and by Farm Hall itself, with its commodious living spaces, two fireplaces, and a library filled with books. Farmar died in 1778, leaving his widow to face the Spanish conquest of Mobile and West Florida in 1780. She abandoned Farm Hall and returned to England, but not before selling those slaves for $14,121.[18]

Farmar's slaves, and those fewer numbers owned by his French and British neighbors, conjure up images of tobacco or cotton fields—the kind of single-crop plantation agriculture that fueled the expansion of slavery throughout much of the South. Many of the landowners in the Mobile-Tensaw delta and up the Tombigbee River during the French and British periods cast about for that kind of profitable crop, but no single one took hold. Some attempted to cultivate sugarcane, but it failed to thrive in the Mobile region the way it did further west in Louisiana. Others devoted extensive acreage in their land grants to tobacco, but it too was not suited to the soil. Indigo seemed more promising. Planters in West Florida shipped just over fifteen thousand pounds of dye from the plant to Britain in 1771, a small percentage of the amount being shipped from East Florida in that period, but a start. Still, indigo was a complicated crop to grow and to process. Farmar tried indigo on his plantation and gave up when he could find no experienced overseers or slaves who knew how to handle the plant.[19]

Instead of a single cash crop, British and French landowners turned to a wide variety of agricultural activities to make a profit. Food crops, from orchard fruits to a diverse array of vegetables, including chickpeas and fava beans, could be consumed at home and, in some cases, sold in Mobile or Pensacola. Corn was a staple for both the white residents and their enslaved Africans, and the surplus was marketable. The rich soil of the Mobile-Tensaw delta yielded sixty to eighty bushels an acre. Rice also thrived in the delta land. Planters often supplemented their slaves' diet with rice and fed the husks removed during threshing to their livestock. The piney woods beyond the more fertile banks of the rivers were not ideally suited for farming but they did serve the economic interests of the residents. Most settlers raised livestock, either to supplement their farming or as their principal economic enterprise, and they allowed the cattle and hogs to forage through the woods. During the winter months when farming chores were limited, many took to the pine forests to extract sap for the production of tar, pitch, and turpentine, used primarily in shipbuilding. Some harvested the pine, cypress, and oak trees themselves to provide clapboards and shingles for houses, masts and planking for ships, and staves for barrels. By the time of the American Revolution a diversified frontier economy had taken hold in the Mobile region.[20]

The Revolutionary War marked a turning point in the settlement history of Tensaw-Tombigbee as the needs of those whose lives were disrupted and the goals of the Spanish Empire coincided. Spain took Mobile and Pensacola during the war and quickly solidified control over West Florida but its claim to the territory stretching north toward the Tennessee Valley was more tenuous, especially with a newly independent and expansionist United States pressing in from the east and the north. Good relations with the Creeks, Choctaws, and Chickasaws was one key but Spanish authorities knew they needed to attract settlers willing to pledge allegiance to the Crown to serve as a buffer against the land-hungry Americans. They found ready takers in former British officers and Loyalists who, despite defeat, were unwilling to leave the continent, and in Americans unsettled by the war. In exchange for free land grants they simply had to swear and sign an oath proclaiming themselves to be "good and loyal subjects of the Catholic Monarch." The new settlers did not even have to convert to Catholicism, although they did have to be circumspect in their religious practices. One group of Tensaw settlers who set up a Baptist church in 1791 tested and found the limits of Spanish tolerance: Juan Vicente Folch, the governor of West Florida, had the minister and several members of the congregation arrested and sent to New Orleans for trial. What happened to them is unknown.[21]

Alexander McGillivray sponsored some of the Loyalist migrants even as he grew uneasy about the arrival of others. The Creek leader wrote to Governor Arturo O'Neill, Folch's predecessor, in 1784 to pave the way for a group of "respectable men all who once possessed ample livings & are now reduced to very little on account of their Loyalty to their King." Since they "have been accustomed to Industry, well Skilled in Farming, raising Stock or any thing in that way," McGillivray said, they would foster "a very flourishing Situation" in

Tensaw, and "become Valuable for its products & Supplys of every kind, whether for the Kings Garrison or shipping."[22] But two months earlier, McGillivray had heard reports that the "Loyalist Corps" in Saint Augustine had broken up and "that above a hundred of them are coming this way & to Pensacola," news he did not welcome. This group had a reputation for banditry, and despite his own Loyalist sympathies, McGillivray was unhappy. "I dont wish for any of them as they can have no means of supporting themselves here," he wrote Governor O'Neill, adding that "we have disorderly people enough already among us."[23]

The Linder family seemed to embody the character of both groups of Loyalists. John Linder Sr. was born in Switzerland but had lived in Charleston for many years and had employed his engineering and surveying skills as an officer for the British during the revolution. His son, John Jr., had also been a Loyalist during the war but ended up leading a group of "disbanded men from the British and American Armies, together with some Vagrants from the different Provinces," according to the British governor of East Florida. Baley Chaney joined his friend, John Jr., after retiring his commission as a lieutenant colonel in the Loyalist militia, and the group of "banditti" staged "repeated acts of robbery and rebellion" from their hideout in the swamps.[24] The last British governor of East Florida suggested that his Spanish successor expel the troublemakers. Whether he took that advice or not, the Linders and Chaney had made their way to Tensaw-Tombigbee by 1785.[25]

The younger Linder and his friend Chaney might have been associated with swamp banditry but they also were men of some means. Chaney received land grants from the Spanish in the late 1780s and early 1790s up along the Tombigbee, where he settled with his wife and children and, with the help of at least eight slaves, cultivated corn and tobacco. The Linders had more substantial property holdings and were the wealthiest residents of Tensaw. Together the father and son and their families owned eighty-two slaves according to the census of 1785, and four years later they had expanded their livestock holdings to 230 head of cattle. The younger Linder died in 1792 but his father continued to prosper, buying land in 1796 on the east side of the Tensaw River.[26]

Other local residents switched allegiance when Spain drove out the British, and they prospered. Cornelius McCurtin, a young Irishman, had come to West Florida in 1769 but ended up serving as an officer in the Spanish militias in both Pensacola and Mobile. In 1787, he petitioned for a land grant in Tensaw and received the plantation that had once been owned by Robert Farmar, the commander of the British forces in Mobile. Farm Hall had lain empty since Farmar's widow had abandoned the property in 1780. McCurtin and his wife, a French woman, lived part of the year there, with eleven slaves who tended to eighty head of cattle and ten horses and grew primarily corn and chickpeas, and part of the year in Mobile, where he owned property.[27]

Samuel Mims represented a different kind of settler in the region, not a direct casualty of the war but one whose life was disrupted by the upheavals of the revolutionary period. Mims, who first appeared in the records of the Mobile district in 1786 as an unmarried forty-five-year-old, had long worked in the Creek towns for George Galphin, the Indian trader from Augusta. Many of the traders, especially the "countrymen" who had married Creek women, had already begun shifting toward farming and especially ranching in the face of declining deerskin sales before the revolution. War sped up that process, in part because Loyalists controlled a number of the trade networks. Mims's allegiance is not known but Galphin was an ardent Patriot who worked to sway Creek warriors to the American cause. He died in 1780, and some years later Mims made his way down the Alabama River to Tensaw.[28]

Like the Linders and Chaney and most other migrants to the region, Mims depended on enslaved labor to survive and prosper. In 1786 he owned sixteen slaves, equally divided between men and women, and by the following year they had produced two hundred barrels of corn and one hundred pounds of tobacco and raised ninety head of cattle and ten horses. He lived in Tensaw but built up his real estate over the next decade, buying land along the Tombigbee and town lots in Mobile. In 1797 he obtained a grant of 524 acres from the Spanish in a northern stretch of Tensaw just below the cutoff. There he embarked on another enterprise made possible by the steady stream of migrants moving to Tensaw and Tombigbee or passing through on their way to Natchez. Westward travelers had to cross both the Alabama and Tombigbee Rivers; between them lay the delta land that often flooded in the early spring. Mims set up a ferry service across the Alabama to Naniaba Island, in the middle of the delta, where he owned land that his slaves farmed, passing travelers off to a partner who ferried them across the Tombigbee. During high-water periods, boatmen had to pole passengers across the entire ten-mile stretch of swamp. Mims and his partner made quite a lot of money, especially after the United States took full possession of the territory and built Fort Stoddert in 1799 a few miles below the ferry on the Tombigbee.[29]

As more settlers arrived, Spanish authorities worked to maintain their allegiance. Governor Folch ordered Fort San Esteban to be built on the Tombigbee in 1789, and soon a growing number of Americans who had pledged loyalty to Spain were farming near what they called Saint Stephens. The fort became the local administrative center. A Georgia shoemaker named Barton Hannon who came to the Tombigbee in 1791 was one of forty-five residents who stopped by Fort San Esteban in 1795 to register their livestock brands, a necessity since the 1,246 head of cattle in the region freely roamed the forests and canebrakes along the river.[30]

West Florida's Spanish leaders got a chance to repay the American settlers for their oaths of loyalty in 1791 when the banks of the Tombigbee overflowed in a massive flood. Governor Folch happened to witness the devastation firsthand since he had traveled upriver to Fort San Esteban to officiate at a ceremony for the priest of the Tombigbee parish. When he arrived that March the residents, alarmed by the rising waters, were already moving their livestock from low-lying meadows and "salvaging their furniture and those personal belongings each regarded as most valuable." He watched over the next few days as the Tombigbee "began to carry away the Negro cabins, warehouses, barns and virtually all the buildings." When the floodwaters receded only Fort San Esteban, the parish house, and a few homes still stood. Reports from Choctaw and Chickasaw Indians who made it to Mobile suggested that their villages and fields along the upper reaches of the Tombigbee had also been inundated.[31]

Some three hundred people, settlers and slaves, had arrived at the Tombigbee region in the weeks just before the flood. Now the swollen rivers blocked their access to Mobile, where they needed to go to swear their loyalty to Spain and to sign the paperwork necessary to get their land grants, leaving them in a kind of legal limbo. Worse, Folch warned, the residents were "without shelter, hardly with enough to eat, and their fields which were expected to provide their sustenance, still under the muddy waters."[32] Those who did have access to corn tried to take advantage. A barrel of corn on the cob in San Esteban, which had sold for $0.65 before the flood, was now going for $5.00. Folch put a stop to the profiteering and fixed the price at $1.25 a barrel. More importantly, he and Esteban Miró, the governor of Louisiana and West Florida, began rounding up shipments of wheat and corn from other parts of the Spanish Gulf to distribute to settlers and Indians alike; they paid for them out of their own pockets with no guarantee of compensation from the Crown.[33] Folch and Miró took seriously their role as agents of a Spanish Empire still intent on dominating the interior and knew that the key to their success was the loyalty of the Indians and of the Americans they enticed to the region.

Satisfying the interests of both the Indians and the new settlers was no easy task. Indian leaders saw the migrants encroaching on their hunting lands as Americans, not as Spanish subjects. McGillivray warned the British trader

William Panton that the "Rapid Settlement of Such Droves of Americans upon Tombigbie" was a "Cause of Alarm and apprehension," since they were "damn vagrants" who were, "as Customary," not willing to obey boundary lines and "have Spread and extended themselves over a great Space of Choctaw and our hunting Grounds."[34] As they had in the Cumberland and western Georgia regions, Indian warriors raided settlements on the eastern side of the Tombigbee to punish those who pushed beyond the boundaries and to steal horses and slaves. Governor Miró rejected the notion that the new settlers were American and told McGillivray that it would "be a dishonor" to Spain "to permit the destruction of these settlements, when all these persons have taken an oath of fidelity to his Catholic Majesty and made themselves his subject."[35]

Doubts about the faithfulness of at least some of the Tombigbee settlers plagued Spanish authorities, despite Miró's protestation. In 1789 one resident named Walton proved adept at playing on those fears of disloyalty. McGillivray described Walton as "a notorious old Rebel Villain from Georgia [who] had found his way thro' Cumberland and the Chickasaws to Tombigbie" and was sowing discord by spying on his neighbors and spreading rumors. "The old Rascall in order to ingratiate himself with his new Masters, employed his Eldest Son & Self to pick up [a] little tattle thro' the Settlements, which kept them in a perpetual State of Animosity and Caused every day some poor Divil to be Clapped into a Dungeon as his most absurd tales were received with Rather too much Eagerness of Belief."[36] Maintaining order on the northern frontier of Florida proved a troublesome task.

━━━━━━━━━━━━━━━━

Loyalists and rebels like the Linders and Walton were not the only settlers in the lands north of Mobile; by the late 1780s, a growing number of Creeks had pushed to the margins of their frontier, clustering near the confluence of the Little River and the Alabama just north of the cutoff. Alexander McGillivray and his sisters formed the nucleus of the Tensaw Creeks and attracted others. His Little River plantation supported extensive herds of cattle tended to by scores of African slaves. Benjamin Durant, who owned cattle herds near Pensacola, married Sophia McGillivray and moved his livestock to the more fertile fields and forests of Tensaw. Sophia's sister, Sehoy III, married an English trader named Charles Weatherford, a Loyalist who had escaped the war in 1780, and they too built a farm near Little River. Each of these families maintained farms in the Upper Creek towns but shifted significant portions of their economic endeavors down the Alabama. The revolution had disrupted old trading patterns, leaving hunters accustomed to looking east to Augusta in the search for new markets. Some Creek families moved to the Tensaw region to be closer to Spanish Mobile and Pensacola—especially because the British firm of Panton, Leslie and Company remained in West Florida—and, as before the war, were ready to exchange deerskins for a variety of consumer goods. Spanish authorities encouraged that resettlement. The Tensaw Creeks could provide beef, corn, and other produce to the residents of Mobile and Pensacola and serve as a buffer against possible American encroachment.[37]

That the Creeks had beef to sell points to deeper changes underfoot in the Alabama interior after the revolution. As the deerskin economy declined, more Creek men shifted to herding, and in some cases farming, especially the families of the old traders who had become countrymen through marriage. But the federal government also promoted that change through its "civilization" policy, a program first articulated in the New York treaty of 1790. The Washington administration promised to "furnish gratuitously . . . useful domestic animals and implements of husbandry" in order to lead the Creek Nation "to a greater degree of civilization."[38] Henry Knox appointed Benjamin Hawkins as the government's agent to the Creeks in 1796, and the former congressman from North Carolina spent the next twenty years advocating economic and social change. As one associate noted, "*Civilizing* the Indians" was Hawkins's "hobby-horse—his passion."[39]

Enlightenment ideas about the cultural malleability of Indians and practical concerns of pacification and land acquisition drove the civilization policy. Men like Knox and Hawkins believed that environment shaped distinctions between peoples; while they unquestionably accepted white superiority, they did not yet see race as fixed and immutable. Changes in the material conditions of life—work, clothing, and housing—could alter social characteristics. Indians could fall into degradation either by clinging to outmoded ways of life, like hunting, or by succumbing to the settlers' worst habits, like alcohol abuse. But they also could rise into "civilization" by adopting the modern practices of a pastoral life. To that end, Hawkins used his agency on the Flint River as a model community to proselytize the benefits of herding, blacksmithing, and farming to Creek men, and of spinning, weaving, and other forms of domestic production to Creek women. He traveled extensively through Creek country, distributing tools and equipment and encouraging economic and social transformation. Thomas Jefferson applauded Hawkins for his work with the Creeks in a letter to the agent in 1803. Herding and farming "will enable them to live

The Plan of Civilization, by an unidentified artist, circa 1800. While it is not certain that this painting depicts Benjamin Hawkins, the livestock and iron tools do illustrate the economic transformation that lay at the center of his vision of "civilization." Courtesy of the Greenville County Museum of Art; Museum purchase with funds from The Museum Association's 1990 and 1991 Collectors Groups and the 1989, 1990, and 1991 Museum Antiques Shows, sponsored by Elliott, Davis & Company, CPAs. Corporate Benefactors: Ernst and Young; Fluor Daniel; Mr. and Mrs. Alester G. Furman III; Mary M. Pearce; Mr. and Mrs. John D. Pellett Jr.; Mr. W. Thomas Smith; Mr. and Mrs. Edward H. Stall; Eleanor and Irvine Welling.

on much smaller portions of land," Jefferson wrote. That would benefit the settlers, whose "increasing numbers will be calling for more land, and thus a coincidence of interests will be produced between those who have land to spare, and want other necessaries, and those who have such necessaries to spare, and want lands."[40]

Because they straddled two worlds, Indian countrymen had the potential to become agents of either improvement or degradation, according to civilization advocates. Jefferson encouraged intermarriage as a tool of assimilation, believing that Indian advancement required letting "our settlements and theirs meet and blend together, to intermix, and become one people."[41] Hawkins shared some of that optimism. He was always eager to note signs of economic progress in his journal and letters and sometimes gave credit to the "outsiders" who had married into Creek society. Zachariah McGirth, the son and nephew of Loyalist bandits from the borderlands of Georgia and East Florida who migrated to the Tensaw region in the 1780s, fit that bill. McGirth moved to Tuckabatchee in 1793 and married Vicey Cornells, the widow of Alexander McGillivray. There the "good fences, a fine young orchard, and a stock of horses, hogs, and cattle" all denoted, in Hawkins's estimation, "a careful, snug farmer."[42]

But Hawkins often doubted the abilities of countrymen to transform Creek traditions. They generally were "lazy, cunning, thievish animal[s], so much degraded in the estimation of the Indians that they are considered a slave of their family and treated accordingly." That was especially the case, he believed, when wives undermined their husbands' authority by exercising the powers granted them in a matrilineal society. Alexander McGillivray's sisters confirmed his suspicions. Despite her owning about eighty slaves, Hawkins found Sophia Durant "poor, and dirty in a small hut, less clean and comfortable than any hut I have seen." He attributed this to "bad management" of the slaves, who, he claimed, "are all idle" and as a result were "a heavy burthen to her." Her sister, Sehoy, "lives well in some taste," but her slaves "do but little, and consume every thing in common with their mistress, who is a stranger to economy." Hawkins blamed the Creek customs that allowed the sisters "to keep the command absolute of every thing from their husbands." Not that he had much respect for Sophia's husband, Benjamin Durant, who, while "a man of good figure," was "dull and stupid, a little mixed with African blood."[43]

The economic ambitions of the métis families created tensions within Creek communities and contributed to the growth of the Little River region of Tensaw. The story of Richard Bailey and his wife, Mary, captures some of the changes underway at the turn of the century. Bailey was an English trader who had lived in the Upper Creek town of Atasi since 1766. He had married a woman from the prestigious Wind Clan and they had five children. When Benjamin Hawkins visited Bailey at Atasi in 1796 he found him living on a prosperous farm with fenced fields, a stable, and lots for 120 horses, 200 head of cattle, and 150 hogs, along with twenty beehives. The family owned seven slaves as well. As a promoter of "civilized" agriculture, it is no surprise that Hawkins approved of Bailey's industriousness, but he clearly laid much of the responsibility for the family's success at Mary's feet. "Mrs. Bailey shares in all the toils of her husband when there was a necessity for it," Hawkins wrote in his journal. "She attended the pack horses to market, swam rivers to facilitate the transportation of their goods, is careful of the interest of her family and resolute in support of it." The one trait reflective of her Creek heritage that separated her and the family from white settlers on the frontier was the ritual of the daily bath. Hawkins attributed the fact that the "whole family are remarkable for being healthy and cleanly . . . to a custom continued by Mrs. Bailey, she and her family every morning winter or summer bathe in cold water."[44]

The Atasi neighbors did not share Benjamin Hawkins's admiration for the ambitions of this Indian countryman and his wife. Mary Bailey might have held to the Creek tradition of bathing but cultural differences still marked the family as outsiders. One son, Richard Dixon Bailey, had been educated in New York under the supervision of Henry Knox, while his younger brother, James, had traveled to Philadelphia for schooling under the tutelage of the Quakers. Sharper points of conflict drove a wedge between the Baileys and their neighbors. Traditionally, Creeks did not fence in the large communal fields of maize along the river bottoms, and Richard, like many traders, often left his livestock to forage in the woods and canebrakes. Inevitably, his cattle made their way into the fields and trampled crops, which angered the town residents, and Bailey, in turn, was aggrieved when Creeks killed the offending livestock. Eventually the residents of Atasi banished the Baileys from their town and the family moved permanently to the Tensaw community. There two of the daughters married white settlers.[45]

Borders divided Indians and settlers in Tensaw and Tombigbee, but they were porous; residents routinely crossed boundaries to exchange goods as all pursued a variety of economic activities. Indians often bartered meat—whether venison, beef, or pork—and corn, beans, and squashes in exchange for homespun cloth or alcohol from migrants passing by or from those who had arrived to claim land but had yet to cultivate their first crops. Others visited Fort Stoddert to trade with the soldiers. Choctaw women frequently traveled to Mobile to sell firewood, vegetables from their gardens, and woven baskets and mats. Indian men served as guides and translators and operated ferries at river crossings. Since their first encounters with Europeans, Indians had proved adept at adapting and using traditional practices to pursue new opportunities. By the turn of the nineteenth century the relentless pressure of American settlers was squeezing them, and the old economy built on the exchange of deerskin was collapsing, but trade still played a role. Sometimes the exchange reinforced old customs and traditional commodities in new forms. In 1801, for example, women in the Upper Creek towns sold Benjamin Hawkins three hundred gallons of hickory oil, which he then shipped to Mobile and sold for two dollars a gallon. Other times, new commodities emerged. That same year, two canoes loaded with 1,500 pounds of cotton made their way from the towns on the Tallapoosa River down to Mobile to be marketed.[46]

Herding also bound Indians and settlers together in a common enterprise. Since plantation crops did not thrive in the Tensaw-Tombigbee region, cattle and hogs played a major role in the economy of the settlements. Washington County's residents owned almost ten thousand head of cattle in 1805, second in the territory only to more heavily populated Adams County, on the Mississippi River, with just over eleven thousand.[47] James Churchill urged his brother in North Carolina to send him cash "by the post as quick as you can as my wish is to purchase some cows for I think Cattle is the best property that a man can be possessed with."[48] Hogs joined the cattle in foraging for food in the piney woods of the rivers' bluffs and the canebrakes along their banks. That free-ranging life produced skinny livestock compared to the coddled cattle and hogs of long-settled regions of the North. Philip Henry Gosse, the English naturalist, was amused by the razorback hogs he saw when he lived in Alabama in the 1830s. "When I have looked on these animals," he said, "with their sharp thin backs, long heads, and tall legs, looking so little like hogs, and so much like greyhounds and have observed the shrewd look, half alarm, half defiance, with which they regard one, I have laughed till the water has run out of my eyes."[49]

Livestock played an increasingly important role in the Indian economy at the turn of the century. The Choctaws encountered and embraced cattle earlier than the Creeks did, in part because of their proximity to the lower Mississippi Valley. By 1732 they were calling a river eight miles west of Mobile the "bayou where cattle pasture," and by the 1770s Choctaw families had begun leaving their towns and settling along the Tombigbee in search of fresh grass and cane to feed their cattle. By the early nineteenth century Choctaw babies, both male and female, received gifts from their families of a cow and calf, mare and colt, and sow and piglet. The Creeks quickly took to horses but were slower to accept cattle and hogs into their lives. It was not until after the revolution that cattle in any significant number had reached their towns. But by the early 1800s some Creek towns had communal herds, and a growing number of countrymen and métis families had significant numbers of cattle.[50]

Settlers and Indians followed similar practices in dealing with their livestock. They rounded them up from the pastures and canebrakes and herded them into cow pens before driving them down trails to Mobile or Pensacola, or to Fort Stoddert or Fort Saint Stephens, to be slaughtered and butchered. The beef was sometimes salted and sold to feed the slaves of the Caribbean sugar islands but there was also a ready market locally, both in the towns and among the steady stream of migrants. The cowhides were also marketable commodities, second only to deerskins.[51]

Many of those tending the cattle or cultivating the crops of the settlers and their Creek and Choctaw neighbors were enslaved Africans. As early as 1785, the 159 slaves in the Tensaw settlement outnumbered the 123 free, white residents.[52] We often associate slavery with the plantations of the cotton kingdom, but the extent to which residents of Tensaw and Tombigbee owned slaves is a reminder of just how common and flexible the institution was, even in frontier regions with a mix of less lucrative enterprises. Few could come close to the large numbers of bound laborers owned by the Linders but many of the region's settlers had at least a few slaves within their households. The men and women toiling in the fields and woods north of Mobile suffered the same indignities accompanying the commodification of human beings as those picking cotton in South Carolina, but their day-to-day life often was different. Tensaw and Tombigbee formed a borderland characterized by blurred boundaries with Indian lands and Spanish Mobile and by a mixed frontier economy, and those factors provided some small measure of autonomy for those bound by enslavement.

People of African descent, most of them enslaved, had long resided on the Alabama frontier, whether owned by French officers or by Carolina traders, but the revolution, and the decades that followed, brought an influx of enslaved men and women to the region. Slaveholders in Georgia and South Carolina, especially those with ties to the deerskin trade, sought to protect their property from the depredations of military campaigns by sending their slaves to the frontier for safekeeping. Others left on their own volition, taking advantage of the chaos of war to run away to Creek country. A few found freedom but most traded one master for another and ended up laboring on Creek farms and ranches. Raids on the settlements of Georgia, Florida, and the Cumberland during and after the war also yielded a rich bounty of black captives. Jack Kinnard, the son of a Scottish trader and Indian mother who lived near the Chattahoochee River, gained influence among the Lower Town Creeks through his raiding. Caleb Swan reported in 1791 that Kinnard owned forty slaves and over a thousand head of cattle, accumulated "entirely by plunder and freebooting, during the American war, and the late Georgia quarrel." That property, according to Swan, had "raised him to the dignity of a chief" by allowing "him to go largely into trade, by which he supplies all the Indians around him, who are dupes to his avarice."[53] More often the enslaved victims of Indian raids were sold. Pensacola provided a ready market for the captives. A former British sailor told an acquaintance, Georgia governor John Martin, that "Indians and White Peple is Constantly Carying Droves of Negroes" to Pensacola, where "the Spanish Govener buyes the Chief of them & Encourages them to fetch the Rest & tell them the[y] schall Receive the Cash for all the[y] fetch."[54] Many of the people sold in Pensacola were transported to Havana but some were passed along to Mobile and the farms to the north.

Both settlers and the African slave trade brought growing numbers of enslaved men and women to Tensaw and Tombigbee after the revolution. Loyalists like the Linders in search of a safe haven brought their slaves with them when they established their farms and ranches, as did the American settlers who arrived a bit later. In small numbers, one by one or ten by ten, groups of African Americans filtered from the east into the frontier north of Mobile, exchanging one life of slavery for another. But a larger percentage of the men and women who were unwilling migrants to that region came directly from Africa and faced enslavement for the first time. The Atlantic slave trade intensified after the war, and while most of the captives found themselves sold to the cotton and sugar plantations proliferating in the Mississippi Valley, quite a few made their way east, first to the markets in Mobile and Pensacola and then to the frontier in the north.[55]

Even as Spanish officials promoted the African slave trade to fuel the labor needs of the plantations along the Mississippi, the population of free people of color grew in the Gulf coast towns of New Orleans, Mobile, and Pensacola. Much of southern society revolved around a two-caste system that created paired binaries of race and status; whiteness signaled freedom, and blackness equaled slavery. But a three-caste system emerged in urban areas, especially those dominated by the French or Spanish, with an intermediate class of free people, most of whom were "creoles" of mixed parentage.[56] Slaves in Mobile could suffer the same brutalities of all the enslaved in the Americas; slaveholders everywhere, after all, wielded the same tools of legal rights and the whip to control their human property. But the fact that 30 percent of Mobile's free population in 1805 was African in ancestry indicated that a different code of race and slavery was at work in that town.[57]

The presence of a significant group of free people of color signaled to slaves that there were potential avenues to freedom. The Spanish authorities had adopted the old French *Code Noir* when they took Mobile from the British in 1781. That set of laws governing Africans restricted slaves by limiting their freedom of movement without passes, prohibiting their carrying firearms, and regulating the conditions under which they could market goods, but they also included relatively relaxed manumission standards. Slaves who amassed enough money had the right to purchase themselves—a difficult, but not impossible, task. Skilled craftsmen or cooks could accumulate a nest egg by hiring out their labor during their free time. Those given plots of land by their masters to grow extra food crops or to raise some chickens, thus reducing the need to provide costly rations, sometimes found ways to market their foodstuffs for profit. Still, most of the manumissions were granted by the slaveholders themselves and sprang from the personal relationships they had with their slaves. Sometimes they singled out favorite servants to reward with freedom, but more frequently they manumitted women with whom they had sexual relations and also freed their offspring. That the sex ratio in Mobile in the late eighteenth century was skewed male among Europeans and female among slaves contributed to those sexual encounters, but the fact that some were conducted openly, within the context of long-term relationships of concubinage and common-law marriage, reflects a more relaxed attitude about interracial relationships in Spanish West Florida.[58]

Mobile's free people of color found room to carve out independent lives in part by maintaining ties to white slaveholders in the community. Masters who manumitted their mistresses and children obviously retained personal connections to their former slaves, but others who manumitted favored slaves or accepted their self-purchase acted as patrons once the slaves gained their freedom. They might help them find employment, serve as witnesses in legal transactions, or loan them money. That patronage is evident in the system of godparentage, an important institution in Catholic Mobile. It was not at all uncommon for free people of color to have white godparents for their children. Those connections to the white community bolstered the ability of those people to claim the rights and responsibilities of freedom. They could own property and testify against white citizens in court, a privilege denied free people of color in the southern United States. And as in other parts of Spanish Florida and Louisiana, free men of color had their own militia to help keep order in the community. That meant they were sometimes used to catch escaped slaves or to roust what the Spanish called *cimarron* communities, encampments of runaways tucked deep in the forests and swamps near Mobile.[59]

The story of Nicolas Mongoula illustrates the ways in which free people of color in Mobile acquired status and privilege through connections with whites while maintaining ties to the slave community. Born into slavery sometime around 1720, Nicolas was listed as a free man in the official records of the 1760s. "Mongoula" was a nickname that meant "my friend" in Mobilian, the lingua

franca of the Indians and traders of the Gulf South. It would not have been un-
usual for an enslaved African in the 1730s and 1740s to have lived and worked
with Indian slaves and for them to have communicated in Mobilian. Just how
Nicolas gained his freedom is unknown but he appears to have prospered in his
adulthood. He worked as a master mason, at least part of the time on the payroll
of the Spanish government in Mobile, married a free black woman, and had children whom they gave Spanish names. At the time of his death in 1798, Nicolas
owned property in Mobile and at Saint Stephens Creek, where he raised some
livestock and grew corn, rice, and beans. He also served as a captain in Mobile's
black militia. Although the record is silent on this subject, Nicolas almost certainly benefited from connections to local whites, at least in terms of finding
masonry jobs. But what is clear is that Nicolas had strong relationships within
Mobile's enslaved community. Baptismal records show that he was named god-
father to three slaves between 1764 and 1781, two children born into slavery and
one adult who was most likely an African who had recently arrived in Mobile.
Being a godparent was not a casual responsibility. Nicolas was expected to work
with the godmothers to offer spiritual guidance and material aid and protection
to his charges. Clearly the bonds forged between people like Nicolas and enslaved Africans did not trouble the white community of Mobile. The free people
of color did not challenge the system of slavery, but neither did they wall themselves off from their enslaved brethren.[60]

The more relaxed racial codes of Mobile spread beyond the city in the late
eighteenth century. In general, the countryside, especially in American territory, maintained a two-caste system of free whites and enslaved blacks, but
there were exceptions. Carlos Lalanda, the free creole man who commanded
the black militia in Mobile, owned multiple properties along the bay and in Tensaw in the late 1790s. Dr. John Chastang, a creole from Mobile, served as a surgeon at Fort San Esteban, where he established a large farm called Harigay Hall.
There he lived with Louison, an enslaved woman with whom he had a sexual relationship and whom he subsequently freed, and who then found employment
as the fort's baking contractor. Together they raised ten children, all of whom
were baptized at the Cathedral of the Immaculate Conception in Mobile. Like
the métis residents of the Little River section of Tensaw, the Chastang children
tended to marry other offspring of mixed-race relationships. When he died in
1812, long after the Americans had claimed control over the Saint Stephens area,
Chastang left Louison, "his beloved friend and companion" of twenty years, his
entire estate, which included livestock, furniture, silverware, and an enslaved
mother, father, and child. Two of Chastang's sons—Basilio, who was an officer

in the black militia like his father, and Zenon—continued cattle ranching north of Mobile.[61] The legacy of French and Spanish control over the region left a more complicated racial landscape in Tombigbee-Tensaw than one might expect on a southern frontier.

The vast majority of enslaved people lived out their lives in bondage on the farms and ranches of the region, but the character of the economy left them some room for day-to-day autonomy. The unremitting routinization of work associated with cotton or tobacco cultivation was absent in Tensaw and Tombigbee at the turn of the century. Instead, enslaved laborers performed a variety of tasks. Clearing land for cultivation was arduous, backbreaking work but most of the bottomlands along the rivers had already been cleared by generations of Indian farmers. Still, slaves planted, weeded, and harvested corn, rice, chickpeas, and vegetable crops, and tended orchards. In the winter months they might go to the pine forests beyond the rivers' bluffs to cut down timber and extract pitch from burning pine logs, perhaps living for days or weeks at a time in work camps. Boatmen transported the surplus corn, timber, and various naval stores down the rivers to Mobile. Many of the slaves herded cattle, riding through the woods roping the free-ranging livestock and checking the brands, then gathering them at the cow pens before driving them to Mobile. Many of those enterprises required that slaves be mobile and independent, free from the close scrutiny of white overseers. In some cases, masters allowed slaves to carry guns to protect themselves and the livestock from thieves and animals. Slaves often received plots of land, provision grounds, to cultivate during their free time, giving them the opportunity not only to augment their diets but also to grow crops and raise animals for barter.[62]

The frontier region north of Mobile offered more opportunities for escape than did long-settled areas like South Carolina. Enslaved men and women from the American settlements on the Tombigbee did not have far to run to cross an international border into Spanish territory, and Choctaw and Chickasaw territory lay just to the west and Creek towns to the east. Masters could appeal to the authorities in those various communities for the return of their absconded property, but that took a lot of effort and time and was not always successful. There was also plenty of uninhabited forest and swampland in which to hide, affording, if not permanent escape, then at least a respite from the pressures of enslavement.

Creek country was increasingly home to slaves but their status and conditions varied. Some of the countrymen and métis like Alexander McGillivray who were most committed to commercial enterprises such as herding and farming treated their slaves as laborers and as commodities, much the way white settlers in the region did. Before he died in 1793, McGillivray had accumulated about sixty slaves, going so far as to commission a small ship to deliver slaves from Jamaica. He hired a white overseer to manage his bound laborers on the Little Creek ranch and was quick to invoke his property rights when challenged. For example, he became embroiled in a legal dispute with John Linder over the ownership of Rachel, a "Molatto wench" working at the Little River plantation under the "management" of McGillivray's overseer.[63] But his sister, Sophia Durant, seemed much less committed to extracting wealth from the large number of enslaved men and women that she owned. Benjamin Hawkins noted with disapproval that her slaves "do nothing the whole winter but get a little wood, and in the summer they cultivate a scanty crop of corn barely sufficient for bread." What was worse in his eyes was the easygoing socializing that brought all the residents of Indian country together. Sophia and her sister Sehoy hosted a regular Christmas gathering of "the black people" that included "a proper frolic of rum drinking and dancing," and local whites and Indians joined in the festivities.[64] Hawkins's account provides a glimpse of a form of frontier slavery that was rapidly disappearing at the turn of the century.

A different sort of frontier developed in the Great Bend to the north, where the Tennessee River swept southwest out of the Appalachian highlands before angling northwest to the Ohio. That arc passed through a region largely devoid of settlements at the time of the revolution, part of the vast hunting grounds of the Cherokees, Creeks, and Chickasaws that stretched far to the north. There were Cherokee towns dotting the headwaters of the Tennessee in the mountains to the east and Chickasaw villages to the west near the series of rapids known as Muscle Shoals. During the Seven Years' War the Chickasaws had established a town further east in the Bend, at the mouth of the Flint River where an important Indian trail crossed the Tennessee, but that location was perilously close to Cherokee territory and they had retreated by the war's end in 1763. Some forty years later, pioneers who followed that same Indian trail south from Tennessee to settle the Great Bend knew the patch of land where the long-abandoned town had stood as Chickasaw Old Fields.[65] In their eyes, this was an empty wilderness waiting to be transformed through clearing and cultivation, a place where they could shelter and sustain their families and perhaps reap profits from commercial crops. Transformation was rapid, with only five years between the arrival of the first American squatters in 1804 and the federal land sale that brought thousands to the newly organized Madison County. Swan's vision of a prosperous frontier devoid of "savages" seemed on its way to being realized in the Tennessee Valley.

Settlement might have been rapid once in progress but the question is why it took so long to begin. After all, the revolution had set all sorts of people in motion, speculators and settlers alike, and many had their eyes on the Great Bend. Since the early eighteenth century the Tennessee River had provided a pathway into the interior as far west as the Mississippi for Carolina and Virginia deerskin traders, but now families began traversing its length, signaling the emergence of a settler frontier in the trans-Appalachian Southwest. John Donelson, whose daughter Rachel would later marry Andrew Jackson, led a flotilla downriver in 1779. They were bound for the French Lick settlement further north on the Cumberland River, but first they had to get past the Muscle Shoals west of the Bend, where the water "made a terrible roaring" and "the driftwood heaped frightfully upon the points of the islands," forcing the current to run "in every possible direction."[66] Many others followed in the 1780s and 1790s but did not stop to homestead the rich lands along the Tennessee. The Great Bend and Muscle Shoals also figured heavily in postrevolutionary speculative ventures. Still, it would be over twenty years from the end of the war before Americans established a foothold in that region.

Indian resistance delayed the opening of the Tennessee Valley, providing a counterweight to the land hunger of both settlers and speculators. The fate of the Brown family, who journeyed by boat down the Tennessee in 1788, is a vivid reminder of the perils of venturing west of the mountains. The Cherokee warriors who took part in the attack were Chickamaugas, a group disaffected from the rest of their nation, unwilling to accept the peace treaty signed by Cherokee leaders in 1777 after a disastrous war against the Carolina frontiersmen. For over fifteen years the Chickamaugas, led by Dragging Canoe, Bloody Fellow, and Doublehead, along with their Creek allies, waged war against the American settlers from their towns along the Tennessee River west of present-day Chattanooga. Loyalists, traders, and countrymen joined them in those Lower Towns and participated in the raids against frontier settlements in Georgia, East Tennessee, and the Cumberland. Pioneering families kept coming over the mountains, but it is no wonder that they preferred the relative safety of rapidly growing settlements in Tennessee and Kentucky to carving out homesteads in the Great Bend just down the river from the Chickamauga towns.[67]

Speculators also had to contend with Indian resistance as they tried to make their visions of frontier settlement real. William Blount and John Sevier, along with other pioneering settlers like John Donelson and Zachariah Cox, sought to gain control over the Great Bend and the Shoals almost immediately after the revolution by negotiating for land grants, openly and secretively, with the Cherokees, Georgia officials, and the Spanish, every power save the new American nation that had some semblance of authority over the region. Overlapping claims to the territory stymied their efforts, but fear of Indian retaliation also made it difficult to establish a tangible foothold on the land. Sevier wrote Georgia's governor in 1786 that "the success of the Muscle Shoals enterprise, greatly depends on the number that will go down to that place," but acknowledged that "a small force will not be adequate to the risk and danger that is to be encountered, and the people here will not venture to so dangerous a place with a few."[68] When Zachariah Cox, a principal in the Tennessee Land Company, which had received four million acres from Georgia in the first Yazoo sale, tried to establish a trading post and settlement at Muscle Shoals, he alarmed Creek and Chickamauga leaders. Warriors attacked boats carrying prospective settlers down the Tennessee, killing twenty-seven men and wounding five others, while a separate war party drove Cox from the blockhouse he had constructed at the shoals.[69]

By the mid-1790s changes were underway that ultimately would pave the way for American settlement of the Great Bend after the turn of the century. The defeat of the Shawnees and their allies at Fallen Timbers and the reversal of Spain's aggressive policy undermined Creek and Chickamauga resistance to American encroachment just as the cotton boom highlighted the economic opportunities of territorial expansion in the Southwest. Cotton transformed the South Carolina upcountry in the second half of the decade as planters took advantage of Eli Whitney's invention of the gin to devote more and more acreage and labor, mostly enslaved, to the crop. Whitney's gin made it cost-effective to plant the hardy Upland strain of cotton, a breed whose short fibers made cleaning the seeds, stems, and debris more difficult but one with the advantage of an extensive geographic range. Cotton took off in the Mississippi River delta around Natchez in the 1790s, piquing interest in the Gulf land that lay to the east. The success of cotton created a new energy among more established planters and slaveholders for venturing west and claiming the fertile soil of the southern frontier. It also helped spark a new round of speculation.[70]

The end of active Indian resistance did not mean that settlers rushed into the Great Bend in the late 1790s, but soon after the turn of the century squatters began filtering south across the Tennessee line. "Old Man" Ditto, an Indian trader, had an outpost on the bend of the river itself, near the site of the abandoned Chickasaw village, and Isaac Criner and his uncle Joseph had built cabins on the Mountain Fork of the Flint River to the north by 1804. John Hunt spent the night at their homestead that year as he traveled south to scout out the land around the Big Spring, the large formation of bluffs and natural spring around which Huntsville would later be built. He began work on a cabin and returned the following year with his family and five slaves. Born in Virginia and a veteran of the Revolutionary War, Hunt and his family had moved frequently, from North Carolina to various counties in East Tennessee. But he was not the stereotypical rootless pioneer searching for free land on which to squat before moving on when settlers arrived. Hunt was well connected to his communities and to political leaders and had served as both a sheriff and a militia captain in Tennessee before moving to the Great Bend. He really was a small-scale land speculator who bought and sold acreage in North Carolina and Tennessee throughout the 1790s and early 1800s. In 1804 he apparently was gambling that the Indian territory south of the state line would soon be in American hands and available for purchase.[71]

The fact that the federal government recognized Indian control over the Great Bend of the Tennessee Valley did inhibit widespread settlement. While they could not prevent squatters from crossing boundary lines to homestead on Indian land, troops did routinely evict settlers in an effort to police those boundaries. It was in the government's interest to placate angry Indians in order to generate goodwill for future negotiations over land cessions, much to the frustration and anger of those pioneering settlers. When troops in 1797 removed settlers from Powell's Valley in East Tennessee after determining that they lay on the wrong side of the Cherokee treaty line, John Hunt and other squatters petitioned John Sevier, now the governor of Tennessee, in protest. "We bought our lands, paid deer for it, both by the sword propertity and money," Hunt wrote, "and to be turned off froom [sic] our lands and livings like a parcel of heathens will look very unhuman and I expect will cause a revelution." Hunt later took the chance to settle on Indian land once again, but most prospective settlers would not risk such an insecure venture. Settlement in that region would require the Indians to sell their land.[72]

Shifts in the Indian economy and in the federal government's civilization program prompted the sale of the Great Bend territory after the turn of the century. For about a hundred years the deerskin trade had shaped the southern frontier, but the continual flow of settlers to the Cumberland River region and East Tennessee, year after year, undermined the Cherokees', Chickasaws', and

Creeks' ability to hunt. Border warfare made it dangerous to travel through the forests near American settlements, places that already were getting crowded with pioneering men hunting their own game, especially in the early years before they had fully established their farms. The free-ranging cattle and hogs that accompanied the families pushing west also drove away the deer by competing for forage. Indian nations saddled with old debts to traders no longer could turn to the hunt as deer grew scarce, leaving land itself as the only valuable commodity they owned. The chronic indebtedness that characterized the old trading economy helped pave the way for settlement by opening new lands for sale.

New economic ventures associated with the federal government's civilization policy divided Indians and generated debts that ultimately benefited settlers. Government officials were quick to point out the diminishing returns brought by hunting. Cherokee men who ventured north into East Tennessee only managed to catch "raccoons, foxes and wildcats" instead of deer, according to Return J. Meigs, the Cherokee agent, and received low prices for their pelts. Still, "those of an idle disposition spend much time rambling there and often return with a stolen horse"—proof, Meigs believed, that "such immense tracts of wilderness" served as "a nursery of savage habits and operates against civilization." He recommended the usual activities associated with the civilization policy: farming and herding for men, and domestic manufactures, especially of cloth, for women. Jefferson echoed that sentiment, telling the Creeks that "a little land cultivated in corn & cotton will go further in providing sustenance and clothing for your people, than the most extensive range of Country can furnish by hunting."[73]

Some Cherokee leaders embraced this policy. When he abandoned his war against the Americans, Edkaqua, or Bloody Fellow, was quick to take advantage of provisions in the treaty of 1791 between the Cherokees and the American government that he had belatedly accepted. "The treaty mentions ploughs, horses, cattle and other things for a farm; this is what we want," he informed President Washington. A sense of resigned recognition of the changing realities of frontier life hung over this request. "In former times we bought of the trader's goods cheap; we could then clothe our women and Children; but now game is scarce and goods dear; we cannot live comfortably," he lamented. "We must plant corn and raise cattle, and we desire you to assist us."[74] Like the Creeks, some Cherokee men, especially those of mixed heritage, took to herding, although they were more resistant to farming, both because it was considered women's work and because it meant leaving towns for private homesteads. Over time some Cherokee families, mainly those of the Indian countrymen and sons of traders, began planting cotton and corn, sometimes with the aid of slave labor.

The Lower Town chiefs, those who had led the Chickamauga raids against the Americans, became the strongest advocates for economic change, none more so than Doublehead. From his village near Muscle Shoals he urged his people to abandon the hunt and take up cotton cultivation and herding, but like Alexander McGillivray, he also actively pursued his own private ventures. He had at least ten slaves laboring in his cotton fields and tending to his large herds of cattle, and he owned sawmills and gristmills and a cotton gin. Doublehead also charged travelers a fee to pilot them through the rapids of the Shoals. He had ambitions to engage in wider trade, telling Meigs that he planned to ship his cattle down to New Orleans and there purchase merchandise to "open a trade with the western wild Indians" along the Red River. Doublehead was eager to embrace the opportunities afforded by the new frontier.[75]

The federal government supported those economic ventures, but "civilization" came at a cost. Meigs kept track of the livestock, hoes, plows, looms, and spinning wheels provided to the Cherokees, as well as the emergency supplies he sent during hard times. When Doublehead and other Lower Town leaders warned in 1804 of imminent starvation in their towns because of drought, Meigs sent three hundred bushels of corn to help them out. Of course, the agent noted the cost in his ledger, as he did again and again during other periods of crop failure and epidemics. Faced with that debt and the reality of the steady, relentless influx of settlers, and committed to an economic future based on cotton fields, gristmills, and sawmills, Doublehead and the other Lower Town headmen considered the sale of the Cherokee hunting lands.[76]

In the fall and winter of 1805–6 a small group of Cherokee headmen sold away a large portion of their nation's hunting territory. The transaction came in two stages. In October 1805, thirty-three chiefs, less than a third of the total number of Cherokee leaders, met at Tellico and agreed to sell five million acres, or just over eight thousand square miles, of their northern hunting territory for $11,000 in cash, $3,000 in merchandise, and a perpetual annuity of $3,000. A couple of months later, a smaller delegation led by Doublehead went to Washington to meet with President Jefferson, and in January 1806 they sold the remaining southern portion of their lands, including the Great Bend. In exchange for the almost seven thousand square miles of land they received $10,000, most of which went to paying off their individual debts. Doublehead received a hundred-square-mile tract of land on the northern banks of the Tennessee River near Muscle Shoals, and several other chiefs were granted smaller cessions to protect their farms. Finally, Jefferson gave Doublehead a special gift of $1,000 "in consideration of his active influence in forwarding the views of Government, in the introduction of the arts of civilization among the Cherokee Nation of Indians, and for his friendly disposition towards the United States and for the purpose of enabling him to extend his useful example among the Red People."[77]

Doublehead, the former leader of the Chickamauga warriors, had engineered a remarkable about-face from implacable foe to informal agent of the expanding American nation, but his leadership in the negotiations exposed deep rifts among the Cherokees. The Upper Town headmen had long been at odds with their Lower Town compatriots. In the late 1780s and early 1790s they had counseled peace while the Chickamaugas waged war. Those roles had reversed by the turn of the century, at least culturally. They rejected the civilization program that the Lower Town Cherokees so eagerly embraced and they were horrified by the betrayals that took place at Tellico and Washington in 1805–6. The shock of the loss of their hunting lands sparked a political reformation of the Cherokee nation and a renewed commitment to resistance to further land cessions. As for Doublehead, he was declared the principal enemy of the Cherokees and was assassinated in the summer of 1807.[78]

The Cherokee cession opened the floodgates, and settlers poured into the Great Bend ahead of the government's efforts to survey and sell the land. Many crossed from Tennessee, drawn by stories of the rich soil of the Bend. The Taylor family of Oglethorpe County, Georgia, loaded up wagons with their nine children and their possessions and, accompanied by a dozen slaves, journeyed to the Elk River region of Tennessee in the spring of 1806. Mia Taylor later penned his childhood memories of his family's frontier settlement. They built a cabin in a place "densely populated with beast and bird, flesh and fowl, everything except man," but within a year others had arrived, some of them former neighbors from Georgia, and "quite a settlement sprang up." Hunters carried back stories of the thick hardwood forests, "well watered by many streams," that lay to the south, and some made plans to relocate. At first the sight of the wagons and packhorses wending their way toward the Bend "attracted as much attention from our little community as a traveler from the Antipodes would not command," but soon "a considerable number" of Tennesseans, new and old, had joined the southward flow. The Taylor family did not immediately join them. Few slaveholders, especially those with more than five slaves, moved to the Bend before the federal land sale of 1809 made landownership secure. But when the Taylors did venture south in 1810 to the Brownsboro settlement of Madison County, they found "a considerable colony" of their old Tennessee neighbors.[79]

The rush of settlers into the Great Bend posed problems for the federal government. The most immediate issue involved those who homesteaded outside the boundaries of the Cherokee and Chickasaw cessions. Some mistakenly found themselves in Indian territory by moving before the lines had been surveyed, but others came later, fully aware that they were squatting illegally. Some used the ambiguity of Cherokee and Chickasaw claims to the hunting lands of the Tennessee Valley to plead their case. One group of squatters on Chickasaw land west of Madison County petitioned Congress in 1810, asking that they be allowed to stay until they could purchase their land from the Indians directly. They argued that they were well within the borders of the Cherokee cession and that they had been unaware that the Chickasaws also claimed this territory. They presented an argument common among squatters who looked upon mile after mile of "wilderness" as open territory, ripe for settlement and cultivation. Why should "a heathan nation" have a right to "nearly 100000 acres of land to each man" who "saunter about . . . like so many wolves or bares whilst they who would be a supporte to government and improve the country must be forsed even to rent poore stoney ridges to make a support to rase their families on whist [sic] there is fine fertile countrys lying uncultivated."[80]

Federal officials would not disagree with that sentiment; they also preferred to see Indian land transformed into American settlements. But that process required Indian cooperation, and squatters interfered with the diplomatic niceties needed to encourage land cessions. Indians understood that and used that knowledge for leverage in removing squatters. Return Meigs, fresh from overseeing the removal of 83 families on Cherokee land and 201 families on Chickasaw land in the Great Bend, reported to the secretary of war that the Chickasaw headmen had told General Robertson that they might be willing to sell the land between the Elk River and Madison County but in the meantime wanted the squatters out. Meigs sympathized with the settlers. "Altho they came under the description of aggressors," he wrote, "it is my duty to say that many of them are reputable well informed, & rich in Cattle & horses—no hunting[,] agriculture their sole pursuit." There were exceptions. One man named Moss, who "was always armed, quarrelsome, & considered by all as a dangerous man," refused to leave his cabin, but escaped to Tennessee before the soldiers could arrest him. Most of those who had settled on Indian land peaceably accepted their fate when confronted by Meigs and made their way into Madison County or Tennessee.[81]

Like John Hunt, many of the early arrivals to the Great Bend had moved from frontier to frontier across the Appalachians and were familiar with the routines of settlement. After building a cabin for shelter the first priority was getting crops in the ground. But in order to do that the hardwood forests that signaled fertile soil to settlers had to be cleared, and that involved backbreaking labor. After girdling the trees by removing a ring of bark to kill the foliage, settlers used light plows or hoes to plant crops around the trunks. Over time dead limbs and trees fell, to be used to build fences to keep livestock out of the cornfields or to be dragged into piles for burning. Grubbing up the stumps and roots out of the ground was difficult but made planting easier. In the meantime, game was plentiful and hogs and cattle could forage in the woods, both providing meat to sustain families. Families tended to cluster together in small squatter communities, some along the Great South Road, the old Indian trail that was now a path for settlers from Tennessee, or on the various forks of the Flint River, or near what was now called Hunt's Spring. Thomas Freeman, the surveyor of Madison County, reported in 1808 that the 353 squatter households had claimed "every spring and convenient spot on the Creeks," adding that "every cottage has its field of corn, from 10 acres up to 50 or 60 acres," along with "small patches of cotton, tobacco, and wheat." The cotton was usually for home consumption; spun and woven into cloth it could be used along with flax and deerskins to make clothing. Tending to basic subsistence needs preoccupied most settlers in those early years.[82]

Commanding enslaved labor eased the hard work of settlement but less than one-quarter of the squatter households brought slaves. The majority of those that did owned between one and three enslaved men, women, or children. Some moderate slaveholders did migrate to the Great Bend but no planter with twenty or more slaves ventured into Madison County before the federal land sale in 1809. The three hundred or so enslaved Africans living in the county in 1808 had been uprooted from family and friends in Tennessee, Georgia, and the Carolinas, and most were scattered across the squatter communities on small farms. There they cleared forests and planted crops, built cabins and fences, tended livestock, and trapped, hunted, and fished, participating in the wide variety of tasks needed to establish homesteads in the new region. Those few owned by larger slaveholders moved quickly beyond dealing with basic subsistence needs and were put to work planting cotton and the foundations of an emerging plantation economy. Littleberry Adams, one of the two largest slaveholders among the squatters, brought seventeen slaves with him to Madison County in 1808. By 1810 he was transporting cotton bales down the Tennessee River bound for the New Orleans market. He was a pioneer in the development of a cotton economy. It would take the security of the federal land sale in the summer of 1809 to attract a large number of slaveholders and planters intent on establishing plantations on the fertile land of the Great Bend.[83]

The government prepared for that sale by ensuring that no competing land claims would impede the smooth transfer of property, especially those springing from the Yazoo speculation of 1795. To nullify the threat of squatters asserting their right to their homesteads, federal officials allowed families to stay as "tenants at will" if they paid a six-shilling fee and renounced any legal claim to the land. That would give them some legitimacy as tenants and allow them time to harvest their crops, better positioning them to purchase their holdings at the sale. "The great object of the President," the secretary of the treasury informed the surveyor, Thomas Freeman, was to weed out "those who under pretence of pretended Georgia titles, intend either forcibly to occupy the lands, or to extort money from ignorant Settlers."[84] None who had purchased land from the Tennessee Land Company could be allowed to challenge the federal government's power by laying claim to the land. Nor could they amass any political or legal power. The governor of the Mississippi Territory, when ready to appoint county judges and sheriffs and other civil officers, was told to pay particular care "that none of those, who lay claim, under Yazoo, or any other supposed titles to the land, may be vested with official authority."[85]

As Freeman moved through the squatter communities, virtually all paid their fees and became tenants at will, with the exception of one settler who had purchased his land from Zachariah Cox. Colonel Michael Harrison had moved from Tennessee to the Great Bend in early 1808 in order to begin surveying forty thousand acres of land stretching twenty-three miles north from the Tennessee River, land that years earlier he had bought from Cox. Many families had claimed homesteads there, including those clustered west of Hunt's Spring, and Harrison insisted that they pay him for their land. He even took out advertisements in the Nashville newspapers during the federal land sale in the summer of 1809 in order to bolster his ownership claims. Most of the squatters on Harrison's land ignored his warnings but some did not, especially after the Supreme Court ruled in *Fletcher v. Peck* in 1810 that the Yazoo claimants deserved indemnification by the federal government. Two speculators purchased the bulk of Harrison's holdings hoping to get government funds, but they were out of luck, despite congressional appropriation of money to pay off the Yazoo debt in 1814. It turns out that Zachariah Cox had relinquished his shares in the Tennessee Company before making what turned out to be a fraudulent sale to Harrison.[86]

The land sale in the summer of 1809 continued the process of settlement begun by the early squatters but also unleashed speculative energies with faint echoes of the Yazoo sales. There were, of course, differences. The land deals of the late eighteenth century were largely confined to vast tracts laid out on maps, imaginary projections into a territory far removed from actual settlement, while the steady flow of settlers across the mountains into Tennessee and then down into the Great Bend fueled interest in Madison County land. But both were rooted in the notion that great profit could be wrung from the transformation of the frontier, especially with the rapid expansion of cotton. Beginning in 1809 and continuing over the next decade, more substantial slaveholders took the chance to leave familiar neighborhoods and livelihoods in Tennessee, Virginia, the Carolinas, and Georgia to settle on this new cotton frontier.

As the sale commenced in August 1809, with others to follow over the next few years, some of the early settlers were able to purchase their homesteads, while others lost out. The sale itself took place in Nashville, where the Madison County land office was first established. Certainly that town could better accommodate the flood of eager purchasers, but its distance from the squatter settlements also appealed to government officials since they feared protests and disorder from settlers unable to purchase their claims. By the end of the year, just over a third of the squatters had secured their holdings at least temporarily by making a down payment, and by 1813, 40 percent of the original settlers owned property in Madison County. John Hunt was not one of them. He made several purchases at the Nashville land sale but for reasons unknown, he allowed them to revert back to the government for resale. By then he was at least sixty years old and perhaps did not have the energy to manage a new farm, instead living out his remaining years with either his daughter and her husband in Madison County or with his son in Tennessee. He left behind a vibrant and rapidly growing community clustered about the spring where he had first built his cabin—a town now known as Huntsville in his honor.[87]

Most of the purchasers at the sale of 1809 bought sections ranging from 160 to 960 acres, but a small number of men belonging to two groups of speculators took almost half the land sold at the public auction. These were not distant capitalists interested only in the profits to be made from resale; rather, they were wealthier pioneers who planned to establish themselves in the new county as men of power. A group of Nashville speculators, many of whom were friends and associates of Andrew Jackson, had experience dealing in Tennessee land and were well positioned to take advantage of the Madison County sale. They included John Brahan and William Dickson, the two principal officials of the land office, and Thomas Freeman, the county's surveyor. Freeman, especially, was an important source of information about the qualities of the land, and he was not hesitant about taking advantage of that knowledge himself. He ended up buying a total of 8,500 acres and becoming the single largest purchaser in 1809.[88]

A second group of speculators from Georgia played an influential role in Madison County and had an impact on the political future of Alabama. After the revolution a number of families left Virginia for newly opened counties at the confluence of the Broad and Savannah Rivers. There they became wealthy tobacco planters and through marriage, business ties, and friendship created a network of political and economic power. Thomas and William Bibb, Charles Tait, Leroy Pope, and his son-in-law John Williams Walker all eventually moved to Alabama, where they became known as the Broad River group, or simply the Georgia faction. They later leveraged their connections back east—especially through William Crawford, who would become the secretary of the treasury after the War of 1812—into political power as Alabama became first a territory and then a state. Pope, Walker, Thomas Bibb, and James Manning all bought large quantities of land during the 1809 sale, although they did not move to the county until the following year. Once there, they concentrated on clearing land, planting cotton, and procuring more slaves and paid less attention to the niceties of life. Manning, the largest slaveholder in the county in 1810, had a two-story log house built for his family that, while undoubtedly larger at thirty-four feet in length than those of his neighbors, was simple in style. Within a few years, once their plantations were established and their careers as lawyers, doctors, and merchants had developed, this "log cabin aristocracy" began constructing fine homes that displayed their status. Leroy Pope, who concentrated his purchases at the 1809 sale on Hunt's Spring and the surrounding countryside, stood at the center of that circle of elite settlers, a group that came to be known as the Royal Party in Madison County.[89]

The foundations of a cotton and slaveholding frontier were laid remarkably quickly in Madison County in the years after the first squatters arrived in the Great Bend. Yeoman farming still predominated before the War of 1812; 77 percent of the households in 1809 owned no slaves, and those families who did had only a few for the most part. But the federal land sales brought settlers intent on planting cotton, and with them came more slaves. By 1815 the percentage of households without slaves had dipped to 61. Five years later just under half of Madison County's population was enslaved, and settlers were busy transforming the hunting lands throughout the rest of the Tennessee Valley into cotton fields.[90]

"Where shall we look for so new a country settled like this," John Williams Walker asked the audience in Huntsville on July 4, 1811. They had gathered at the county seat to celebrate the founding of their own community as much as the birth of the nation. "It is not two years since the American citizen could legally fix his habitation here; yet look at the population, how numerous, how orderly, how decent, how opulent, how responsible!" Those who had settled there were not the "hunters and herdsmen" of a "rude frontier," the "mere precursors" of farmers, but "the tillers of the earth themselves" who brought "with them the pleasures of social life, the arts of industry, the abundant means of easy and comfortable subsistence."[91] The rapid transformation of the Great Bend from the first squatters in 1804 and the Cherokee cession two years later to the federal sales that began in 1809 was astounding. It was as if all the pent-up energy generated by the opportunities of frontier land since the revolution—the relentless press of settlers across the mountains, the speculative schemes, and the excitement of the cotton boom—played out in the rapid settlement of Madison County.

Walker's speech echoed Swan's vision of Alabama in his report of 1790. Swan had looked at the Creek land through a prism of future development of cash crops, manufacturing, and commerce, erasing the presence of the Indians who retarded progress. In a sense, in Walker's eyes at least, Madison County had leapfrogged over the frontier stage, bypassed the typical progression of more rudimentary societies of hunters and herdsmen, and was fast becoming a settled community. The presence of planters like himself suggested that soon cotton and commerce, and not just subsistence, would drive the growth of the region. Walker's self-congratulatory optimism reflected America's vision of the frontier as a place of opportunities and as an open field for the replication of the economic and social structures of eastern society. Walker connected the settlement of the Great Bend to the grand American story of progress, a story that emphasized the integration of frontier regions into the broader American landscape.

Of course, "the tillers of the earth" were not just the yeoman farmers seeking shelter for their families; increasingly they were masters of bound labor, whose toil in the fields paid for the comfort and opulence of the settlers. Settlers could take solace in the fact that they were rapidly rebuilding what they had left behind. But the enslaved, the unwilling migrants to this frontier who left familiar families, friends, homes, and routines for a new land with new work demands, faced separation and hardship, not integration or opportunity. They would have to find their own ways of forging new connections and relationships on this frontier.

In many ways Tensaw-Tombigbee was a more open frontier, especially for Native Americans and people of African descent. Opportunities for trade and interaction abounded in that borderland region as all residents scrambled to make a living. Those pursuits encouraged more freedom of movement, even among the enslaved, than was true in the emerging cotton region to the north. The presence of Spanish West Florida and Mobile, with more substantial populations of free people of color and more relaxed racial codes, also softened the hierarchical rigidities more common in plantation regions. The métis Creeks and the mixed-race children of John Chastang and Louison reflected the fluidity of the Gulf borderlands.

Yet American settlers in Tensaw and Tombigbee felt constricted by the Spanish and Indian presence and isolated from the rest of the nation. Their frontier seemed pent-up, rather than being an open and expansive field of opportunity. As early as 1799 they complained to Congress that they were squeezed between the Indian line to the north and the Spanish line to the south and asked that the government push the Indians for land cessions between the Tombigbee and Alabama Rivers. There was no room to spread out, they said, since "within two miles of the rivers, the Country is a continual pine-Barren in many places not arable, and every where steril and unproductive."[92] The 12 percent tariff on goods passing through Mobile stifled trade and impeded economic progress. Compounding the limitations on available land and the free flow of goods was the profound sense of isolation. "The people inhabiting this section of the Mississippi Territory, are peculiarly cut off, from all communication with other parts of the United States," Ephraim Kirby informed President Jefferson in 1804. Whether traveling east to Georgia or west to Natchez, "the traveler must go through several hundred miles of wilderness, possessed by savages, and be compelled to encamp in the woods, and swim unfordable streams." The region was strategically important. "A strong American settlement on this river," Kirby suggested, "will afford an excellent barrier, against the approach of a foreign enemy at the southwestern point of our territories." But it was also fragile, and American control over this corner of the frontier was not guaranteed. "So long as these people continue in their present insulated condition," Kirby told Jefferson, "it cannot be expected that they will possess that degree of moral or political virtue, which is essential to the existence of a free government." Instead of bringing civilization, the settlers would inevitably devolve. "Indeed," he said, "they will naturally become a banditti, fugitives from justice, and disturbers, of the peace of our frontiers."[93]

All of those same grievances filled the petition to Congress from residents of the eastern portion of the Mississippi Territory in 1809. "Are we Americans or Spaniards?" they asked before railing against the tariff in Mobile and the Creek and Choctaw lands that hemmed in their settlements. Frustrated by the indifference of a distant territorial government they asked Congress to split Mississippi in two so that the eastern settlers could govern themselves. Do that, and negotiate the navigation and trade issues with Spain, and new families would come to the Tensaw and Tombigbee frontier. With "a strong settlement between Georgia and the Mississippi . . . the Indian nations themselves, would be obliged to adopt civilized habits, or to abandon their country," they said. Within "a few Years, a chain of settlements extending thro a country, now an almost unexplored wilderness, would connect together the state of new-hampshire and the Territory of Orleans."[94] Erase the muddled borderland complexities, the petitioners argued, and Congress could help build a frontier integrated into the larger national whole.

By 1810, discontent in the Tensaw and Tombigbee settlements of Washington County was growing and patience with the federal government was wearing thin. Judge Harry Toulmin warned President James Madison that "the peculiar local position of this settlement, surrounded by Indians,—cut off and entirely detached from & unknown to the main body of the territory of which it is a part,—[and] adjacent to the province of an European power, bearing daily oppressions from it," had created "a fairer field open to unprincipled intrigue & restless ambition than in any spot of equal extent."[95] Toulmin owed his position as a superior court judge to his friendships and political relationships with Virginia leaders like Madison. An intellectual free-thinker who was an Englishman by birth, Toulmin was an outsider who competed for the allegiance of the residents with local leaders whose authority sprang from neighborhood connections. Men like John and James Caller, who were officers in the militia, and Joseph Kennedy, a prominent lawyer, harnessed the growing resentment among settlers to their own ambitions. Boasting that they could take Mobile from the Spanish themselves, Kennedy and the Callers began recruiting followers at militia musters. They found sympathetic supporters among American settlers who had more recently arrived and who found the Spanish duties on goods particularly galling. Rumors flew of a planned expedition into Spanish West Florida, much to the alarm of federal officials. Colonel Richard Sparks, the commander of Fort Stoddert, paid grudging respect to Joseph Kennedy when he wrote that, when it came to "seditious intrigue, or for the low arts that secure popularity, he must be acknowledged eminent." Kennedy and the Callers assured prospective supporters that they had the federal government's tacit approval to take Mobile, a suggestion that Toulmin worked hard to counter. Either way, sentiment in favor of the expedition seemed to be growing as summer gave way to fall.[96] One of the conspirators, a justice of the peace, said that while "they hoped to have the countenance of government . . . *they were determined not to be cramped.*"[97]

Restless intrigue was endemic throughout the Gulf borderlands as American settlers confronted a weakening Spanish regime in West Florida. The Louisiana Purchase in 1803 eroded Spanish control over the Gulf and emboldened settlers in the western portion of the Mississippi Territory to launch raids south across the international boundary. Called "filibusters," these raids were part looting expeditions, part efforts to spark insurrection among residents fed up with Spanish rule. Never having been able to attract many Spaniards to the Gulf and preoccupied with its military conflict with France, Spain maintained only a tenuous hold on the loyalty of the largely Anglo-American population of West Florida. That became clear in the summer of 1810 when delegates from the four districts of Baton Rouge met to discuss a reformation of the colonial administration, while still insisting on their loyalty to the Crown. That pretense fell away in September when rebels stormed the Spanish fort in Baton Rouge and placed the commandant under arrest. President Madison declared American control over Baton Rouge and argued that all of West Florida belonged to the United States as part of the Louisiana Purchase.[98]

The ease with which the rebels to the west took Baton Rouge and the administration's tacit acceptance emboldened those planning an expedition against Mobile. They had the support of Reuben Kemper, a representative from Baton Rouge who had a long history of border raiding in the company of his two brothers. In December 1810, a force of about one hundred men led by Kennedy marched south to a site they renamed Bunker Hill and set up camp to await reinforcements and a supply boat from Saint Stephens. Once resupplied, the ragtag army made their move in early December. Kemper led a few of his compatriots back to Tensaw to try to drum up new recruits while a second small force rowed across the bay to raid a small Spanish settlement at Sawmill Creek, about twelve miles north of Mobile. There they paused, proceeding to get drunk on the liquor they had confiscated, while Governor Vicente Folch took the offensive. He sent two hundred soldiers to attack at midnight on December 10, catching the expedition forces unawares, and routed the Americans, killing four and capturing ten unlucky settlers who soon found themselves languishing in a

Havana prison for the next five years. John Caller, Reuben Kemper, and several others were arrested when they made their way to Fort Stoddert, but the grand jury refused to indict them.[99]

The ill-conceived expedition against Mobile intensified American efforts to deal with the problem of Spanish control of the Gulf. Toulmin, after all, did tell the conspirators, "The day, I hope, is fast approaching when our neighbours will become one with us," even while reminding them that "genuine *unity* cannot be *produced by force*."[100] American officials' greatest fear was that Britain would take advantage of the chaos of restless settlers and weakened Spanish authority to claim West Florida for itself. So an American naval expedition sailed into Mobile in January 1811 and occupied the city without attacking the Spanish fort, setting up a stalemate.[101] The Tensaw and Tombigbee settlers were closer to breaking through the Spanish obstacle to their progress, but in the coming years continued efforts to consolidate American authority over the southwestern frontier sparked more dangerous conflicts with their Creek neighbors.

Notes

1. Swan to Knox, "Position and State of Manners and Arts in the Creek, or Muscogee Nation in 1791," Philadelphia, April 29, 1795, in *Information respecting the History, Condition and Prospects of the Indian Tribes of the United States: Collected and Prepared under the Direction of the Bureau of Indian Affairs, Department of the Interior*, by Henry R. Schoolcraft (Philadelphia: J. B. Lippincott, 1855), 251–55.

2. Ibid., 251.

3. Ibid., 251–52.

4. Ibid., 258.

5. Ibid., 257–58.

6. Ibid., 255, 257–58.

7. "Treaty with the Creeks, 1790," August 7, 1790, in *Indian Affairs: Laws and Treaties*, ed. Charles J. Kappler, vol. 2, *Treaties* (Washington, DC: US Government Printing Office, 1904), 25–27, http://digital.library.okstate.edu/kappler/Vo12/treaties/creo025.htm.

8. Andrew Ellicott, *The Journal of Andrew Ellicott, Late Commissioner on Behalf of the United States . . . for Determining the Boundary between the United States and the Possessions of His Catholic Majesty. . . .* (1803; repr., Chicago: Quadrangle Books, 1962), 200–201.

9. Ellicott, *Journal of Andrew Ellicott*, 198.

10. Ephraim Kirby to President Thomas Jefferson, Fort Stoddert, May 1, 1804, in *The Territorial Papers of the United States*, ed. Clarence Edwin Carter, vol. 5, *The Ter-*

ritory of Mississippi, 1798–1817 (Washington, DC: US Government Printing Office, 1937), 323.

11. Lorenzo Dow, *History of Cosmopolite; or, the Four Volumes of Lorenzo Dow's Journal....* (Wheeling, VA: Joshua Martin, 1848), quoted in Alan Gallay, ed., *Voices of the Old South: Eyewitness Accounts, 1528–1861* (Athens: University of Georgia Press, 1994), 203.

12. Kirby to Jefferson, Fort Stoddert, May 1, 1804, in Carter, *Territorial Papers*, vol. 5, 323–24.

13. Kirby to Jefferson, Fort Stoddert, May 1, 1804, in Carter, *Territorial Papers*, vol. 5, 325.

14. Ibid., 324.

15. Gregory A. Waselkov and Bonnie L. Gums, *Plantation Archaeology at Rivière aux Chiens, ca. 1725–1848*, report prepared for the Alabama Department of Transportation (Mobile: Center for Archaeological Studies, University of South Alabama, June 2000), 7–21, 32–33.

16. Karl Davis, "The Founding of Tensaw: Kinship, Community, Trade, and Diplomacy in the Creek Nation," in *Coastal Encounters: The Transformation of the Gulf South in the Eighteenth Century*, ed. Richmond F. Brown (Lincoln: University of Nebraska Press, 2007), 86; Gregory A. Waselkov, "Formation of the Tensaw Community," in *Red Eagle's Children: Weatherford vs. Weatherford et al.*, ed. J. Anthony Paredes and Judith Knight (Tuscaloosa: University of Alabama Press, 2012), 36.

17. William Bartram, *Travels through North and South Carolina, Georgia, East and West Florida....* (Philadelphia: James and Johnson, 1791), 405, quoted in Waselkov and Gums, *Plantation Archaeology*, 83.

18. Waselkov and Gums, *Plantation Archaeology*, 82–85.

19. Ibid., 63–66.

20. Ibid., 63–68.

21. Jack D. L. Holmes, "Alabama's Forgotten Settlers: Notes on the Spanish Mobile District, 1780–1813," *Alabama Historical Quarterly* (Summer 1971): 88; David H. White, "A View of Spanish West Florida: Selected Letters of Governor Juan Vicente Folch," *Florida Historical Quarterly* 56 (October 1977): 145.

22. McGillivray to O'Neill, Little Tallassee, February 5, 1784, in *McGillivray of the Creeks*, by John Walton Caughey (Norman: University of Oklahoma Press, 1938), 69.

23. McGillivray to O'Neill, Little Tallassee, December 5, 1783, in Caughey, *McGillivray of the Creeks*, 63.

24. Patrick Tonyn to Vicente Manuel de Zéspedes, Saint Augustine, July 5, 1784, in *East Florida, 1783–1785, a File of Documents Assembled and Many of Them Translated*, by Joseph Byrne Lockey, ed. John W. Caughey (Berkeley, CA: University of California Press, 1949), 235–36, quoted in Holmes, "Alabama's Forgotten Settlers," 89.

25. Holmes, "Alabama's Forgotten Settlers," 88–89.

26. Ibid., 90.

27. Waselkov and Gums, *Plantation Archaeology*, 84; Holmes, "Alabama's Forgotten Settlers," 96.

28. Gregory A. Waselkov, *A Conquering Spirit: Fort Mims and the Redstick War of 1813–1814* (Tuscaloosa: University of Alabama Press, 2006), 20.

29. Ibid., 20–21, 28–29.

30. Holmes, "Alabama's Forgotten Settlers," 96–97; Waselkov and Gums, *Plantation Archaeology*, 67.

31. Vicente Folch to Miró, Mobile, April 11 [17?], 1791, copy enclosed in Las Casa to Campo de Alange, July 29, 1791, quoted in Jack D. L. Holmes, "Observations on the 1791 Floods in Alabama," *Alabama Historical Quarterly* 40 (Fall/Winter 1978): 122; Holmes, "Observations on the 1791 Floods," 119, 122–25.

32. Folch to Miró, Mobile, April 11 [17?], 1791, quoted in Holmes, "Observations on the 1791 Floods," 124.

33. Holmes, "Observations on the 1791 Floods," 123–24.

34. McGillivray to Panton, Little Tallassee, May 20, 1789, in "Papers Relating to the Georgia-Florida Frontier, 1784–1800," by D. C. Corbitt, *Georgia Historical Quarterly* 21 (September 1937): 283, 285.

35. McGillivray to Miró, Little Tallassee, May 26, 1789, in Corbitt, "Papers," 234.

36. McGillivray to Panton, Little Tallassee, May 20, 1789, in Corbit, "Papers," 284–85.

37. Davis, "Founding of Tensaw," 82, 87–90; Waselkov, *Conquering Spirit*, 42, 48–49, 56–59.

38. "Treaty with the Creeks, 1790," August 7, 1790, in *Indian Affairs: Laws and Treaties*, ed. Charles J. Kappler, vol. 2, *Treaties* (Washington, DC: US Government Printing Office, 1904), 25–27, http://digital.library.okstate.edu/kappler/Vol2/treaties/cre0025.htm.

39. Issac Brigs to President Thomas Jefferson, Washington, Mississippi Territory, May 18, 1805, in Carter, *Territorial Papers*, vol. 5, 403–4.

40. Jefferson to Hawkins, February 1803, in *The Writings of Thomas Jefferson*, ed. Albert E. Bergh (Washington, DC: Thomas Jefferson Memorial Association, 1907), 9:361–63, quoted in Anthony F. C. Wallace, *Jefferson and the Indians: The Tragic Fate of the First Americans* (Cambridge, MA: Harvard University Press, 1999), 222–23.

41. Ibid.

42. Benjamin Hawkins, *Letters, Journals and Writings of Benjamin Hawkins*, ed. C. L. Grant (Savannah, GA: Beehive, 1980), 291–92, quoted in Waselkov, *Conquering Spirit*, 57; also see Waselkov, *Conquering Spirit*, 56–59.

43. Benjamin Hawkins, *The Collected Works of Benjamin Hawkins, 1796–1810*, ed. Thomas Foster (Tuscaloosa: University of Alabama Press, 2003), 43; Theda Perdue, *"Mixed Blood" Indians: Racial Construction in the Early South* (Athens: University of Georgia Press, 2003), 32.

44. Hawkins, *Collected Works*, 39–41, 47; Waselkov, *Conquering Spirit*, 49.

45. Waselkov, *Conquering Spirit*, 52–53; Hawkins, *Collected Works*, 40, 48.

46. Robbie Ethridge, *Creek Country: The Creek Indians and Their World* (Chapel Hill: University of North Carolina Press, 2003), 152, 175–77, 179, 186–87; James Taylor Carson, *Searching for the Bright Path: The Mississippi Choctaw from Prehistory to Removal* (Lincoln: University of Nebraska Press, 1999), 72.

47. John D. W. Guice, "Cattle Raisers of the Old Southwest: A Reinterpretation," *Western Historical Quarterly* 8 (April 1977): 177.

48. James Churchill to William Churchill, Tombigbee, July 24, 1811, William Churchill Letters, Duke University Library, Durham, NC, quoted in Guice, "Cattle Raisers," 181.

49. Philip Henry Gosse, *Letters from Alabama (U.S.), Chiefly Relating to Natural History* (1859; repr., Tuscaloosa: University of Alabama Press, 1973), 63, quoted in Ethridge, *Creek Country*, 163.

50. James Taylor Carson, "Native Americans, the Market Revolution, and Culture Change: The Choctaw Cattle Economy, 1690–1830," in *Pre-removal Choctaw History: Exploring New Paths*, ed. Greg O'Brien (Norman: University of Oklahoma Press, 2008), 185–86; Carson, *Searching for the Bright Path*, 75; Ethridge, *Creek Country*, 159–61.

51. Carson, "Native Americans," 187.

52. Jack D. L. Holmes, "The Role of Blacks in Spanish Alabama: The Mobile District, 1780–1813," *Alabama Historical Quarterly* 37 (Spring 1975): 7–8.

53. Swan to Knox, "Position and State," 260–61.

54. Patrick Carr to Governor John Martin, December 13, 1782, in "Creek Indian Letters, Talks, and Treaties, 1705–1839: In Four Parts," typescript, ed. Louise F. Hays, Georgia Archives, Morrow, GA, part 1, 40, quoted in Christina Snyder, "Conquered Enemies, Adopted Kin, and Owned People: The Creek Indians and Their Captives," *Journal of Southern History* 73 (May 2007): 280.

55. Ira Berlin, *Many Thousands Gone: The First Two Centuries of Slavery in North America* (Cambridge, MA: Harvard University Press, 1998), 344.

56. Ibid., 326.

57. Richmond F. Brown, "Colonial Mobile, 1712–1813," in *Mobile: The New History of Alabama's First City*, ed. Michael V. R. Thomason (Tuscaloosa: University of Alabama Press, 2001), 58.

58. Holmes, "Role of Blacks," 14; Berlin, *Many Thousands Gone*, 202; Brown, "Colonial Mobile," 58.

59. Virginia Meacham Gould, "The Parish Identities of Free Creoles of Color in Pensacola and Mobile, 1698–1860," *U.S. Catholic Historian* 14 (Summer 1996): 3, 7; Holmes, "Role of Blacks," 17.

60. David Wheat, "My Friend Nicolas Mongoula: Africans, Indians, and Cultural Exchange in Eighteenth-Century Mobile," in Brown, *Coastal Encounters*, 120–29.

61. Holmes, "Role of Blacks," 10–11; Gould, "Parish Identities," 8; Waselkov and Gums, *Plantation Archaeology*, 83.

62. Berlin, *Many Thousands Gone*, 200–202.

63. McGillivray to Linder, Little Tallassee, December 28, 1788, in Caughey, *McGillivray of the Creeks*, 212–13; Saunt, *New Order of Things*, 88, 117.

64. Hawkins, *Collected Works*, 48–49.

65. Frances Cabaniss Roberts, "Background and Formative Period in the Great Bend and Madison County" (PhD dissertation, University of Alabama, 1956), 45–47.

66. Donald Davidson, *The Tennessee*, vol. 1, *The Old River, Frontier to Secession* (New York: Rinehart,1946), 164.

67. William G. McLoughlin, *Cherokee Renascence in the New Republic* (Princeton, NJ: Princeton University Press, 1986), 19–24.

68. J. G. M. Ramsey, *The Annals of Tennessee* (1853; repr., Kingsport, TN: Kingsport Press, 1926), 380, quoted in Roberts, "Background and Formative Period," 75.

69. Thomas D. Clark and John D. W. Guice, *Frontiers in Conflict: The Old Southwest, 1795–1830* (Albuquerque: University of New Mexico Press, 1989), 69; Shaw Livermore, *Early American Land Companies: Their Influence on Corporate Development* (New York: Octagon Books, 1968), 147–50; George R. Lamplugh, *Politics on the Periphery: Factions and Parties in Georgia, 1783–1806* (Newark: University of Delaware Press, 1986), 66–71; McGillivray to William Panton, Little Tallassee, May 8, 1790, in Caughey, *McGillivray of the Creeks*, 259–60, 262; Roberts, "Background and Formative Period," 93.

70. Gregory Evans Dowd, *A Spirited Resistance: The North American Indian Struggle for Unity, 1745–1815* (Baltimore: Johns Hopkins University Press, 1992), 112–13; McLoughlin, *Cherokee Renascence*, 24–25. See also Adam Rothman, *Slave Country: American Expansion and the Origins of the Deep South* (Cambridge, MA: Harvard University Press, 2005), 37–70.

71. David Byers, "Two Hundred Years—The Big Spring and John Hunt," in *The Huntsville Historical Review: A History of Early Settlement; Madison County before Statehood, 1808–1819* (Huntsville, AL: Huntsville–Madison County Historical Society, 2008), 53–56; Joseph M. Jones, "New Market—First and Fairest of Them All?," in ibid., 60–63.

72. Hunt to Sevier, Powell's Valley, July 17, 1797, Governor's Correspondence, John Sevier, 1796–1809, Book 1, p. 104, Tennessee State Library and Archives, Nashville, quoted in Roberts, "Background and Formative Period," 117–18.

73. Return J. Meigs to Benjamin Hawkins, February 13, 1805, Records of the Cherokee Indian Agency, Tennessee, 1801–1835, Records of the Bureau of Indian Affairs, National Archives and Records Administration, Washington, DC, quoted in McLoughlin, *Cherokee Renascence*, 62; Thomas Jefferson, "President's Talk to the Creeks," November 2, 1805, RG 75.2, Records of the Bureau of Indian Affairs, quoted in Angela Pulley Hudson, *Creek Paths and Federal Roads: Indians, Settlers, and Slaves and the Making of the American South* (Chapel Hill: University of North Carolina Press, 2010), 68.

74. Edkaqua, quoted in McLoughlin, *Cherokee Renascence*, 61.

75. Doublehead to Return J. Meigs, November 20, 1802, Records of the Bureau of Indian Affairs, quoted in McLoughlin, *Cherokee Renascence*, 85; also see McLoughlin, *Cherokee Renascence*, 71, 84–85.

76. McLoughlin, *Cherokee Renascence*, 67–68.

77. Henry Dearborn to Return J. Meigs, January 8, 1806, Letters Sent by the Secretary of War Relating to Indian Affairs, 1800–1824, Records of the Bureau of Indian Affairs, quoted in ibid., 106; also see ibid., 104–7.

78. McLoughlin, *Cherokee Renascence*, 120–21.

79. Mia Taylor, "Early Recollections of Madison County," *Huntsville Historical Review* 2 (1972): 23–27, quoted in Daniel S. Dupre, *Transforming the Cotton Frontier: Madison County, Alabama, 1800–1840* (Baton Rouge: Louisiana State University Press, 1997), 19–20.

80. "Petition to the President and Congress by Intruders on Chickasaw Lands," Mississippi Territory Elk River Sims'es settlement, September 5, 1810, in *The Territorial Papers of the United States*, ed. Clarence Edwin Carter, vol. 6, *The Territory of Mississippi, 1809–1817* (Washington, DC: US Government Printing Office, 1938), 106–7.

81. Return J. Meigs to John Smith, Highwassee Garrison, June 12, 1809, in Carter, *Territorial Papers*, vol. 5, 739–740.

82. Thomas Freeman to Secretary of the Treasury Albert Gallatin, camp on Flint River, August 25, 1808, quoted in Roberts, "Background and Formative Period," 148–49; Dupre, *Transforming the Cotton Frontier*, 20–21.

83. Roberts, "Background and Formative Period," 147–48; Dupre, *Transforming the Cotton Frontier*, 20–22.

84. Gallatin to Freeman, Washington, DC, October 25, 1808, quoted in Carter, *Territorial Papers*, vol. 5, 658–59.

85. Albert Gallatin to Governor Robert Williams, Washington, DC, November 5, 1808, quoted in Carter, *Territorial Papers*, vol. 5, 660.

86. Roberts, "Background and Formative Period," 169–70, 173, 195; Dupre, *Transforming the Cotton Frontier*, 23.

87. Dupre, *Transforming the Cotton Frontier*, 26–27; Roberts, "Background and Formative Period," 200; Byers, "Two Hundred Years," 46, 57.

88. Dupre, *Transforming the Cotton Frontier*, 27.

89. Ibid., 28–38.

90. Ibid., 33–35, 126.

91. "Fourth of July Address Made Here One Hundred and Four Years Ago," *Weekly Mercury* (Hunstville), July 7, 1915, quoted in Roberts, "Background and Formative Period," 234–35.

92. "Petition to Congress by Inhabitants of Tombigbee and Tensaw," August 1, 1799, in Carter, *Territorial Papers*, vol. 5, 69–70.

93. Kirby to Jefferson, Fort Stoddert, April 20, 1804, in Carter, *Territorial Papers*, vol. 5, 317–18.

94. "Petition to Congress by a Convention East of Pearl River," November 11, 1809, in Carter, *Territorial Papers*, vol. 6, 28–30.

95. Toulmin to Madison, Fort Stoddert, July 28, 1810, in Carter, *Territorial Papers*, vol. 6, 84–85.

96. Sparks to Secretary of State Robert Smith, Fort Stoddert, July 12, 1810, in Carter, *Territorial Papers*, vol. 6, 82, quoted in Clark and Guice, *Frontiers in Conflict*, 57; Clark and Guice, *Frontiers in Conflict*, 56–57, 61; Secretary of War William Eustis to Wade Hampton, Washington, DC, August 22, 1810, in Carter, *Territorial Papers*, vol. 6, 101–2; Governor David Holmes to James Caller, Joseph Carson, and James Patton, Washington, Mississippi Territory, September 8, 1810, in ibid., 113–14; Holmes to Caller, July 31, 1810, in ibid., 92–93; Toulmin to Madison, Fort Stoddert, July 28, 1810, in ibid., 84–90; Toulmin to Madison, Fort Stoddert, November 22, 1810, in ibid., 135–39; Toulmin to Madison, Fort Stoddert, November 28, 1810, in ibid., 140–43.

97. Toulmin to Madison, Fort Stoddert, July 28, 1810, in Carter, *Territorial Papers*, vol. 6, 88.

98. Clark and Guice, *Frontiers in Conflict*, 46–55.

99. Clark and Guice, *Frontiers in Conflict*, 59–60; Robert V. Haynes, *The Mississippi Territory and the Southwest Frontier, 1795–1817* (Lexington: University Press of Kentucky, 2010), 274–78; Toulmin to Madison, Fort Stoddert, November 28, 1810, in Carter, *Territorial Papers*, vol. 6, 141–43; Toulmin to Madison, Fort Stoddert, December 6, 1810, in ibid., 149; Toulmin to Madison, Fort Stoddert, December 12, 1810, in ibid.,153.

100. Toulmin to the Captains of Militia, Washington County, Fort Stoddert, November 4, 1810, in Carter, *Territorial Papers*, vol. 6, 131.

101. Thomas Cushing to William Claiborne, governor of Orleans, Mobile, January 8, 1811, in Carter, *Territorial Papers*, vol. 6, 167–68; Clark and Guice, *Frontiers of Conflict*, 60.

7

The Creek War

In the summer of 1813, Samuel Mims's plantation, one of the largest in the Tensaw settlements, became a fort. The frame house with two porches, built in the "creole" style popular on the Gulf coast, shared grounds with three horse stables, a blacksmith shop, and a number of other outbuildings, all testaments to the economic success of the old Indian trader. Since arriving in the region in the mid-1780s, Mims had grown wealthy dabbling in land speculation along the Tombigbee, raising cattle and crops, and operating his ferry across the Alabama River. By 1808 he owned forty-six slaves who labored on 524 acres of land near Boatyard Lake and was one of the richest men in the Tensaw and Tombigbee settlements. In July 1813 his neighbors, alarmed by rumors of impending attacks by the militant Creeks known as Red Sticks, gathered at his place and began building defensive walls. Others across the settlements in the forks of the Alabama and Tombigbee were doing the same: fortifying the strongest houses they could find. By August some four hundred people were cooped up behind the vertical pickets of logs that turned the site, just a little more than one acre, into a stockade. There they struggled with the summer heat, illnesses, and an anxious boredom, waiting to see if the violence of the civil war that had recently engulfed the Creek nation would spill into their corner of Alabama's frontier.[1]

The image of scared settlers huddled in a fort while hostile Indians threatened assault is deeply embedded in our popular culture through films and television. That scenario captures the violence that accompanied westward expansion, blamed in earlier generations on the savagery of the Indians. Today we would more likely acknowledge the underlying grievances that fueled the hostility of the Native Americans. In either case the image reinforces a simplistic notion of a binary frontier occupied by settler and Indian, with the fort's walls serving as a material reminder of the imaginary "frontier line" dividing civilization from wilderness. But frontiers were rarely, if ever, that neat.

The hundreds of people gathered in Fort Mims that summer of 1813 were a mixed group that reflected the complex population of the Tensaw-Tombigbee frontier. Certainly there were many men, women, and children who fit the traditional image of American settlers: single men and families who had pulled up stakes in the Carolinas or Georgia and pushed west to try their luck in the Southwest. Some, like Mims, had been longtime residents who had witnessed the slow transformation of the old trading frontier, while others were more recent arrivals. The Rigdon family traveled from Georgia in 1811 to settle in Tensaw, eager to join their two teenage sons who were serving as drummer boys at Fort Stoddert. Other Americans were part of the Mississippi Territorial Volunteers who had recently been sent from the Natchez region by Governor David Holmes to defend "the eastern frontier." Not surprisingly, given the international character of the borderlands, some at the fort had French ancestry, and even a small group of Spanish residents, soldiers who had deserted their posts, had made their way to Mims's plantation. The métis Creeks of the Little River region of Tensaw composed a major portion of the fort's refugees, a legacy, like Mims himself, of the old trading frontier that had slipped away. Creek countrymen like Zachariah McGirth and his wife, Vicey Cornells, Alexander McGillivray's widow, sought shelter at the fort with their families. Dixon Bailey and his brothers and sisters, wife, and children were there. Bailey's father had been banished from Atasi and had moved his family to Tensaw, and Dixon had now taken up the planter's life in the Little River community. The fifty or so members of the Tensaw militia company at Fort Mims, white Americans and métis alike, thought highly enough of Bailey to elect him captain that August. Polly Jones, a métis Creek, and her American husband were at the fort along with their three children. That family must have embraced Benjamin Hawkins's civilization programs, since they named their youngest Jeffersonia Hawkins Jones. Finally, perhaps as many as one hundred enslaved Africans were there, brought by their owners to seek protection from attack. Fort Mims, like the Tensaw borderland itself, was a jumble of races and ethnicities.

The lines between Indian and settler blurred at Fort Mims but recent events were sharpening divisions on the southwestern frontier in 1813. The residents of

Tensaw and Tombigbee had been on edge since the previous summer, following a spate of settler murders by Creek militants who opposed the civilization agenda of Hawkins and his Creek allies. Those militants were loosely allied with Tecumseh and his brother Tenskwatawa, Shawnee leaders who called for resistance to American encroachment through a pan-Indian military alliance across the west from the Great Lakes to the Gulf, and through a cultural and spiritual revival. The declaration of war against Britain in June 1812 heightened tensions, as everyone looked to see if the Creeks would follow Tecumseh's lead and join the British in common cause against the Americans. Andrew Jackson, angered at the slaughter of two families by Creeks on Tennessee's Duck River, blamed Tecumseh: "That incendiary, the emissary of the *Prophet,* who is himself the tool of England, has caused our frontier to be stained with blood." He begged Tennessee's governor, Willie Blount, for permission to lead the militia south, since the frontiersmen "burn to carry fire and sword to the heart of the Creek Nation, and to learn these wretches in their own Towns and villages what it is to massacre Women and Children at a moment of profound peace."[2]

Those anxieties deepened in the spring of 1813 as Creek country plunged into civil war. The Red Sticks focused on attacking their enemies within Creek towns, but rumors that the British or Spanish would begin arming the militants intensified fears that the American settlements would be the next target. When a party of Red Sticks traveled to Pensacola in July seeking guns and ammunition from West Florida's governor, those fears seemed to be confirmed. Tensaw militiamen, both white and métis, sought a preemptive strike and intercepted the Creeks at Burnt Corn Creek on the path back to the Upper Towns. The brief skirmish left dead on both sides but the Red Sticks claimed victory by routing the much larger militia forces, leaving the settlers more anxious than ever as they waited in makeshift forts all along the Tensaw and Tombigbee Rivers.

The divisive tensions and antagonisms of the Creek civil war shifted to Tensaw after the battle at Burnt Corn Creek. Even here the blurred lines of Alabama's southwestern frontier seemed to sharpen divisions. Many of the Red Sticks viewed the Little River settlement as a wayward "daughter" community that had broken away from the traditional talwas and aligned itself too closely with American interests. Clan and kinship ties bound many of the métis at Little River to the Red Sticks. William Weatherford, for example, was one militant leader who was very familiar with the Little River Creeks since he had spent time among them when visiting a number of his relatives. Those connections intensified the sense of betrayal. Burnt Corn Creek confirmed the suspicions of the Red Sticks; the Tensaw métis had thrown their lot in with the Americans and needed to be punished. In town after town along the Coosa, Tallapoosa, and Alabama Rivers, warriors danced their war dances and drank their purifying tea to prepare for battle before setting out on different paths toward Tensaw, with plans to gather before striking back against those who had betrayed them.

As August wore on without an attack, fear gave way to complacency among the refugees at Fort Mims. Those accustomed to the heightened sense of vulnerability that came with living on isolated farms must have been reassured by the strong picket walls of the stockade and the presence of both the Tensaw militiamen and the Mississippi Volunteers. Who could imagine that the Creeks would assault such a formidable fort? Some began to venture out to attend to chores or to visit family and friends who, in the panic of the rumors earlier in the summer, had fled to other makeshift forts in the Tensaw and Tombigbee. Imagine the relief of escaping, even just for a few hours, the noise and chaos generated by the four hundred people crowded together behind the stockade walls.

Those forays brought troubling reports of large numbers of Creeks gathering in the vicinity of Fort Mims. Zachariah McGirth sent three of his slaves up the Alabama River to his plantation to gather ripe corn from the fields for the hungry refugees. Red Sticks captured the men, but although one escaped and rushed back to raise the alarm, the commander of the Mississippi Volunteers, Major Daniel Beasley, did not believe him. That pattern continued through the last week of August, as various slaves and métis Creeks reported sightings of the militants. Major Beasley wrote to the Mississippi Volunteers' General Ferdinand Claiborne about "a false alarm" raised by "two negro boys belonging to Mr. Randon" who had left the fort to tend to some cattle and said "they Saw a great number of Indians Painted, running and hallooing."[3] Beasley again refused to believe the story and had one of the slaves whipped for spreading rumors.

It is hard to understand why Beasley discounted the Red Stick sightings. Perhaps the fact that he was an outsider on the Tensaw borderlands played a role. He was born and raised in Virginia but had lived for the past ten years near Natchez, working as a sheriff and jailer. That part of the Mississippi Territory was dominated by cotton plantations and had been for some time, and it was a place of sharper racial lines and tighter control over slaves. He was less familiar with the frontier world of mixed races and of slaves whose work herding cattle or hunting or collecting timber allowed a bit more freedom to roam the delta lands. Beasley mistrusted the motives of the métis Creeks and the slaves at Fort Mims. But he also likely fell prey to overconfidence in the fortifications and in his soldiers, and dismissed an enemy that he thought of as raiders and not a formidable military force.

The refugees and soldiers at Fort Mims began the morning of August 30 in familiar ways, unaware that 750 Red Stick warriors hid in the nearby woods. A group of women, including Peggy Bailey, Dixon's sister, took washing to nearby Boatyard Lake. Zachariah McGirth and two of his slaves went down to the Alabama River to prepare his flatboat for a trip to his plantation to bring back corn and pumpkins, while Peter Durant and Viney Randon, two teenage métis, slipped away to pick wild grapes on an island in the river. The enslaved boy owned by Viney's father, the one who had been whipped the day before for trying to raise an alarm, left the fort with a companion to tend to his master's cattle. Once again, they spied Indians. Fearing a second whipping, Randon's slave refused to return to Fort Mims and instead ran to another fortified house in the vicinity. His friend, a slave owned by Josiah Fletcher, went back to report what they had seen. Even that warning had an air of familiarity about it, as did Major Beasley's reaction. He scoffed and ordered the slave boy whipped, despite Fletcher's protests. One final alarm was rung when James Cornells, Zachariah McGirth's brother-in-law, rode up to the fort to warn of his having seen a group of Red Sticks, only to depart in disgust when Beasley dismissed his account. So the warriors waited in the woods on that ordinary day at Fort Mims, waited as soldiers tied the boy to a post to prepare for his whipping and the rest of the inhabitants went about their business. The sentry at the eastern wall, busy watching a card game, seemed not to care that the gate was open.

The paths to that August morning at Fort Mims were long and complex but they had converged two years earlier in Tuckabatchee when two men came to speak before the Creek National Council. Several thousand people had gathered in that town on the Tallapoosa River in September 1811, mostly Creeks but also a scattering of frontier residents: Choctaws, Cherokees, Americans, and Africans. One of the visiting speakers was Benjamin Hawkins, a familiar figure at the National Council meetings and thus no particular draw to the throngs in attendance. The other visitor had come from further away, and it was he who stirred the most excitement among the spectators. Tecumseh, the Shawnee leader, had traveled from Indiana Territory to the South to recruit supporters for a pan-Indian alliance of tribes. With him were fifteen warriors and a religious prophet named Seekaboo, a proselytizer in the movement of cultural and spiritual revival initiated by Tecumseh's brother, Tenskwatawa. Tecumseh had not had much luck gathering support among the Choctaws or Chickasaws but he hoped things would be different in Tuckabatchee. This was an ancestral home-coming of sorts; his parents had grown up in Shawnee refugee communities among the Upper Creek towns before moving north beyond the Ohio River at the time of the Seven Years' War. Some suggested that his mother might even have had Creek blood. The two speakers arrived in Tuckabatchee at a time of economic hardship and division, when an increasing number of Creeks were growing skeptical of the benefits of economic progress promised by the civilization policy and angry about the loss of political autonomy.[4]

Hawkins came before the National Council in 1811 to talk about roads, a topic fraught with tension. The federal government had long been intent on connecting the eastern states and Tennessee and Kentucky to American settlements in the Southwest, with an eye toward improving communication and promoting settlement. Travelers had relied on Indian paths through Alabama because bushwhacking, as historian John C. Hall puts it, "was likely to lead one into an impassable hell of beaver ponds, bogs, sloughs, precipitous cliffs . . . back-swamps, canebrakes, gum ponds, cypress domes, pine barrens, alligator holes and briar patches."[5] But wagons needed roads, not paths, and the government needed Indian approval to build those roads through their territories. That took diplomatic work. In 1805 Creek leaders had agreed to allow the construction of a postal road that came to be known as the Federal Road. The path, measuring four to six feet wide, generally followed an old Indian trail, passing the Chattahoochee near Coweta and continuing on to New Orleans via Fort Stoddert. Now Hawkins was back making new demands for roads before the skeptical members of the National Council.[6]

The Federal Road alarmed many Creeks since it encapsulated so many of the troubling changes transforming their society at the turn of the century. First and foremost, the road facilitated the relentless flow of settlers through Creek country. Benjamin Hawkins reported that about 800 people traveled through Creek lands along a variety of trails in the winter of 1801–2, but during the months between October 1811 and the following March, 3,700 people passed along the Federal Road. Those travelers brought trouble by providing tempting targets for young warriors intent on harassment or theft, or, at times, by getting into fights or stealing from the Creeks themselves. Even peaceful migrants who managed to pass through Creek territory to Tensaw, the Alabama forks, or Natchez without conflict proved unsettling, as they were reminders of the rapid transformation of the southwestern frontier. The Creeks did not have to read the petition sent to Congress by the residents of Washington County in 1809 asking for their own territorial government—the one that promised "a chain of settlements extending thro a country, now an almost unexplored wilderness," connecting "together the state of new-hampshire and the Territory of Orleans"—to understand the American vision of the future. They had only to watch the men, women, and children—on foot, on horseback, or in wagons— pass by along the Federal Road. And where did the Creeks fit in that imagined future? The petitioners answered that question. With "a strong settlement between Georgia and the Mississippi . . . the Indian nations themselves, would be obliged to adopt civilized habits, or to abandon their country."[7]

The fact that some Creeks seemed ready to embrace that future shook their society more deeply than did the settlers, who were, after all, passing through. Here too the Federal Road came to embody more general divisions and corruptions within Creek society. Hawkins had solidified his authority as agent by distributing cash gifts and agricultural tools to favored headmen who would support his civilizing mission in the National Council. Those micos alienated other Creeks by sharing their gifts with relatives and supporters rather than following the traditional custom of distributing goods widely through their communities.[8] The Federal Road also seemed to many to be a corrupting influence. The headmen who granted permission for the postal road in 1805 in the Treaty of Washington immediately faced the withering criticism of their people. The treaty stipulated that taverns and ferries were to be operated by Creek men, and at least two of the signers, William McIntosh and Alexander Cornells, one of Benjamin Hawkins's assistants, stood to gain from that provision. Cornells's farm near the Tallapoosa River stood next to the proposed route and could serve as a tavern, and McIntosh had made plans to operate a ferry across the Chattahoochee where the road crossed near Coweta.[9]

Hawkins was back before the National Council meeting in Tuckabatchee in 1811 because administration officials were worried about the vulnerabilities of the Gulf frontier as tensions with Great Britain grew. The old Federal Road had limitations. If postal riders had difficulty fording the rivers and navigating the swampy muck along the route, what hope would troops have of using the road to mobilize in the event of war? Widening the road and building more bridges over the deeper rivers and log causeways through the swamps would allow mounted soldiers and wagons loaded with provisions to reach Fort Stoddert and New Orleans and the points in between more rapidly. The first of Hawkins's demands, then, was the improvement of the Federal Road. The National Council leaders were reluctant to acquiesce, knowing full well that a wider road with better bridges would only mean more and more American families traversing their land. But it was Hawkins's request for a road from the eastern Tennessee Valley to the Coosa River and free passage down that river and the Alabama to the Gulf that alarmed the Creeks the most. The previous year, Secretary of War William Eustis had sent General Edmund Gaines with a party of soldiers from Fort Saint Stephens to survey routes, only to have Creek warriors intercept them and force their return to the Tombigbee. President Madison responded with a message telling the Creeks that "good pathways and roads are equally useful to his white and to his Red Children. Rivers & Water courses are made by the Great Spirit to be used by the Nations to and thro' which they run." Dropping the flowery language, Madison revealed the bottom line: Tennesseans "have to go a great way to carry their produce and to bring home necessaries from the sea," and they required a direct route to the Gulf.[10] The settlement, prosperity, and security of the southwestern frontier necessitated transportation routes through Indian land. But the prospect of both migrants and East Tennessee farmers transporting their agricultural goods along a road and on the rivers that passed through many Upper Creek communities was too much to tolerate. Headmen at the National Council meeting in 1811 agreed that allowing that would prove too stark a violation of their territorial sovereignty.

Hawkins's response laid bare the erosion of Creek autonomy. He told the headmen that while he would like their cooperation, the government had decided that the Federal Road would be widened and the new road from the Tennessee Valley would be built whether they agreed or not. "The period has now arrived when the white people must have roads to market and for traveling wherever they choose to go," he told the Council.[11] Indeed, troops had already begun the repair work on the Federal Road a couple of months earlier. Hawkins tried to sweeten the bitter pill with promises of the usual implements of civilization: a thousand spinning wheels and a thousand pairs of cotton cards for Creek women and iron farming tools for the men. William McIntosh, Alexander Cornells, and some other headmen whose power stemmed from their close relationship with Hawkins reluctantly accepted, while others at the council meeting seethed with resentment.[12]

Tecumseh sought to channel that anger into an alliance with the Creeks. He spoke to the council after Hawkins had left and discussed his efforts to unite the Indians of the West from the Great Lakes to the Gulf of Mexico to prevent any further land cessions, and most likely mentioned the support provided by the British. But those military and political goals were embedded in the spiritual movement begun by his brother, Tenskwatawa, several years earlier. Two years after the Tuckabatchee council, Benjamin Hawkins wrote down a secondhand account of a portion of Tecumseh's speech: "Kill the old chiefs, friends to peace; kill the cattle, the hogs, and fowls; do not work, destroy the wheels and looms, throw away your ploughs, and every thing used by the Americans. Sing 'the song of the Indians of the northern lakes and dance their dance.' Shake your war clubs, shake yourselves; you will frighten the Americans."[13]

Tecumseh took aim at the livestock and tools of Hawkins's civilization program and at the "old chiefs" who had failed to stand up to the Creek agent. But his was not simply a message of rejection; the Shawnee leader was promoting Tenskwatawa's movement by calling on those assembled to adopt the song and dance of the Great Lakes Indians. Those were important rituals of purification designed to spark a cultural and spiritual revival, signaling a deeper resistance to acculturation.

Creek cosmology emphasized the importance of maintaining balance through purifying rituals. The Creeks drank the emetic "black drink" before holding councils, for example, and cleansed their bodies and spirits before and after battle. The goal was to rid themselves of corruptions that could upset the natural balance of life. For many Creeks, the erosion of traditional customs over the past decades marked an imbalance that proved demoralizing. The decline of the deerskin economy, the burdensome debt, the loss of hunting territory, the relentless drumbeat of civilization, the growing power of Hawkins over the chiefs of the National Council, the Federal Road, and the pursuit of new economic opportunities by some Creek families—all were "corruptions" that angered many. Those tensions existed before Tecumseh came to Tuckabatchee. But his articulation of his brother's movement placed those resentments, anxieties, and tensions within a sacred context and promised a path toward purification.

Over the next month or so Tecumseh and Seekaboo, Tenskwatawa's emissary, spoke at one Upper Creek town after another about the benefits of political alliances and spiritual revival. A comet blazed in the night sky during the period of Tecumseh's visit, and since his Shawnee name meant "shooting star," that celestial display seemed to be a sign of supernatural blessing. Not all were impressed, however. The Lower Creeks overwhelmingly dismissed talk of alliances with the northern Indians, as did some of the chiefs of the Upper Creeks, especially those with the closest connections to Hawkins. But Tecumseh's talk of unity and Seekaboo's message of cultural revitalization drew many of the Upper Town Creeks, particularly those of Alabama ancestry. The Shawnees left later that fall of 1811, but Seekaboo stayed behind to continue proselytizing. One headman, Little Warrior, and some of his men returned with Tecumseh on his journey home, and by the end of 1812, as fighting on the northwestern frontier broke out, others traveled north until as many as two hundred Creek warriors had joined the Shawnees.[14]

Some reported that, before he departed, Tecumseh told the Creeks that he would demonstrate his power by climbing the highest mountain and stamping his foot three times to make the earth shake. Late that fall and winter, the New Madrid earthquakes shook large portions of the Midwest and South with a series of violent tremors.[15] Margaret Eades was traveling with her family from Georgia to settle western lands when she experienced the quake, a once-in-a-lifetime event that she remembered clearly, years later, when she wrote her memoir. She and her family were already on edge since they had passed into Creek country. The Cherokees they had encountered earlier had been friendly, but now they "could see the terrible hatred" in the eyes of Creeks they passed, and as a precaution they circled their wagons at night with the men keeping guard. "One night after a fearful day," she wrote, "the Indians had followed us for miles, we camped in an old field. Just as supper was announced, a most terrific earthquake took place, the horses all broke loose, the wagon chains jingled, and every face was pale with fear and horror." Margaret recalled that "the next day some of the Indians came to us, and said it was Tecumseh stamped his foot for war."[16]

Whether awed by Tecumseh's supposed power to make the earth shake or simply by the clarity of Seekaboo's message in a time of tension and demoralization, Creeks gravitated toward the nativist movement. They came to be known as Red Sticks because of their painted war clubs. Some asserted their own supernatural powers as prophets, building on traditional practices of conjuring and communing with the spirit world through trances. One of them, Captain Isaacs, claimed to be able to spend days at the bottoms of rivers speaking with a serpent to learn "future events and all other things necessary for a man to know in his life." Shaking became associated with Red Stick prophets. Kasita Hadjo, or High-Head Jim, shook hands with Sam Moniac, a métis Creek from Tensaw who was skeptical of the prophetic movement, "and immediately began to tremble and jerk in every part of his frame, and the very calves of his legs would be convulsed, and he would get entirely out of breath with agitation."[17] The shaking, they believed, was in reaction to the presence of impurities, whether a nonbeliever like Moniac or simply a person who had consumed something like salt pork or beef, forbidden products associated with Americans. Most who aligned with the Red Sticks claimed no special powers but were drawn by the promise of a resurrection of old traditions. Many already led lives distant from white men's ways and joined to affirm their hostility toward the civilization program and their suspicion of Hawkins's favorite chiefs, and simply committed to avoiding raising livestock or drinking alcohol.[18]

The broad contours of the division within Creek society were clear in 1812, but the details were more complex. The Red Stick Creeks tended to live in the Upper Towns and be more traditional in their economic practices and gender roles. Those who eschewed the movement tended to live in closer proximity to the American frontiers and to be more immersed in American ways of life. They included Lower Town Creeks and especially the Tensaw Creeks and métis families who herded livestock and planted cotton, often using slave labor, and traded among and socialized with their white neighbors. But the categories were not always neatly binary, as William Weatherford's family ties illustrated. Despite a close connection with his Tensaw relatives and his own economic pursuits, Weatherford became a leader of the Red Stick faction. Unlike his brother David Tate, who was educated at schools in Philadelphia and Scotland, William remained deeply rooted in Creek culture and was committed to traditional religious values. His belief system determined his path when it came time to choose sides. Alabama's frontier was a muddled place where residents held complex identities, but the emerging civil war forced sharper divisions.[19]

The roots of that civil war were deep but the catalyst was the heavy-handed response by Hawkins's allies within the National Council to a series of murders in 1812–13. It was no coincidence that the murders focused on travelers: either Creeks moving through American settlements or white settlers journeying through Creek lands. The frontier borders between settler and Indian country were permeable. That often resulted in connections, both social and economic, but in the increasingly tense atmosphere of 1812–13, as war broke out with Great Britain, travel could prove dangerous.

The headmen opposed to the construction and widening of the Federal Road often predicted violence between angry Creeks and settlers passing through, and that prediction came true. Thomas Meredith, an elderly man traveling with his extended family and slaves from South Carolina to settle in Mississippi in March 1812, was killed at Pinchona Creek by "an old chief" named Maumouth "who appeared to be in liquor," according to reports Hawkins received.[20] Margaret Austill remembered that her family encountered Creek men who "demanded toll a high price for every soul that crossed a bridge," and that when the settlers refused and instead "would make their negroes cut trees and make a bridge," the warriors "would threaten us with death."[21] That might have been what happened to Thomas Meredith when he encountered Maumouth. A short time later, a former Georgia legislator named Lott was killed on the Federal Road in present-day Macon County.

Violence also broke out when Creeks traveled through white settlements. In May 1812 Hillabee Hadjo was leading a small group of four Creek warriors back south after visiting with Tecumseh's Shawnees when they attacked members of the Manley and Crawley families on the Duck River on Tennessee's frontier. Jesse Manley and John Crawley were away but the Creek warriors killed and scalped five children and two adults and took Martha Crawley captive. Mrs. Manley, despite being "shot in the knee and shot through the jaws" and "scalped and arrows left in her," survived for some hours before succumbing and was able to provide some details of the attack. She claimed that the attackers grabbed her newborn baby and swung him against the wall, and that when her older son tried to run away, he "was overtaken by the Indian dogs, that they danced around him and then killed him, and killed the rest of her family." The Creeks took Martha Crawley to Tuscaloosa on the falls of the Black Warrior River. By June rumors of the captive had reached George Gaines, the factor of the Choctaw Trading House in Saint Stephens, and he sent Tandy Walker, a blacksmith who had lived for many years in Creek country, to rescue her. When he returned with Martha, Gaines noted that "she was in bad health, her mind a good deal impaired by her suffering; her limbs and feet were still in a wounded condition, caused by the brush, briars, etc., she was forced to walk through" during her captivity. Gaines's wife, Ann, took charge of her care and after a few weeks she was able to return home to Tennessee.[22]

The murders on the Duck River angered and scared settlers on the Tennessee frontier. Lurid stories about Martha Crawley's captivity circulated freely in the absence of firm information about her fate, including the assertion in the *Nashville Clarion* in July that "a half-breed Cherokee" informed the newspaper that "she has been severely whipped, exhibited naked in circles of warriors, who danced around her; and that at present she is at Tuckabatchee, beating meal for the family to whom she belongs."[23] The outrage spilled over into passionate calls for retaliation. Andrew Jackson was in Georgia when the attack occurred but upon his return to Tennessee he was quick to express his anger with the murder of "our innocent, wifes and little babes." War had just been declared against Britain, and like most on the frontier at this time, Jackson had "no doubt" that the Creek warriors were "urged on by British agents." The time was right to strike, he told Governor Blount, since "the sooner the[y] can be attacked, the less will be their resistance, and the fewer will be the nations or tribes that we will have to war with." He proposed that they "march into the creek na-

tion [and] demand the perpetrators, at the Point of the Bayonet—if refused—
that we make reprisals—and lay their Town in ashes."[24]

War did not break out, but Hawkins, as the government agent among the
Creeks, pushed hard to have the offenders responsible for all of those murders punished. Although frontiersmen like Jackson never trusted Hawkins and
saw him as too close an ally of the Creeks, the agent was rigorous in his insistence that the provisions of the Treaty of 1790 be upheld. Alexander McGillivray had consolidated some of his power through the National Council and a
group of warriors who acted as a police force, and Hawkins, once named agent,
continued that practice. In response to the murders in the spring of 1812 he ordered the National Council to send policing parties in pursuit of the offenders.
Lott's murderer "had fled to the white town" of Tallassee, according to Hawkins,
and had sat himself down on the honored seat of Hopoithle Mico "as a sanctuary." The square grounds of Creek towns, especially of white towns, often were
places of refuge for those accused of crimes, places removed from violence. But
Hawkins was told that "the leader of the armed party pursued and shot him on
the seat, through the head and body." The Creek police found Hillabee Hadjo in
the council house of Hickory Ground. After shooting him they tossed his body
into the Coosa River. By the end of August 1812, nine Creeks involved in the
spate of murders had been executed by the National Council's police.[25]

The relentless pressure that Hawkins put on the council to kill the murderers,
and the old chiefs' acquiescence, angered many Creeks who had not been sympathetic to the Red Stick movement. The executions represented a further cor-
ruption of traditional ways. White towns were supposed to be sanctuaries, not
places of summary judgment. Clan leaders, not a police force under the thinly
veiled command of the Creek agent, were supposed to punish violators of laws.
As historian Gregory Dowd points out, the executions were not "ritualized affairs designed to awe the public" or "performances dramatizing state power and
justice," but "surprise attacks ... whose very lack of ritual or order revealed the
council's weakness more than its strength." The retaliatory actions encouraged
by Hawkins, like his insistence on the new road from East Tennessee to the Alabama River, was a stark reminder that Creek autonomy was fast slipping away.[26]

Early in the spring of 1813 another frontier outrage prompted yet more punishment. Little Warrior, the Creek leader who had traveled north with Tecumseh after the Tuckabatchee meeting, was returning south after fighting with the
Shawnees in the Great Lakes region. He and his party of warriors, inspired perhaps by rumors that the Creeks had joined in the war against the Americans,
killed and mutilated seven white settlers near the mouth of the Ohio River.

They then continued on to Tuckabatchee, where Little Warrior spoke out in favor of war in council with other Creek headmen. They rejected his pleas and, according to Hawkins, told Little Warrior "to leave the council house as a man unworthy to have a seat in it."[27] Within weeks the National Council had raised a large force of warriors from both Upper and Lower Creek towns to find and execute Little Warrior and his compatriots. The militants had barricaded themselves in a house at Hickory Ground, and when they discovered that they had been spotted they "gave the war whoop, began their war dance, and fired on the warriors" who had come to apprehend them. The house was set on fire, driving some out. Two suffering from the smoke crawled from the burning house pleading for help and were "put to death with tomahawks." Others ran and were overtaken and killed, but Little Warrior, while wounded, managed to escape. Captain Isaacs, the Creek prophet who earlier had joined Tenskwatawa's spiritual movement, had shifted to the old chiefs' corner. He, along with James Cornells and David Tate, métis Creeks from the Tensaw region, led the search party and tracked Little Warrior to a nearby swamp, "decoyed him out, and put him to death."[28]

The killing of Little Warrior and his followers triggered the Creek civil war. Red Stick militants first struck back against those directly responsible by attacking Captain Isaacs's home. Once commanding great authority as a prophet, Captain Isaacs now was denounced as a witch deserving of death. Although he managed to escape, two of his allies were killed and his house was burned to the ground. Creeks began choosing sides. Most of the Lower Towns joined forces with the old chiefs who had now been labeled the "peace" faction, while the Upper Town residents divided. The Alabamas overwhelmingly sided with the militant Red Sticks while the Abihkas remained loyal to the National Council. A number of towns split, sometimes with deadly results. In Okfuskee, militants killed five headmen who resisted their call to join Tecumseh's war against the Americans. Everywhere, the Red Sticks slaughtered cattle and left their bodies on the ground to rot. Witnesses reported seeing militants with severed cow tails lashed to their arms, often painted red, trophies of their assault on the corrupting influence of acculturation.[29]

Upper Creeks allied with the peace faction scrambled to find refuge. Some fled to the Chattahoochee River communities or to Benjamin Hawkins's agency on the Flint River in Georgia. Others stayed in the region and gathered at Tuckabatchee, home of Hawkins's ally Big Warrior (or Tustanagee Thlucco) and the site of the National Council meetings. There they built a picket stockade around the town to protect as many as three thousand people, only six hundred of whom were warriors, while a large force of militants laid siege. Corn was ripening in the town's fields that July but the women could not go out to harvest it without being attacked, and hunger spread in Tuckabatchee. Facing starvation, Big Warrior appealed to General James Wilkinson for aid. The prospect of battle with the Americans convinced the Red Sticks to allow the town's residents to retreat to Coweta before they burned Tuckabatchee to the ground. Rumors spread that July about where the Red Sticks would strike next—Coweta, or Hawkins's agency, or the Tensaw and Tombigbee settlements—heightening anxieties in Indian, métis, and white communities alike.[30]

diff b/w 1800s & 1760s

Fifty years earlier a series of murders in Creek country also took place in the context of imperial war. On a single day in May 1760 warriors staged a coordinated attack, killing eleven traders in several Upper Creek towns. British officials in South Carolina and Georgia were quick to blame allies of a nativist Creek headman named Mortar who, like Tecumseh and Tenskwatawa, rejected European trade, and at the same time they believed that France, currently at war with Britain, was pulling the strings. But the outcome then was different. The diplomatic rituals of talks sent between Augusta and the Creek towns on the Coosa and Tallapoosa prevailed and no retaliatory punishments followed. Comparing the different reactions to those violent episodes reveals just how much the middle ground of Alabama's frontier had slipped away.

The relentless pressure of settlers and the federal government's expansionary thrust in the decades following the revolution had created an Indian world of compromised and ambiguous boundaries, sharpening both Creek antagonism and American reactions to atrocities. The murdered traders of 1760 had lived and worked in Creek towns that, while connected to the broader transatlantic world of trade, diplomacy, and war, were emphatically Indian. They had assumed risks by entering the extensive southeastern interior, far from the European settlements in Augusta, Pensacola, or Mobile, and that fact muted colonial responses to their deaths. The men, women, and children killed by the Creeks in 1812–13 had come to settle the interior. Meredith and Lott died on the Federal Road, the thread stitching together the far-flung communities on the southern frontier that many Creeks believed violated their territorial integrity. The Crawleys and Manleys and those anonymous settlers on the Ohio died at the hands of militants who perceived the entire West as Indian land and who were determined to drive away those who intruded. Those murders

sparked outrage because, far from being distant, American settlements surrounded and pressed hard against the boundaries of Creek country. Residents
with memories of the Creek and Chickamauga raids of the 1780s and 1790s
feared a renewal of hostilities and called for retaliation, confident that the decades of pioneering had honed the military power of their militias. Newspapers
and politicians in Tennessee and the Mississippi Territory amplified the anger
over the attacks and lobbied the federal government for support. The *Nashville
Clarion*, for example, responded to the Crawley-Manley murders by urging its
readers to "act as your forefathers, and at the point of the bayonet subdue or ex-
tirpate the savage foe."[31] Instead of messages of reconciliation passed between
colonial and Indian leaders along forest paths, letters traveled between federal,
state, and territorial officials, demanding justice.

Reconciliation in 1760 was built on the mutual dependence at the heart of
Indian-colonial relations. The majority of the Creeks wanted the guns, powder,
shot, and other goods provided out of the deerskin trade and could not afford to
alienate their trade partners. Headmen were quick to rein in those who had attacked the traders and to send word to Augusta and Charlestown that they still
shared one fire with the British. Georgia's governor worked within the framework of Indian diplomacy; he pretended to believe the familiar excuse that rash
young warriors had been to blame, and didn't insist on punishment. South Carolina's governor did not arrest Handsome Warrior when he rode to Charlestown
with a Cherokee scalp to make amends for killing the traders. In the midst of
war with France, the colonial authorities could not afford to antagonize the Indians and push them into closer alignment with their enemy, even as they suspected that the French lay behind the attacks. The potential for a French alliance gave the Creeks power, and the presence of Fort Toulouse in the heart of
Creek country gave substance to that British fear.

Indian diplomacy had disappeared by 1812. The Treaty of 1790 stipulated the
responsibility of the entire Creek nation for murders of Americans committed by individuals, and Benjamin Hawkins had power over the National Council. No amount of rhetorical dancing would absolve those who had killed the
settlers, and besides, who would make the effort? The decentralized nature of
Creek politics in 1760 gave headmen room to maneuver, but that had changed
in the early nineteenth century. The pressures of Hawkins's efforts to central-
ize his authority and further his civilizing mission through favored chiefs had
hardened divisions within Creek society, and that, in turn, escalated the violence. Red Stick militants might have rejected all things American, but those
headmen allied with Hawkins had little choice but to strike back at those ac-

cused of murder because their authority depended on American support. And so they sent police and warriors out to execute the militants, bringing their nation to the brink of civil war.

In 1760, then, the Creeks were able to manipulate British fears of an Indian-French alliance to bolster their negotiating power; war sharpened their ability to play both imperial powers off one another. But in 1812–13, war with Britain heightened American suspicion of Indian intentions without giving the Creeks any real advantages in terms of alliances or material support. Frontiersmen and politicians alike assumed that the British were manipulating the southern Indians, and the popularity of Tecumseh's pan-Indian movement among the Red Sticks gave that idea just enough plausibility. Vestiges of the imperial frontier lay primarily in the imaginations of Americans who feared that a British-Creek alliance threatened the vulnerable Gulf South and their own dreams of a southwestern empire.

The murders of 1812 presented opportunities that never existed in 1760. The killing of the traders decades earlier had disrupted the frontier order built on trade and imperial alliances, and leaders on both sides focused on restoring those ruptured relationships. The frontier of the early nineteenth century was rooted in the acquisition of land and the expansion of American power. An article in the *Nashville Clarion*, likely written by Andrew Jackson, anticipated the imminent occupation of Mobile and the rest of Florida by Americans and argued that "a part of the country inhabited by the Creeks will be indispensable" to "strengthen" those new settlements. Imagining "the moment when all the southern indians shall be pushed across the Mississippi," the author envisioned "a city, the emporium of a vast commerce," flourishing "on the spot where some huts, inhabited by lawless savages, now mark the junction of the Alabama and Tombigbee rivers." Why was it "a favorable moment" for "accomplishing a part of this great design"? Because "the crimes of this [Creek] nation have supplied us with a pretext for the dismemberment of their country."[32]

Settlers in the Tensaw and Tombigbee region were scared and panicky in the summer of 1813, "in a state of the utmost confusion and alarm," according to General Claiborne of the Mississippi Volunteers. They had fled to makeshift forts on the western side of the Tombigbee, "leaving behind them rich and highly cultivated farms, with immense crops & stocks of cattle."[33] Margaret Austill remembered the scene from her childhood many years later. When rumors of Creek war parties on the move reached her family's farm near the Tombigbee, they fled to Carney's Bluff on the river, where settlers were building a fort—"all hands, negroes and whites," working "with superhuman exertion": "When we arrived at the river it was a busy scene, men hard at work chopping and clearing a place for a Fort, women and children crying, no place to sit down, nothing to eat, all confusion and dismay, expecting every moment to be scalped and tomahawked." A week later, the fort was built and chaos had subsided. "The tents [were] all comfortable," Margaret remembered, and "the streets full of soldier boys drilling, drums beating, pipes playing, but no Indians yet."[34]

Jittery nerves encouraged altercations. Judge Harry Toulmin reported back in 1812 that the militia "acted as if they were anxious to bring on an Indian war." Colonel James Caller of the Washington County militia had sent out rangers "without any occasion,—& whose avowed design is to murder indians." One "party of indians were wantonly & without provocation fired upon by others,—and some peacable Choctaws were almost beaten to death in Washing[n] County." Toulmin worried that "such things will excite jealousies if not resentments & vengeance, and the Indians will be induced by these to listen to the overtures of the Spaniards."[35]

Fears that Spanish officials were recruiting Creek allies on behalf of the British had spread by 1813, and Pensacola, the home of Forbes and Company, the trading firm formerly known as Panton, Leslie and Company, seemed a logical channel for the funneling of British arms and ammunition to Creek militants. When reports reached Tensaw in July 1813 that a party of Red Stick warriors had journeyed to that town, burning a few plantations of Little River métis along the way, those fears seemed confirmed. Colonel Caller mobilized six companies with about 150 militiamen and Dixon Bailey gathered thirty Tensaw Creeks to march east to prevent the Red Sticks from returning to their towns with guns and ammunition.

The Pensacola trip had not met the expectations of the Red Sticks. Led by the métis Peter McQueen and High-Head Jim, the party had hoped to acquire large supplies of guns, powder, and shot and had reason to think the Spanish might be obliging, despite Spain's neutrality in the ongoing war between the United States and Britain. They had heard that Britain was eager to arm its Indian allies in the South in preparation for an assault on the Gulf coast, and Spanish officials might be willing accomplices given West Florida's vulnerabilities. American forces had occupied Mobile in April, and West Florida's governor, Mateo González Manrique, was anxious to maintain the goodwill of the Creeks in the event of aggression against Pensacola. But hopes did not match reality.

The British were not ready to take the war to the South, the people of Pensacola were struggling to feed themselves, and the governor was not in a position to offer much. After three days of cajoling and threatening the governor, McQueen gave up and accepted only a small portion of what he had hoped to receive. The Red Stick party left Pensacola and headed north toward the Federal Road with barrels of flour and corn, blankets, a few heads of cattle, and about a thousand pounds each of gunpowder and shot.[36]

Caller and Bailey's militiamen intercepted the Red Sticks a few days' north of Pensacola where the Wolf Trail crossed Burnt Corn Creek. The militia caught sixty or so Creeks, including McQueen, High-Head Jim, and Josiah Francis, resting and eating a midday meal, and the surprised warriors fled after a brief skirmish. Some of the militia and Tensaw Creeks pursued the Red Sticks but most stayed behind to rummage through the goods carried by the packhorses and to celebrate their easy victory. Caller's militia was poorly trained since their usual musters were devoted more to drinking than to drilling. McQueen and the other leaders circled their warriors back around through the woods and staged a counterattack, sending most of the militia running for their lives. Only a few, including Dixon Bailey, stood their ground and fought back before finally being repulsed. Two militiamen were killed at the battle of Burnt Corn Creek and fifteen were wounded, while the Red Stick contingent lost ten to twelve. Caller's horse fled during the melee and he ended up wandering in the piney woods of South Alabama for fifteen days before being found.[37]

The skirmish at Burnt Corn Creek was a turning point. The Red Stick warriors were at once proud of their ability to defeat a militia that was three times as large as their forces and angry at their losses, which included a portion of their supplies. The target of their ire was the Tensaw métis who had played a prominent role in the battle, especially Dixon Bailey. After the battle he had led a small group of warriors deep into Creek country to burn and loot Red Stick plantations, including McQueen's. Instead of attacking Coweta next, to begin cleansing the Lower Creek towns of the pro-American faction, the Red Sticks shifted their attention west to the Tensaw Creeks and their settler allies.[38]

The refugees at Fort Mims celebrated the "victory" at Burnt Corn Creek even as they braced for retaliation. The militia unit, so undisciplined in battle, stayed true to form and scattered, while Caller, after being rescued from the woods, went back to Saint Stephens. Bailey returned to Fort Mims a hero and was promptly elected captain of the Tensaw militia. But some of the other most prominent local métis, like Sam Moniac and David Tate, did not come to the fort; instead they left to attend to business elsewhere. Both men seemed to share some sympathies with the Red Stick cause even as they tried to stay neutral in the civil war, and they probably did not want to kill or be killed in battle against fellow Creeks.[39]

The large force of about a thousand Red Stick warriors moving southwest along different paths took advantage of the settlers' panic and helped themselves to the corn and pumpkins ripening in the abandoned fields. They gathered together, and one party of about 200 warriors split off to travel to the settlements in the fork of the Tombigbee and Alabama Rivers while the rest, numbering about 750, moved toward Little River and Fort Mims. William Weatherford and Josiah Francis, both métis with connections to the Tensaw Creeks, led the war party. Weatherford had gathered intelligence of the fort's defenses from some captured slaves, but the night before the scheduled attack he decided to check for himself. Leaving the campsite he snuck up to the walls of the stockade and discovered that the loopholes through which the fort's defenders could shoot were only four feet high. That information, plus the obvious lack of vigilance that allowed him to approach during the night, gave him his plan of attack. The warriors would rush the fort without firing a shot in order to take command of the portholes and force their way inside. Paddy Walsh, an Alabama métis who served the Red Stick movement as a prophet, added a spiritual element to the tactics. One part, Gregory Waselkov notes, involved Walsh running "around the fort three times, after which the Redsticks could handily slay all within with their knives and war clubs, 'as all the men would be in a state of torpitude and paralised.'"[40]

Fort Mims's defenders were caught off guard when the assault began around noon on August 30. The warriors sprinted across the open ground and were within thirty feet of the walls before the sentry near the open east gate, who was preoccupied watching a card game, spotted them and raised the alarm. Most of the Mississippi Volunteers were in that part of the fort and tried unsuccessfully to get the gate closed. Almost half of them, including Major Beasley, were killed within minutes as Red Sticks poured into the fort. Other warriors took command of the portholes and began firing into the compound, creating a deadly fusillade that forced those inside to seek shelter in the buildings. One group gained control of the blockhouse on the western side and began taking axes to the inner gate and wall that barred their entrance to the interior of the fort. An enslaved African man named Siras, or Cyrus, who had been staying at Mims's plantation, aided the Red Sticks in that effort.

The initial onslaught overwhelmed the defenders, but as time went on they began to regroup and inflict serious damage on the attacking Red Sticks. Dixon

Bailey gathered the Tensaw militiamen together on the north side of the stockade and they poured bullets into their Creek enemies. After two hours of battle the Red Sticks retreated for a time to confer and decide how to proceed. Their casualties troubled some; Paddy Walsh had promised that the white man's weapons could not harm them. He himself was wounded as he ran around the fort a third time. But they abandoned thoughts of retreating and decided to renew the attack, while Weatherford slipped away to his brother's Little River plantation to ensure the safety of Tate's slaves.

With the second assault, the Red Sticks overwhelmed Fort Mims. They set fire to the buildings and killed those retreating from the flames and smoke. Some of those inside the fort managed to pry loose several of the pickets, squeezed through, and ran toward safety in the woods. But most of the refugees and militiamen died. Precise figures are hard to come by since it would be just over a week before General Claiborne sent soldiers of the Mississippi Volunteers to inspect the site, and three weeks before they returned to bury the dead. During the first visit, Captain Uriah Blue and Major Joseph Kennedy reported seeing "Indians, Negroes, men, women and children in one promiscuous ruin,"[41] and the bodies partially consumed by fire, dismembered by the Red Sticks, or torn up by animals in the intervening days made it very difficult to get an accurate count. The burial party interned 247 men, women, and children, none of them identified as enemy Red Sticks. Scholars agree that about a hundred captives were taken, primarily African slaves and métis women and children, and about fifty people managed to escape the fort. The Red Sticks suffered high casualties as well, with approximately one hundred killed during the battle.[42]

Word of the attack filtered out quickly. Although Judge Toulmin reported on August 30 that "the smoke of burning houses" in Tensaw could be seen at Fort Stoddert,[43] it was not until refugees began straggling into the fort that the enormity of the attack registered. The first were those lucky few who had left Fort Mims the morning of the battle, such as Peter Durant and Viney Randon, who were picking grapes, and the group of women doing wash down at the lake. But they did not know the fate of those who remained behind. Zachariah McGirth and his two slaves had heard the gunfire from their flatboat a couple of miles up the Alabama River and were the first to arrive after the battle later that night. There they saw their comrades, "some still bleeding, all scalped & mutilated, and smoked with fire," but they could not find McGirth's wife, Vicey, or his children. No one commented on whether his enslaved companions also searched in vain for loved ones they had lost. The three men made their way to Fort Stoddert to add their tale to the deadly accounts already collected.[44]

Panic descended on the delta region and north to the forks of the Alabama and Tombigbee Rivers. Judge Toulmin captured some of the chaotic scene in a long letter sent on September 7 from Mobile to the *Raleigh Register*, later reprinted in Baltimore's *Weekly Register*. The gruesome details and the fear of further attacks drove hundreds to flee, "and such was the hurry of a flight conducted almost at midnight, that few took anything with them." Some "fled by land in the darkness of the night," while others "pushed off by water," and "the river was strewed with boats from fort Stoddert to Mobile." Toulmin seems to have counted himself among the refugees when he wrote that "we have abandoned our houses, our crops and our herds, and wherever the Indians have appeared, they have involved the whole within their reach in one scene of desolation."[45] Rumors of impending attack spread to faraway Madison County, causing "a large majority of the population of that once flourishing settlement to abandon their farms," according to the governor of Tennessee.[46]

Over the next few weeks, more settlers began flowing south from the Tensaw and Tombigbee regions, until Mobile's population of five hundred had swelled by several thousand hungry and homeless people. Harvest time was approaching and there were plenty of crops in the fields, but few dared confront the roving bands of Red Sticks who ranged up and down the delta land and the forks gathering corn and slaughtering livestock. General Claiborne, who had been at a fortified house near Saint Stephens at the time of the attack on Fort Mims, reflected on his own pioneering days in Ohio, when settlers took "their guns in their hands" to work in the fields. Alabama's settlers lacked that fortitude, he lamented: "Never in my life did I see a Country given up without a struggle for it before. . . . Here are the finest crops my eyes ever beheld . . . immence stocks, negros and other property, abandoned by their owners almost on the first alarm."[47] After the war residents of Tensaw and Tombigbee entered claims for compensation from the federal government and listed losses totaling 5,400 cattle, almost half as many hogs, eight thousand bushels of corn, and fifty-five slaves.[48]

The loss of those enslaved laborers in particular stirred fears. Some might have taken advantage of the chaos and run away, but the Red Sticks captured many and were quick to recognize the value of slaves in contradictory ways. They could be treated as contraband and sold in Pensacola for needed supplies, but they also could be allies in the fight against the Americans. The specter of an Indian-slave alliance hung over the Gulf coast after the battle of Fort Mims, especially as rumors of the approach of five hundred British and Spanish troops swirled. During the revolution the British had sought Indian support and had enticed slaves to run away, and they had every incentive to mobilize Indian and African forces once again in 1813. But the Red Sticks were reluctant to embrace the opportunity to forge connections with the enslaved residents of the borderlands. While a few Africans joined their cause, the Creeks generally mistrusted enslaved men; they executed a number captured at Fort Mims even as they kept enslaved women and children.[49]

As word of the tragedy at Fort Mims spread, first in rumors and reports and then in newspaper accounts, shocked Americans confronted lurid details of Indian savagery that sparked cries for vengeance. Those descriptions both reflected and intensified the trauma felt by the settlers of Tensaw and Tombigbee. The soldiers sent by Claiborne about a week later to inspect the site set the tone. Major Kennedy described one spot at the fort where they "found forty five men, women and children in one heap, they were stripped of their clothes without distinction of Age or sex, all were scalped, and the females of every age were most barbarously and Savage like butchered, in a manner which neither decency nor language can convey." The soldiers went on to report that "women pregnant were cut open and their childrens heads Tomahawked."[50] The burial party that came a couple of weeks later echoed the general description of mutilation, scalping, and nudity and again singled out women for particularly graphic detail. "There were many women in the family way & all such the infants were cut out of their bellies, and fence rails run up their privates," one witness reported.[51] The first detailed reference to the violence committed at the fort, in a letter from Tombigbee printed in Baltimore's *Weekly Register* in December, noted that "the women were butchered, then stripped and subjected to every brutal indignity that the savages could think of." After repeating the story of pregnant women cut open and their unborn babies tomahawked, the writer observed that "many of the women had *two* scalps taken from them."[52]

The emphasis on the violation of women's bodies and the violence committed against unborn children, a common feature in accounts of frontier wars, heightened the juxtaposition of savage Indians and innocent, defenseless settlers. Creek warriors did scalp and mutilate their enemies, as did frontier soldiers, and they did kill a large number of women and children at Fort Mims, perhaps as many as seventy-five. But the majority of those killed were men, soldiers of the Mississippi Volunteers and the Tensaw militia, who were armed and fought a hard, pitched battle for survival. Some accounts briefly described that struggle. A letter writer from Saint Stephens, after noting that the fort's defenders were surprised by the attack, said that "all was done that could be effected by cool determined bravery; but overpowered by numbers, they were literally

Martyred' of a Children

butchered, the house set on fire, and the old men, women and children (who were in an upper room) burnt to death."[53] But beyond generalized references to scalping and mutilation there were no detailed descriptions of men's bodies. Women and children became the symbol of Fort Mims.[54]

The accounts of the battle offered two sources for the savagery of that day. The first was British manipulation of the Creeks. One of the early reports that made its way east, a letter from Saint Stephens reprinted in the *Weekly Register* on October 2, briefly described the battle and slipped in the aside that "under the double influence of British gold and furious fanaticism, the savages fought in a manner scarcely to be credited." A fuller account printed in December blamed "*the agency of the British government*" for the Creek "*murders*" at Fort Mims.[55]

The notion that Indians were the puppets of scheming imperial powers had deep roots reflecting the long-standing perception of vulnerability on the southern frontier. The Carolinians back in the eighteenth century worried about French machinations among the Creeks and Cherokees, especially during periods of war. Accusations of British manipulation of Indians in the northwest and fears that that influence might spread to the powerful southern tribes contributed to the calls for war in 1812 and, once declared, offered a context through which all Creek actions were filtered. The shock of Fort Mims only intensified that perception. Governor Blount of Tennessee even cast doubt on the Creek civil war in October, writing that Hawkins's contention that the "nation was pretty equally marshaled against itself . . . was altogether fudge—a mere tub for the whale—thrown out by the hostile party of the Creeks, through the contrivance and suggestion of the British and Spaniards at Pensacola, as a blind to the credulous."[56] The very real threat of a British invasion of the Gulf territories only heightened the belief that they controlled, or at the very least influenced, the Red Sticks.

The accounts of the battle at Fort Mims also suggest that the innate characteristics of the Creek people were the second factor that led to the savagery on display that day. While contradicting the emphasis on British manipulation, this theme hints at a sense of betrayal and a deeper disillusionment with and skepticism of "civilization" and the place of Native Americans on the frontier. The "butchery at *Tensaio*" had led to "the annihilation" of the civilization program, the *Weekly Register* argued. "Many of the chiefs had fully fallen into the plan of civilization; cultivating their lands in regular order; and, in their domestic or household affairs, approaching us so nearly that the difference could hardly be discovered." Assimilation seemed to be working, at least on the surface. One traveler, the editor recounted, said "that he had dined at one of the chief's houses where the whole business of eating and drinking was done in a stile and manner that might be compared with that of any private gentleman in the best settled states." But Fort Mims stripped away the veneer of civilization, revealing the savagery underneath. "All the pleasant prospects we had are clouded by blood, and forever blasted by that treacherous people, for whom we have done so much," the *Register's* editor lamented, before adding "that *mercy* itself seems to demand their extermination, to prevent greater calamity." A second article highlighting a letter from Tombigbee excoriated Benjamin Hawkins for the failure of his program: "Is this the nation of savages on whom thousands have been expended . . . ? And, good God! is this the point at which they have arrived?" Among the Red Sticks were "*hundreds*, who spoke the English language, had a constant intercourse with the whites, and many of them were raised among the white people," yet "the scheme of humanity . . . HAS COMPLETELY FAILED, through the native propensity of the *Indians* to rapine, and the universal disposition of BRITAIN to encourage it."[57]

The various rumors, reports, and articles recounting the destruction of Fort Mims and the slaughter of its defenders crystallized sentiments already at work on Alabama's frontier, even as they carried America into war with the Creeks. Vestiges of the old imperial frontier echoed in the fears of British influence but it was the tensions generated by settlement that shaped the reactions to the battle. Stories of women and children being mutilated resonated because many had lived through or heard tales about the border wars of the 1780s and early 1790s. Those women and children embodied the most benign character of westward expansion: family, community, and civilization. The stories of old battles celebrated frontiersmen as defenders of family who unleashed their martial prowess and terrible vengeance in reaction to violations of their women and children. In late September 1813, Andrew Jackson rallied Tennesseans after word of Fort Mims reached Nashville by announcing the "invasion of the savage foe! Already do they advance towards your frontier with their scalping knifes unsheathed, to butcher your wives, your children, and your helpless babes."[58]

Land hunger was the ever-present backdrop to skepticism about the assimilation of Indians and to an emerging racialized belief in their innate primitivism. Tennessee's governor, Willie Blount, predicted in October "that the Creeks will be not only whipped, but that the Floridas, from whence they derive their counsel and support, to mar our frontier will be ours." Then "each southern and western inhabitant will cultivate his own garden of Eden, and will, through the natural channels placed by a wise and just Creator . . . export his own produce, and import such comforts as he may think desirable, by the shortest routes of communication with the ocean." The previous July, before the attack on Fort Mims, Andrew Jackson had reminded Tennesseans that "the country to the South is inviting" as he mobilized his troops for the possibility of war with the Creeks. "The soil which now lies waste and uncultivated," he said, could be transformed "into rich harvest fields, to supply the wants of millions."[59]

If the refugees who crowded into Fort Mims embodied the messiness of Alabama's frontier, then the reactions to the brutal attack drew sharper lines. That is not to say that the presence of métis Creeks and of Africans was ignored in the aftermath of the battle. Slaves served as witnesses to the slaughter and appeared as potential instigators of rebellion in official letters and as stolen property in claims for compensation. Early accounts by local residents such as Judge Toulmin recognized the valiant role that "half-breeds" like Dixon Bailey played in defending the fort. Their presence at Fort Mims lived on in the Indian allies—Cherokees, Choctaws, and Creeks—who helped defeat the Red Sticks during the coming months. So in many ways the complexity of the southern frontier persisted. But the memory of the "massacre" at Fort Mims became a powerful symbol of an imaginary frontier structured around a neater division of settler and Indian. The manipulations of the British, the treachery of "civilized" Indians raising the tomahawk, and, above all, the mutilated bodies of defenseless women and children left little room for people like Dixon Bailey.

───────────────────────────

It is easy in hindsight to see in the Red Stick victory at Fort Mims the defeat that lay ahead. Benjamin Hawkins had told the "fanatical chiefs" back in July that "the power of your prophets to make thunder, earthquakes, and to sink the earth . . . cannot frighten the American soldiers" with "their cannons, their rifles, and their swords." He had warned, "War with the white people will be your ruin."[60] Ultimately, Hawkins was right. But too easy an acceptance of the inevitability of America's conquest of the Creeks obscures the complexities of the six months that followed the assault on Fort Mims. The Red Sticks had reasons to be confident, while many obstacles faced the Americans as panic among the settlers shifted to outraged cries for war. Paying attention to why that confidence turned to ashes and how those obstacles were overcome reveals much of what Alabama's frontier had become and where it was heading.

The Red Stick forces traveling the paths back to their homes with their scalps and their captives had much to celebrate as they looked back over the past few months. They had driven their Creek enemies to the Chattahoochee, consolidating their control over the towns along the Alabama, Coosa, and Tallapoosa Rivers. They had routed a larger force of Americans and métis warriors at Burnt Corn Creek even after being taken by surprise. Most significantly, they had burned a garrisoned fort to the ground, killing or capturing virtually all of those sheltering behind its walls, and forcing thousands of settlers to flee the rich lands of Tensaw and Tombigbee. That was an extremely rare feat in the history of Native American warfare. Now they were returning home to the vast interior of Alabama, a land that had not seen war since the days of Hernando de Soto. Still they knew that the assault on Fort Mims meant that the Americans would be coming, that they had to prepare for invasion.

The first priority was food for the approximately eight thousand men, women, and children living in the Red Stick talwas. The civil war had disrupted the normal agricultural patterns in the spring and summer of 1813. The chaos and violence made planting difficult in some towns and livestock became a target for Red Stick militants, both because they symbolized the intrusion of American economic practices and because their slaughter deprived the Red Sticks' enemies of meat. That meant that the Upper Creek towns faced food shortages going into the fall. The settlements at Tensaw and Tombigbee provided the solution, at least temporarily. In September the fields were full of ripening corn and the gardens tangled with pumpkins, beans, and other vegetables, while the settlers themselves were scattered to the wind. Armed bands of Red Sticks systematically gathered the crops from the forks of the Tombigbee and Alabama down to the eastern shore of Mobile Bay, sending canoe loads up the river to their towns. Some of the first skirmishes in the Creek War took place in those fields as small parties of hungry settlers tried to take back control of their land.[61]

Anticipating invasion, the Red Sticks moved many of their families from their traditional talwas to defensive havens. Some flocked to the isolated towns of the Black Warrior River on the northwestern frontier of Creek country, which seemed removed from the probable paths of invading armies. Others gathered in areas more easily defended. Tohopeka, for example, was situated on a sharp curve in the Tallapoosa River known as the Horseshoe Bend, creating a natural barrier on three sides of the town. Holy Ground, a third haven for Red Stick families, located in thick woods and marshes near the Alabama River, had defensible terrain, but Josiah Francis boosted protection by using his prophetic powers to create a supernatural barrier preventing white intrusion. Despite the failure of Paddy Walsh's charms at Fort Mims, Red Stick belief in the spiritual power of their cause remained strong and bolstered their confidence.[62]

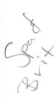

Any chance of defeating the Americans hinged on gaining access to weaponry and military supplies, and here the Red Sticks had some reason to hope. The Creeks had a long history of playing imperial powers off one another to their advantage, and there were two nations that might benefit from an alliance with the Red Sticks against the Americans. Rumors of an impending British invasion along the Gulf coast were as rampant among the Indians as they were among the American settlers, and it was not much of a stretch to imagine the British paving the way by first arming the Creeks, just as they had done with Tecumseh's Shawnees in the Northwest. In the meantime, Spanish West Florida was a possible source of military aid. Governor Manrique had given McQueen's party some gunpowder and shot, albeit reluctantly, in July. Spain remained neutral in the ongoing war, but officials in Pensacola, still smarting at the presumptuous ease with which the Americans had taken Mobile the previous spring, applauded the Red Stick victory at Fort Mims. Josiah Francis and other Red Stick leaders sent a letter to Manrique boasting of the number of enemies killed and captives taken, which they exaggerated, and pleading for more guns, powder, and lead to replace their depleted stockpile. Then they promised to conquer Coweta and to burn Mobile to the ground if the Spanish had not yet retaken it from the Americans. But by December a letter from John Durant, a Red Stick whose father, Benjamin, was killed defending Fort Mims, revealed that "the spanards do not seem incline to supply us they and the inglish is one and the inglish has rote on to them to supply us but we see no supply."[63]

The difficulty in acquiring weaponry doomed the Red Stick cause and marked a significant shift in Alabama's frontier history. For almost 150 years, the southeastern Indians had had choices in their pursuit of trade and alliances. The imperial competition between England, France, and Spain generated war and slave raiding, to be sure, but it also gave the native people room to maneuver. When they lashed out against the Carolinians in the Yamasee War, for example, they could turn to the Spanish or French to maintain a flow of arms. That world was all but gone, replaced by an expansive American empire intent on building roads and settling land. Spanish Florida was a ghost of its former glory and only a trickle of supplies flowed north from Pensacola during the Creek War. Britain's threatened invasion reawakened Alexander McGillivray's dreams of a European check against American aggression but came too late to help the Red Sticks. When British forces finally came to the Gulf late in 1814 they arrived hundreds of miles west near New Orleans, and Andrew Jackson's army was ready for them. Instead of a frontier of contesting empires the Red

Sticks faced a frontier of American settlements encircling them on three sides, with an impotent Spanish colony to the south.

The peril of that encirclement became obvious as American forces mobilized to invade Creek country following the attack on Fort Mims. General John Floyd, commanding an army of 950 Georgia Volunteers and militiamen, with an additional force of almost four hundred allied Creek warriors, mostly from the Lower Towns, pushed against the Red Stick strongholds from their base near the Chattahoochee River. General Claiborne, the man who had stationed his Mississippi Volunteers in the various Tensaw and Tombigbee forts, commanded a thousand men, including a small contingent of the US Army Infantry. His approach would be up the Alabama River from the southwest. Finally, Andrew Jackson's army, supplemented with troops from East Tennessee commanded by John Cocke, would drive south to the Creek settlements along the Coosa River.[64]

Three armies pushing into Creek country from different directions threatened the Red Stick warriors, but Indian control of the interior posed a problem for the Americans. Compounding the already complicated process of coordinating between commanders was the difficulty in communicating across Creek territory. That was exactly why the federal government had pushed so hard for a postal and military road to link settlements, and it was one justification given for Indian removal in the coming decades. In the meantime, messages between Claiborne and his colleagues in Tennessee and Georgia had to be carried by riders through Red Stick territory. Zachariah McGirth volunteered for the dangerous duty. According to family stories, McGirth "painted himself like a hostile warrior & shaved his head" before mounting "upon a good horse with 3 pecks of shelled corn for his animal & 2 quarts of cold flour for himself."[65] Three times in September and October and then again in January, McGirth rode to Georgia and back carrying messages. While McGirth was in Georgia, Hawkins passed along news that the Indian countryman's wife and daughters were captives and had not died at Fort Mims.[66]

Much of the hardship experienced by the American soldiers in the coming months sprang more from the logistical difficulties of frontier warfare than from actual battle. Mobilizing thousands of men and keeping them fed, clothed, and sheltered while marching across often difficult terrain proved a complicated task. One soldier in Floyd's Georgia forces already complained that the army had been "badly provisioned with victuals" while they were encamped on the Ocmulgee River at the eastern border of the Creek nation. Rains, poor shelter and food, and hard marching led to sickness, and by the time the Georgians had reached the allied Creek town of Coweta, some 250 of them had been left behind because of illness. Floyd established Fort Mitchell near the Chatta-hoochee River, but it would be late November before he moved against the Red Sticks on the Tallapoosa River. Meanwhile Claiborne's Mississippi Volunteers were making their way west from Saint Stephens across the forks, slowed by frequent skirmishes with small bands of enemy Red Sticks. They finally crossed the Alabama in the middle of November and established a stockade called Fort Claiborne, about twenty miles downriver from Holy Ground.[67]

Andrew Jackson's Tennessee forces faced the most daunting logistical challenges of the war, but he was also the most determined commander. Tennesseans had responded enthusiastically to the recruitment calls after Fort Mims. John Coffee, Jackson's friend and cavalry officer, wrote his wife in October that once the troops had been mobilized, "we shall be able to over run the Creek nation, and I fear we shall never see an Indian for, as they hear of our strength, they will fly before us and never risque an action." Jackson, he was convinced, "will have an army that can drive the Creek nation like a flock of bullocks."[68] But first the soldiers had to get to Creek country, and a series of highland ridges south of the Tennessee River blocked their way. Following an ancient Indian path, one to two hundred fatigue troops with axes pushed ahead of Jackson's main forces up one steep climb and down another, across ridge after ridge, cutting a wagon road. The goal was to carve out a supply route linking Madison County to the newly built Fort Strother, on the Coosa. Even with the road Jackson faced difficulties feeding his troops. He sent Coffee to raid Creek villages on the Black Warrior River in October, but they had been deserted and there were no stores of corn or livestock to be found. Coffee burned the towns to the ground and came back empty-handed. Jackson's forces had more luck later that month when they took the small town of Littafuchee. The few residents of this isolated village surrendered without a fight and Jackson had them sent as prisoners, first to Huntsville and then to Nashville. His troops were disappointed to discover that the corn was still in the field.[69]

These early experiences created a pattern that Jackson followed for the rest of the war. In between the major battles his forces routinely took small towns, some empty and others with primarily women, children, and elderly men. They would appropriate the food supplies, burn the town to the ground, and either take the residents prisoner or relocate them east of the Coosa River. Part of his mission was to feed his troops, but Jackson also wanted to clear the Creeks from the land to the west, in what historian Kathryn Braund calls a "purposeful ethnic cleansing." It is worth remembering that the home front was the battlefield for the Creeks.[70]

Late in the fall all three American armies engaged in battle with the Red Sticks. Jackson's forces under General Coffee's command struck first in early November when they attacked the town of Tullushatchee. Fierce fighting took place between the Americans and the two hundred warriors in the town, but the Creeks were outgunned. They were primarily using bows and arrows, evidence of the ways in which limited access to Spanish or British weaponry hampered their military cause. Many of the women in Tullushatchee also fired arrows. David Crockett, the Tennessean who would later become a congressman and something of a celebrity as a frontiersman, was at the battle and reported seeing a Creek woman kill one of the soldiers, which "so enraged us all, that she was fired on, and had at least twenty balls blown through her."[71] Most of the warriors were killed, as were an undetermined number of women and children. Eighty-four prisoners were taken, all women and children, and many of them were severely wounded. Jackson was eager to follow up by pushing further south toward Tohopeka, or Horseshoe Bend, on the Tallapoosa River, where he knew a large settlement of Red Sticks had congregated. But the lack of food and the discontent and desertion among his soldiers convinced him to retreat back to Fort Strother to await new recruits.[72]

The other two American armies struck important Creek towns in the fall of 1813, but like Jackson, they were then forced to retreat because of a lack of supplies. General Floyd led his army to the Tallapoosa River, where they attacked Atasi in late November. Cannon fire and bayonets killed close to two hundred Red Stick warriors but fewer women and children were killed than at Tullushatchee. They had built caves into the banks of the river and found shelter there during the battle. Floyd was wounded and, facing severely limited food supplies, decided to return to Fort Mitchell on the Chattahoochee River. To the west, General Claiborne's army of about a thousand soldiers, including Choctaw warriors, marched across difficult terrain to reach Holy Ground. As they maneuvered closer to the town in late December a Red Stick man out hunting discovered their presence and raised the alarm back in the town. William Weatherford, who commanded the defenses for the town, was able to evacuate most of the women and children, and some of the warriors, across the Alabama River to safety, leaving behind a small force to hold off the Americans. Some of those fighting included Africans who had joined the Red Stick cause. Weatherford was able to escape by, as legend has it, mounting his pony and jumping off a fifteen-foot bluff into the river. Most of the other warriors slipped through the American encirclement and only thirty or so were killed. To the delight of the American soldiers they found 1,200 barrels of corn in Holy Ground, but that

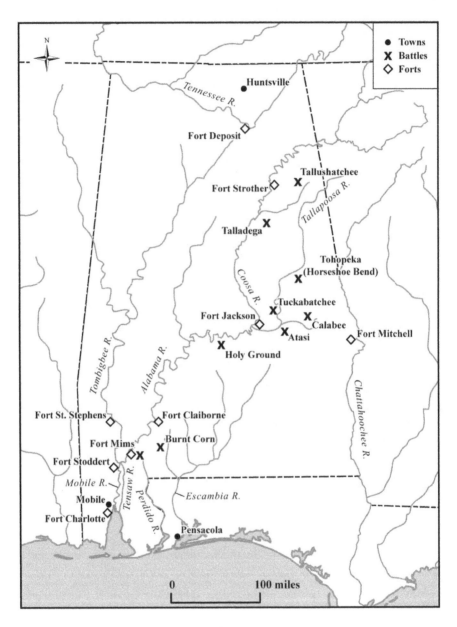

The Creek War, 1813–14. Drawn by Patrick Jones.

was not enough to sustain them. The army left Indian country and Claiborne retired.[73]

The final stages of the war came with the new year, as both Jackson and Floyd took to the field with new recruits and more plentiful supplies. The Georgians and allied Creeks, numbering about 1,700, set up a fortified camp on Calebee Creek, near the now-burned town of Atasi. In late January 1814 a large force of about 1,300 Red Stick warriors attacked the encampment from all sides in the dark hours before dawn. It was not until daybreak, when there was enough light to use their artillery, that the tide of battle turned in favor of the Americans. In March, Jackson pushed his three thousand troops, comprising Tennessee Volunteers and about five hundred Cherokee and Creek warriors, south toward Tohopeka, the refugee town on the Horseshoe Bend of the Tallapoosa River. Tohopeka was the largest settlement of Creeks left in Alabama, with about a thousand warriors and probably four times as many family members. The site was well defended, a peninsula with water on three sides and a barricade on the landside. That barricade was so heavily fortified that Jackson could not breach it after a two-hour artillery barrage. While that was distracting the defenders, Cherokee warriors swam across the Tallapoosa, untied the Red Sticks' canoes, and shot burning arrows into the town to set it on fire. Jackson's troops charged the barricade with bayonets, finally breaking through the Red Stick line and pushing them back toward the river. General Coffee's cavalry sealed the constricting circle by riding along the Tallapoosa and shooting any Indians trying to swim to safety. After five hours the battle ended, with more than eight hundred warriors killed and three hundred women and children captured. The battle at Horseshoe Bend was the final major engagement of the Creek war.[74]

Horseshoe Bend was a decisive victory for the Americans, but Creek resistance did not end with a clear-cut surrender. Instead, most Red Stick warriors either fled south to Florida to continue fighting with the Seminoles or simply found places to hide away. In April, Jackson built a fort near the old site of Fort Toulouse at the confluence of the Coosa and Tallapoosa Rivers, in the heart of the Upper Creek country. A growing stream of refugees poured into Fort Jackson and other American forts, mostly women and children who were starving. Their towns were destroyed; almost sixty in all had been burned to the ground, and with their livestock and crops decimated there was little food to be had. With the refugees came captives from Fort Mims, mostly métis and African women and children. Then, at the end of April, William Weatherford walked into Fort Jackson to surrender. Jackson spared his life and in the months to come Weatherford helped to convince other Red Stick warriors to surrender, along with their starving families.

One who surrendered was Hopoithle Mico, of Tallassee, an elderly man in his nineties with a long history on Alabama's frontier. The Tallassee King had supported the Americans during the revolution and had joined Alexander McGillivray in the Creek delegation to New York in 1790. But he had grown increasingly angry at the encroachment of American settlers and the construction of roads and threw in his lot with the Red Sticks. He died under guard at Fort Jackson in June 1814 and was buried along the Coosa River. Reports suggested that Hopoithle Mico had been beaten or abused in some way at the fort.[75]

Preparations for a treaty had been underway even before the American victory at Horseshoe Bend. The secretary of war had appointed Benjamin Hawkins and General Thomas Pinckney, whose South Carolina troops had replaced General Floyd's exhausted Georgians in the field, as commissioners for the negotiations they anticipated would follow the Red Sticks' certain defeat. Pinckney's original outline in April demanded from the Creeks land cessions to pay for the cost of war, free navigation of rivers, the right to build roads with forts and trading houses, and the surrender of all Red Sticks. They would also be forced to cut off all trade with foreign nations. In many ways those preliminary demands were an extension of the federal government's goals before the war and reflected a realization that the Creek nation was divided and that allied Creeks had sought American aid in fighting the Red Sticks. When Andrew Jackson replaced Pinckney as the principal negotiator, the terms shifted.[76]

Jackson's magnanimity with Weatherford did not extend to the Creek nation as a whole. He was a westerner who, like many, remained skeptical of Hawkins's civilizing mission and demanded vengeance for what he perceived to be a long history of violent raids, culminating in the attack on Fort Mims. Land would be the instrument of that vengeance. He called Creek leaders together at Fort Jackson in August 1814, and those who came were overwhelmingly Creek headmen who had allied with the Americans. The Red Stick leaders were either in hiding or in Florida preparing to continue the war. Jackson kept many of Pinckney's original demands but the one change he made was significant. Instead of a land cession to cover the cost of the war, Jackson called for twenty-three million acres of Creek land: a broad strip along the Georgia border with Florida and

about three-fifths of Alabama. What remained for the Creeks was a vastly reduced territory east of the Coosa. Thirty-five headmen, only one of whom had
been an enemy of the United States, reluctantly signed the treaty in August.
Hawkins resigned his position as Creek agent in protest over the harsh terms of
the Treaty of Fort Jackson and died in 1816.[77]

The Creek War and the Treaty of Fort Jackson were major turning points
in the transformation of Alabama from a diverse borderland to an American
settlers' frontier. Vestiges of the old imperial frontier remained in the ongoing
Seminole resistance. Josiah Francis, one of the principal prophets of the Red
Stick movement, fought with them and continued to pursue support from the
British. Four years after the conclusion of the Creek War he was captured by
Jackson's forces and summarily executed. Florida retained a borderland character for years to come, with Seminoles, Red Sticks, and runaway African slaves
resisting American control over their land. But the death of thousands of Creek
warriors and civilians, the destruction of homes and fields and livestock, and the
stripping away of the land that constituted much of the heart of Creek country
opened the door to waves of American settlers.

Notes

1. The following account of Fort Mims is drawn primarily from Gregory A. Waselkov, *A Conquering Spirit: Fort Mims and the Redstick War of 1813–1814* (Tuscaloosa:
University of Alabama Press, 2006).

2. Jackson to Blount, Hermitage, June 5, 1812, in *The Papers of Andrew Jackson*, ed.
Harold D. Moser and Sharon Macpherson, vol. 2, *1804–1813* (Knoxville: University of
Tennessee Press, 1984), 301.

3. Beasley to Claiborne, Mims' Block House, August 30, 1813, letterbook F, J. E. H.
Claiborne Collection, Mississippi Department of Archives and History, Jackson,
quoted in Waselkov, *Conquering Spirit*, 125.

4. Claudio Saunt, *A New Order of Things: Property, Power, and the Transformation
of the Creek Indians, 1733–1816* (Cambridge: Cambridge University Press, 1999), 233;
Waselkov, *Conquering Spirit*, 77.

5. John C. Hall, "Landscape Considerations for the Creek War in Alabama, 1811–
1814," *Alabama Review* 67 (July 2014): 232.

6. Henry DeLeon Southerland Jr. and Jerry Elijah Brown, *The Federal Road through
Georgia, the Creek Nation, and Alabama, 1806–1836* (Tuscaloosa: University of Alabama
Press, 1989), 12, 32.

7. Angela Pulley Hudson, *Creek Paths and Federal Roads: Indians, Settlers, and Slaves
and the Making of the American South* (Chapel Hill: University of North Carolina Press,

2010), 54, 91; "Petition to Congress by a Convention East of Pearl River," November 11, 1809, in *The Territorial Papers of the United States*, ed. Clarence Edwin Carter, vol. 6, *The Territory of Mississippi, 1809–1817* (Washington, DC: US Government Printing Office, 1938), 28–30.

8. Waselkov, *Conquering Spirit*, 73.

9. Hudson, *Creek Paths*, 64; Saunt, *New Order of Things*, 216–18.

10. James Madison, "Talk to the Chiefs of the Creek Nation," January 14, 1811, Records of the Bureau of Indian Affairs, National Archives and Records Administration, Washington, DC, quoted in Hudson, *Creek Paths*, 84.

11. Hawkins to William Eustis, October 3, 1811, in *Letters, Journals and Writings of Benjamin Hawkins*, ed. C. L. Grant (Savannah, GA: Beehive, 1980), 2:593–94, quoted in Hudson, *Creek Paths*, 92.

12. Hudson, *Creek Paths*, 92–93.

13. Hawkins to Big Warrior, Little Prince, and other chiefs, Creek Agency, June 16, 1814, in *American State Papers, Indian Affairs*, vol. 1, ed. Walter Lowrie and Matthew St. Clair Clarke (Washington, DC: Gales and Seaton, 1832), 845, https://memory.loc .gov/cgi-bin/ampage?collId=llsp&fileName=007/llsp007.db&recNum=4.

14. Gregory Evans Dowd, *A Spirited Resistance: The North American Indian Struggle for Unity, 1745–1815* (Baltimore: Johns Hopkins University Press, 1992), 171; Waselkov, *Conquering Spirit*, 79.

15. Waselkov, *Conquering Spirit*, 79–80.

16. [Margaret Austill], "Life of Margaret Ervin Austill," *Alabama Historical Quarterly* 6 (Spring 1944): 93.

17. George Stiggins, "A Historical Narration of the Genealogy Traditions and Downfall of the Ispocage or Creek Tribe of Indians, Written by One of the Tribe," vol. 1, ser. 5, Georgia, Alabama, and South Carolina Papers, Lyman Draper Manuscript Collection, Wisconsin Historical Society, Madison, quoted in Waselkov, *Conquering Spirit*, 83; "Deposition of Samuel Manac, of lawful age, a Warrior of the Creek Nation . . . 2d day of August, 1813," in H. S. Halbert and T. H. Ball, *The Creek War of 1813 and 1814* (Chicago: Donohue & Henneberry, 1895), 91–93, quoted in ibid.

18. Waselkov, *Conquering Spirit*, 83.

19. Waselkov, *Conquering Spirit*, 42–47, 92–95.

20. Gary Burton, "Pintala's Cold Murder Case: The Death of Thomas Meredith in 1812," *Alabama Review* 63 (July 2010): 163–91.

21. [Austill], "Life of Margaret Ervin Austill," 93.

22. Tom Kanon, "The Kidnapping of Martha Crawley and Settler-Indian Relations Prior to the War of 1812," *Tennessee Historical Quarterly* 64 (Spring 2005): 3–4, 7–8; James P. Pate, ed., *The Reminiscences of George Strother Gaines: Pioneer and Statesman of Early Alabama and Mississippi, 1805–1843* (Tuscaloosa: University of Alabama Press, 1998), 50–53.

23. *Nashville Clarion*, July 8, 1812, quoted in Kanon, "Kidnapping of Martha Crawley," 7.

24. Jackson to Blount, Hermitage, June 4, 1812, in Moser and Macpherson, *Papers of Andrew Jackson*, vol. 2, 300.

25. Extract of a letter from Benjamin Hawkins to Secretary of War William Eustis, Creek Agency, July 13, 1812, in Lowrie and Clarke, *American State Papers*, 812; Saunt, *New Order of Things*, 242–43.

26. Waselkov, *Conquering Spirit*, 88–89; Dowd, *Spirited Resistance*, 157.

27. Hawkins to John Armstrong, March 29, 1813, in *Letters, Journals and Writings of Benjamin Hawkins*, 2:632, quoted in Saunt, *New Order of Things*, 250.

28. Report of Nimrod Doyell, assistant agent for Indian affairs, to Hawkins, Creek Agency, May 3, 1813, in Lowrie and Clarke, *American State Papers*, 843. Also see Saunt, *New Order of Things*, 250–52; Waselkov, *Conquering Spirit*, 89–90.

29. Waselkov, *Conquering Spirit*, 90; Saunt, *New Order of Things*, 252, 256–57.

30. Saunt, *New Order of Things*, 256; Dowd, *Spirited Resistance*, 157; Kathryn E. Holland Braund, "Reflections on 'Shee Coocys' and the Motherless Child: Creek Women in a Time of War," *Alabama Review* 64 (October 2011): 266–67.

31. *Nashville Clarion*, May 23, 1812, quoted in Kanon, "Kidnapping of Martha Crawley," 9–10.

32. Sketch from the *Nashville Clarion*, in *Weekly Register*, September 26, 1812, 52–53, quoted in Waselkov, *Conquering Spirit*, 97.

33. Claiborne to the governor of Georgia, David B. Mitchell, cantonment near Fort Stoddert, August 14, 1813, quoted in John Innerarity and Elizabeth Howard West, "A Prelude to the Creek War of 1813–1814: In a Letter of John Innerarity to James Innerarity," *Florida Historical Quarterly* 18 (April 1940): 263.

34. [Austill], "Life of Margaret Ervin Austill," 94–95.

35. Toulmin to John Graham, Fort Stoddert, August 5, 1812, in Carter, *Territorial Papers*, vol. 6, 306–7.

36. Robert P. Collins, "'A Packet from Canada': Telling Conspiracy Stories on the 1813 Creek Frontier," in *Tohopeka: Rethinking the Creek War and the War of 1812*, ed. Kathryn E. Holland Braund (Auburn, AL: Pebble Hill Books, 2012), 53–58; Waselkov, *Conquering Spirit*, 99–100; John Innerarity to James Innerarity, July 27, 1813, in Innerarity and West, "Prelude to the Creek War," 254.

37. Collins, "'Packet from Canada,'" 71; Waselkov, *Conquering Spirit*, 100.

38. Waselkov, *Conquering Spirit*, 110.

39. Karl Davis, "'Remember Fort Mims:' Reinterpreting the Origins of the Creek War," *Journal of the Early Republic* 22 (Winter 2002): 630–31.

40. Waselkov, *Conquering Spirit*, 112–14.

41. *Washington Republican*, October 3, 1813: 3, quoted in Waselkov, *Conquering Spirit*, 149–50.

42. Waselkov, *Conquering Spirit*, 149–50, 152–53, 226; Davis, "'Remember Fort Mims,'" 631–32.

43. Toulmin to General Thomas Flournoy, Mount Vernon, Mississippi Territory, August 30, 1813, in "Letters Relating to the Tragedy of Fort Mims: August–September,

1813," ed. James F. Doster, *Alabama Review* 14 (1961): 269–85, quoted in Waselkov, *Conquering Spirit*, 136.

44. Testimony of Col. Robert James to Albert Pickett, Pickett Papers, Alabama Department of Archives and History, Montgomery, quoted in Waselkov, *Conquering Spirit*, 136; Waselkov, *Conquering Spirit*, 137.

45. Henry Toulmin, "Indian Warfare," *Weekly Register*, October 16, 1813.

46. Willie Blount to Brigadier General Thomas Flournoy, Nashville, October 15, 1813, in Lowrie and Clarke, *American State Papers*, 855.

47. Claiborne to unknown recipient, cantonment at Mount Vernon, September 6, 1813, letterbook F, J. E. H. Claiborne Collection, Mississippi Department of Archives and History, Jackson, quoted in Waselkov, *Conquering Spirit*, 143.

48. Waselkov, *Conquering Spirit*, 141, 143.

49. Ibid., 144, 147–48.

50. Major Joseph Kennedy and Captain Uriah Blue to Claiborne, Mount Vernon, September 9, 1813, Pickett Papers, Alabama Department of Archives and History, quoted in Waselkov, *Conquering Spirit*, 150.

51. Notes of Dr. Thomas G. Holmes, Pickett Papers, Alabama Department of Archives and History, quoted in Waselkov, *Conquering Spirit*, 153.

52. "The Destiny of the Creeks," *Weekly Register*, December 18, 1813.

53. "The Creek Indians," *Weekly Register*, October 2, 1813.

54. Braund, "Reflections on 'Shee Coocys,'" 269–70.

55. "Creek Indians"; "Destiny of the Creeks."

56. Blount to Flournoy, Nashville, October 15, 1813, in Lowrie and Clarke, *American State Papers*, 855.

57. "Creek Indians"; "Destiny of the Creeks."

58. Andrew Jackson to the Tennessee Volunteers, headquarters, Nashville, September 24, 1813, in Moser and Macpherson, *Papers of Andrew Jackson*, vol. 2, 428.

59. Blount to Flournoy, Nashville, October 15, 1813, in Lowrie and Clarke, *American State Papers*, 856; Andrew Jackson, *Nashville Democratic Clarion and Tennessee Gazette*, July 27, 1813, quoted in Tom Kanon, "Before Horseshoe: Andrew Jackson's Campaigns in the Creek War Prior to Horseshoe Bend," in Braund, *Tohopeka*, 106.

60. Benjamin Hawkins to Hoboheilthle [*sic*] Micco et al., Creek Agency, July 6, 1813, in Lowrie and Clarke, *American State Papers*, 848.

61. Waselkov, *Conquering Spirit*, 160–61.

62. Ibid., 144–45.

63. John Durant to Alickander [Sandy] Durant "at the Apperlachcola," n.d., Ferdinand Leigh Claiborne Papers, Alabama Department of Archives and History, quoted in Waselkov, *Conquering Spirit*, 167; also see ibid., 146.

64. Waselkov, *Conquering Spirit*, 164–65.

65. "Notes Taken from the Lips of Col Robert James," Pickett Papers, Alabama Department of Archives and History, quoted in Waselkov, *Conquering Spirit*, 160.

66. Waselkov, *Conquering Spirit*, 159–60.

67. Peter A. Brannon, "Journal of James A. Tait for the Year 1813," *Georgia Historical Quarterly* 8 (September 1924): 230, 233; Waselkov, *Conquering Spirit*, 161–62, 164.

68. John Coffee to Mary Coffee, Camp Batey near Huntsville, undated, "Letters of John Coffee," *Tennessee Historical Magazine* 2 (December 1916), reprinted in History of Alabama, Alabama Genealogy Trails, accessed March 28, 2016, http://genealogy trails.com/ala/history_jcoffee1.html.

69. Hall, "Landscape Considerations," 230–31; T. R. Henderson, "The Destruction of Littafuchee, and a Brief History of American Settlement," *Alabama Review* 67 (July 2014): 233–53.

70. Braund, "Reflections on 'Shee Coocys,'" 283.

71. David Crockett, *A Narrative of the Life of David Crockett of the State of Tennessee* (Lincoln: University of Nebraska Press, 1987), 88.

72. Braund, "Reflections on 'Shee Coocys,'" 276–77; Kanon, "Before Horseshoe," 110, 113.

73. Waselkov, *Conquering Spirit*, 165–66.

74. Ibid., 170–71; John E. Grenier, "'We Bleed Our Enemies in Such Cases to Give Them Their Senses': Americans' Unrelenting Wars on the Indians of the Trans-Appalachian West, 1810–1814," in Braund, *Tohokepa*, 178.

75. Hudson, *Creek Paths*, 28, 82, 85, 97, 110; Gregory A. Waselkov, "Fort Jackson and the Aftermath," in Braund, *Tohopeka*, 162.

76. Thomas D. Clark and John D. W. Guice, *Frontiers in Conflict: The Old South-west, 1795–1830* (Albuquerque: University of New Mexico Press, 1989), 147–48.

77. Ibid., 148–49; Hudson, *Creek Paths*, 122–23.

8

The Cotton Frontier

Newton Cannon, a Tennessee congressman, traveled through territory west of Madison County in 1816 and visited many homesteaders, squatters who had "been driven there from different parts by the failure of their crops." The Chickasaws had just ceded their hunting territory in the Tennessee Valley when the families began arriving. They came because their cattle could roam "the finest range both winter and summer" and they hoped "the increase of their Stock in this country" would allow them "to purchase a small spot of Soil on which to make a more independent support for their families in the future." Frontier land offered a haven for poorer settlers, a place to carve out subsistence and perhaps, if they were lucky, set down roots.[1]

Further south and a year later, another settler ventured into the frontier, eager to make a new start for his family. The conquest of the Red Stick Creeks had opened lands along the Alabama, Cahawba, and Black Warrior Rivers, and James Tait was one of thousands who crowded into the region in anticipation of sales. He had left his home in Georgia in December 1817 to scout out land where he and his new wife "would feel ourselves more independent and more at home, than we have ever done yet."[2] Tait, a veteran of General Floyd's campaigns in the war, had some familiarity with the frontier and staked out a spot about ten miles up the Alabama River from Holy Ground. There, according to a letter home to his father, he built his "humble cabbin on cane creek, entirely alone, in a wilderness" and began "preparing a few acres for the cultivation of indian corn."[3] The letter carried a whiff of youthful self-dramatization, but distance from family and homesickness probably did heighten Tait's sense of isolation. Still, he was not alone. Brunswick, Wily, and Gloster, three enslaved men, came along and helped Tait build his cabin and plant his corn on Cane Creek. Soon the rest of his twenty slaves, wedding gifts from his in-laws and his father, would journey west with his bride. Eager to escape the shadow of his father, a United States senator from Georgia, James intended to establish his own household and find financial success as a planter on Alabama's frontier. The land stripped from the Creeks and the labor of his slaves afforded him that possibility. By 1821 they were cultivating and picking over one hundred bales of cotton.[4]

James might have wanted to stake out his own claim of independent manhood but he ended up serving as the forward agent of his father's dreams. A year after his son settled on Cane Creek, Charles Tait decided to move west. He had helped push through the Senate a bill creating a separate territory for Alabama in 1817, and by the winter of 1818–19 he was determined to relocate to a more expansive field to pursue his political and economic ambitions. James would serve as his scout. Charles wrote many letters that winter detailing the kind of land he desired. First there needed to be "a stream near at hand for a mill and machinery" and "a never failing spring at the foot of a hillock, on the summit of which" he could build "a mansion house." The "back range" should be "extensive" so that "our cattle and hogs can graze and fatten without the aid of corn houses." There should also be good land on either side of the plantation "where will settle a number of good neighbors" to provide "the pleasures and benefits of society."[5] He further instructed James that, above all, he should keep "in mind at all times the unity of Fertility, Salubrity, & Navigation" when selecting land.[6] Charles was speculating about a prosperous future in a new land even as he dreamed of transplanting the social ties that created home. As it turned out, he would get to choose his plantation himself; when he arrived in 1819, the year Alabama became a state, the land along the river had not yet been surveyed and brought to market. He and James remained squatters for a while more.

The eagerness with which settlers flowed into Alabama after the war, whether poor families seeking a place to forage their cattle or young and old planters following dreams of prosperity, posed problems for federal officials. The land could not be put on the market until it was surveyed, and that process was moving slowly. Lost horses, inhospitable terrain, and illness were common difficulties, but more pressing was the scarcity of food. The surveyors working west of the Chattahoochee River "were compel'd to give five dollars a bushel for Indian corn, & Meat of every description, *when to be had*, was equally dear," Thomas

Freeman, the chief surveyor for the southern Creek lands, wrote to the head of the Land Office in 1817. That scarcity boded ill for the settlers in the "Creek Purchase." Freeman warned "that a large portion of the present Intruders will be compel'd to abandon their improvements, and seek existence in the older settlements to prevent starvation, yet there are hundreds of families arriving there daily."[7]

The scarcity of food was the direct result of a war that had transformed a settled land into a kind of wilderness. In the past, traders and travelers could count on purchasing corn and meat from the Creeks. Towns with fields of maize and herds of cattle had dotted the rivers and streams of the Alabama River system. But Jackson had destroyed the towns and farms west of the Coosa River, forcing the refugees east to a shrinking Creek homeland that straddled the Georgia border. In 1817 surveyors were moving through ruined settlements, overgrown fields, and forests where no cattle roamed, save a stray here or there left behind by the retreating families. Their tasks of measuring and parceling out sections were contingent on the conquest of the Creeks, of course, but were also made more difficult by the emptying of the land.

The squatters themselves created headaches for federal officials but also offered great opportunities. William Barnett, who reported on the surveying of the Creek lands, commented on the numerous families he saw clustered around one spring after another and fretted about the inevitable quarrels and possible bloodshed that would occur when the sales came and legal ownership hung in the balance. He warned the secretary of war that the continued growth of the squatter settlements would hurt the price of land and disturb "the peace, comfort & good order of the future Settlers." But the large numbers of squatters boded well for profitable sales in the future. John Read, the land register in the Huntsville office, hoped that the Chickasaw cession could be sold while cotton prices were high and "while such a Spirit of emigration from the East to the west, prevails," and he predicted that the land "would sell generally as high, & perhaps higher than any lands of the united States ever sold." Barnett agreed that the Tennessee Valley land should sell first; he hoped that high prices for the Chickasaw lands would "give a tone to those below" and attract the right kind of settlers to the Creek lands along the Alabama River and its tributaries. A successful sale there in a couple of years would "introduce into these Settlements the sway of the laws," Barnett argued, "& they will soon be purified & regenerated."[8]

The squatters who settled in the Tennessee Valley, along the Alabama River, and in valleys at points in between sought refuge and opportunity, impulses that had a long history on this frontier. Poor families searching for a tucked-away corner of land to graze their cattle were not much different from the Koasatis escaping the slave raids of the Westos, African slaves running away from the British, French, and Spanish colonies on the perimeter, or Loyalists fleeing defeat in the revolution. All had hoped to begin again, to feed and shelter themselves and their families with the resources of the land, to create a life not unlike that of the countless generations of Indians who had called Alabama home. Others who arrived in 1817 had dreams of wealth far beyond some acres of corn and forage for their cattle, but that too was not new. Ever since Hernando de Soto crashed his way through the Southeast, outsiders had pursued riches in one form or another, whether gold, captives, deerskins, or land. In the past, those seeking refuge or opportunity or both had to contend with the fact that Alabama was Indian country. Outsiders of various kinds entered and imperial powers pressed inward from the perimeter, but the Indians, especially the Creeks, controlled the interior.

War shattered Alabama's frontier by stripping away the Indians' possession of most of the interior land. Andrew Jackson's conquest of the Red Sticks and his ruthless treaty negotiations transferred over fourteen million acres of the Creek heartland in Alabama to the United States. His defeat of the British at New Orleans and his subsequent incursions into Spanish Florida drove a nail into what remained of the old imperial borderlands, leaving the southern Indians with no allies and limiting their ability to find trading partners. By 1816 the Choctaws had signed a treaty relinquishing their lands east of the Tombigbee River and the Chickasaws had ceded their lands north and south of the Tennessee River. Military victories also cemented American control over the Southwest and guaranteed navigation on the region's rivers and access to the Gulf. Millions of acres of available land drew tens of thousands of settlers, free and enslaved. The 9,000 non-Indian people who lived in the eastern portion of the Mississippi Territory in 1810 grew to 30,000 in 1816, and swelled to 144,000 by 1820, one year after Alabama became a state.[9]

The Indian cessions in Alabama would have attracted settlers no matter how great the hunger for land was, but rising cotton prices turned settlement into a kind of mania. That too was a legacy of the War of 1812. Jackson's victory at New Orleans and news of peace in 1815 unleashed a spirit of patriotic nationalism after the gloom of war and a new confidence in economic expansion. Fueling that was a resurgent commercial trade between the United States, Britain, and Europe, released after years of being bottled up by hostilities. The pent-up demand for British textiles sparked factory production, which in turn required ever-increasing amounts of cotton. Settlers pushed into the Creek, Chickasaw, and Choctaw lands of Alabama just as cotton prices soared as high as thirty cents per pound. Plenty of yeoman farmers and herdsmen migrated to Alabama in the years after the war, but so too did small slaveholders and planters like Charles and James Tait who were willing to pull up stakes in Virginia, the Carolinas, Georgia, and Tennessee to take a chance on the cotton frontier, bringing with them increasing numbers of enslaved men, women, and children.

The federal government facilitated those migratory waves. Federal officials had long struggled to find the right balance between encouraging and controlling settlement of the Southwest. Since the revolution they had understood that consolidation of the frontier as a stable part of the American nation would ultimately require settlers on the ground. But unregulated flows of squatters had threatened that stability by provoking Indian attacks and, at times, separatist schemes involving the Spanish Empire. The War of 1812 erased that tension, at least within Alabama, by weakening both the Creeks and the Spanish, leaving the government free to encourage settlement by surveying land, parceling it out, and selling it on credit.

The end of Alabama's frontier lay in the intersection of war, migration, cotton, and land policy. The process was not smooth; the collapse of the postwar boom in the Panic of 1819 complicated settlement. But through the 1820s streams of settlers and slaves cleared land and planted cotton, integrating Alabama not just into the nation of states but into the burgeoning southern plantation economy.

They called it the "Alabama fever." In 1817 Samuel McDonald wrote a letter describing the "disease" that had become "prevalent" in his corner of Georgia. It began with people talking about "the new country, Jackson's Purchase," continued with the sale of livestock and plantations, and concluded when it "carrie[d] them off to the westward."[10] Sometimes the contagion was spread by letters extolling the prime quality of the frontier land or by those visiting home, and then "a panic or moving fever would soon break out" among the neighbors.[11] Those left behind could only look on in wonder. A resident of North Carolina wrote that "the *Alabama Feaver* rages here with great violence and has *carried off* vast numbers of our citizens," and he feared that "if it continues to spread as it has done, it will almost depopulate the country." He agreed that it was "contagious." When "one neighbour visits another who has just returned from the Alabama he immediately discovers the same symptoms . . . as the person who has seen the allureing Alabama."[12] Augustin Harris Hansell remembered that when he was a boy living near Milledgeville, Georgia, on the Federal Road, "We met almost daily, caravans of fifteen and twenty one-horse covered carts, going westward, each containing a whole family and with a spinning will [wheel] on the back and usually a dog underneath." When asked where they were going they all would say they were "bound for the 'New Purchase,' or bound for the 'Alabam.'"[13] Everyone seemed to be on the move, eager to take advantage of new lands.

A "contagion" of some sort must have been at work since it was not easy to pick up a life and move it five hundred miles away. Some were poor enough to walk, driving a few heads of cattle and some hogs along the roads with their meager possessions atop a packhorse. Others loaded wagons or even stuffed their goods into large hogshead barrels with rods running through the centers attached to shafts hitched to mules or oxen, and rolled their way to Alabama.[14] Adam Hodgson, an English traveler, remembered seeing in 1820 "a curious collection" of vehicles, people, and animals piled up on the banks of one of Alabama's rivers waiting to ford or be ferried, including "sulkies, carts, Jersey waggons, heavy waggons, little planters, Indians, Negro[es], horses, mules, and oxen." The women sat and the children played "while the men were engaged in the almost hopeless task of dragging or swimming their vehicles and baggage to the opposite side."[15] Some men went ahead to claim land and then returned for their families. Williamson Hawkins left Tennessee in May 1815 with one packhorse and some of his slaves and ventured south across the mountains to the Jones Valley in north-central Alabama. They cleared land, planted corn, and built a shelter before he left to fetch his family, leaving his laborers behind to guard the homestead. Hawkins returned with one wagon loaded high with people and possessions, chickens in baskets tied to the sides, and some hogs trotting alongside.[16] Those wealthy enough could send an overseer and slaves ahead to prepare the way. One traveler recounted passing six wagons in 1820, filled with ninety slaves belonging to a planter "removing from his plantation in Georgia, to his settlement on the Cahawba, in Alabama."[17]

Some approached the move with a spirit of adventure. Gideon Lincecum, a young man in his early twenties who grew up in the Georgia-Creek borderlands, traveled to Alabama in 1818 and later reminisced that he had "looked upon the long journey, through the wilderness, with much pleasure." The large party of settlers included his wife and two little sons, his parents and eight siblings and a brother-in-law, and ten slaves. "We had good horses and wagons and guns and big dogs," he said, adding, "I felt as if I was on a big camp hunt." The six weeks it took to travel was "the most delightful time I had ever spent in my life." In his memory, the forests and streams were not obstacles but places of abundance. He and his brother walked in the woods flanking the road "as the wagons rolled along and killed deer, turkeys, wild pigeons, and at nights, with pine torches, we fished and killed a great many with my bow and arrows."[18]

John Owen had a very different experience on his journey from Virginia to Tuscaloosa, Alabama, in 1818; his terse journal records privations and hardships that were common among the migrants. Four days after the "Sale of all my goods," Owen set off in late October with his wife and two children along with his mother-in-law and a few slaves. After two days they were forced to stop when the "Cart broke down." That was the first of eleven times that the cart was damaged and needed repair. Wheels came off, bolts and axles broke, and on one memorable occasion, their "horse Runaway with cart broke it all to peaces & alarm us very much." Owen worried about his mother-in-law, who was sick much of the time, but they all periodically suffered illnesses, at times brought on by exposure to unfamiliar environments. "Got to the limestone watter which is disagreeable to the taste makes bad Coffee & opperates on the bowels," Owen noted on November 10. The next day "all well but Lucy & Sam," his slaves. They had "the limestone fever." Food was often scarce, as was fodder for the horses, and they all went hungry.[19]

Physical hardships took their toll but so too did the unsettled nature of human companionship on the road. Owen took a dim view of the people he met in southwestern Virginia and eastern Tennessee, beginning with the man he found "to mend" his cart tire "who half done it & charg[d] double price." Abington, Virginia, was "A sorry looking place & a poor set," while he found "No cleaver people all shifting and mean" across the line in Tennessee. Owen "set up all night apprehensive of Robbers" at one spot in Virginia, and while passing through Cherokee territory encountered an "Indian drunk" who came to their campsite and "plagued us all night." The day before, their "horses got away" and he "had to walk 6 miles to look for them in the wilderness found them at an indian house." At times the party "fell in with many families" on the roads, "met several droves of hogs," or were "pestered" by "negro drivers," but rarely was Owen comforted by fellow travelers.[20]

Owen seemed to reach his breaking point about a month into the trip when the "Old mair fell down" and the "carriage run back" down a hill, which "very much alarm[d] Mother & Ann" and left the "Coupling Bolt broke." He confessed to his journal that he was "much distress[d] & low spirited almost wish I was dead or that fate had bloted the day in which I was born out of the calendar & left a perfect Blank." Owen admitted, to himself at least, that his wife, Ann, had "more fortitude than myself." But he mended the bolt and continued on, finally arriving at "Joneses Vally" on December 22, 1818, where they found "Good land corn & fodder." Four days later they reached Tuscaloosa, "thankful to kind Heaven that after 9 weeks traveling & expos^d to Every danger that we arriv^d safe and in good health." Owen prospered in Alabama by buying land and more slaves and practicing medicine. His prominence within the local community was evident in his appointment as a director of the state bank and his election as mayor of Tuscaloosa.[21]

The routes into Alabama confronted travelers with many hardships. The Tennessee Valley was relatively accessible, either by passing south down roads from Nashville or Knoxville or by boating down the Tennessee River. But settlers coming from Virginia, North Carolina, or Tennessee seeking land further south in Jones Valley or Tuscaloosa had a more difficult time. They used the military roads cut by Jackson's soldiers through the forests and up and down the mountains south of the Tennessee River, an arduous journey on foot or with wearied horses pulling wagons. Some boated down the Tennessee to Muscle Shoals and then packed their belongings on horses and made their way overland to the Black Warrior or Tombigbee Rivers.

Most of those migrating into the former Creek lands of central Alabama or to the Choctaw land along the Tombigbee took the Federal Road, a more established route that nonetheless had its own perils and hardships. When the road passed through sandy soil, deep ruts developed through erosion and washouts, especially on hills, making it a challenge to move loaded wagons. In swampy areas wagons got mired in mud. Getting past rivers and streams was the most difficult and dangerous task for travelers. Smaller waterways could be forded, although during rainy season when streams were high, the cargo and occupants of carriages and wagons often got wet. Larger rivers posed more problems. Flatboats ferried passengers across for a toll but they were not always available. Some of the most memorable descriptions of the multitudes pushing west into Alabama were of occurrences at riverbanks. The Goode family, for example, discovered at the Chattahoochee that "the flat was gone, the rope broke" when the river was high from winter rains, leaving twenty-two wagons and carriages and hundreds of cows and hogs waiting to cross. The livestock could swim but vehicles had to be broken down and carried across in canoes, a painstaking process that took two days.[22]

The recent war was evident not just in the forts strung along the road that served as way stations for travelers, but also in echoes of the old divisions within Creek society. Former allies like William McIntosh and Alexander Cornells maintained public houses along the road through the Creek nation and also managed ferries. McIntosh even built a road from his plantation near Coweta up to the Coosa River, the boundary between Creek territory and Alabama, and advertised the route in a Georgia newspaper. "There are good ferries and bridges," he noted, "so that travellers need not be apprehensive that they will be detained on the road by high waters."[23] But some of the remaining Red Sticks who had fled south across the Florida border to fight with the Seminoles made periodic raids along the road through the Creek nation and even in Alabama, killing or stealing cattle, horses, and hogs. Those attacks intensified local support for the military campaign against the Seminoles and their allies.[24]

Dreams of a new, more prosperous life might have helped settlers cope with the hunger, hardship, and dangers of the road, but arrival brought new disappointments and difficulties. Benjamin Porter and his wife faced the frustrations of the road when they left South Carolina in 1829 bound for the Alabama River near Claiborne. They complained of price gouging, first in the Creek nation by Indians demanding tolls at the "bridges" across the many small streams and then by whites who sold them corn, and of their encounters with "half-naked savages and beastly Negroes" drunk on rum. But what sustained them on their journey was a vision of their uncle, "an early settler," and the home he surely had managed to create in this new land. "We indulged in golden dreams of his appearance and that of his house," Porter wrote. "We pictured him a portly, well-looking old man; and his homestead the very abode of comfort." They imagined "a large white house" with "piazzas and green blinds" and could almost sense "the vapors of benevolence which rose from his face, and the savory smells from his kitchen." Those dreams were dashed when they arrived. "We found our uncle a small man," Porter recalled, "with a very lean girdle—his house was a rail pen, full of squalling, mischievous babes, and snapping bull puppies, and our supper a rasher of bacon with boiled greens."[25]

The Porters had to build their own, more rustic life on the frontier. Benjamin took satisfaction in constructing a "not contemptible bedstead, table, and arm chair" from a poplar tree, but frontier isolation made life difficult during his wife's pregnancy. The nearest midwife was ten miles away in Claiborne and Benjamin found himself "continually swimming the two large creeks" between their farm and town to fetch her in the final weeks before delivery. Then the midwife charged the astronomical fee of thirty-five dollars, instead of the five dollars that Benjamin was able to bargain for when his later children were born.[26]

The thousands who poured into Alabama in the years following the war, who endured the tedium and toil, and sometimes the danger, of the road in order to claim a piece of land, then faced considerable hardship in creating a new home. Food supplies were depleted during the journey and often were scarce or costly in the newly emerging settlements. Unless the settler lucked into a claim that included Indians' old fields, the hard labor of clearing trees in order to plant corn and other food crops lay ahead. Cabins had to be constructed, often crude shelters with few amenities. William Ely visited Tuscaloosa in 1821 and noted the growth of the community, now populated with perhaps as many as "800 souls" only "4 or 5 years since the *first* white Family settled." But he was not impressed with the quality of the town. "What they call their houses," he observed, "are either the most despicable rough dirty and uncomfortable rotting log Cabins, or less durable and more mean buildings, most of them without a single pane of glass . . . and almost as destitute of furniture. . . . Some have no floor but the bare Earth." The persistence of crude frontier conditions might have reflected the fact that the land in Tuscaloosa still had not been legally sold—the inhabitants were squatters.[27]

Migrations offered new beginnings, even if crude ones, but they also entailed loss. An editorial in the *Southern Agriculturalist* warned fathers who moved their families west that they would be condemning "their posterity for two or three generations, to the ills and hardships to which frontier countries are necessarily exposed, to a state short of barbarism, destitute of the amenity which has been the delight of their lives."[28] While frontier "barbarism" surely did not persist for generations, settlers did miss the social connections of home. In 1820 Adam Hodgson encountered "a very pleasing family in the middle of the forest" near the intersection of the Federal Road and the path to Pensacola, the one that passed Burnt Corn Creek. They told him that they missed their old home in Georgia, especially because their new neighbors were "rough and ill suited to their tastes." But they were happy that Sabbath laws were beginning to be enforced and had heard that a free public school would be opening before long— signs, they hoped, that life on the frontier would soon improve.[29]

Traveling with neighbors and kin eased the transition to frontier life, both emotionally and materially. One cannot help but wonder if Benjamin Porter's unnamed wife had any family members to comfort her and ease her fears of labor and childbirth while her husband was off searching for the midwife. Earlier depictions of pioneers as restless wanderers striking out into the wilderness to escape the confines of families and communities have given way to a deeper understanding of the ways in which kinship ties shaped migrations. Historian Carolyn Billingsley uses genealogical methods to trace the movement of Thomas Keesee and his family across the South. Keesee was born in Virginia in 1778, moved to upcountry South Carolina, and then moved to Tennessee with his father and siblings. He might have traveled through Alabama in 1813–14 since he later claimed to have served under Andrew Jackson during the war, or perhaps he simply caught a case of the Alabama fever. Either way, in 1821 Keesee decided to move to lands on the Black Warrior River not far from Tuscaloosa. None of his siblings made that move, but all of his eight children joined him there, and when the land was finally surveyed and put on the market in 1825, he purchased 960 acres. That same year his father died in Tennessee and his estate was divided, including fifty slaves, a cotton gin, and 570 acres planted in tobacco and cotton in Sumner County. Keesee probably already owned some slaves, but that year he received six enslaved men and women from his father's estate: Booker, Big Isram, Clock, Minnie, Gabriel, and China. He must have prospered in Alabama as a cotton planter; in 1840, just three years after he moved on to Arkansas, Keesee owned thirty-one slaves. During his sixteen years in Alabama, his children married, mostly among neighbors and fellow church members, and Keesee formed connections with those in-law families. When he moved to Arkansas, many of his children, their spouses, and their wider families joined him, a testament to the bonds of blood and marital kinship that had developed in Alabama.[30]

Kin connections had the potential to make life easier on the frontier and to pave the way toward economic success. Men could assist one another in clearing land or building houses, or lend out their slaves to help, shortening the time it took to establish a homestead. Women could count on siblings, in-laws, and cousins to help with childbirth or illness. Family members could provide loans or cosign security bonds or simply offer advice to those entering into financial transactions. Even as he was leaning on his son to scout out land for his new plantation, Charles Tait was urging James to seek counsel from his wife's family, who also had moved to Alabama. Those kinds of family alliances could also foster political careers on the frontier. As Billingsley notes, "In a world where political and economic power frequently was contingent on a network of kin, where having a baby was a dangerous business, and where a trip by wagon to a new territory was a long and arduous venture . . . kinship groups stuck together."[31]

The decision to pick up and move hundreds of miles west to start a new life was a cornerstone of American ideals of independence. That choice was often a male prerogative since the motivations for resettlement were usually economic. Women could find themselves forced into journeys and new homes not of their making, bereft of the kind of social connections with family and friends that gave meaning to their lives. Historians disagree about the extent to which women were active participants in decisions to move, but if Billingsley is right that kinship structured migration patterns then frontier life ruptured fewer relationships than previously believed. Westward settlement might have meant autonomy to some and the transplantation of the familiar and familial to others.[32]

Enslaved settlers had neither autonomy nor secure relationships; for them, migration embodied their very powerlessness as human property. Almost 10,000 enslaved people lived in Alabama in 1816, and that number more than doubled to 21,384 by 1820. Because so many free white settlers were also pouring into Alabama during those years, the proportion of the population that was enslaved remained at just under 32 percent. That percentage would grow over the next decade as white settlement slowed and the importation of slaves increased. But the density of slaveholdings in 1820 varied across the new state, with concentrations in the Tennessee Valley and along the Alabama River. Madison County's slave population, for example, grew from just under 30 percent of the total in 1816 to just under 50 percent four years later. While white settlers moved west into the new Valley counties, enslaved laborers poured into Madison.[33]

Those unwilling pioneers made their way to Alabama in different ways. Slave traders brought some to the region in the years following the war, confident that the demand for labor to clear land and plant cotton while prices were high would ensure sales of their inventory. Owen mentioned in his journal seeing "negro drivers" on the roads from Virginia and Tennessee, and other travelers witnessed large groups of slaves moving west, the men chained together in a coffle while the women and children rode in wagons. But since the interstate slave trade did not fully develop until the 1830s, most came with their masters or were purchased from neighboring states by Alabama's settlers. The road sometimes imposed a rough frontier equality among enslaved and free travelers, especially those with just a few slaves. Owen, his family, and his slaves, Lucy and Sam, all suffered the ill effects of "the limestone fever" while passing through the mountains of southwestern Virginia. Williamson Hawkins probably worked with his slaves to clear land and plant corn and trusted them enough to leave them in the Jones Valley while he returned to Tennessee to get his family.[34]

Migrations could also highlight the difference in status between slaves and masters. The disruption of routines and travel through rough and isolated terrain and Indian territory heightened fears that slaves might run away. That could lead to tighter restrictions, especially among large groups of enslaved men and women. An observer noted that "when there is a gang of from twenty to a hundred, the poor creatures are arranged two abreast, secured by a long chain that passes down between them, and in this manner are driven forward; all prospect of escape being cut off, by the loaded rifles on either hand."[35] One large group of migrants from North Carolina traveling with sixty slaves made their way to the headwaters of the Tombigbee River. There they loaded everyone into canoes and set off downriver to settlements further south. Before they got very far, their canoes capsized and they lost all of their possessions, including twenty-one of their enslaved companions who drowned. Only one of the white settlers, a little child, died in the mishap. One wonders whether those who lost their lives were bound or chained in some way to keep them under control.[36]

The enslaved men and women brought to Alabama were stripped away from familiar communities of kin and friends. This was especially true of those ensnared in the formal slave trade, most of whom came from the Chesapeake region, but also of those traveling with their owners. Because frontier slaveholders preferred young slaves for their strength in performing the hard physical labor needed on new farms and, in the case of women, for their reproductive labor, adolescent slaves were often separated from their parents before being sent west. An Alabama planter asked his brother in Virginia to send him youthful slaves, "excepting 2 or 3 healthy old women to cook and a trusty old man to attend to the hogs,"[37] while a newly arrived planter in Mississippi was advised "to buy *none in families*, but to *select only choice, first rate, young hands from 14 to 25 years of age*."[38] Planters migrating to Alabama sometimes maximized their workforce by selling those too young or too old to work, or leaving them with family back east. Even when entire slaveholding establishments pulled up stakes in Georgia or South Carolina and made their way to Alabama, the people forced along left behind familiar homes and probably relationships with people on neighboring farms and plantations.[39]

Think about the different meanings that migration had for Thomas Keesee and the six slaves whom he inherited from his father in 1825. Keesee did leave his father and siblings behind in Tennessee but came to Alabama with all of his children. They in turn married and forged such strong connections between families that when Keesee decided to move on to the Arkansas frontier, those in-laws joined him. Thomas probably welcomed the six inherited slaves for their additional labor, since he received them just as he was purchasing 980 acres of land. But they might also have served as an emotional connection back to his siblings and his father and to his old home in Tennessee. Perhaps he grew up among them. But those six men and women were stripped from a community of fifty slaves when his father's estate was settled. Most of those fifty went to Thomas's siblings, who lived near each other in Tennessee. Those six were sent to Alabama and surely left family and loved ones behind. Thomas chose to leave his family in Tennessee; Booker, Big Isram, Clock, Minnie, Gabriel, and China had no choice. And sixteen years later they again had no say when the Keesee family decided to move to Arkansas, tearing their slaves from whatever broader community they had established in Tuscaloosa.

———————————————————

The settlers who flocked to Alabama after the war, whether poor herdsmen or wealthy planters, all shared one thing in common when they arrived: they were squatters. The first acres of the Creek cession would not be sold until August 1817, while the Tennessee Valley land would not go on the market until November. Much of the rest of the land recently acquired from the Indians would remain unsold for several years. The federal government's mission was to turn those squatters into settlers. That was necessary to impose order on the frontier so that the lands taken from the Indians would, in the words of William Barnett, "be purified & regenerated." But federal officials also had their eye on the potential profits to be made from land sales, especially as cotton prices rose in the heady atmosphere of the postwar boom. A political order began to emerge at the same time, as local leaders with connections to national politicians like Charles Tait created a territorial government in 1817 and then the state of Alabama in 1819. The collapse of the boom in the Panic of 1819 shattered the postwar optimism that had fueled Alabama fever. For a time the settlement process seemed to unravel as settlers became squatters again, and the economic dislocation shook the foundation of Alabama's early political system.

The federal government confronted the issue of squatters with some flexibility, balancing its need to impose order with a realistic mixture of pragmatic humanitarianism. Since the 1790s the government had taken a dim view of squatters, especially those encroaching on Indian land, and had not hesitated to use troops to remove violators. The squatters disrupted relations with the Indians and impeded negotiations for land cessions. But the families who rushed west after the War of 1812 crowded onto land already purchased, or taken, from the Indians; they did not threaten efforts to acquire more territory. In one effort to create some order the Mississippi Territorial Legislature organized all of the Creek cession into Monroe County in the summer of 1815, almost one year after the Treaty of Fort Jackson. By 1816 just over 3,500 white settlers and 1,600 slaves lived in this vast county stretching between the Coosa and Tombigbee Rivers from the Florida border north to the Tennessee Valley. Ignoring the fact that the residents were illegally residing on public land, the territorial officials decided to create an administrative and judicial apparatus and offer representation to the new settlers. Letting the squatters remain seemed the humane thing to do. William Barnett argued that forcibly removing those families would cause "incalculable distress" since "many of these unhappy people have expended almost the whole of their little all in reaching the forbidden land; and are utterly incapable of returning." Besides, who would round up the families? The entire county was made up of illegal residents. As Harry Toulmin wrote to President Madison in 1816, "How can a jury be found in Monroe county to convict a man of intrusions,—where every man is an intruder."[40]

Leniency also grew out of a sense that the postwar squatters were not obstacles but precursors to settlement, paving the way toward an imminent sale. The congressional representative Newton Cannon, who sympathized with the poor families in the Tennessee Valley, saw no evidence of conflict between them and the wealthier planters scouting out land in preparation for the 1817 sale. On the contrary, he said, "they have opened roads and paths through the different parts of the country, by which it can be more easily and accurately explored by others," and provided shelter and hospitality to emigrants viewing the land.[41] Other western politicians touted the role that pioneers played in the recent war in defeating both the British and the Indians, lauding their martial valor as just cause for leniency. Congress passed a law in 1816 allowing settlers to stay on public lands if they applied to their local land office in order to relinquish any claim to their holding during the sale. Few bothered to do so.[42]

Surveying dragged on, even as more and more squatters arrived. Thomas Freeman, who was charged with surveying the various Indian cessions in Alabama, detailed exactly what made the process so difficult in apologetic letters back to his impatient superiors. The territory was vast and the terrain difficult in places. Each surveying party included axemen to clear the way and chainmen to assist the surveyors, and those underlings often grew weary of the work and left, forcing Freeman and his assistants to search among the squatter settlements for replacements. The scarcity of food and a wide variety of illnesses compounded those difficulties, as did Freeman's constant worry about Indian attack. Tired of Freeman's complaints and slow pace, the land office decided to split Alabama into northern and southern sections and hired John Coffee to survey the Tennessee Valley lands. Andrew Jackson had recommended his old friend who had served as his cavalry officer in the Creek War and at the battle of New Orleans, and Coffee did not disappoint. He and his surveying parties moved quickly through the Valley.[43]

The auctioning of the Creek lands in August 1817, followed by the Tennessee Valley lands in early 1818, generated one of the greatest land booms in the nation's history. The government usually set aside a couple of weeks for public auction, when buyers could bid on tracts, the smallest being a quarter section of 160 acres. Any land not sold during that time could then be purchased for the minimum price of $2 an acre. Only one-quarter of the purchase price had to be paid up front, with the rest due in three annual installments. The land sold in August, primarily rich bottomlands close to the present site of Montgomery, went for more than $5 an acre. The Tennessee Valley lands brought in more profits when they were sold the following year. Some tracts fetched between $50 and $100 an acre at the auction and even average land reached $20 to $30 an acre. Of course, much of the land sold privately, after the auction, at the much lower rate of $2. By the end of the year one million acres of Valley land had been sold for over $7 million, averaging $7.50 an acre.[44]

A number of factors converged to drive up the price of land, the first and foremost being the booming cotton economy. The wealth generated by the expansion of cotton was evident to the prospective buyers who flocked to Huntsville in anticipation of the land sales. Brick buildings, including the county courthouse and the Planters' and Merchants' Bank, had replaced many of the crude wooden structures, and by 1818 Huntsville had approximately 260 residences and at least a dozen mercantile businesses. Leroy Pope, who owned over one hundred slaves in 1815, looked down on the town and the bank that he directed from his mansion on a hill, complete with a colonnaded porch. He and Thomas Bibb, who owned fifty-three slaves in 1815, rode through the town in four-wheeled carriages. They stood at the head of a group of planter elite who had prospered on this frontier. One visitor to Madison County in 1818 declared the cotton fields "astonishingly large; from four to five hundred acres in a field!" adding, "To a stranger, coming suddenly amongst these fields, it has the appearance of magic."[45] The 20 gins in the county in 1817 had multiplied to 149 in 1819, and cleaned almost 4,500,000 pounds of cotton to be sent down the Tennessee River for sale in New Orleans. That transformation was made possible by the increasing availability of slaves being transported from the East.[46]

With cotton prices pushing toward thirty cents a pound and the rapid success of Madison County as a model, it is no wonder that prospective settlers were intensely interested in the Tennessee Valley lands to the west. John Campbell came to Huntsville in 1817 to scout out the region and wrote that Huntsville's "growth with that of the whole surrounding country in population and in wealth exceeds anything I have ever heard of." The young Virginian had heard rumors that farmers were "clearing between four and five hundred dollars to the hand," and was convinced that "any person settling in this country who has had anything of a capitol" was sure to "become wealthy in a few years." He wrote his brother that he wanted "to turn all of my energies towards the acquisition of wealth" and that he thought North Alabama "will favour my views better than any country that I have yet seen." John Hardie, a young Scottish immigrant who worked as a clerk in Richmond, made the trek to Huntsville because a friend who had journeyed there earlier assured him that the Tennessee Valley, "being in its infancy," was "one of the best places in the United States for making money."[47]

Other factors besides the rising price of cotton fueled inflationary pressures on the eve of the land sale. One, a legacy from the past, was part of the legal settlement over the tangled Yazoo sale of 1795. The federal government agreed to pay the Yazoo claimants $5 million in what was known as Mississippi stock or scrip, which could only be used to purchase land. Most of those holding claims on the original Yazoo land had no interest in settling in Alabama or Mississippi, but they could sell their stock to those who were eager to move to the southwestern frontier. The irony is that the funds used to sort through the mess created by a fraudulent and grandiose speculative scheme back in 1795 ended up helping to spark a new speculation twenty-three years later.[48]

Political and economic forces within Alabama also created an environment conducive to profiteering off land hunger. The elite planters who had migrated from the Broad River region of Georgia before the War of 1812 had come to dominate the economic landscape of Madison County. Extensive slaveholdings and landholdings were sources of power for men like Leroy Pope, his son-in-law John Williams Walker, and Thomas Bibb, but so too was their leadership of the Planters' and Merchants' Bank of Huntsville. But their connections to old neighbors like Senator Charles Tait and Secretary of the Treasury William Crawford afforded opportunities to extend their power once Alabama gained territorial status in 1817. One of the first acts of the new territorial legislature was the repeal of the Mississippi Usury Act of 1805, which had limited interest rates on loans. Banks like the Planters' and Merchants' Bank would still have to cap interest on loans at 6 percent, but there would be no limit to the interest charged for private lending. Advocates of the repeal argued that money remained tight despite the flurry of notes from almost seventy newly chartered Tennessee and Kentucky banks flooding the Tennessee Valley before the sale. Walker wrote to Tait to explain his sponsorship of this "bold experiment," claiming that his intent was to let money "find its level of value" instead of artificially restricting it.[49]

Private loans could be a lucrative investment. John Hardie asked his brother to send him money and was willing to pay 8 percent interest on it since it would "be of more value to me here for a *short time* than I ever had any idea of." He explained that in Huntsville, "30 to 40% could be got" for loaned money, since it was "much wanted to buy land," and those loans became "a speculation many a one has made their fortune at."[50] Wealthy merchants and planters like Walker who were stockholders and directors of the Planters' and Merchants' Bank were better positioned to take advantage of the law. They could borrow the limited supply of the bank's funds at 6 percent and then loan it out at exorbitant rates to recent settlers looking to buy land or slaves. In the heady atmosphere of the postwar boom, payment of all debts seemed possible if a cotton crop could be sent off to market.[51]

Some of those same men associated with the bank in Huntsville organized speculation companies to take advantage of the Tennessee Valley sales. One such group was the Cypress Land Company, established in 1818 as an alliance between the former Nashville and Georgia elites. Leroy Pope, Thomas Bibb, and John Coffee, among others, combined forces to buy up potential town sites along the northern banks of the Tennessee. They focused their efforts on the foot of Muscle Shoals, long a focus for speculators as the head of easy navigation along the river and for its relatively close proximity to the upper stretches of the Black Warrior and Tombigbee Rivers. There they purchased over five thousand acres for just over $85,000, with each trustee of the company receiving shares commensurate with the amount of land he bought. Coffee, using his surveying skills, laid out the town of Florence, and the Cypress Land Company quickly put the town lots on sale in the summer of 1818. Speculators, most of whom never intended on settling in Florence, bought lots. Some were local planters like John Williams Walker, who was a stockholder in the company and bought six lots, and others were more distant, like Andrew Jackson and James Madison. All of them hoped to turn a profit down the road when they could sell their holdings in the town. Meanwhile, the Cypress Land Company made a profit by selling the four hundred town lots for over $280,000.[52]

Not everyone who purchased Tennessee Valley land in the 1818 sale was a well-connected planter; yeoman farmers with few or no slaves also participated. Many of those settlers probably waited out the public auction where prices soared, hoping that their chosen tracts made it through unsold so that they could purchase them at the private sales for two dollars an acre. But prosperity and ever-rising cotton prices enticed many to overreach and risk debt for the chance of owning fertile land. As John Hardie noted, a "number of emigrants" flocked to the valley because the "price they receive for one year's crop will pay for the price of the land."[53] Of course, that depended on the market for Alabama cotton.

The optimism of the postwar boom that drove Alabama fever collapsed in the Panic of 1819 and threatened to unravel the settlements of the Indian lands. Triggered in part by a shift in policies by the Bank of the United States and a contraction in the money supply, the Panic drove down cotton prices from about twenty-five cents per pound in the winter of 1818–19 to twelve cents the following summer. Banks closed their doors or suspended paying specie—gold and silver coins—in exchange for their banknotes, which depreciated in value. Those most integrated into the cotton economy were hurt first. John Taylor and Philip Foote, for example, were partners in a Huntsville mercantile business. They had the bad luck of having recently purchased, as Taylor recounted, "a very large quantity" of cotton from Madison County's planters "at the highest prices." Taylor was in New Orleans on business when he heard "of the immense and unparallelled [sic] fall in the price of cotton." The firm of Taylor & Foote owed money to eastern merchants for merchandise it had bought on credit and carried substantial debts to the Huntsville Bank and to a bank in Tennessee. The partners ended up having to auction all the goods from their store, several lots in Huntsville, and a cotton gin, and Foote was forced to sell his own house with its "new brick kitchen and meat house . . . framed stable and carriage house, and a large inclosed garden."[54]

Soon smaller farmers in frontier settlements were feeling pinched. Many were bound together by a network of mutual obligation and debt, with various personal notes keeping account of who owed what to whom in place of an exchange of money. People hired out a slave for a day's labor, utilized the services of a doctor or lawyer, or bought a drink at the local tavern, all on credit with a personal bond or note sealing the deal. In good times there was some flexibility in the payment of those debts, but as the economic depression filtered into Alabama's settlements, pressure built. People needed the debts owed them to be paid so that they could pay off their own debts during hard times. "FAIR WARNING!!" read the newspaper notice from Alexander Campbell in Madison County. He announced that because he was "hard pushed for cash," those who owed him should settle those debts by March 1820 or "expect to settle with an officer." Campbell was forced to take "this last resort" out of "imperious necessity."[55]

The Alabama fever that compelled so many to make the hard trek to the newly opened Indian lands must have felt like a delirium dream in the wake of the Panic. Some wondered why they had paid so much for their land, and even why they had left home to come to Alabama in the first place. William Harris left Virginia in early 1819 and purchased land in Madison County just before the Panic hit. In a series of letters to his brother beginning in the fall of 1820 he recounted his hardships and regrets. "In the first place you know that the d——d land cost me $26,000," Harris wrote, adding that a poor cotton crop and falling prices left him unable to pay off that debt. He was able to sell his property for $10,800 and believed he would "submit" to the loss "cheerfully" if he did not have other financial obligations weighing him down. His sense of failure is palpable in his letters. "If I had never left Virginia," he wrote, "I might perhaps been better off... and it grieves me to think that I have, perhaps, to go still farther." In a letter that he asks his brother to show "to no person but the family," Harris reveals the depth of his shame. "The embarrassment of mind I have suffered for some time . . . causes reflections which almost unmans me, those *feelings* I hope you never may experience." Harris thought of moving to Cuba or Florida and becoming a merchant. Others picked up and moved further west. "Would you believe it?" one visitor to the Tennessee Valley asked in 1822. "The people are leaving this beautiful country, and going, some to Texas, some to Missouri, and some to Red River, and others, the plague knows where."[56]

The Panic of 1819, coming so closely on the heels of the cotton boom that drove much of the settlement of Alabama, complicated the process of frontier development. The depression shattered the confidence of settlers like Harris and contributed to a demonization of the speculative excesses of the postwar period. That, in turn, roiled the political waters of early Alabama by strengthening populist assaults against the Georgia faction, the group of landowners also known as the Broad River group. The boom and bust also generated a tremendous land debt that threatened to unravel settlement, forcing settlers and their political leaders to turn to the federal government for relief.

The Georgia faction was riding high when the Panic of 1819 hit Alabama, in part because their migratory streams bridged North and South Alabama. While the earlier group of Broad River settlers had chosen Madison County, later arrivals from Georgia took advantage of the opening of Creek and Choctaw lands and settled to the south. William Bibb, Thomas's brother, moved to Saint Stephens on the Tombigbee and Charles Tait joined his son on the Alabama River. William Crawford remained in Georgia but used his influence with President Monroe to get William Bibb appointed Alabama's first territorial governor. John William Walker presided over the constitutional convention held in Huntsville in the early summer of 1819, just before news of the Panic began filtering through the region. Four other directors of Leroy Pope's bank, including Thomas Bibb, joined the constitutional delegation that was dominated by members from Madison County. Thomas Bibb then became president of the state senate, which promptly elected Walker to the United States Senate. Voters elected William Bibb the state's first governor. Still, the Georgia faction's power was not limitless. Charles Tait lost his bid to be elected Alabama's other senator because legislators from southern Alabama thought he was too closely allied with the Georgians from the Tennessee Valley.[57]

Bibb waded into the morass of sectional tension with his selection of the new town of Cahawba as the state capital. A commission had suggested Tuscaloosa, which was far enough north to satisfy the Tennessee Valley legislators, but Bibb bucked that recommendation in favor of the new settlements of South Alabama. The delegates at the constitutional convention accepted Bibb's choice but determined that the assembly would have the power to change the capital's location in 1825 without the governor's approval. Bibb did not live long enough to see the capitol building completed in Cahawba. Weakened by tuberculosis, he died in 1820 from injuries he sustained from a fall from his horse and was replaced by his brother Thomas, who was not as skilled a politician.[58]

Sectional tensions undermined the unity of the Georgia faction, but it was the Panic and the subsequent depression that gave the most potent ammunition to its political enemies. The members of the Broad River group were too tainted by the speculative frenzies of the postwar settlement period, especially their association with both the repeal of the Usury Act and the Planters' and Merchants' Bank of Huntsville. Alabama's first state legislature met in late 1819 as the Panic spread, and although they repealed the experiment in unrestricted private loans, they did not invalidate the existing contracts. That left some debtors facing crippling charges because of excessive interest rates. Those so-called "big interest" cases went to the state supreme court over a period of years in the 1820s and became fodder for a populist press. The *Huntsville Democrat*, for example, railed against the Royal Party, depicting the men surrounding the Planters' and Merchants' Bank as aristocrats who had defrauded the people, especially by ensnaring them in usurious loan contracts. The trauma of frontier settlement in postwar Alabama lived on deep into the 1820s.[59]

The demise of the Huntsville bank came at the hands of two unlikely foes. William Crawford had been a crucial and well-positioned ally as secretary of the treasury, selecting the bank to be the depository of federal funds from the Tennessee Valley land sales. But his support crumbled when hard times forced Leroy Pope's bank to suspend specie payments. Crawford insisted that the monies generated by the land sales be withdrawn and sent east, but Pope dragged his feet in complying, prompting the secretary to accuse the Huntsville bankers of being "a set of public swindlers."[60]

The loss of Crawford's powerful patronage wounded the Planters' and Merchants' Bank, but it was Israel Pickens who finished it off. The North Carolinian had served in Congress from 1811 to 1817, but decided to forgo another term and instead move to Alabama like so many others that year. He used his political connections to get a job as register of the Saint Stephens land office and within a year he had amassed 3,500 acres of land in southwest Alabama, after which he became the first president of the Tombigbee Bank of Saint Stephens. The speculator and banker was a supporter of William Bibb and seemed a natural ally of the Georgia faction and the Huntsville bank. But Pickens, an adept politician, recognized the growing hostility toward the Broad River group and by 1820 he began to distance himself. When Thomas Bibb declined to run for governor in 1821, Pickens stepped into the race and defeated Henry Chambers, a director of the Planters' and Merchants' Bank. He made the creation of a state bank the centerpiece of his administration and maneuvered to ensure the demise of the Huntsville bank. Pickens threatened an investigation into the bank's suspension of specie payments in 1822, prompting the bank's directors to promise a full resumption of payments by the end of 1823. If they failed, they would forfeit their charter. After again defeating Chambers for reelection in 1823, Pickens pushed through a bill establishing the Bank of Alabama. Two years later, the Huntsville bank folded.[61]

While populists attacked the Georgia faction and rival elites challenged its authority, political leaders in both Alabama and the federal government confronted the tremendous land debt generated by the boom and bust. That debt threatened the solvency of the national Treasury and the livelihoods and stability of the farmers and planters who had migrated west after the war. Alabama far outstripped the other western states in this regard. Recent purchasers of land throughout the trans-Appalachian West owed the government $21 million by the end of 1820, and settlers in Alabama carried more than half of that burden at over $11 million, with Ohio coming in second at just over $2.5 million. The sales in the Tennessee Valley left purchasers owing just over $6 million, but the Alabama River region was not far behind at just under $4 million. The question was how the Treasury could recoup money owed from the sale of land without stripping vast numbers of settlers of their landholdings. No one wanted to see a return to the early years after the war when squatters prevailed. Some sort of relief was needed, argued Huntsville's newspaper, the *Alabama Republican*.

Adopting the persona of a settler unable to pay the installments on his land, the editor detailed for the government the impact of the debt: "Your timber will be destroyed, your land will be withheld from market, and the particular spot on which I now reside, instead of becoming a snug and cheerful retreat, under my prudent management, will only be my place of sojourning, until I am driven from it by force."[62]

Congress found a solution in March 1821 when it passed a relief bill that gave land debtors two options. They could either relinquish portions of their land to complete payment on what they retained, or they could apply for an extension of credit for four, six, or eight years, depending on how much they had already paid. The *Alabama Republican* applauded this action and painted a rosy picture of the future to contrast with its gloomier assessment of a reversion to squatter settlements. "We shall now see lands highly cultivated, orchards planted, comfortable dwellings erected, and a spirit of public improvements pervade the whole community," the newspaper predicted. In a kind of parody or mirror image of the scene three years earlier during the sale of 1818, the *Republican* described the "bustling" crowd that filled the Huntsville land office "from sun rise till dark" in order to meet the relinquishment deadlines.[63]

The land relief bill of 1821 succeeded in reducing debt by almost half, but at a cost. Settlers had to relinquish about a third of the land purchased in the Tennessee Valley between 1818 and 1820. Many were likely able to hold on to homesteads while forfeiting portions of their land, but others found themselves once again squatting on land they no longer owned. Residents of the new counties of Franklin and Lawrence in the western valley petitioned Congress in 1821 for preference rights to their land, arguing that speculators had driven up prices back in 1818 and threatened once again to steal away their land. Throughout the decade Alabamians argued over the disposition of the relinquished land, a reminder of the persistent problems associated with settlement in a period of boom and bust.[64]

———————————————

Frontier settlement seemed incomplete and insecure when viewed through the lens of the political controversies generated by the Panic of 1819. Beneath that tumult, however, a steady progression of settlers and their slaves were cultivating land formerly occupied by Creeks, Choctaws, and Chickasaws, and in the process were transforming Alabama. Small farmers and herdsmen found homes in the hill country below the Tennessee Valley and in other isolated corners of the state, but much of the newly settled land in other regions was devoted to cotton. The settlement of Creek lands along the Alabama River and Choctaw lands on the Tombigbee, for example, is evident in the increasing number of bales of cotton passing through Mobile: the 16,000 bales exported in 1820 had grown to 102,684 by 1830. Planters in North Alabama extended the cotton kingdom already established in Madison County to the Chickasaw lands of the western Tennessee Valley.[65]

Steamboats facilitated the emergence of the cotton kingdom in Alabama. The first run from Mobile to Montgomery was in 1821 and took ten days, but the boats soon became a familiar sight on all the state's rivers. They were smaller than those plying the Mississippi River, with shallow drafts that allowed them to navigate deeper inland than they otherwise would have been able to go. Some towns along the rivers, such as Montgomery and Selma, became inland ports, regular stops along the route, but often steamboats put in at the private landings of planters to take on cotton. Those plantations on bluffs high above the water often had chutes down to the river so that cotton bales could be slid to the waiting decks below. The federal government assisted in the development of the cotton business in 1826 by funding the dredging of a channel through a bar of sand and silt at the mouth of the Mobile River so that boats could more easily pass. Muscle Shoals proved a greater obstacle. For decades Valley residents debated and lobbied for and against various schemes, from a canal to a railroad, to solve the shipping problems along the Tennessee River.[66]

A business culture centered on cotton quickly emerged in Alabama's towns. One letter to a Huntsville newspaper in 1825, penned by someone using the name Amanda Heartfree, challenged the priorities of planters and merchants whose mouths were "stuffed with cotton." All of them were too preoccupied with "the attainment of wealth, with the most immediate excess" to "pursue . . . the improvement of society." None discussed "the advancements of sciences and literature," but "you are certain to catch the price of cotton."[67] Mobile's entire economy revolved around the cotton trade. Planters in the interior used the city's cotton brokers to market their crops and purchase supplies and relied on its banks and insurance companies to finance and protect their livelihoods. During the winter months, when cotton was shipped, the population of Mobile often tripled or quadrupled in size, only to empty during the hot, sleepy months of summer. Even the city's streetscape changed because of cotton's demands. The marshy muck that bordered the waterfront had always impeded trade. Long wharves had to be constructed to extend to water deep enough for ships, and those were limited in number. Fort Charlotte, known by the French who constructed it as Fort Conde, provided at least a partial solution. The federal government had no more use for it and sold it to a local group of private developers in 1820. The city paid to have it demolished to open access to more of the waterfront and used the rubble to fill in the wetlands. The decrepit symbol of the old imperial frontier served to shift Mobile closer to the water and to the ships laden with cotton bales.[68]

The cotton kingdom arose out of the Creek, Chickasaw, and Cherokee lands acquired by the federal government and from the Alabama fever that drew countless settlers west, but not without the labor of tens of thousands of enslaved migrants to that frontier. The slave trade drew disproportionately from the Chesapeake region, an area once dominated by tobacco but which by the early nineteenth century had increasingly been given over to grains and mixed farming. There slaves performed a wide variety of tasks associated with cultivating and processing different crops and tending livestock, including artisanal work like carpentry and blacksmithing. They had no experience with cotton and faced great hardship as they learned a new labor regimen.[69]

Charles Ball's description of his time in the cotton fields of South Carolina offers a window into the difficulty of that transition. Ball, a strong man who took pride in his skills, was sold south from Maryland and found, "when we came to the picking of cotton, that I was not equal to a boy of twelve or fifteen years of age." He worked as hard as he could but when the cotton was weighed at the end of the day, Ball was "ashamed" to find that his was less than that of most, "even of the women, who had heretofore regarded me as the strongest and most powerful man of the whole gang." Ball anticipated "something still more painful" than that embarrassment, "for I knew that the lash of the overseer would soon become familiar with my back, if I did not perform as much work as any of the other young men."[70]

Conditions for new settlers, both free and enslaved, were often primitive for a time, even several years, but the burdens fell more heavily on the slaves. It took a tremendous amount of labor to clear land and plant crops in the first years of settlement when provisions were scarce and shelter was crude. The feverish rush to claim land, to make enough to purchase those claims, and to prosper on this new cotton frontier spilled over onto the enslaved laborer who made it possible. One settler who passed through an area west of Montgomery captured some of the intensity of settlement in his reminiscences. "Farmers were picking cotton and clearing land,—the axes were cutting until midnight, and an hour before day next morning," he wrote. "Camped near Marion Saturday night. Negroes were cutting timber all night until sunrise Sunday. Marion was thronged with people on Sunday, talking about cotton and 'niggers.'"[71] William Ely visited Tuscaloosa in 1821 and described the settlers as "indolent" and "lazy" but also as "a very avaricious People—Money is their God and *Cotton* the *Idol* of their devotions." Because their energies were focused on clearing land and planting cotton, they paid little attention to the niceties of life. Settlers lived in primitive conditions by choice with the knowledge that they were building a future, but they also forced privations on their slaves. One kitchen in Tuscaloosa was "the filthiest place you can conceive of," according to Ely. It "contains two beds, in which and on the floor, from 6 to 10 Negroes of both Sexes and various ages all unmarried sleep Promiscuously."[72]

When Charles Tait arrived in Alabama in 1819, his son James was busy establishing a plantation, on land he did not yet own, through the labor of his slaves. His workforce actually comprised men and women owned by both him and his father. After his initial settlement in 1818, when he and three slaves began "preparing a few acres for the cultivation of Indian Corn," his father sent sixty slaves who arrived in January 1819. Forty of them were Charles's and the remaining twenty were a wedding present to James, but only twenty-five of them were old enough to be working hands. They expanded the amount of cleared land and planted 80 acres of corn and 175 acres of cotton in 1819, and once those were harvested and picked, they continued clearing "a big field on the upland . . . and some in the swamp." James and Charles worked them hard, putting "two or three more ten year olds" into the fields, and their reward in 1820 was eighty bales of cotton.[73]

The extent of white settlers' dependence on the enslaved pioneers is evident in Charles Tait's preoccupation with the mood of his labor force as they anticipated leaving their Georgia home. He wrote his daughter-in-law, already in Alabama, that "our black people" looked ahead to the move "cheerfully" and therefore "deserve to be treated well; not only with justice but with tenderness." But some concern crept into his letter when he wrote, "I have strong hopes that every one will go without a murmur." After his slaves were sent ahead to join James and Caroline Tait in Alabama, Charles wrote that he was sure "that they will give cheerfully all their exertions to our establishment in the Alabama," but again revealed a tickle of doubt by adding, "I hope there will be no discontents, no murmurings."[74] Historian James David Miller, cautioning against accepting at face value Tait's awareness of his slaves' feelings about migrating west, makes the salient point that "cheerful or murmuring, they still had to go."[75] Tait's dream of reestablishing and improving on his life on the cotton frontier depended on that.

Notes

1. Newton Cannon to Acting Secretary of War George Graham, January 17, 1817, in *The Territorial Papers of the United States*, ed. Clarence Edwin Carter, vol. 18, *The Territory of Alabama, 1817–1819* (Washington, DC: US Government Printing Office, 1952), 24.

2. James A. Tait to Elizabeth Caroline Tait, February 6, 1818, Tait Family Papers, Alabama Department of Archives and History, Montgomery, quoted in James David Miller, *South by Southwest: Planter Emigration and Identity in the Slave South* (Charlottesville: University of Virginia Press, 2002), 63.

3. James A Tait to Charles Tait, February 7, 1818, Tait Family Papers, quoted in Miller, *South by Southwest*, 72–73.

4. Miller, *South by Southwest*, 60–65, 72–73; James Benson Sellers, *Slavery in Alabama* (University: University of Alabama Press, 1950), 32.

5. James A. Tait to Charles Tait, December 15, 1817, Tait Family Papers, quoted in Thomas D. Clark and John D. W. Guice, *Frontiers in Conflict: The Old Southwest, 1795–1830* (Albuquerque: University of New Mexico Press, 1989), 166.

6. Charles Tait to James A. Tait, November 7, 1818, Tait Family Papers, quoted in Miller, *South by Southwest*, 4–5.

7. Thomas Freeman to Josiah Meigs, Washington, Mississippi Territory, January 29, 1817, in Carter, *Territorial Papers*, vol. 18, 35; Freeman to Meigs, April 17, 1817, in ibid., 89.

8. William Barnett to Acting Secretary of War George Graham, Huntsville, March 12, 1817, in Carter, *Territorial Papers*, vol. 18, 71–72; John Read to Josiah Meigs, Huntsville, April 17, 1817, in ibid., 84.

9. "Census of the Mississippi Territory Taken in 1816," in *The Territorial Papers of the United States*, ed. Clarence Edwin Carter, vol. 6, *The Territory of Mississippi, 1809–1817* (Washington, DC: US Government Printing Office, 1938), 730; "Abstract of the Territorial Census," in Carter, *Territorial Papers*, vol. 18, 462; Sellers, *Slavery in Alabama*, 17; Clark and Guice, *Frontiers in Conflict*, 164.

10. Samuel McDonald to Ann Brantley, May 27, 1817, Elizabeth Furman Talley Papers, University of North Carolina, Chapel Hill, quoted in Miller, *South by Southwest*, 2.

11. "Recollections" of 1836, chap. 2, James Rowe Coombs Papers, Duke University Library, Durham, NC, quoted in James Oakes, *The Ruling Race: A History of American Slaveholders* (New York: Vintage Books, 1983, 77.

12. James Graham to Thomas Ruffin, November 9, 1817, in Thomas Ruffin, *The Papers of Thomas Ruffin*, ed. J. G. de Roulhac Hamilton (Raleigh: North Carolina Historical Commission, 1918), 1:198, quoted in Malcolm J. Rohrbough, *The Trans-Appalachian Frontier* (New York: Oxford University Press, 1978), 196.

13. Augustin Harris Hansell, "Memoirs, 1817–1906," Augustin Harris Hansell Memoirs, Southern Historical Collection, University of North Carolina, Chapel Hill,

quoted in Angela Pulley Hudson, *Creek Paths and Federal Roads: Indians, Settlers, and Slaves and the Making of the American South* (Chapel Hill: University of North Carolina Press, 2010), 125.

14. Everett Dick, *The Dixie Frontier* (New York: Capricorn Books, 1948), 58–59.

15. Adam Hodgson, *Remarks during a Journey through North America in the Years 1819, 1820, and 1821 in a Series of Letters* (New York: Samuel Whiting, 1823), 146–47, quoted in James Eyre Wainwright, "Both Native South and Deep South: The Native Transformation of the Gulf South Borderlands, 1770–1835" (PhD dissertation, Rice University, 2013), 354.

16. William Warren Rogers et al., *Alabama: The History of a Deep South State* (Tuscaloosa: University of Alabama Press, 1994), 58.

17. Adam Hodgson, *Letters from North America, Written during a Tour in the United States and Canada* (London, 1824), n.p., quoted in Miller, *South by Southwest*, 1.

18. Gideon Lincecum, "Autobiography of Gideon Lincecum," in *Publications of the Mississippi Historical Society* (Oxford: Mississippi Historical Society, 1904), 8:464–65, quoted in Henry DeLeon Southerland Jr. and Jerry Elijah Brown, *The Federal Road through Georgia, the Creek Nation, and Alabama, 1806–1836* (Tuscaloosa: University of Alabama Press, 1989), 105.

19. Thomas McAdory Owen, ed., *John Owen's Journal of His Removal from Virginia to Alabama in 1818* (Baltimore: Friedenwald, 1897), 4, 6, 8.

20. Owen, *John Owen's Journal*, 5–7, 9–10.

21. Owen, *John Owen's Journal*, 7–8, 11.

22. Rogers et al., *Alabama*, 57.

23. *Georgia Journal*, September 24, 1822, quoted in Hudson, *Creek Paths*, 138–39.

24. Hudson, *Creek Paths*, 124–25, 135, 138–39; Edmund Gaines to Acting Secretary of War George Graham, Montgomery, Mississippi Territory, August 25, 1817, in Carter, *Territorial Papers*, vol. 18, 138; Governor Bibb to Secretary of War John C. Calhoun, Fort Claiborne, April 30, 1818, in ibid., 318.

25. Benjamin Porter, *Reminiscences of Men and Things in Alabama*, ed. Sara Walls (Tuscaloosa, AL: Portals, 1983), 29–30, quoted in Southerland and Brown, *Federal Road through Georgia*, 106.

26. Ibid.

27. William Ely to "Dear Clarissa," June 2, 1821, Ely Letters, folder 1, W. S. Hoole Special Collections Library, University of Alabama, Tuscaloosa, quoted in Wainwright, "Both Native South and Deep South," 303–4.

28. *Southern Agriculturist* 8 (1835): 243, quoted in Oakes, *Ruling Race*, 89.

29. Hodgson, *Letters from North America*, 1:143–44, quoted in Southerland and Brown, *Federal Road*, 96.

30. Carolyn Earle Billingsley, *Communities of Kinship: Antebellum Families and the Settlement of the Cotton Frontier* (Athens: University of Georgia Press, 2004), 36–38, 43–44, 47, 59.

31. Ibid., 42.

32. Joan E. Cashin (*A Family Venture: Men and Women on the Southern Frontier* [New York: Oxford University Press, 1991]) is the leading proponent of the idea that migration was a masculine venture that often stripped women of their familiar worlds.

33. "Abstract of the Territorial Census," in Carter, *Territorial Papers*, vol. 18, 462; Sellers, *Slavery in Alabama*, 17; Daniel S. Dupre, *Transforming the Cotton Frontier: Madison County, Alabama, 1800–1840* (Baton Rouge: Louisiana State University Press, 1997), 126.

34. Robert H. Gudmestad, *A Troublesome Commerce: The Transformation of the Interstate Slave Trade* (Baton Rouge: Louisiana State University Press, 2003), 8–9; Edward E. Baptist, *The Half Has Never Been Told: Slavery and the Making of American Capitalism* (New York: Basic Books, 2014), 92–93.

35. William Tell Harris, *Remarks Made during a Tour through the United States of America, in the Years 1817, 1818, and 1819* (Liverpool: Henry Fisher, 1819), 21, quoted in Hudson, *Creek Paths*, 132.

36. Dick, *Dixie Frontier*, 57.

37. Henry A. Tayloe to Benj. Ogle Tayloe, July 29, 1839, Tayloe Family Papers, Virginia Historical Society, Richmond, quoted in Steven F. Miller, "Plantation Labor Organization and Slave Life on the Cotton Frontier: The Alabama-Mississippi Black Belt, 1815–1840," in *Cultivation and Culture: Labor and the Shaping of Slave Life in the Americas*, ed. Ira Berlin and Philip D. Morgan (Charlottesville: University Press of Virginia, 1993), 157.

38. Jno. Knight to William M. Beall, January 17, 1844, John Knight Papers, Perkins Library, Duke University, quoted in Miller, "Plantation Labor Organization," 157.

39. Miller, "Plantation Labor Organization," 156–57; Baptist, *Half Has Never Been Told*, 102–3.

40. Sellers, *Slavery in Alabama*, 17; Rhoda Coleman Ellison, *Bibb County, Alabama: The First Hundred Years, 1818–1918* (Tuscaloosa: University of Alabama Press, 1984), 2; Malcolm J. Rohrbough, *The Land Office Business: The Settlement and Administration of American Public Lands, 1789–1837* (New York: Oxford University Press, 1968), 94; Barnett to Acting Secretary of War George Graham, Huntsville, March 12, 1817, in Carter, *Territorial Papers*, vol. 18, 71; Toulmin to Madison, Fort Stoddert, January 20, 1816, in Carter, *Territorial Papers*, vol. 6, 647, quoted in Dick, *Dixie Frontier*, 67–68.

41. Cannon to Acting Secretary of War George Graham, January 17, 1817, in Carter, *Territorial Papers*, vol. 18, 24.

42. Rohrbough, *Land Office Business*, 94–95.

43. Thomas Freeman to Josiah Meigs, Washington, Mississippi Territory, January 29, 1817, in Carter, *Territorial Papers*, vol. 18, 35; Freeman to Meigs, Washington, Mississippi Territory, April 22, 1817, in ibid., 88–89; Rohrbough, *Land Office Business*, 97–100.

44. Rohrbough, *Land Office Business*, 118–20; Dupre, *Transforming the Cotton Frontier*, 43–44.

45. Anne Newport Royall, letter of December 24, 1817, in Anne Newport Royall, *Letters from Alabama, 1817–1822*, ed. Lucille Griffith (University: University of Alabama Press, 1969), 114–15.

46. Dupre, *Transforming the Cotton Frontier*, 38–39.

47. John Campbell to Col. David Campbell, December 16, 1817, in Campbell Family Papers, Duke University; John Hardie to his brother, March 26, 1818, in *John Hardie of Thornhill: His Life, Letters, and Times*, ed. B. Palmer Lewis (New York: Avondale, 1928), 47–51. Also see Hardie's letters of July 28, September 17, October 28, and December 10, 1818, in ibid., 63–68, 72–77.

48. Dupre, *Transforming the Cotton Frontier*, 43.

49. John William Walker to Charles Tait, September 22, 1818, Tait Family Papers.

50. John Hardie to his brother, October 28, 1818, in Lewis, *John Hardie*, 73.

51. Dupre, *Transforming the Cotton Frontier*, 43, 86–87.

52. Ibid., 44–45.

53. See John Hardie's letters to his brother, March 26, July 28, September 17, October 28, and December 10, 1818, in Lewis, *John Hardie*, 47–51, 63–68, 72–77.

54. John Taylor to Daniel Boardman, June 25, 1829, Daniel Boardman Correspondence, 1818–31, Alabama Department of Archives and History; *Alabama Republican*, November 13, 1819, quoted in Dupre, *Transforming the Cotton Frontier*, 50–51.

55. Alexander Campbell, notice in *Alabama Republican*, January 29, 1820; Dupre, *Transforming the Cotton Frontier*, 51–53.

56. William Harris to Frederick Harris, November 15, 1820, and April 25, 1821, Harris Family Papers, Duke University; Anne Newport Royall, letter of June 8, 1822, in Royall, *Letters from Alabama*, 247.

57. Dupre, *Transforming the Cotton Frontier*, 47–48, 76, 84; Daniel S. Dupre, "William Wyatt Bibb, 1819–1820, and Thomas Bibb, 1820–1821," in *Alabama Governors: A Political History of the State*, ed. Samuel L. Webb and Margaret E. Armbrester (Tuscaloosa: University of Alabama Press, 2001), 13–14; Rogers et al., *Alabama*, 68–71.

58. Dupre, "William Wyatt Bibb," 15–16.

59. Dupre, *Transforming the Cotton Frontier*, 75–97.

60. Crawford to Charles Tait, November 7, 1819, Tait Family Papers.

61. Dupre, *Transforming the Cotton Frontier*, 92–93.

62. *Alabama Republican*, November 3, 1820. Also see Dupre, *Transforming the Cotton Frontier*, 101–2.

63. *Alabama Republican*, March 16, 1821, September 28, 1821. Also see Dupre, *Transforming the Cotton Frontier*, 103.

64. Dupre, *Transforming the Cotton Frontier*, 104–5.

65. Harriet E. Amos, *Cotton City: Urban Development in Antebellum Mobile* (University: University of Alabama Press, 1985), 21.

66. John S. Sledge, *The Mobile River* (Columbia: University of South Carolina Press, 2015), 87, 92, 98–99, 102; Dupre, *Transforming the Cotton Frontier*, 107–12.

67. *Southern Advocate*, May 20, 1825.

68. Sledge, *Mobile River*, 84, 95; Harriet E. Amos Doss, "Cotton City, 1813–1860," in *Mobile: The New History of Alabama's First City*, ed. Michael V. R. Thomason (Tuscaloosa: University of Alabama Press, 2001), 66, 69–73.

69. Baptist, *Half Has Never Been Told*, 75–144.

70. Charles Ball, *Fifty Years in Chains* (Mineola, NY: Dover, 1970), 132–33.

71. *Marion Standard*, April 9, 1909, quoted in Weymouth Jordan, *Hugh Davis and His Alabama Plantation* (Tuscaloosa: University of Alabama Press, 1948), 5.

72. Ely to "Dear Clarissa," quoted in Wainwright, "Both Native South and Deep South," 303–4.

73. James A. Tait to Charles Tait, January 21, 1818, February 7, 1818, January 19, 1819; Charles Tait to James A. Tait, October 14, 1818, November 10, 1818, Tait Family Papers, quoted in Miller, "Plantation Labor Organization," 160–61.

74. Charles Tait to Elizabeth Caroline Tait, [n.d.] 1818, December 13, 1818, Tait Family Papers, quoted in Miller, *South by Southwest*, 5.

75. Miller, *South by Southwest*, 6.

Epilogue

Years after he first arrived in Barbour County in 1837, John Horry Dent sketched out a familiar pioneering tale of deprivation and opportunity when he recalled his migration to Alabama. The young South Carolinian and his family had "embarked in a life of hardship" in "a Wild unsettled" land devoid "of accustomed comforts and habits." While his "prospects ahead were dark and gloomy," Dent "was blessed with a stout heart and strong resolution to do my best and contend against difficulties." That determination, coupled with the labor of the forty-five slaves who migrated with him, promised a more prosperous future. When he arrived, Dent rented a "one-room shanty" in the tiny village of Clayton so that his wife "would not be isolated in the woods among the roughest class of frontiers men ever seen" and the few "Indians still remaining in the Nation," and set about searching for land on which he could build a plantation and a new life. He found it on the South Cowikee Creek "in the swamp, and in the Wilderness" about ten miles north of Clayton, a place with only "a small patch . . . cleared on it and a small log hut built." But that unprepossessing purchase was "rich and exceedingly productive." Oblivious to the backbreaking work needed from his enslaved laborers to clear swamp and forestland, Dent marveled that "cotton, corn and what else were planted . . . grew nearly spontaneously." He accumulated more slaves, eighty-five by 1856, and weathered the upheaval of the Civil War and emancipation. In 1880 he proudly stated that his "was said to be one of the best plantations in Barbour."[1]

Dent knew he had not settled in a pristine wilderness, of course. Someone had built that log hut and had cleared the "small patch." He actually was a relative latecomer to the region known as New Alabama, a crescent wedge stretching from the Coosa River to the Chattahoochee and the Georgia line. Squatters began pushing into that last remnant of the Creek nation a decade before Dent ventured west, and the Indians' surrender of their Alabama homeland to the federal government in 1832 sparked a frenzy of speculation and settlement. Dent differentiated himself from those who had preceded him, however. Hunters and Indian traders had come to escape "civilized and moral society," while planters and farmers like him, who had migrated to "increase their fortunes" by cultivating cotton, actually transformed the wilderness. They had had "to open roads, clear the lands, and erect the habitations" in order to accomplish the "First stages of redemption from a land of Barbarians to a land of civilization."[2]

One year before John Horry Dent and his family arrived in Barbour County, another couple left New Alabama for lands further west. Katy Grayson and her husband, Johnnie Benson, grew up in Creek country. Her father, Robert Grierson, a Scottish trader who lived in Hilabi, had married Sinnugee, a refugee from Florida of Indian, Spanish, and perhaps African descent who had been taken in by the Creeks. Together they raised eight children. Johnnie's mother had also been adopted as a child after being captured in a raid on an American settlement and had married a Creek man and raised a family. A former Red Stick warrior, Johnnie was also known as Tulwa Tustanagee. Katy's family was prosperous, singled out by Benjamin Hawkins as exemplars of the civilization policy. In the 1790s, when Katy was born, Robert began supplementing his trading with herding and farming, raising over three hundred head of cattle and cultivating over two thousand pounds of picked cotton. By 1812, Robert owned between seventy and one hundred slaves, whom he bequeathed to his children upon his death in 1825. But that wealth did not save Katy's family as pressures to leave their homeland grew. In 1836, a small faction of Creek warriors attacked and killed settlers along the Chattahoochee, triggering what came to be known as the Second Creek War. The army easily quelled the resistance and the federal government stepped up its efforts to remove the Indians. Katy, Johnnie, their families, and most of the native inhabitants of the Creek nation were rounded up and forced to migrate to the Indian Territory west of the Mississippi.[3]

One family's departure and another's arrival marked the final closure of Alabama's frontier, erased by an expanding cotton kingdom and the forced removal of the Indians. The shifting identities and boundary-crossing relationships exemplified by the Grierson/Grayson family, vestiges of the eighteenth-century trading frontier, depended on a clear demarcation of Indian territory. Borderland fluidity, in other words, required strong borders. But Creek country collapsed in the 1830s, replaced by a New Alabama filled with settlers like the Dent family, eager to establish homes, make a living, and prosper with the help of enslaved labor. White masters and black slaves brought with them the more rigid racial hierarchies of the southeastern plantation society. That transition, one of the last steps toward integrating the Old Southwest into the broader nation, was not a smooth process. Confronted with fraud and violence, the federal government tried to bring order to the chaotic transfer of land but found itself at odds not just with squatters but with a state government eager to assert its rights. Ultimately the common desire to be rid of the Creeks bridged the divisions between state and federal governments and the settlers of New Alabama.

By the late 1820s some twenty-three thousand Creek men, women, and children remained in the over five million acres of their ancestral homeland. Stripped of their Georgia territory in 1826, refugees had crossed the Chattahoochee, creating severe strains in the Lower Towns on the western side of the river. Famine and smallpox ravaged Creek communities. The Upper Towns along the Coosa and Tallapoosa Rivers retained more extensive hunting lands and faced less crowding from refugees, but they had their own problems. Americans began slipping across the Georgia border and squatting in the territory north and east of their towns. Using the presence of those settlers as an excuse, Alabama's leaders extended the legal jurisdiction of neighboring counties across Creek territory to the Georgia border. That was the first step, on paper at least, toward turning the Creek homeland into New Alabama.[4]

Indians faced with squatter intrusions and violations of tribal sovereignty in the past might have turned to the federal government for support, but that avenue was less promising in the late 1820s with Andrew Jackson occupying the White House. Jackson had fought against and alongside Creek, Cherokee, Chickasaw, and Choctaw warriors for much of his life in order to open the Old Southwest to American settlement and had long scoffed at the notion of tribal sovereignty. He supported the right of states like Georgia and Alabama to extend their laws over the Cherokees and Creeks and said as much in his first address to Congress in 1829. The focus of his administration's first year in office was the Indian problem, culminating in the passage of the Indian Removal Act in 1830. The law gave all Native Americans east of the Mississippi two choices:

move, with government assistance, to Indian Territory in the West to live under tribal law and custom, or stay as individuals on private plots of land under state and federal law. Jackson believed that the second option would prove intolerable to most Indians.

The Treaty of Cusseta, signed in 1832, emerged out of the pressures facing the Creeks: the influx of refugees and squatters; famine and disease; Alabama's legal intrusion on tribal sovereignty; and an unsympathetic federal administration. Creek negotiators abandoned efforts to hold on to the 5,200,000 acres of land in common and agreed to accept a system of allotments. Each head of household would receive 320 acres, while ninety headmen would receive 640 acres, which they could keep or sell. Government agents would take a census of Creek households and survey out the allotments before opening the remaining 3,000,000 acres to settlement by outsiders. The administration pledged to protect Indian landholders from encroachment by squatters for five years while overseeing any sales during that period. American negotiators made no bones about the fact that they wanted the Indians to leave. The treaty insisted that "they shall be free to go or to stay as they please," but also promised that "as fast as the Creeks are prepared to emigrate, they shall be removed at the expense of the United States."[5]

Clarifying land ownership under the allotment system was tangled and slow because of ambiguities in the treaty and complications on the ground. The decisive statement that "all intruders" on the ceded land "shall be removed . . . until the country is surveyed" was followed by the qualification that "those white persons who have made their own improvements, and not expelled the Creeks from theirs" could "remain till their crops are gathered."[6] Squatters and their political allies used that qualifier in the coming years as ammunition in their battles to resist removal. Determining the legitimacy of Creek households was complicated in part because there was no easy fit between the Alabamians' notions of male ownership of land and Creek matrilineal traditions. The commissioners conducting the census generally accepted white countrymen who had long-standing marriages with Creek women, but what to do with the men who, after the treaty was signed, rushed to "marry" Creek women, some coerced and some colluding, in order to claim land allotments? They also were reluctant to elevate free African Americans married to Creek women to head-of-household status. Then there were the descendants of mixed-race relationships. Samuel Brashears, a distant relation of Alexander McGillivray, lived in Tuckabatchee with a white wife. Despite assurances from Tuskenea, the town's headman, that he was Creek, the commissioner rejected Bashears's claim to an allotment. He

This 1830s engraving of the Chattahoochee River at Columbus, Georgia, illustrates the ways in which slavery and cotton were transforming the final remnants of the Creek homeland. The illustration appears in Francis de Castelnau, *Vues et souvenirs de l'Amérique du Nord*, plate 13, "Pont de Columbus, (Georgie et Alabama)." Courtesy of General Collections, Beinecke Rare Book and Manuscript Library, Yale University, New Haven, CT.

simply looked too white. Samuel's brothers had better luck; they had darker skin and were married to Creek women. It took time to sort through such complexities, and when the census was completed in June 1833, speculators had overrun much of Creek country.[7]

With cotton prices on the rise in the early 1830s, speculators were ready to make money off the Americans' land hunger. They could wait until Creek lands had been allotted and the roughly three million acres left over had been surveyed and put up for sale, but that would take time. The Creek allotments themselves were a ripe target ready for plucking. One group of speculators in particular led the way. Just a few days after the treaty was signed, twenty wealthy residents of Columbus, Georgia, formed the Columbus Land Company. Located at Coweta Falls on the Chattahoochee River, Columbus was fast becoming the shipping center for western Georgia. The first steamboat had reached the falls only four years earlier but now the town's merchants were busy shipping cotton bales down the river to the Gulf. Soon, they hoped, burgeoning plantations in New Alabama would expand cotton exports through Columbus, but in the meantime great profits could be made snatching up Creek homesteads.[8]

The Columbus Land Company introduced a variety of fraudulent practices that soon became common throughout the region. Taking a cue from the old deerskin traders, the Columbus speculators set up trading posts in New Alabama stocked with goods and whiskey, sold on credit to Creek men. Once indebted, and often inebriated, they could be pressured into selling titles to their allotments. They also sent men called "strikers" into Creek communities to harass landholders into selling their claims or to pay Creek men to impersonate allotment holders initiating sales at the land office. Often the strikers were free or enslaved African Americans familiar with the Muskogee language and customs. Creek men also sometimes joined forces with speculators. Katy Grayson's brother, Watt, colluded with a small group of speculators and helped round up neighbors and friends willing, for ten dollars, to claim false identities to receive allotments that they then signed over to his companions. By 1835 the Columbus Land Company owned title to seven hundred allotments, primarily in the settlements of the Lower Town Creeks, and other speculators, acting alone or in groups, had snatched up more. The enthusiastic admonition of one member of a speculative cabal captures the spirit of the times in New Alabama: "Now is the time, or never! Hurrah boys! here goes it! let's steal all we can. I shall go for it, or get no lands! Now or never!"⁹

Alabama's extension of state laws over Creek country complicated efforts to bring order to the new territory and ended up encouraging intrusions. In 1827 Alabama made it more difficult for Creek men to feed their families by prohibiting Indians from hunting, fishing, and trapping within state boundaries. Then, early in 1832 before the Treaty of Cusseta was signed, they invalidated the authority of the National Council and placed Creeks under state law. Designated free people of color, or second-class citizens, Creeks, like African Americans, could not testify against white Alabamians in court, including the speculators and squatters who cheated them out of their allotments. As an ardent states' rights advocate, Dixon Hall Lewis, the Alabama House representative from Montgomery, supported the extension of state law on philosophical grounds, but he also made clear the underlying intent. When the Creeks "see and feel" the full impact of state law, he said, "their veneration for their own law and customs will induce them speedily to remove to that region of the country west of the Mississippi."¹⁰ To drive that point home, Alabama criminalized any effort to impede or discourage Creek removal to Indian Territory. By the end of 1832, Alabama had carved out nine new counties from the Creek land.¹¹

Andrew Jackson's administration found itself in a jurisdictional bind. On the one hand, the federal government shared Alabama's interest in pushing the

Indians westward, and state authority was a convenient excuse for inaction on its part. Back in 1830 when Creek leaders complained to Secretary of War John Eaton about Alabama's violations of their sovereignty, he replied, "Congress has no power over the subject. Your Great Father has none. It belongs to the State . . . to regulate and to direct all affairs within her limits, and nothing can prevent it."[12] On the other hand, the Treaty of Cusseta obligated the federal government to protect Creeks from intruders as they oversaw the process of dividing up allotments and surveying and selling the remaining land. While Jackson might have sympathized with Alabama's leaders and shared their interest in Indian removal, he did not take lightly any challenges to his authority.

The extent to which the political landscape had shifted became clear when federal officials tried to remove squatters from the new town of Irwinton, in Barbour County, located on the Chattahoochee River. Settlers hoped that Irwinton would compete successfully against Columbus as a trade center for the farms and plantations that soon would be popping up in the region. The problem was that Irwinton was situated on the site of the Lower Creek town of Eufaula. Settlers had driven away the Indian residents and claimed their cabins and crops. The Treaty of Cusseta mandated that squatters on Indian land be removed, so Secretary of War Lewis Cass ordered Robert Crawford, the US marshal for Alabama's southern district, to head up that project. Crawford came to Irwinton in July 1832 accompanied by troops from Fort Mitchell, and ordered the soldiers to drive the squatters out of the town and to torch the cabins so the intruders would not return. "Rough men require rough treatment," Crawford explained, and Cass quickly sent word back of his approval.[13] After being rousted from the town, the squatters soon returned armed with guns and, more importantly, with a sheriff in tow bearing legal documents as ammunition. The grand jury had issued writs of trespass for the Creeks who had returned to their old town of Eufaula, and a civil warrant against the officer in charge of the Fort Mitchell soldiers. Federal officials proved impotent as settlers began to rebuild Irwinton. Jeremiah Austill, Crawford's deputy marshal, admitted defeat in November. The former hero of the Creek War was disgusted by "the acts of cruelty and imposition imposed upon the Indians" but acknowledged that, while it would only take "fifty men" to "drive" away the "outlaws" in Irwinton, "it would take Five Hundred to keep them off."[14]

Tensions escalated the following summer when federal officials tried to remove Hardiman Owens, a particularly violent and disorderly man who had appropriated Creek land in Russell County. Responding to numerous complaints, Deputy Marshal Austill demanded that Owens leave the Creek lands in July

1833, and when he refused, ordered his arrest. Feigning compliance, Owens invited the marshal into his house but Austill hesitated when several Creek bystanders urged caution, a fortuitous decision since a short time later the house exploded. Owens had apparently packed it with gunpowder to create a trap. He ran and the soldiers followed, killing Owens after a brief skirmish. When the Russell County grand jury indicted the soldiers and officer involved, some of Alabama's politicians and newspaper editors championed Owens. Most locals regarded him as a violent and cruel scoundrel but his death at the hands of soldiers became a symbol of unwarranted federal intrusion.[15]

The controversy over Owens and federal efforts to remove squatters from New Alabama played out in political waters roiled by South Carolina's nullification of the federal tariff in 1832. The threats of disunion contained in the nullifiers' challenge alarmed even the many opponents of the tariff in Alabama, but so too did Andrew Jackson's assertion of the right to use military force to ensure compliance with federal law. There remained an appetite for more limited assertions of states' rights, and the specter of federal troops burning cabins and killing a settler fit the bill. Governor John Gayle acknowledged that South Carolina's actions had "brought into disrepute" the notion of state sovereignty, but he argued that the principle was "still worth preserving." On a more practical level, championing the rights of New Alabama's settlers became a way to break the hold that Jackson's allies had on state politics.[16]

States' rights advocates transformed squatters into virtuous and innocent settlers while stripping away Creek claims to federal protection. Who are the "thirty thousand people" who "have been commanded to leave their homes," the editor of Tuscaloosa's *State Rights Expositor* asked. "Are they enemies? No, they are citizens of the United States" who "were encouraged" to settle in ceded territory "by all the acts of this government from its inception" to further "the rapid conversion of savage wastes into cultivated fields."[17] Gayle explained that "while they retained their character of a tribe," the Creeks "had an unqualified indefeasible right to their immediate improvement," but that was no longer the case. They were citizens of Alabama and "were subject to its laws," and could sell their allotments at will. If they had complaints of fraud then they could appeal to the state courts, Gayle argued, ignoring the fact that they could not testify against whites. The flood of settlers, the treaty, and the extension of state law all reinforced the diminution of the Creeks as an autonomous people. "In their present situation they cannot be regarded as a distinct tribe," Gayle wrote to Secretary Cass in August 1833, "for as such they have disappeared, and been lost in the large community now in possession of their ancient birth-right."[18]

Public meetings organized by states' rights leaders ratcheted up tension that fall as federal officials prepared to remove the squatters. Citizens at a meeting in Lowndes County near Montgomery complained of "a band of armed soldiers ... trampling on the rights of our fellow citizens" who were living "in the bosom of a peaceful and orderly community." Those efforts to remove the settlers, they resolved, was "unconstitutional, oppressive and utterly subversive of the sovereignty of the state." But not all agreed. The settlers in Creek country were "intruders," the *Mobile Register* insisted, scoffing that "all this verbiage about, 'the sacred rights of property,'" was no more than "mere flourishes of rhetoric." Still, Gayle issued a proclamation in October denouncing federal efforts to remove the squatters and calling on "all civil officers" in the New Alabama counties "to be attentive to the complaints of the people" and "to bring offenders to justice, particularly such as are guilty of murder, false imprisonment, house-burning, robbery, forcible entries, and all such like heinous offences." State law, he said, would provide settlers "a shield, impenetrable to the sword and the bayonet." Montgomery's *Alabama Journal* encouraged the settlers to form militias to resist removal. Alarmed, the commander at Fort Mitchell ordered additional arms and ammunition, and Major General Winfield Scott began planning a naval blockade of Alabama.[19]

Andrew Jackson had no intention of provoking a confrontation with Alabama, especially when he agreed that the Creeks would ultimately have to leave their homeland. He sent Francis Scott Key, the district attorney for the District of Columbia, to negotiate a settlement. Key spoke to settlers and Creek residents of New Alabama and then traveled to Montgomery to interview political leaders, including Gayle and his Jacksonian opponents. The latter wanted to put an end to the controversies, but even the states' rights minority, once they had loudly proclaimed their principles, saw no advantage to escalating tensions; they too were anxious to remove the Creeks. Key worked out a compromise. The federal government would temporarily suspend the removal of squatters while officials finished determining the allotment boundaries, and the state would drop the charges against the soldiers who killed Owens and their commanding officer.

This political resolution did not result in the mass emigration of Creeks, for a number of reasons. Since the Indian Removal Act promised support for transport to the western territory, the government bid out contracts to private groups to enroll emigrants and arrange for the food and transportation needed for the journey. Disorganization hampered those efforts since the low bidders selected by the administration were often ill prepared to mobilize and transport thousands of people. One group was led by some of the principal speculators of Columbus, Georgia, which only heightened Creek suspicions. Divisions and demoralization within Creek society sparked some interest in emigration, but there were countervailing pressures. As early as 1828, Creek leaders vowed to kill anyone who signed on with an emigration agent and backed up that threat with violent intimidation. Some Creeks simply hoped to stay on their allotments, while others fled to the Cherokee nation. By the spring of 1835, one year after all of the Creek lands had been surveyed and allotted, only one group of Indians had moved west.[20]

The varied decisions of members of the Grayson family reveal the pressures generated by the transformation of Creek country into New Alabama. Many of Sinnugee's children and grandchildren seemed resigned to leaving their homeland, but under their own terms and not as dupes of the speculators. Eleven members of the large métis family sold their allotments for an average of six hundred dollars each, about twice as much money as the typical Hilabi allotment fetched in sales. Katy's sister Elizabeth, however, not only did not sell; she purchased two of her neighbor's allotments. Perhaps she planned on later reselling them for a profit, but she might also have intended to stay. She owned a valuable plantation, commanded the labor of a large number of slaves, and was accustomed to navigating the commercial world. The hostility of many of her Indian neighbors in Hilabi reinforced her identity as a white resident of Creek country. Why not become a citizen of Alabama?[21]

Katy and Elizabeth's brother, William, followed a different path. He had been a bit of an outsider in the family since just after the War of 1812 when he crossed racial bounds by establishing a relationship and fathering children with Judah, one of his father's slaves. When Robert Grierson died in 1825, he left slaves for Katy and Elizabeth but bequeathed none to William. Elizabeth became the owner of Judah and her children, forcing William to visit the slave quarters when he could. Over the years the couple had more children, seven in all by 1834. But racial boundaries were hardening, threatening a relationship whose security was already tenuous. Creek warriors—traditionalists who wanted nothing to do with slaves they saw as symbols of an encroaching plantation society—whipped William when he came to visit Judah at his sister's place. Creek assimilationists were no happier with the situation; they wanted to inoculate themselves against charges of fraternization with the enslaved lest suspicions be raised about their loyalties among the increasing numbers of white settlers. William finally persuaded Elizabeth to transfer ownership of Judah and their children to him, and the family struck out for Indian Territory in 1834. When they arrived William freed his wife and children.[22]

The pressures of speculators and squatters and the divisions within Creek communities sparked violence in 1835–36, which ultimately gave the federal government the excuse to move beyond encouraging emigration to forcing removal. Reports of attacks on travelers between Columbus and Montgomery filtered out of New Alabama in the summer of 1835. Gayle, in a letter to the secretary of war asking for troop reinforcements at Fort Mitchell, blamed both the frauds committed by the speculators and the famine that encouraged Creek men to "prey upon the property of their neighbours."[23] He used the occasion to argue that only removal "could render a residence in that part of the state tolerable for the white men." Worries intensified in the spring of 1836 as rumors spread that Lower Town warriors were gathering in swamps, painting their faces, and preparing for war. Continued resistance by the Seminoles in Florida only fueled those fears. Alabama's new governor, Clement Clay, sent military supplies and several militia companies to Montgomery to prepare for the possible outbreak of war. In May, Creek warriors struck, killing several settler families and attacking stagecoaches passing along the Federal Road and steamboats on the Chattahoochee. Residents of New Alabama fled east to Columbus and west to Montgomery but they remained homeless for only a short period. Retaliation was swift. Federal troops, Alabama militias, and Creek warriors from the Upper Towns swept through the Lower Towns. By July 1836 they had rounded up over two thousand men, women, and children who were then marched to Montgomery and sent down to Mobile in boats. There the prisoners embarked on a long journey to New Orleans, up the Mississippi, and then west to Indian Territory. Eliminating those who had fought in the Second Creek War was not enough. Gayle had told Lewis Cass the previous summer that the Creeks and whites "cannot live together, and, if attempted, the Indians must perish."[24] The army began informing the remaining Creek families that the time had come to emigrate. Later that summer into the fall of 1836, thousands of Creeks left New Alabama to start new lives in the West.[25]

The Graysons' wealth, their mixed-race status, and the fact that five of their men had fought against the Creek "rebels" did not protect them from removal. The family, including their slaves, were among the 2,830 people who left in September 1836, the last major group organized by the Alabama Emigration Company. They first walked to Memphis, some three hundred miles away, and then to the White River, where steamboats waited to transport them to Little Rock. From there they walked again, finally reaching Indian Territory in late January 1837. The hardships of the road, made worse by the inadequate provisions of an emigration company interested in cost-cutting and profits, paled in comparison to the harsh life that awaited them in the first months in their new homeland. Almost ten thousand Creeks clustered around Fort Gibson, camped out in the snow with little in the way of protection. Each family received only one blanket and food supplies were minimal, making a mockery of the federal government's promise to provision the Creeks for the first year. Over time the children and grandchildren of Sinnugee and Robert Grierson carved out new lives in Indian Territory.[26]

Settlers replaced the Creeks, flocking to New Alabama seeking land on which to support their families and prosper. Many, like John Horry Dent, tied their individual stories of migration and new beginnings to America's grand frontier tale and saw themselves as pioneers taming a wilderness. Soon after he arrived in Barbour County, Dent paid a visit to his uncle in Tuscaloosa, located in what he called "a rich and beautiful Country." Land only recently wrested from the Creeks in the Treaty of Fort Jackson after the Red Stick War had been, he said, "settled by an intelligent enterprising population" that had grown "wealthy from Cotton planting," and now Tuscaloosa "presented an appearance of wealth, refinement and elegance." Thinking, perhaps, of the swampland he had just purchased, Dent acknowledged that New Alabama lagged behind Tuscaloosa; it had "yet to be cleared up, built up, and settled by civilized people." But he had no doubt that his region would follow the same path now that "pioneer farmers ... were moving in to settle fresh plantations to make cotton."[27]

The removal of the Creeks opened land to enterprising settlers but it was slaves who provided the labor to transform the soil into the cotton from which, according to Dent, all the blessings of civilization flowed. Many who settled in New Alabama, especially in the northern counties, were smaller farmers who owned no slaves, but the cotton boom drew large numbers of slaveholders as well. When Dent arrived in Barbour County about one in five of the households owned slaves, an unusually high percentage for a frontier region. At least two settlers each had over one hundred enslaved men, women, and children toiling on their plantations. By 1840, slaves made up about one-third of the county's population. Often settlers brought their slaves with them when migrating to the frontier, but others flowed into the region through the markets and coffles of the slave trade. The firm of Pickett & Williamson advertised sixty slaves for sale in New Alabama as early as 1833, both field hands and skilled laborers like cooks, seamstresses, and carpenters. Surplus laborers could always be hired out since there was a brisk rental market in slaves on the frontier. Dent, for example, hired out slaves to the turpentine industry in the region. Traders stood to make a great profit given the high demand. One trading partnership operating out of Montgomery sold thirteen slaves in New Alabama in 1837 for an average profit of $429 each, the equivalent of over $10,000 today. Whether transported from home or purchased in Alabama, slaves were invaluable both for the hard physical labor of clearing land and cultivating cotton and for performing the tasks necessary to present the "appearance of wealth, refinement and elegance" so prized by Dent.[28]

Vestiges of old frontiers haunted the settlement of New Alabama, often clothed in new garb. The rousting of Irwinton's residents was not the first time federal troops had pushed squatters from Indian land, although in the past those squatters did not respond with a sheriff carrying writs of trespass. The Columbus Land Company was part of a long lineage of speculators who had eyed Alabama land. While the eighteenth-century gentlemen who drove the Yazoo speculation might have cringed at the grubby deals to steal Creek allotments made over whiskey bottles, they would have recognized the impulse to turn land and the dreams of settlers into cash. The pressures of those squatters and speculators were familiar to the Creek men and women who were trying to hold on to the last pieces of their homeland. For generations they had fought, through diplomacy and war, to maintain the integrity of their territory. But the acceptance of allotments to be doled out to individual families obliterated the boundaries of Creek country. Alabama's frontiers had always been defined by the interplay of outsiders and indigenous peoples, but by the mid-1830s there was no more "inside" or "outside." Removal punctuated a closure of the frontier that was already a foregone conclusion.

The outsiders who came to Alabama over the centuries pursued private goals within imperial contexts. Hernando de Soto fused the two roles; his pursuit of riches and the greater glory of Spain were one and the same. The traders who followed 150 years later created an uneasy balance. They forged the connections with Indians that became the foundations of the alliances sought by the English, Spanish, and French empires competing over the flow of captured slaves, deerskins, guns, and trade goods. But traders were unreliable agents whose unruly behavior and unbridled pursuit of profits often generated tensions on the frontier. "Beloved men" from both the colonial periphery and the South's indigenous interior worked hard at maintaining the alliances that served their interests. After the revolution, the new American nation contended with the unruly energies of their settlers. They too, in a sense, were agents of an American empire whose goal was territorial expansion. The flow of pioneers across the Appalachians could further those goals by pressuring Indians to negotiate treaties and tempering Spanish claims to territory north of Florida. But they also complicated the process of acquiring, surveying, and selling frontier land and, more importantly, threatened to engulf the fledgling nation in an Indian war it could ill afford. The task for the government, then, was to manage the chaos of westward expansion, to establish boundaries and authority over a frontier it did not control.

Throughout the long history of Alabama's frontiers, government officials had feared fractures. South Carolina's leaders in the early eighteenth century and again in the 1750s and 1760s believed that Creek country was a pivot point in the competition between Britain and France. If the French succeeded in gaining the allegiance of the Creeks, Britain would lose the Southeast. George Washington, late in that same century, also worried that the trans-Appalachian frontier would break away, seduced by the Spanish or the British into abandoning the new country. Much of federal policy from the 1790s on reflected efforts to integrate the expanding frontier into the broader nation: systems of land surveying and sales, the civilization policy, negotiated treaties with Spain and Indian nations, road building, and war. Victories over the Creeks and the British and the acquisition of Spanish Florida in 1819 completed the Americanization of the Gulf and put an end to the long history of imperial competition in the region. Indian removal marked the eradication of the final impediment to the full integration of Alabama and the rest of the Southwest into the nation.

Integration created its own complications, however. Slavery and cotton expanded, settling Alabama's frontier as the government had hoped but also forging strong connections to a South increasingly sensitive to its own sectional interests. The prickliness of Alabama's politicians about federal encroachment in the Creek cession reflected newly emerging sensitivities to threats to state sovereignty, and more was at stake than Indian land and squatter rights. Dixon Hall Lewis, the state legislator who championed the extension of Alabama law over the Creeks, argued that if the federal government could tell the state "that Indians cannot be citizens," then it could also "say that Negroes shall not be slaves."[29] That fusion of states' rights and the sectional protection of slavery hinted at new fractures to come, not between East and West but between North and South. But in the mid-1830s, the federal and state officials, and the settlers eager to set their slaves to work, shared a common goal that muted antagonism. They all united over the removal of the last Creek families from their land.

You can sketch the contours of Alabama's many frontiers through lines of movement. Hernando de Soto's intrusion deep into the interior of La Florida initiated the interplay of indigenous and imperial, the interaction of insiders and outsiders that would come to define the frontier. In his wake, chiefdoms collapsed or moved and native peoples came together in new towns, but those kinds of fluctuations had always characterized life in the South. Traditional seasonal rhythms—the journey to and from winter hunting camps, for example—still governed the patterns of movement in the decades following de Soto's entrada. But by the turn of the eighteenth century, raiding parties, slaves, and refugees traveled the Indian trails to new European outposts on the Gulf and Atlantic coasts, marking a shift in Alabama's frontier. As the century wore on, fewer warriors and more packhorses laden with deerskins, guns, and cloth followed the paths, along with delegations of Indian and colonial beloved men journeying to and from Creek towns and Mobile, Pensacola, and Charlestown for diplomatic parlays. A map of those routes would reveal the ligaments of an imperial frontier built on the pursuit of profit and alliances. After the revolution, many of those same trails became the paths and roads that carried the American settlers who once again transformed Alabama's frontier.

No history books trace the route of John Horry Dent's migration to South Cowikee Creek in Barbour County. It was one of tens of thousands of journeys that embodied the restless ambitions of American settlers as they left familiar homes for new lives in new lands. Enslaved pioneers followed those same routes from Virginia, the Carolinas, and Georgia, taken or sold from their homes to make real their masters' dreams through their blood and sweat. Draw each journey of the free and the bound in the decades following the American Revolution on an imaginary map, and in that tangle of blackened lines you would see the weight of outsiders transforming Alabama's frontier. But the end of that frontier could only come when there were no more insiders, when the indigenous no longer occupied the land. The forced removal of the Creeks and other native peoples to lands west across the Mississippi marked the full closure of Alabama's frontier.

In 1937, an elderly Creek woman recounted a story she had heard as a young girl "of an old lady whose name was Sin-e-cha," who had left Hilabi and come west with just "a small bundle of her few belongings." On the steamboat, she had sung "a sad song" while "reopening and retying her pitiful bundle." "I have no more land," Sin-e-cha lamented. "I am driven away from home, driven up the red waters, let us all go, let us all die together and somewhere upon the bank we will be there."[30]

It is likely but not certain that Sin-e-cha was Sinnugee. Born in Spanish Florida of mixed parentage, adopted into the Creek nation, and married to a Scottish trader, Sinnugee had witnessed and participated in the great transformations of Alabama's frontiers. She and her husband had raised a large family, purchased slaves, herded cattle, and planted cotton, prospering through adaptation and a willingness to seize opportunities. But that world had slipped away; Sinnugee and her children and grandchildren had been driven out, pushed west across the Mississippi. There, most likely, she died. The elderly storyteller claimed that she could still find Sin-e-cha's grave; it was located near Fort Gibson, "upon the banks of the Grand River."[31] A thread connected South Cowikee Creek to that grave, spun out of Dent's dreams and ambitions, the toil and pain of his slaves, and Sinnugee's exile, a thread that helped stitch together a new society that came to be called the Old South.

Notes

1. Ray Mathis, Mary Mathis, and Douglas Clare Purcell, eds., *John Horry Dent Farm Journals and Account Books, 1840–1892* (microfilm publication) (University: University of Alabama Press, 1977), 2:256, 259, 275, 355; 13:256–57, 259, quoted in Ray Mathis, *John Horry Dent: South Carolina Aristocrat on the Alabama Frontier* (University: University of Alabama Press, 1979), 28, 30, 85.

2. Mathis, Mathis, and Purcell, *John Horry Dent Farm Journals*, 2:256–59, quoted in Mathis, *John Horry Dent*, 30.

3. Claudio Saunt, *Black, White, and Indian: Race and the Unmaking of an American Family* (New York: Oxford University Press, 2005), 11, 14–16, 32, 49–53.

4. John T. Ellisor, *The Second Creek War: Interethnic Conflict and Collusion on a Collapsing Frontier* (Lincoln: University of Nebraska Press, 2010), 21–23; Michael D. Green, *The Politics of Indian Removal: Creek Government and Society in Crisis* (Lincoln: University of Nebraska Press, 1982), 145–46.

5. "Treaty with the Creek Indians," reprinted in *Niles' Weekly Register*, April 14, 1832; Mary Elizabeth Young, *Redskins, Ruffleshirts, and Rednecks: Indian Allotments in Alabama and Mississippi, 1830–1860* (Norman: University of Oklahoma Press, 1961), 38; Ellisor, *Second Creek War*, 47.

6. "Treaty with the Creek Indians."

7. Ellisor, *Second Creek War*, 50–57.

8. Ellisor, *Second Creek War*, 63; Young, *Redskins, Ruffleshirts, and Rednecks*, 74–75; Lynn Willoughby, *Flowing through Time: A History of the Lower Chattahoochee River* (Tuscaloosa: University of Alabama Press, 1999), 48–50.

9. Benjamin P. Tarver to M. A. Craven, March 1, 1835, in *The New American State Papers, Indian Affairs* (Wilmington, DE: Scholarly Resources, 972), 9:513, quoted in Saunt, *Black, White, and Indian*, 42; Ellisor, *Second Creek War*, 62–63, 103–5; Young, *Redskins, Ruffleshirts, and Rednecks*, 74–76; Saunt, *Black, White, and Indian*, 41–42.

10. Dixon Hall Lewis, Alabama House *Journal, 1828–29*, Debates (January 21, 1829), 220–23, quoted in Green, *Politics of Indian Removal*, 147.

11. Green, *Politics of Indian Removal*, 145–48; Saunt, *Black, White, and Indian*, 37; Ellisor, *Second Creek War*, 49.

12. John Eaton to Creek Indians East of the Mississippi, March 20, 1830, Letters Received, 1824–1881, Creek Agency, Records of the Bureau of Indian Affairs, National Archives and Records Administration, Washington, DC, 6:343–46, quoted in Green, *Politics of Indian Removal*, 163.

13. Crawford to Robb, September 15, 1832, Letters Received, 1824–1881, Creek Agency, Records of the Bureau of Indian Affairs, National Archives and Records Administration, reel 223, 54–59, quoted in Green, *Politics of Indian Removal*, 176.

14. Austill to Cass, November 15, 1832, Letters Received, 1824–1881, Creek Agency, Records of the Bureau of Indian Affairs, National Archives and Records Administration, reel 223, 162, quoted in Green, *Politics of Indian Removal*, 176–77; Young, *Redskins, Ruffleshirts, and Rednecks*, 77; Ellisor, *Second Creek War*, 58–59.

15. Green, *Politics of Indian Removal*, 179–80; Ellisor, *Second Creek War*, 84–85.

16. Gayle to Lewis Cass, October 2, 1833, in *Niles' Weekly Register*, October 26, 1833; Ellisor, *Second Creek War*, 49; Young, *Redskins, Ruffleshirts, and Rednecks*, 78; J. Mills Thornton III, *Politics and Power in a Slave Society: Alabama, 1800–1860* (Baton Rouge: Louisiana State University Press, 1978), 28–30.

17. "The Indian Question in Alabama," reprinted in *Niles' Weekly Register*, October 26, 1833.

18. Gayle to Cass, October 2, 1833, in *Niles' Weekly Register*, October 26, 1833; Gayle to Cass, August 20, 1833, in *Niles' Weekly Register*, September 21, 1833.

19. "Excitement in Alabama," *Niles' Weekly Register*, October 19, 1833; excerpt from the *Mobile Register*, in *Niles' Weekly Register*, November 2, 1833; John Gayle, "A Proclamation—By the Governor," *Niles' Weekly Register*, October 26, 1833; Ellisor, *Second Creek War*, 85–91; Young, *Redskins, Ruffleshirts, and Rednecks*, 78–79.

20. Ellisor, *Second Creek War*, 113, 118–19; Saunt, *Black, White, and Indian*, 38, 43.

21. Saunt, *Black, White, and Indian*, 40, 42–43.

22. Ibid., 26, 32–35, 43–45.

23. "The Indians in Alabama," *Niles' Weekly Register*, July 4, 1835.

24. Ibid.

25. "Indian Hostilities," *Niles' Weekly Register*, May 28, 1836; Ellisor, *Second Creek War*, 170–71, 177–78, 185–93; Saunt, *Black, White, and Indian*, 50–53.

26. Saunt, *Black, White, and Indian*, 52–54.

27. Mathis, Mathis, and Purcell, *John Horry Dent Farm Journals*, 13:257, quoted in Mathis, *John Horry Dent*, 29–30.

28. Anthony Gene Carey, *Sold down the River: Slavery in the Lower Chattahoochee Valley of Alabama and Georgia* (Tuscaloosa: University of Alabama Press, 2011), 43–46.

29. Lewis, Alabama House *Journal*, 220–23, quoted in Green, *Politics of Indian Removal*, 147.

30. Interview with Elsie Edwards, September 17, 1937, Indian-Pioneer Papers, Oklahoma Historical Society, Oklahoma City, 27:189–93, quoted in Saunt, *Black, White, and Indian*, 54.

31. Ibid.

Index

Page numbers in italics refer to illustrations and maps.

DANIEL S. DUPRE is Associate Professor of History at
the University of North Carolina at Charlotte and author
of *Transforming the Cotton Frontier: Madison County,
Alabama, 1800–1840.*

CPSIA information can be obtained
at www.ICGtesting.com
Printed in the USA
BVHW081255080519
547715BV00005B/598/P